Economic Development in Modern China Since 1949

As the second volume of a two-volume set on Chinese economic history, this book investigates Chinese economic development since 1949, uncovering the momentum, unique models, and general laws of the economy in China.

From the perspective of development economics, the two-volume set studies the economic history and development of China since 1912, with a focus on the quantitative analysis of economic activities. This volume describes the historical process and characteristics of the economy since 1949, then looks into the momentum and inner logic that underpin the economic development. The former part covers issues of agriculture, industry, population and labor force, urbanization and mobility, income distribution and poverty, and price changes. The latter part includes analyses on capital formation, human resources, technological progress, institutions, macro policies, international trade, and direct investment.

This title will interest scholars and students working on Chinese economic history, the Chinese economy, and modern Chinese society.

Guan Quan is Professor at the School of Economics of Renmin University of China. His research interests include development economics, international economics, Chinese economy, and Japanese economy. His recent publications with Routledge include the two-volume *Industrial Development in Modern China: Comparisons with Japan*.

China Perspectives

The *China Perspectives* series focuses on translating and publishing works by leading Chinese scholars, writing about both global topics and China-related themes. It covers Humanities & Social Sciences, Education, Media and Psychology, as well as many interdisciplinary themes.

This is the first time any of these books have been published in English for international readers. The series aims to put forward a Chinese perspective, give insights into cutting-edge academic thinking in China, and inspire researchers globally.

To submit a book proposal, please contact the Taylor & Francis Publisher for the China Publishing Programme, Lian Sun (Lian.Sun@informa.com)

Titles in economics include:

The Emission Reduction Effects of Spatial Agglomeration
Zhang Ke

China's Economic Development
Implications for the World
Cai Fang

State-Owned Enterprise's Ownership Reform
A Chinese Modernization Approach
Zhigang Zheng

Comprehensive Land Consolidation in China
Yan Jinming, Xia Fangzhou

Economic Development in Modern China Before 1949
Guan Quan

Economic Development in Modern China Since 1949
Guan Quan

For more information, please visit www.routledge.com/China-Perspectives/book-series/CPH

Economic Development in Modern China Since 1949

Guan Quan

LONDON AND NEW YORK

First published in English 2024
by Routledge
4 Park Square, Milton Park, Abingdon, Oxon OX14 4RN

and by Routledge
605 Third Avenue, New York, NY 10158

Routledge is an imprint of the Taylor & Francis Group, an informa business

© 2024 Guan Quan

The right of Guan Quan to be identified as author of this work has been asserted in accordance with sections 77 and 78 of the Copyright, Designs and Patents Act 1988.

All rights reserved. No part of this book may be reprinted or reproduced or utilised in any form or by any electronic, mechanical, or other means, now known or hereafter invented, including photocopying and recording, or in any information storage or retrieval system, without permission in writing from the publishers.

Trademark notice: Product or corporate names may be trademarks or registered trademarks, and are used only for identification and explanation without intent to infringe.

English Version by permission of China Renmin University Press.

British Library Cataloguing-in-Publication Data
A catalogue record for this book is available from the British Library

Library of Congress Cataloging-in-Publication Data
Names: Guan, Quan, 1955– author.
Title: Economic development in modern China since 1949 / Guan Quan.
Description: Abingdon, Oxon ; New York, NY : Routledge, 2024. |
  Series: China perspectives | Includes bibliographical references and index.
Identifiers: LCCN 2023020780 (print) | LCCN 2023020781 (ebook) |
  ISBN 9781032531182 (hardback) | ISBN 9781032531212 (paperback) |
  ISBN 9781003410393 (ebook)
Subjects: LCSH: Economic development—China—History. |
  China—Economic conditions—1949–
Classification: LCC HC427.9 .G795 2024 (print) | LCC HC427.9 (ebook) |
  DDC 338.951/05—dc23/eng/20230511
LC record available at https://lccn.loc.gov/2023020780
LC ebook record available at https://lccn.loc.gov/2023020781

ISBN: 978-1-032-53118-2 (hbk)
ISBN: 978-1-032-53121-2 (pbk)
ISBN: 978-1-003-41039-3 (ebk)

DOI: 10.4324/9781003410393

Typeset in Times New Roman
by Apex CoVantage, LLC

Contents

List of figures   *vii*
List of tables   *ix*
Preface to the Chinese edition   *xii*

PART I
Preparatory investigation   1

1 Overview of China's economic development   3

PART II
Processes and characteristics   25

2 Development and change in agriculture   27

3 Industrial development and upgrading   50

4 Development and significance of the service industry   71

5 Demographic changes and labor supply   85

6 Urbanization and labor mobility   97

7 Income distribution and poverty issues   110

8 Price changes and citizens' lives   126

vi *Contents*

PART III
Conditions and causes 139

9 Formation of capital: savings and investment 141

10 Human resources: education and health 157

11 Technological advancement: introduction and innovation 169

12 Institution building: government and market 181

13 Macro policy: fiscal and finance issues 192

14 International trade: closed and open 207

15 Direct investment: "invite in" and "go global" 226

PART IV
Summary and outlook 239

16 China's experience and prospects 241

References 256
Index 261

Figures

1.1	Growth rate of real GDP and GDP per capita	16
2.1	Growth rate of real added value of the primary industry	31
2.2	Significance and role of township and village enterprises	47
3.1	Real growth rate of added value of the secondary industry	52
3.2	Approximate production function of industry (net value per capita)	57
3.3	Labor coefficient and capital coefficient in industry (net output value)	58
3.4	Labor coefficient and capital coefficient in secondary industry (1982–2013)	59
3.5	Proportions of heavy industry, state sector of the economy, and collective economic operations	60
3.6	Relationship between per capita fixed assets and per capita gross output value of industrial enterprises (2011)	67
3.7	Relationship between the total asset's contribution rate and the ratio of profits to cost of industrial enterprises (2011)	68
4.1	Real growth rate of added value of tertiary industry	72
5.1	Demographic transition in China	88
5.2	Growth rate of labor supply	93
6.1	Urbanization in China (1949–2013)	99
6.2	Todaro model under the household registration system	103
6.3	Todaro model under the dual roles of household registration system and family planning policy	104
7.1	Distribution of the proportion of urban worker households grouped by monthly income in China (1964 and 1981)	116
7.2	Distribution of the proportion of urban resident households grouped by monthly income in China (1986 and 1990)	117
7.3	Distribution of the proportion of rural households in China grouped by income (1980, 1985, and 1990)	119
7.4	Distribution of the proportion of rural households in China grouped by income (1995, 2000, and 2005)	120
7.5	Distribution of the proportion of rural households in China grouped by income (2005 and 2011)	121
8.1	Changes in the procurement price index of agricultural products and the producer price index of industrial and mining products (1950–2000)	132

viii *Figures*

9.1	Change in investment rate	146
9.2	Change in marginal output/capital ratio	147
9.3	Changes in capital coefficients of various industries	150
9.4	Changes in the capital/labor ratio of various industries	151
9.5	Changes in labor productivity of various industries	152
9.6	Changes in gross savings rate, household savings rate and investment rate	153
10.1	Process of universal access to education	163
11.1	Types of technologies imported by China	176
12.1	Institutional transformation after 1949	185
13.1	Proportion of fiscal revenue to GDP and proportion of tax revenue to fiscal revenue	196
13.2	Proportion of fiscal revenue by economic types	197
13.3	Money supply	205
14.1	Actual import and export growth rate after the reform and opening up	211
14.2	Changes in China's trade dependency as well as import and export structure	214
14.3	Relationship of proportions of heavy industry for production and trade	219
14.4	Changes in terms of trade, ratio of China's export price to world export price, and ratio of import price to domestic price	221
15.1	Proportion of imports and exports of foreign-invested enterprises to total imports and exports as well as the proportion of industrial output value of foreign-invested enterprises to the total industrial output value	229
15.2	Proportion of foreign direct investment to fixed asset investment (capital formation)	230
16.1	Factors influencing economic development	248

Tables

1.1	Changes in GNP per capita in developed countries	5
1.2	China's real GDP and its comparison with those of the United States and Japan	10
1.3	China's per capita real GDP and its comparison with those of the United States and Japan	12
1.4	Several estimates of China's economic growth rate	14
1.5	GDP growth rate and its breakdown	17
1.6	Comparison between China and the world (1950–2010)	19
1.7	China's industrial structure	20
1.8	Contribution made by the three industries to GDP and their pulling effect on GDP	21
2.1	Status of agriculture in the national economy	29
2.2	Growth rate of primary industry	33
2.3	Partial investment in agricultural production	35
2.4	Growth rate of primary industry and its breakdown	37
2.5	Development of mutual aid cooperatives for agricultural production	40
2.6	Implementation of Household Contract Responsibility System in rural areas	41
2.7	Changes in fixed assets of rural organizations at all levels	42
3.1	Growth rate of secondary industry	54
3.2	Growth rate of secondary industry and its breakdown	55
3.3	Proportion of various types of economy in gross value of industrial output	63
3.4	Changes in the proportion of enterprises in industry	64
3.5	Basic situation of industrial enterprises by forms of ownership (2015)	66
4.1	Growth rate of tertiary industry	73
4.2	Growth rate of tertiary industry and its breakdown	75
4.3	Composition of output value of the tertiary industry	77
4.4	Sources and distribution of aggregate purchasing power in the planned economy period	78
4.5	Proportion of private commerce and transport	79

4.6	Number of employees in various sectors of the service industry	80
4.7	Number of employees in the financial sector	81
4.8	Total retail sales of consumer goods by economic types	82
5.1	China's population after 1949	87
5.2	Age structure and dependency ratio of China's population	89
5.3	Population of people aged above 15 years, labor force, employed persons, the unemployed	94
7.1	Income and expenditure of urban as well as rural residents	114
7.2	Basic situation of urban residents by income grade	115
7.3	Basic situation of rural households by income level (2011)	118
7.4	Rural poverty in China	122
7.5	Income and expenditure of urban households in financial difficulties in China	123
8.1	Retail price index of commodities grouped by urban and rural areas	128
8.2	Agricultural product procurement price index	129
8.3	Producer price index of industrial and mining products	131
8.4	Changes in various price indexes after the reform and opening up	133
8.5	Per capita income of urban and rural residents as well as Engel coefficient	134
8.6	Proportion of per capita cash outlays of urban and rural residents	135
8.7	Per capita consumption amount of major food by urban and rural residents	136
9.1	Composition of GDP by expenditure approach	144
9.2	Calculation of investment function of the secondary industry	145
9.3	Capital coefficient, capital/labor ratio and labor productivity	149
9.4	Calculation of personal consumption function and saving function	154
10.1	Proportion of secondary and elementary school graduates entering schools of a higher level as well as enrollment rate of elementary schools	158
10.2	Basic situation of education in China	159
10.3	Length of schooling as shown in previous censuses	161
10.4	Diseases as the top 10 causes of death among urban and rural residents in 1990 and 2018	165
10.5	Total spending on health	166
11.1	Construction of key projects aided by the Soviet Union	171
11.2	Complete projects introduced in 1972 and 1978	174
11.3	Introduction of equipment from 1950 to 1985	175
11.4	Number of domestic and foreign patent applications and authorized patents	178
12.1	Number of employees during the period of socialist transformation	187
12.2	Structure of employees by ownership	189
13.1	Government revenues and expenditures	195
13.2	Main tax revenue	198
13.3	Main items of fiscal expenditure	200
13.4	Deposits of financial institutions	204

14.1	Total import and export trade	209
14.2	Calculation results of the trade dependency function	213
14.3	Import and export structure of primary products after the reform and opening up	217
14.4	Import and export structure of manufactured goods during the reform and opening up period	218
14.5	Calculation of export and import functions	224
15.1	Foreign investment and foreign-invested enterprises introduced after the reform and opening up	227
15.2	Changes in China's trade mode	228
15.3	Distribution of industries for foreign direct investment enterprises	231
15.4	Calculation results of the foreign investment demand function	233
15.5	Distribution of industries for China's outward direct investment	235

Preface to the Chinese edition

Purpose and significance

The world has changed in various subtle ways since humanity entered the 21st century. For example, the September 11 incident in the United States was the nation's first attack on its homeland since its founding. The attacks were particularly devastating in New York and Washington, two cities that represent the United States' might, thus magnifying its influence. Only Hawaii (which became the 50th state in the United States in 1959), a possession far away from the continental United States, was attacked by Japanese Kamikaze in the early stages of the Pacific War. This partially confirmed Samuel P. Huntington's prediction about the clash of civilizations and also prompted the United States to step up its global counterterrorism efforts, which has severely depleted U.S. people, material resources, and energy. This has presented both opportunities and challenges to the development and expansion of other countries and regions.

A prominent case is China's rise. China ultimately joined the World Trade Organization in 2001, after 15 years of tough talks, providing a significant boost to China's burgeoning economic and trade exchanges around the world. Since then, Chinese goods have been sold all over the world, and China's development has accelerated. China overtook Germany in 2008 and Japan in 2010 to become the world's second largest economy. This is similar to what happened in the second half of the 20th century, when Japan overtook the United Kingdom, France, and the Federal Republic of Germany to become the second largest economy in the Western world from 1967 to 1969 (the Soviet Union was nominally the world's second largest economy at the time). China will soon overtake the United States as the world's largest economy if current trends continue. If the method of purchasing power parity is used for calculation, China's aggregate economic output exceeded that of the United States in 2014–2015.

It is impossible for China to maintain an average yearly economic growth rate of more than 9 percent, as it has done for the past 40 years, for a variety of reasons, but there is every possibility of a moderate growth rate (4 to 5 percent). China's aggregate economic output will eventually exceed that of the United States, whether in 10 or 20 years, resulting in massive global influence and changes.

The emergence of the "BRIC countries" [Brazil, Russia, India, China, South Africa (the latest to be accepted)] is another notable example. Following the inception of this concept in 2001, these countries united and aired their views on many key global concerns. These countries have their own challenges, some of which are serious in some countries, but they are in the second tier of the global economy and share common goals and interests and therefore will strengthen cooperation on many issues. BRIC countries aim to become global powers, but they find it difficult to do so on their own. There are a lot of unknowns and variables in this process. Some countries may be eliminated, while others, such as Indonesia and Mexico, may emerge and join them. As a result, the term "BRIC countries" may be only symbolic and does not ensure a country's success. We believe that the second tier is essential in the world economy, that is, countries that compete with the first-tier countries.

In first-tier countries, developed economies such as the United States, European countries, and Japan face the pressure of being overtaken and challenged. In fact, numerous situations that are unfavorable to them do exist. To begin with, aside from the September 11 attacks (2001), the United States saw the worst financial crisis since World War II (2008), which had a devasting impact on the global economy. Second, Japan, which was once the world's second biggest economy, has been stuck in a rut since the economic bubble burst in the early 1990s and is unable to find the way forward. The fact that Japan has the greatest life expectancy (with an average life expectancy of 84 years) and is the first country with an oversized aging population (the elderly account for 28.4 percent) casts a shadow over the Japanese economy's recovery. The scarcity of workers may be the most pressing issue Japan faces in the next decades. Third, while the EU has expanded to 27 member states (after BREXIT in the United Kingdom), compromising the vast majority of European countries, the economic environment has not improved as a result of its increased size. Instead, it is plagued by high unemployment and slow long-term growth with no clear solution. These developed economies continue to be the world's economic leaders, with highly developed science and technology, top-tier human resources, as well as other soft power, such as international influence and a say in international affairs. However, as a result of the challenges posed by emerging countries and the natural laws, their standing comes under threat, and their say in international affairs has dwindled. Although former U.S. President Barack Obama declared that the United States will continue to lead the world for the next 100 years, he may have merely been giving lip service. Former President Donald Trump adopted an extraordinary method to safeguard the interests of the United States, such as America First-ism, but it is uncertain whether that succeeded.

Another important change to the global economy as a result of globalization is regional economic integration. Since the European Union (EU) set a precedent for European integration, attempts to foster economic integration in various regions have been made, notably the Association of Southeast Asian Nations (ASEAN) and the North American Free Trade Agreement (NAFTA). As things stand, it is difficult to evaluate how successful these regional economic integration efforts are, but they do cause a domino effect. A salient example is the free trade agreement negotiations between the United States and the EU, as well as between Japan and the EU. These agreements, if implemented, would drastically alter the global economic landscape. In this way, two economic groups would be formed, with the first-tier countries at the center, to compete against other countries that are not linked. Countries that are united obviously have more advantages, while countries that are not united are at a disadvantage. In particular, the united countries include the most developed countries, while other countries are not. It is self-evident who is the more powerful. In this regard, the United States is truly ruthless. Some may believe that this is yet another U.S.-led conspiracy. We are not totally against it. The world is constantly changing. It may not be a bad thing if it is done in a fair and reasonable manner. China's rise has also altered global patterns. A variety of variables exist in the pattern of international economic relations.

These trends reveal some noteworthy phenomena. On the one hand, developed countries are experiencing sluggish growth and rely more on the cooperation of newly industrialized countries. On the other hand, developed countries, which are concerned about their own status, tend to exclude newly industrialized countries. This can be seen from the previously mentioned trend of restructuring regional economic integration. On the contrary, newly industrialized countries represented by the BRIC countries are also experiencing a slew of conflicts. On the one hand, newly industrialized countries require capital and technology from developed countries in order to develop. On the other hand, if they rely too heavily on developed countries, their economy will stagnate, and it will be difficult to make breakthroughs. The real issue is that these countries in the second and third tiers find it difficult to develop independently of first-tier countries because first-tier countries have the most cutting-edge science and technology. Given the complex international environment and global economic changes, how China should skillfully respond and develop becomes a touchstone. Today's situation is not the same as it was 10, 20, or even 30 years ago. Thirty years ago, the world witnessed the Cold War, and the developed countries, led by the United States primarily, faced the strategic threat posed by the Soviet Union, providing opportunity for China's development. More than 20 years ago, the Soviet Union disintegrated, major changes took place in Eastern Europe, and Japan's economic bubble burst, giving opportunity for China's progress. The United States was hit by the September 11 attacks more than 20 years ago, and China's accession to the World Trade Organization provided international circumstances for China's development. China is currently confronted with greater uncertainties and adverse factors.

First of all, as China progresses, favorable factors such as latecomer advantages and demographic dividends are gradually dwindling, while unfavorable factors such as inequality of income distribution, rising labor costs, lack of technological innovation, insufficient economic reform, and population aging become more prevalent. Second, although having a huge total economic output and an increasing share of the global economy, China does not dominate in high-end fields, with many industries still reliant on developed countries. Finally, China's economic reforms are progressing slowly. As the economy develops and globalization advances, this system will become a stumbling block to development, resulting in inefficiency and a lack of competitiveness.

Of course, China still has many favorable economic conditions. First, China is still a developing nation. The per capita national income is not high (US$10,000 in 2019), social security is inadequate, and people are still eager to work hard, all of which contribute to increased productivity. Second, despite the fact that the demographic dividend is declining, a large number of young people (more than 15 million new births in China each year) enter the labor market, injecting vitality into economic growth. China has begun to implement the two-child policy, which help to alleviate the issues of population aging and labor shortage. Third, China's urbanization is still limited. Hundreds of millions of rural people will become urban residents for some time in the future, providing a tremendous driving force for economic development. China's economy will be a topic that attracts great attention for a long time to come. There have long been various viewpoints in the world regarding China's rapid development and significant influence in world affairs, including the China's Rise Theory, the China Threat Theory, and even the China Collapse Theory. China's Rise Theory is a generally objective view of China's development. According to the China Threat Theory, some countries believe that once China becomes powerful, it will become a threat to them. The China Collapse Theory is a variant of the China Threat Theory, and proponents of this view wish for China to fail or disintegrate. The latter two arguments, which are obviously subjective and biased, are baseless clichés and do not deserve a debunking effort.

Features of this book

China's tremendous economic growth and development in recent years has drawn great attention from many global and domestic researchers. As a result, they have published numerous related research findings. These studies are divided into the following categories. First are works that introduce and comment on China's economy comprehensively, including textbooks. The majority of these works focus on China's economic development since reform and opening up, and some cover the planned economy period. Second are studies on specific professional fields, such as population, labor mobility, finance, agriculture, private sector of the economy, reform of state-owned enterprises, income distribution, regional economy, and international trade and investment. Of course, there are comprehensive studies as well. Third are studies on current events and hot topics, such as reform of state-owned enterprises, new countryside development, pension insurance system, real estate market, and migrant worker-related issues. Fourth are books on economic history, including economic history from the planned economy period to the reform and opening period, such as the *Economic History after the Founding of the People's Republic of China*. Special studies were conducted on the economic history of the reform and opening period, such as the economic history of 40-year economic reform.

However, there is a lack of academic work that comprehensively reflects China's economic development after 1949. The content should include the following aspects. To begin with, China has gone through two periods in more than 70 years since 1949, namely the planned economy period and the reform and opening up period. The vast majority of studies on the Chinese economy focus on the latter period, with a view covering only the former period and even fewer combining the two periods. What is significant is that if a study only looks at the 40 years of reform and opening up while ignoring the 30 years prior to that, you cannot see the groundwork for progress because the economic achievements made during the reform and opening up period are built on a solid foundation laid during the planned economy period. China would not have achieved its current economic performance without the industrial structure and corresponding talents in the preceding 30 years.

Second, economic development research involves more than just a study of economic history. It must be explained using economic theories. Quantitative analysis, which entails applying theories and methodologies to explain economic changes over time, requires methods and instruments such as statistics and econometrics. For example, reform and opening up aid China's economic development tremendously. What are the manifestations of these? What role does China's WTO membership play in the internationalization and development of its economy? What has been the impact of the influx of migrant workers on urban development? What function do township and village enterprises play? These topics need to be studied for economic development, and the majority of them can be described using economics. Some issues may involve other disciplines, such as political science, sociology, and science of international relations.

Third, it is difficult to include both the research achievements of numerous scholars, as well as the authors' individual opinions and research findings. It is impossible for a scholar to give unbiased comments on every section of a book that comprehensively covers China's economic development, let alone to accomplish anything in all areas. This is a significant challenge because this book is not devoted to the study of specific areas. A book is merely introductory reading material if the author does not provide individual, independent opinions and viewpoints. It is not easy for the author to present independent opinions and viewpoints in a book that discusses China's economic development comprehensively because it is impossible for a single person to perform in-depth research on all issues.

Structure of this book

This book consists of 16 chapters in four parts. Part I, "Preparatory Investigation", deals with the general situation of China's economic development. It comprises one chapter. Chapter 1, "Overview of China's Economic Development", introduces the basic framework of China's economic development from 1949 to the present, including a comparison of growth rates of economic development, as well as structural changes in the planned economy period and the reform and opening up period.

Part II examines the processes and features of economic development. This part consists of seven chapters. Chapter 2, "Development and Change in Agriculture", examines the changes in and roles of agriculture in the course of economic development. After 1949, China's agricultural sector experienced a complex and volatile process. Particularly, during the planned economy period, farmers were bound to the people's communes and couldn't bring into play their individual initiative for work, causing long-term stagnation in agricultural production. After the reform and opening up, individuals enjoy higher initiative, and agriculture has seen rapid development. Chapter 3, "Industrial Development and Upgrading", focuses on the processes and characteristics of industrialization. China's industry has also experienced a tortuous process – the emphasis was on heavy industry during the planned economy period in order to balance development after reform and opening up, leading to the present status as the world's factory. However, the extensive mode of growth and inefficiency in China's industry have not been thoroughly solved, and China still lags far behind developed countries. Chapter 4, "Development and Significance of the Service Industry", examines the issues concerning the development of the service industry. In China, the service industry lags behind in development as a result of cognitive and institutional limitations. The service sector was once considered dispensable. However, China recognizes the importance of the service sector, which has also become a significant sector of economic growth on a par with industry. Chapter 5, "Demographic Changes and Labor Supply", discusses population growth and structural changes in economic development. China's population changes demonstrate prominent characteristics. On the one hand, the population is large, making China the world's most populous country. On the other hand, due to economic development and policy orientation, China once experienced a population boom, and then the population growth rate was reduced through forceful family planning policies. This has led to unique changes to China's population. Chapter 6, "Urbanization and Labor Mobility", examines urbanization, a key link in China's economic development. Industrialization and urbanization generally reinforce each other, but in China, the two are not unified because urbanization lags far behind industrialization. This largely stems from the household registration system, which limits the movement of people and even impedes balanced development between urban and rural areas. This is still a significant stumbling block to China's economic development. Chapter 7, "Income Distribution and Poverty Issues", discusses the issue of the widening income gap that is prone to occur in the process of economic development. According to Kuznets' Inverted U hypothesis, as the economy develops, a country will experience a process in which the income gap widens and then narrows again. This law basically describes China's current situation, which refers to a widening income gap. This also has a significant negative impact on the economy. Chapter 8, "Price Changes and Citizens' Lives", discusses improving the quality of life of people, one of the outcomes and achievements of economic development. China is unique in this regard. In the planned economy, neither prices nor income rose. After reform and opening up, it is the opposite, with rapidly rising prices and significantly increased incomes. China has done a good job in this regard, and there is no serious inflation, which may gnaw away the achievements of economic development.

Part III examines the conditions and causes of economic development. This part consists of seven chapters. Chapter 9, "Capital Formation: Savings and Investment", examines the issues of capital accumulation and capital raising in the course of economic development. China's economic development also follows the law of "savings = investment" – relying on high savings to drive investment and stimulate economic growth. This mode of growth is universal and necessary, but, as the economy grows, there is a shift. The rule of diminishing marginal returns will come into play, and China has reached a stage at which investment-driven growth is replaced by consumption-led growth. Chapter 10, "Human Resources: Education and Health", discusses the issues of talent cultivation as well as people's nutrition and health that are more important to economic growth than natural resources and physical capital. In this regard, full attention should be paid to China's special situation, because China has a large population, but the quality of life is low, which impedes not only China's development but also social progress. It can be said that the income gap primarily stems from a gap in human resources. Chapter 11, "Technological Advance: Introduction and Innovation", examines the issue of technological advance, one of the drivers for economic growth and development. China has made great strides in this regard, but it also faces serious problems. We have mastered the basic technologies and skills in a great many fields, but the lack of innovation remains a fatal weakness that restricts China's further development. This concerns the question of whether China can overcome the "middle-income trap" and compete with the developed countries. Chapter 12, "Institution Building: Government and Market", discusses an eternal topic that is important for developed countries but is even more important for developing countries with imperfect markets and inexperienced government. China is such a country. Therefore, how to establish efficient and fair institutions is essential for the effective operation of the market economy. China has made some progress in this regard, but it still has a long way to go. This must be achieved primarily through further reforms. Chapter 13, "Macro Policy: Fiscal and Financial Issues", discusses fiscal and financial topics. When it comes to a country's economic development, fiscal and financial issues are linked to capital and monetary issues, and they are also the principal means of macro regulation. The application of these two systems and means is not only necessary but also effective. However, many developing countries have inadequate strength in this regard. China also faces a host of problems, particularly in respect to institutional reforms, regulatory mechanisms, and opening up the market. Chapter 14, "International Trade: Closed and Open", focuses on the role of international trade in developing countries. It discusses the benefits of developing economies while opening up the market to the world. China has been successful in this regard. After the reform and opening up, China has implemented the outward-looking development strategy, which has made good use of China's advantages of a large population and abundant labor. This paves the way for China to become the largest trading country. China's accession to the World Trade Organization (WTO) promoted its integration into the world market and gave full play to its economies of scale effect that other countries do not enjoy. Chapter 15, "Direct Investment: 'Bring In' and 'Go Global'", examines the role of introduction of foreign capital and outbound investment. China has been tremendously successful in introducing foreign investment since the reform and opening up. In this regard, China has gained far more benefits that other BRICS countries have. As China's economy develops and internationalization deepens, outbound investment has become inevitable. However, China is still in its infancy in this regard, and truly transnational operations are nonexistent. China lags far behind developed countries in this regard.

Part Four, "Summary and Prospects", consists of one chapter. Chapter 16, "China's Experience and Prospects", summarizes China's experience in economic development, including a development model in which the government and market jointly play a role, outward-looking development strategies, the economies of scale effect for a large country, the use of late-mover advantages, and the improvement of social capabilities. Finally, the conditions necessary for economic development are summarized, which may be of reference value for the economic development of other countries.

Feelings and acknowledgments

The reason for writing this book first emerged in 1988. At that time, I was admitted to the Department of Economics Research at Hitotsubashi University in Japan as a government-sponsored overseas student to pursue a master's program under the tutelage of the well-known economist Ryoshin Minami. Under the master's program, we studied our tutor's book, *The Economic Development of Japan*, at a seminar. This influential book has been translated into English, Chinese, Korean, and other languages. From the standpoint of development economics, the tutor conducted an in-depth analysis of Japan's long-term economic development and presented opinions from diverse sources as well as his unique insights. The book contains theoretical explanations and empirical analysis, with a focus on the latter. He also pointed out the general and unique nature of Japan's economic development through comparison with other developed countries. I was involved in the translation of the second edition of the book into Chinese. As a result, I have a deeper understanding of the tutor's intention and methods and am also impressed by his profound research competence. Thereafter, I nurtured an idea of writing a similar book on China's economic development. However, due to a hectic schedule of my master's and doctoral studies and research (the main focus of research at that time was Japan's economy) and my limited knowledge of the Chinese economy, this idea was mothballed until 30 years later.

After I returned to China in 2002, I released some publications while studying China's economy. Publications related to this book are as follows: (1) Guan Quan, "What Does Foreign Investment Bring? The Role of Foreign Investment", in Ryoshin Minami and Makino Fumio, eds., *Introduction to China's Economy*, 2nd ed., translated by Guan Quan. (China Water&Power Press, May 2007); (2) Guan Quan, "The Current Situation of China's Modernization and Development", *Dokkyo Economics* (Faculty of Economics, Dokkyo University), No. 85, 2008; (3) Guan Quan and Kong Jian. "A Study on Trade Dependency", *Open Economic Review* (School of Economics, Renmin University of China), No. 1, 2008; (4) Guan Quan. "Political Economy Analysis of Economic Integration in East Asia", in Yang Dongliang and Zheng Wei, eds., "Progress of East Asian Integration and Its Path of Regional Cooperation" (Tianjin People's Publishing House, March 2008); (5) Guan Quan and Wang Hanru, "How to Get Out of the Poverty Alleviation Dilemma", *Annual Research Report of the Institute of Asian Cultures* (Tokyo University, Japan), No. 43, February 2009; (6) Guan Quan and Wang Hanru. "Poverty and Income Gap in China's Economic Development", *Annual Research Report of the Institute of Asian Cultures* (Tokyo University, Japan), No. 44, February 2010; (7) Guan Quan, "Crossing the Lewis Turning Point: The Japanese Experience and Its Inspiration", Japan Institute of Nankai University (2010) (Beijing: World Affairs Press, 2010); (8) Guan Quan, *China's Reform and Opening Up as Well as the Formation of an Industrial Society*. Song Zhiyong and Zheng Wei, editors-in-chief, *Institutional Change in East Asia in the Era of Globalization* (Tianjin: Tianjin People's Publishing House, 2011); (9) Guan Quan, "The Cycle and Grade of Economic Take-off as Well as Late-mover Advantage", *Academic Frontiers*, No. 29, 2013; (10) Guan Quan, Makino Fumio, and Wang Hanru, "The Transfer of Surplus Rural Labor in China: Literature Outlook", in Ryoshin Minami, Makino Fumio, and Hao Renping, eds. *China's Economic Turning Point* (Beijing: Social Sciences Academic Press, 2014); (11) Guan Quan. "'Dual Structure' More Suitable for China", *PKU Business Review* (Peking University), No. 8, 2015; (12) Guan Quan. "China Must Coordinate Eight Relationships in Its Economy", *People's Forum*, July 2016 (I); (13) Guan Quan, "The Nature of China–U.S. Trade Conflicts and the Significance of Promoting Balanced Trade, *People's Forum*, October 2018 (II); (14) Guan Quan. "Challenges and Prospects of Global Trade Liberalization", *Academic Frontiers*, October 2018 (III); (15) Guan Quan. "Trends in Global Trade Liberalization and Chinese Countermeasures", *World Economic Survey* (Institute of World Economics and Politics, Chinese Academy of Social Sciences), No. 20, May 2019; (16) Guan Quan. "China's Industrial Development over 70 Years", *Economic Theory and Business Management* (Renmin University of China), No. 9, 2019; (17) Guan Quan. *China's Economic Development: Centennial Course* (China Renmin University Press, 2019). This book is equivalent to the part of this book on modern China.

In the process of writing, graduate students Zhang Mingxia, Du Yuming, Peng Yutao, Wang Li, Yin Sisi, et al. provided a wealth of references. Zhang Mingxia also performed econometric analysis. Professor Wang Zhigang of Renmin University of China and his doctoral student Zhou Haiwen, as well as Meng Haoqi from the Guizhou Insurance Society, read the book in its entirety and gave valuable comments. I hereby express thanks to them.

Finally, I would like to thank the editors of China Renmin University Press. This book would not be published without their recommendation and careful review.

Guan Quan
June 2020

Part I
Preparatory investigation

1 Overview of China's economic development

1.1 Introduction

Before 1949, particularly from 1912 to 1949, China had realized economic development to some extent, including a period of economic growth and structural changes.[1] During this period, China's economy was in a state of change, some modern industries were introduced, and growth was achieved in some regions, particularly coastal cities such as Shanghai and the northeast region. Quite a few new industries emerged, such as textile and weaving, flour milling, papermaking, tobacco, matches, pharmaceuticals, rubber, and machinery. On the whole, these new industries were weak in competition and few in number, and they accounted for a small share of the Chinese economy at that time. However, this trend was needed and also vitally important for economic development. In this sense, it can be said that this period laid somewhat of a foundation for economic development after 1949, and this must be recognized. Many countries (such as India) with national conditions similar to those of China were still in a state of being colonized. Despite a lack of modern economic growth and a state of stagnation as a whole during this period, China took on a new look[2] and even experienced a "failed take-off" compared with most poor and backward countries.[3]

This first chapter gives an overview of China's economic development after 1949. Compared with the Republic of China period, China has seen a wholly different picture in economic development after 1949, evolving from a poor and weak country into a country that has built a moderately prosperous society and that has become the world's second largest economy. This great difference in economic development is due to the great basic and strategic differences between the two periods. To begin with, the political structure has significantly changed – from a presidential republic to a socialist country and from a weak government to a strong one. Secondly, the economy reverted from the market economy to the planned economy and then to the market economy again. Finally, the country has achieved independence and unity and has the will and capacity to catch up with the developed countries.

Actually, China's economic development strategy was significantly adjusted during the long-term development even after 1949. First of all, although the government is powerful in terms of the economic system, the market plays an increasingly bigger role and will continue to play a key role. Second, the development strategy has shifted from a simple focus on heavy industrialization to a strategy under which China strikes a balance among agriculture, light industry, heavy industry, and service industry and from a domestically oriented development strategy to an outward-looking development strategy. Third, the international environment has undergone significant changes. In the early period (the planned economy period, 1949–1978), China was greatly impacted by the Cold War. In the later period (the period of reform and opening up, after 1979), China has achieved great success by riding the wave of globalization.

During this period, China has not only seen an economic take-off but also has become a middle-income country. It is believed that this trend of development will continue, despite a gradual decline in economic growth rate. This chapter mainly discusses several issues concerning China's economic development as a whole. The first issue is when China began its modern economic growth. The second is the growth rate of China's economy. The third is to conduct preliminary observations and discussions on the industrial structure. An analysis of the three industries is detailed in Chapters 2 to 4.

1.2 China's economic take-off

China had made some progress in economic development before 1949, but it did not start modern economic growth. It only introduced some modern industries, and a certain degree of growth was achieved in some regions. When did China's modern economic growth begin? Although there are few research findings on this issue, two views are noteworthy. One is Walt Whitman Rostow's view that both China and India realized economic take-off in 1952.[4] The other is the view of the Japanese scholar Makino Fumio that China began to see modern economic growth after 1978.[5] No matter whether these two views are correct, one thing is certain that China's modern economic growth began after 1949. Judgments and explanations will be made in this chapter based on these studies. Before doing so, the author first introduces the concepts of modern economic growth and economic take-off and their connotations, as well as the findings of studies by Japanese scholars on Japan.

1.2.1 Modern economic growth

The concept of modern economic growth was coined by Simon Smith Kuznets. This term compares the modern economic era with the era of commercial capitalism or feudalism. He argues that modern economic growth is still continuing, and therefore its full characters are not very clear, but the key is to apply science to solve problems in the economy and work. This in turn has led to industrialization, urbanization, and explosive population growth. After collecting and analyzing statistics from developed countries over a long term, Kuznets believes that economic growth since the 18th and 19th centuries is essentially different from preceding economic growth, and the later growth is called "modern economic growth".[6]

He believes that "epoch-making economic development" has occurred several times in the long history of mankind, such as the medieval urban economy of Western Europe from the 11th to the 15th centuries, and the commercial capitalism of the late 18th century. The epoch-making economic development is characterized by innovation. In the epoch-making development of the commercial capitalist economy, the expansion of Western Europe into the New World is an innovation. The epoch-making characteristics of modern economic growth are the wide application of modern science and technology in economic activities. The earliest and all-important innovation was the steam engine, which was essentially the product of advances in steam dynamics, followed by electricity, the internal combustion engine, chemistry, electrons, and atomic energy. The economic application of science has also promoted scientific progress. Factories that use new scientific and technological equipment are also plants for science and technology experiments. This mutual promotion of science and economy is the essence of modern economic growth. Industry plays a core role, and therefore modern economic growth and industrialization are in fact the same thing.[7]

Kuznets argues that modern economic growth shows the following characteristics: (1) rapid growth in population and per capita productivity; (2) rapid changes in industrial structure and concentration of population in cities (urbanization); (3) the sustaining of these changes, that is, "self-sustaining growth".[8] According to his research, the changes in gross national product (GNP) at the beginning of modern economic growth in today's developed countries are shown in Table 1.1. Since the First Industrial Revolution occurred in Britain, only Britain registered modern economic growth during this period. Thereafter, it successively took place in Northern Europe, Western Europe, Southern Europe, North America, and Japan. The Second

Table 1.1 Changes in GNP per capita in developed countries, Unit: US$

Country	GNP per capita at the beginning	1965	1978	1989	1999	2013
Australia	760 (1861–1869)	2,023	7,920	17,388	20,773	65,400
Switzerland	529 (1865)	2,354	12,100	26,348	36,347	90,680
Canada	508 (1870–1874)	2,507	9,170	20,783	21,146	52,210
United States	474 (1834–1843)	3,580	9,700	20,629	34,047	53470
Denmark	370 (1865–1869)	2,238	9,920	20,402	32,760	61,670
The Netherlands	347 (1831–1840)	1,609	83,90	15,061	24,899	51,060
Belgium	326 (1831–1840)	1,835	9,070	15,393	24,457	46,340
Germany	302 (1850–1859)	1,939	9,600	19,183	25,727	47,250
Norway	287 (1865–1869)	1,912	9,510	2,1500	34,292	102,700
Italy	261 (1861–1869)	1,100	3,840	15051	20,421	35,620
France	242 (1831–1840)	2,047	8,270	1,7061	24,228	43,520
United Kingdom	227 (1765–1785)	1,870	5,030	14,646	24,548	41,680
Sweden	215 (1861–1869)	2,713	10,210	22,303	26,939	61,710
Japan	136 (1886)	876	7,300	23,296	35,715	46,330

Sources of data: For 1965–1999: Ryoshin Minami (1981, 1992, 2002); for 2013: *World Development Indicators 2015*.

Notes:
(1) The numbers in parentheses refer to the years when modern economic growth began in each country.
(2) The numbers in the table refer to the exchange rates of the current year.

6 *Preparatory investigation*

Industrial Revolution occurred as a result of this process. Scientific and technological revolution gradually spread from Britain to other regions thanks to this spread and diffusion effect. It is consistent with the phenomenon just stated in this regard.

The characteristics discussed next can be seen from Table 1.1. First, modern economic growth in today's developed countries began in the 19th century with the exception of Britain (which began in the 18th century). It shows that economic development takes a long time, far longer than eight or ten years. As for the whole process of modern economic growth, or when it began and when it was completed, there is no definite standard for making an accurate judgment. However, according to Kuznets's data ending in the mid-1960s, it can be seen that the aforesaid countries had completed modern economic growth at that time. In other words, it took these countries nearly 100 years to meet the criteria of developed countries. Second, with the exception of Japan, per capita income at the beginning of modern economic growth was more than US$200. This demonstrates that it takes some accumulation to kick off modern economic growth, which cannot start from scratch. The per capita income of the New World countries in the initial period was relatively high. Third, due to the different rates of economic growth, the changes in GNP per capita also vary greatly. In 1965, GNP per capita was the lowest in Japan, followed by Italy, and it was the highest in the United States. In 1978, it was the lowest in Italy, followed by the United Kingdom; Japan was nearly on a par with Australia; it was the highest in Switzerland, followed by Sweden. In 1989, Switzerland had the highest GNP, followed by Japan and Sweden, with the United Kingdom having the lowest GNP. There was little change in 1999 and 1989, with Switzerland ranking first, followed by Japan, Norway, and the United States, and with Italy at the bottom. In 2013, the Nordic countries had obvious advantages.

1.2.2 *Economic take-off*

After studying the process of economic development in various countries, Walt Whitman Rostow put forward the theory on the stages of economic growth. He wrote: "From an economic viewpoint, it is possible to classify all societies into five types: the traditional society, the preconditions for take-off, the take-off, the drive to maturity, and the age of mass production".[9] He argues that, "for a traditional society, it means that its structure develops within a finite production function. It is based on pre-Newtonian science and technology as well as the attitude of pre-Newtonian human beings towards the material world. . . . They share a common feature: progress in economic and technological productivity is limited."[10] "Take-off is the period when the obstacles and resistance to steady growth are overcome, and when the forces that spur economic progress expand and begin to dominate society". "Growth becomes normal. . . . The basic structure of the economy as well as the structure of society and politics have changed in 10 or 20 years, so that the stable growth rate can be maintained".[11] He stressed that three interrelated conditions must be met to achieve take-off. (1) A high rate of capital accumulation, that is, the rate of investment increasing from 5 to over 10 percent, is needed. (2) One or many key manufacturing sectors must dominate development. (3) Institutional, social, and political changes must be realized.[12]

Rostow judged the beginning of modern economic growth in various countries using the concept of economic take-off: 1783–1802 in Britain, 1830–1860 in France, 1833–1860 in Belgium, 1843–1860 in the United States, 1850–1873 in Germany, 1868–1890 in Switzerland, 1878–1900 in Japan, 1890–1914 in Russia, 1896–1914 in Canada, 1935 in Argentina, 1937 in Turkey, and 1952 in India and China.[13] Despite slight differences in the definitions and connotations, there is not much difference between Rostow's findings and Kuznets's conclusions, except for a large span. Moreover, Rostow developed his doctrine by dividing the stages of economic development into four levels and adjusted and enumerated the development status of various countries, including some new countries. The beginnings of economic take-off for only some countries are introduced here: 1933 in Argentina, Turkey, and Brazil; 1940 in Mexico; the early 1950s in India, China, and Iran; South Korea and Thailand in 1960.[14] Judging from Rostow's research, economic take-off and development originated in Western Europe and gradually spread to southern Europe, North America, and then to Asia. He predicted that it would also spread to the least developed regions such as sub-Saharan Africa. He is highly optimistic about developing countries with good development status.

Despite the fact that Rostow's theory on stages of economic growth is flawed in many parts and is also much criticized, it is nevertheless widely recognized and accepted. In particular, the concept of economic take-off is well known.[15] Rostow's observations, which are based on experience rather than on economic theories, cannot fully explain the patterns of economic development in all countries, but they are basically consistent with the facts of economic development in developed countries and can be used to predict the prospects for the economic development of developing countries, despite exceptions. As each country has its unique national circumstances, the experience of all countries in economic development is never exactly the same, but there should be certain similarity.

1.2.3 Views on China

The preceding discussion is an introduction to Kuznets's concept of modern economic growth, Rostow's explanation of economic take-off, and Ryoshin Minami's judgment on Japan's modern economic growth. What is the situation in China? Rostow holds that China achieved economic take-off in 1952, while Makino Fumio believes that 1978, when the reform and opening up were initiated, saw the beginning of China's modern economic growth. Although Rostow did not directly discuss the reasons for China's economic take-off, the following description shows that each country has its own characteristics and cannot be generalized. He wrote:

> I have discussed many key non-economic forces that determined the time span of the preconditions for take-off: a short time in Japan (32 years from the landing of Matthew Perry, or only 17 years from the Meiji Restoration); a long time in China (110 years from the Opium War); longer in Mexico (120 years from its independence). Obviously, there can be no definite and consistent time frame for the preconditions for economic take-off. My conclusion is

that peoples with their respective cultural, social and political traditions will decide whether, when and how to begin to achieve sustained growth.[16]

Makino Fumio did not specifically explain why the period around 1978 was set as the beginning of China's modern economic growth, but he discussed the relationship of reform and opening up with the beginning of modern economic growth. He cited rural reform, market reform, enterprise reform, and opening up to the outside world, among other things, as the basis for judgment.[17]

It is necessary to determine when China began to see modern economic growth, that is, the year for economic take-off. This involves two time points: one is the time to begin modern economic growth, such as 1886 in Japan. The other is the formal type of modern economic growth, that is, the year of progress toward normal industrialization and economic development, such as the early 20th century in Japan.[18] Based on China's economic development before 1949, we argue that it is impossible to pinpoint the starting point of China's modern economic growth, but it can only be seen as a background, at most as a transitional period. For example, Japan's period from the Meiji Restoration (1868) to 1885 can be seen as a transitional period at most.[19] Therefore, China's modern economic growth can only begin after 1949, which corresponds to Rostow's "theory of 1952" and Makino Fumio's "theory of 1978".

According to Rostow, each country has its respective national circumstances, and there is no certain basis for studying economic take-off, but some conditions must be met, such as institutional changes and an appropriate rate of investment. Regarding institutional reforms, China has experienced several changes of different forms and natures since modern times. The first change was the Opium War, which promoted China into a modern era and into the international community. However, this cannot be seen as an institutional reform because China still maintained feudal rule. What brought change to China is "seeing the world with eyes open" and knowing the progress of the outside world. We disagree with Rostow's view that China's take-off began with the Opium War. The second time was the establishment of the democratic republic in 1912. The third time was the founding of socialist China in 1949. The fourth time was the initiation of reform and opening up in 1978. The status in 1949 was essentially different from that in 1912, while the year 1978 saw significant changes compared to 1949, but both had a profound impact on social progress and economic development. The changes in 1912 and 1949, though different in the essence, produced similar effects because the former overthrew feudal dynasty and founded a republic, and the latter began a transition to a socialist society. The two can be used as the basis for the institutional change as described by Rostow. They both laid a somewhat institutional basis for promoting economic development, but they are not perfect. Therefore, it is justified to regard the early 1950s as the starting point for take-off, and the rest depends on whether other conditions are met.

Despite the fact that China began to transition to a socialist society after 1949, followed the Soviet model in its economic system, and operated the planned economy, it did promote economic development. In particular, the first five-year plan, which began to be implemented in 1953, clearly set economic development as a national goal. Therefore, we basically agree with Rostow's "theory of 1952", but it only initiated modern economic growth, equivalent to what Japan had in 1886. Before the reform and opening up in 1978, China's economy was full of twists and turns for a host of factors, which seriously restricted normal development. Nevertheless, it achieved a high growth rate, although not comparable to those of Japan and the "Asian Tigers" in the same period. The reform and opening up in 1978 pushed China's economic development on the right track. China not only gradually transitioned to a market economy but also integrated into the world economy. Despite many ups and downs thereafter, the overall direction of development remained unchanged, and the growth rate remained at a high level. It can be said that China embarked on a trajectory of normal economic development. Therefore, the period from the late 1970s to the early 1980s can be seen as the official beginning of modern economic growth, equivalent to what Japan had in the early 20th century. In this way, the nearly three decades from the early 1950s to the late 1970s saw the initial form of modern economic growth in China. It was equivalent to Japan's period from 1886 to the early 20th century. Developments after the 1990s belong to formal manifestation of modern economic growth, corresponding to Japan's period after the early 20th century.

1.3 Analysis of the rate of economic growth

The previous section introduces the beginning of China's economic take-off or modern economic growth, when it embarked on the right track of development. It hopes to inform people that China's economic development got off to a very late start, and China lagged far behind developed countries in terms of starting point. However, we also know the hypothesis of "late-mover advantage":[20] backward countries can realize rapid growth by drawing on technologies developed by advanced countries without the need to start from scratch. However, many backward countries in the world have failed to make full use of the late-mover advantages to achieve economic development for a host of reasons. Strictly speaking, only the Asian Tigers realized this vision in the decades after World War II. Of course, many countries, including China, achieved rapid growth to some degree and were closer to developed countries. We will analyze the changes in GDP and GDP per capita and examine them through comparisons with other countries.

1.3.1 GDP and GDP per capita

It is no exaggeration to describe China in the period from 1949 to 1952 as "having a huge population and a weak economy" or "poor and backward" because China had not yet recovered from the wounds of war, nor did it have the ability to recover. Needless to say, China has been the most populous country in the world, and ensuring that people are adequately fed and clad is a top priority and a strategic issue. Because of a weak economy, the people lived in straitened circumstances, and there was a lack of quality goods and services.

Table 1.2 shows China's real GDP from 1952 to 2010 using several prices and also compares it with the real GDP of the United States and Japan. It shows the following respects. First, China's total GDP has increased many times in about 60

10 *Preparatory investigation*

Table 1.2 China's real GDP and its comparison with those of the United States and Japan, Unit: US$100 million (%)

Year	Government Statistics (US$ 100 million)	Estimate by Hitotsubashi University (US$ 100 million)	Estimate by Maddison (US$ 100 million)	United States (US$ 100 million)	Japan (US$ 100 million)	China/ United States (Government statistics, %)	China/ United States (Hitotsubashi estimate, %)	China/ United States (Maddison estimate, %)	China/ Japan (Government statistics, %)	China/ Japan (Hitotsubashi estimate, %)	China/ Japan (Maddison estimate, %)
2005 price											
1952	940	1,551	—	22,439	2,969	4.19	6.91	—	31.66	52.24	—
1960	1,924	3,062	—	28,309	5,571	6.80	10.82	—	34.54	54.96	—
1970	2,814	4,264	—	42,700	1,3460	6.59	9.99	—	20.91	31.68	—
1980	5,142	7,136	—	5,8390	2,0827	8.81	12.22	—	24.69	34.26	—
1990	12,487	14,468	—	8,0339	3,2765	15.54	18.01	—	38.11	44.16	—
2000	33,684	30,241	—	11,2164	36,652	30.03	26.96	—	91.90	82.51	—
2010	91,264	91,264	—	130,630	39,548	69.86	69.86	—	230.77	230.77	—
2000 price											
1952	335	615	—	19,908	3,832	1.68	3.09	—	8.74	16.05	—
1960	685	1,214	—	25,117	7,192	2.73	4.83	—	9.52	16.88	—
1970	1,001	1,690	—	37,884	17,374	2.64	4.46	—	5.76	9.73	—
1980	1,829	2,828	—	51,805	26,885	3.53	5.46	—	6.80	10.52	—
1990	4,443	5,734	—	71,279	42,295	6.23	8.04	—	10.50	13.56	—
2000	1,1985	1,1985	—	9,9515	4,7312	12.04	12.04	—	25.33	25.33	—
2010	32,471	36,662	—	115,898	5,1050	28.02	31.63	—	63.61	71.82	—
1990 international dollar											
1952	1,625	2,131	3,059	16,201	2,103	10.03	13.15	18.88	77.27	101.33	145.44
1960	3,326	4,208	4,417	20,439	3,947	16.27	20.59	21.61	84.27	106.61	111.91
1970	4,864	5,859	6,369	30,829	9,535	15.78	19.00	20.66	51.01	61.45	66.80
1980	8,889	9,804	10,411	42,158	14,755	21.08	23.26	24.70	60.24	66.45	70.56
1990	21,585	19,879	21,239	58,005	2,3212	37.21	34.27	36.61	92.99	85.64	91.50
2000	58,229	41,551	43,193	80,983	25,965	71.90	51.31	53.34	224.26	160.03	166.35
2010	157,766	127,106	—	94,316	28,016	167.27	134.77	—	563.13	453.69	—

Data sources: Ryoshin Minami and Makino Fumio (2014), pp. 468–473; government statistics data from *China Statistical Yearbooks*.

Note: The international dollar in 1990 is multilateral purchasing power parity (PPP) years. According to government statistics, GDP in 2010 was nearly 97 times that of 1952, regardless of the type of prices used. Over the same period, the GDP of the United States increased by 4.8 times, and that of Japan increased by 12.3 times.

Japan's economy grew rapidly for quite a long time after World War II, with an economic growth rate of over 9 percent in the 28 years from 1945 to 1973. Nevertheless, Japan's growth rate is not comparable to that of China, which has achieved a growth rate of 9 percent over 40 years after the reform and opening up.[21] Second, we must be aware that due to China's weak economy, it is difficult to surpass these two economic powers even if China has achieved long-term ultra-high-speed growth. Although China surpassed Japan and even the United States in 2010 based on recent prices and the purchasing power parity (PPP) calculated in international dollars in 1990, there is still a gap according to the prices for 2000.

Third, the right column of the table shows the ratio of China's GDP to the United States' GDP during various periods calculated at different prices. China's GDP only accounted for 4 to 7 percent of the United States' GDP (the range calculated using different statistical methods) in 1952, and recently this proportion reached nearly 70 percent. Despite a gap, it is clear that the Chinese economy has grown and been approaching the U.S. economy (at 2005 prices). Even when measured using the 2000 prices, China's proportion has increased from the range of 1–4 to the range of 28–32 percent. This figure has soared from the range of 10–19 to the range of 134–168 percent if calculated at the PPP in 1990. China also lagged far behind Japan in terms of GDP. The proportion of China's GDP to Japan's GDP soared from just 30–53 to about 230 percent (at 2005 prices). Even calculated at the 2000 price, this figure jumped from 8–17 to 63–72 percent. If calculated based on the PPP in 1990, it soared from 77–146 to 453–564 percent.

Of course, we are aware that a key feature of economic aggregate is that it is veiled by the population. If a population is huge, the economic aggregate is also large, even if the GDP per capita is not necessarily high. Since China's population is several times or even a dozen times that of the United States or Japan, we cannot ignore the huge gap that still exists even if China catches up with or even surpasses them in terms of GDP. Table 1.3 shows several estimates of China's real GDP per capita as well as its gaps with the United States and Japan. For the convenience of comparison, the U.S. dollar is used for calculations. There is a large difference due to the different base years used. Prices in 2005 are closer to the present prices and relatively match what people perceive now. The results calculated at the 2000 prices are too low, while the results calculated at the PPP international dollars in 1990 are too high. Therefore, China's GDP per capita reflected by the 2005 prices in 1952 was US$165 (government statistics) and US$273 (Hitotsubashi estimate). In 2010, it reached US$6,822 (government statistics) and US$6,916 (Hitotsubashi estimate) using two statistical methods, which were 41 times and 25 times higher than that of 1952, respectively. The GDP per capita in 1952 calculated at the 2000 prices was only US$59 (government statistics) and US$108 (Hitotsubashi estimate). In 2010, it reached US$2,427 (government statistics) and US$2,741 (Hitotsubashi estimate), which were 41 times and 25 times higher than the former, respectively. Over the same period, the United States and Japan saw an increase of about 3 times

12 *Preparatory investigation*

Table 1.3 China's per capita real GDP and its comparison with those of the United States and Japan

Year	Government Statistics (US$ 100million)	Estimate by Hitotsubashi University (US$ 100million)	Estimate by Maddison (US$ 100million)	United States (US$ 100 million)	Japan (US$ 100 million)	China/United States (Government statistics, %)	China/United States (Hitotsubashi estimate, %)	China/United States (Maddison estimate, %)	China/Japan (Government statistics, %)	China/Japan (Hitotsubashi estimate, %)	China/Japan (Maddison estimate, %)
2005 price											
1952	165	273	—	13,820	3,486	1.19	1.98	—	4.73	7.83	—
1960	288	459	—	15,190	6,023	1.90	3.02	—	4.78	7.62	—
1970	344	521	—	20,344	12,899	1.69	2.56	—	2.67	4.04	—
1980	524	727	—	25,368	17,835	2.07	2.87	—	2.94	4.08	—
1990	1,100	1,274	—	31,567	26523	3.48	4.04	—	4.15	4.80	—
2000	2,668	2,395	—	39,412	28,889	6.77	6.08	—	9.24	8.29	—
2010	6,822	6,916	—	41,835	31,030	16.31	16.53	—	21.99	22.29	—
2000 price											
1952	59	108	—	12,262	4,499	0.48	0.88	—	1.31	2.40	—
1960	103	182	—	13,477	7,775	0.76	1.35	—	1.32	2.34	—
1970	122	206	—	18,049	16,651	0.68	1.14	—	0.73	1.24	—
1980	186	288	—	22,507	23,022	0.83	1.28	—	0.81	1.25	—
1990	391	505	—	28,007	34,237	1.40	1.80	—	1.14	1.48	—
2000	949	949	—	34,967	37,292	2.71	2.71	—	2.54	2.54	—
2010	2,427	2,741	—	37,118	40,055	6.54	7.38	—	6.06	6.84	—
1990 international dollar											
1952	286	375	538	9,978	2,469	2.87	3.76	5.39	11.58	15.19	21.79
1960	499	631	662	10,968	4,267	4.55	5.75	6.04	11.69	14.79	15.51
1970	594	716	778	14,688	9,138	4.04	4.87	5.30	6.50	7.84	8.51
1980	906	999	1,061	18,315	12,634	4.95	5.45	5.79	7.17	7.91	8.40
1990	1,901	1,751	1,871	22,791	18,789	8.34	7.68	8.21	10.12	9.32	9.96
2000	4,612	3,291	3,421	28,456	20,466	16.21	11.57	12.02	22.53	16.08	16.72
2010	11,794	9,502	—	30,205	21,982	39.05	31.46	—	53.65	43.23	—

Data sources: Ryoshin Minami and Makino Fumio (2014), pp. 468–473; government statistics data from *China Statistical Yearbooks*.

Note: The international dollar in 1990 is multilateral purchasing power parity.

and 9 times, respectively. Obviously, China saw much faster growth than these two countries. Of course, due to a low starting point, the difference in minimum values between China and the two countries is still large, and China has not yet exceeded the level of the United States in 1952 and Japan in 1970. Even after having achieved rapid growth, China still lags far behind developed countries in terms of GDP per capita. Based on the 2000 prices, the proportion of China's GDP to the United States GDP increased from 0.48–0.88 to 6.54–7.38 percent. Based on the 2005 prices, it increased from 1.19–1.98 to about 16.31–16.53 percent. Based on the international dollars in 1990, it increased from 2.87–3.76 to 31.46–39.05 percent.

1.3.2 Economic growth rate

Next, we observe and analyze the growth rate of the Chinese economy. Table 1.4 shows the growth rates of the Chinese economy estimated using several different approaches. Growth rates are different because several estimates are based on different baseline times and different methods. In general, the growth rate calculated based on the early time is biased toward the early stage, which is unfavorable to the later stage. Similarly, if a later benchmark year is used, it is favorable to the later stage but not to the early period. In addition, the data used here are calculated based on indexes, and the growth rates are continuous rather than based on a certain year alone. Therefore, appropriate comparison can be conducted. The Angus Maddison estimate is based on PPP and therefore differs slightly from other estimates. However, any method or benchmark year is a form of reflecting China's economic growth rate, only that each has a certain tendency or bias.

According to government statistics, China's economy grew fast in the 1950s, with a growth rate of 9.56 percent, but the rate of economic growth was low in the 1960s and 1970s. Particularly, it registered negative growth from 1960 to 1962 and from 1967 to 1968. After the reform and opening up, economic growth increased significantly, exceeding 9 percent in each period and even 10 percent in some periods. This is an eye-catching achievement compared with the previous period and even dwarfs those of Japan and the Four Asian Tigers during their high-growth period.

The Hitotsubashi estimate (1) is close to government statistics, except that estimates for the 1980s and 1990s are obviously lower, while estimates for years after 2000 are on the high side. Other estimates mostly reduced the previous growth rate but raised the growth rate in the later stage, especially after 2000. Despite different emphases, other estimates have the same tendency: too low in the early period and too high in the late stage. Specifically, it is low under the planned economy but high during the reform and opening up period. The most conservative estimate of growth for the previous stage was 4.75 percent, and the highest estimate was 6.87 percent, with an average of 5.50 percent. The lowest estimate for the later period was 8.03 percent, and the highest estimate was 10.09 percent, with an average of 9.08 percent. The difference in average growth rates between the two periods was 3.58 percentage points, which was a large difference. While these data cannot account for all the problems, it at least proves that the economy has grown rapidly

14 *Preparatory investigation*

Table 1.4 Several estimates of China's economic growth rate, Unit: %

Period	Government statistics (1)	Government statistics (2)	Government statistics (3)	Hitotsubashi estimate (1)	Hitotsubashi estimate (2)	Hitotsubashi estimate (3)	Hitotsubashi estimate (4)	Maddison estimate (1)	Maddison estimate (2)
1953–1960	9.56	4.63	4.86	9.09	8.16	6.76	4.79	5.33	6.58*
1961–1970	4.99	4.43	4.68	4.55	4.87	4.77	4.56	4.69	4.08
1971–1980	6.59	5.16	5.38	5.38	5.49	5.15	5.08	5.52	5.18
1953–1980	6.87	4.75	4.98	6.14	6.03	5.48	4.81	5.17	5.28*
1981–1990	9.35	9.41	9.25	7.38	7.11	7.19	7.43	9.28	7.30
1991–2000	10.13	10.17	10.45	7.71	7.89	7.71	7.44	10.64	7.47
2001–2010	9.60	10.51	10.58	10.84	11.80	11.48	9.53*	9.30*	–
1981–2010	9.69	10.03	10.09	8.98	8.93	8.79	8.03*	9.87*	7.29*
1953–2010	8.33	7.48	7.63	7.61	7.53	7.19	6.42*	7.29*	6.11*

Data sources: Ryoshin Minami and Makino Fumio (2014), p. 474; government statistics data from *China Statistical Yearbooks*. Maddison estimate (2) from Maddison's (2009).

Notes:
(1) Government statistics (1) are based on index calculations; government statistics (2) refer to prices in 2000; government statistics (3) refer to prices in 1990; Hitotsubashi estimate (1) is based on index calculations; Hitotsubashi estimate (2) refers to prices in 2000; Hitotsubashi estimate (3) refers to prices in 1990; Hitotsubashi estimate (4) refers to prices in 1987; Maddison estimate (1) refers to prices in 1987; Maddison estimate (2) refers to prices in 1990. For details of the various methods, see Ryoshin Minami and Makino Fumio (2014), pp. 222–242.

(2) "*" indicates that the years indicated by the number are slightly different from those in the table. For example, in the Maddison estimate (2), the years 1953–1960 should be 1951–1960; the years 2001–2010 are 2001–2008 in the Hitotsubashi estimate (4), and 2001–2003 in the Maddison estimate (1). For the years 1953–2010, it is 1953–2008 in the Hitotsubashi estimate (4), 1953–2003 in the Maddison estimate (1), and 1951–2001 in the Maddison estimate (2).

after the reform and opening up, which is not only far higher than the previous period but also higher than that of the vast majority of countries in the world.

For the period of 1953–2010, China's economic growth was estimated at no less than 7 percent or was estimated to be as high as more than 8 percent. This is an enviable figure. There is probably no other country – even post-war Japan and the Four Asian Tigers – that can achieve an average economic growth of 7 to 8 percent over nearly 60 years. It is no exaggeration to say that China has performed a world miracle in terms of economic growth. China's economy still remains in the upper middle level of development, and the full course of economic development is yet to be achieved. However, this rapid growth has brought tremendous benefits to China after all. It is no mean achievement to transform a least developed country in the world into a country with the upper middle level of development. However, when today's developed countries have achieved this status after more than 100 years of 2 to 3 percent growth rate,[22] how come China has not become a developed country? In simple terms, if the average growth rate of 8 percent in 60 years is converted into a growth rate of 4 percent over 120 years, China should have achieved the goal of economic development, but this is not the case. This situation cannot be fully accounted for, but we can consider the following areas.

First, China's economic base may not be as good as those of today's developed countries when they initiated modern economic growth. While it is difficult to make a direct comparison and a simple measure can only be made based on Kuznets and Maddison statistics, it is basically certain that China's economic base is relatively poor. When studying the economic development of developed countries, Kuznets found that the GDP per capita of such countries at the beginning of modern economic growth was above US$200 (at 1965 U.S. dollars), with Japan having the lowest GDP per capita of US$136 and Australia having the highest GDP per capita of US$760 (see Table 1.1). China's GDP per capita in the early 1950s was given in Table 1.3 but not at 1965 U.S. dollar prices. We can see that the GDP per capita in 1952 calculated at 1960 domestic prices was US$133.3. With reference to the figures in Table 1.3, it is sure that China's GDP per capita around 1952 was far lower than those of today's developed countries. Second, even if these estimates are credible, there are still uncertainties. Government statistics may be flawed. According to the preceding comparison, the figures of government statistics are the highest, and these may be overestimated. Of course, this is only speculation that is not proved by sufficient evidence. Third, China's economic growth mode is "extensive" rather than "restrained" or "intensive", which may compromise the rate of economic growth. In other words, there is inefficient and wasteful economic growth, which inevitably leads to superficial high growth. For example, steel produced by steelworks may be used to manufacture defective machine tools, but steel is already counted as GDP. This phenomenon was common under the planned economy and also existed to varying degrees after the reform and opening up. Fourth, it is the quality problem related to the third point. As a result of China's long-term pursuit of quantity rather than quality in the previous period, the output was of low quality, and new products and new processes were lacking. It resulted in quantitative growth, low quality, or repeated manufacturing. GDP may be high

16 *Preparatory investigation*

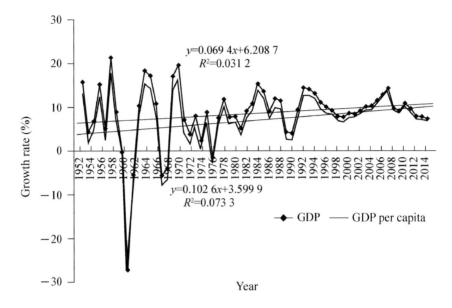

Figure 1.1 Growth rate of real GDP and GDP per capita
Data source: *China Statistical Yearbook* over the years.

in the absence of innovative growth, but production level and quality of life were rarely improved.

Figure 1.1 shows the growth rates of China's GDP and GDP per capita. The changes in the two are generally consistent, with the per capita value slightly lower than the total value. This should be linked to the fact that the population grew faster than GDP for a long time. Moreover, we can see economic fluctuations. The economy fluctuated greatly and frequently before the reform and opening up, and the difference between peaks and troughs was large, exhibiting great instability. This can be construed that China's economy just got off the ground during this period, and it was uncertain in many areas, including objective factors and human factors. Objective factors include the unstable economic base and an unsettled society in the early period. With regard to the subjective factors, the government knew little about economic laws and was inexperienced in implementing a planned economy. Coupled with bureaucracy, it was prone to make wrong decisions. The "Great Leap Forward" is a case in point, and the "Cultural Revolution" played havoc with normal economic activities.

Economic growth rates have rarely fluctuated during the period of reform and opening up, except for a few events in a few years. This is conducive to the long-term development of the economy. As far as the growth rate is concerned, it is certainly good news that the rate of economic growth is high and sustained. The two trend lines show that China's economy belongs to the "trend acceleration". Although this concept was advanced by a Japanese scholar when studying Japan's economic growth, it is also applicable to China's economic growth.[23] In other words, an economy on track will experience what Kuznets calls "self-sustaining growth" under the influence of many factors, hence more in-depth economic development.

1.3.3 Breakdown of growth rates

Long-term changes in the growth rates of China's economy after 1949 have been examined. Next, the growth accounting method is used to break down the growth rate and find the contribution of various factors to economic growth. The rate of economic growth $G(Y)$ can be broken down into the growth rate of labor force $G(L)$ and the growth rate of productivity $G(Y/L)$:

$$G(Y) = G(L) + G(Y/L) \tag{1.1}$$

with the production function of

$$Y = F(L, K, t)$$

$G(Y/L)$ can be broken down as follows:

$$G(Y/L) = \lambda + E_K G(K/L) \tag{1.2}$$

where K and L indicate capital and labor, respectively, and E_K is the productive elasticity of capital. λ indicates all forms of technological progress and is also the movement of production function caused by changing demand for products. The contribution of λ can be obtained by deducting the increased contribution of input from $G(Y/L)$. The results of breakdown based on equations (1.1) and (1.2) are shown in Table 1.5. Due to limited data, only the situation from 1953 to 2014 is calculated. It should be noted that the growth rate of GDP per capita here uses the

Table 1.5 GDP growth rate and its breakdown, Unit: %

Period	G (Y)	G (L)	G (K)	G (Y/L)	G (K/L)	EKG (K/L)	λ	λ/G (Y/L)
1953–1962	4.36	2.32	15.32	2.04	12.82	4.06	−2.01	−98.73
1963–1972	9.35	3.31	8.42	6.05	4.97	1.57	4.47	74.00
1973–1982	6.61	2.37	8.11	4.25	5.63	1.78	2.47	58.08
1983–1992	10.32	3.95	8.56	6.37	4.62	1.46	4.90	77.04
1993–2002	9.85	1.03	2.02	8.82	0.98	0.31	8.51	96.47
2003–2014	10.00	0.44	1.36	9.56	0.92	0.29	9.27	96.97

Notes:
(1) Y = GDP (1952 = 100 before 1978, and 1978 = 100 after 1979). The data are from *Data of Gross Domestic Product of China 1952–1995* and *China Statistical Yearbook* over the years.
(2) K = capital stock (1952 = 100); data for the 1952–1994 period from Zhang Jun et al. (2003); data for the 1995–2014 period are estimated based on China's total fixed asset investment on this basis.
(3) L = the number of employees; data from *China Labor Statistical Yearbook* over the years.
(4) G = growth rate.

data on labor, not population (GDP per capita). Therefore, the concept here should be "GDP per producer".

In terms of the economic growth rate $G(Y)$, it is significantly higher after the reform and opening up than during the planned economy period, although the growth rate was not low in the 1960s. This shows that after the reform and opening up, people's initiative for production and labor was stimulated, and efforts were made to conduct international trade and attract foreign investment, which has greatly promoted China's economic growth. In terms of the growth rate of the labor force $G(L)$, it was significantly higher during the planned economy period than during the reform and opening up period, which is exactly the opposite of the economic growth rate. In other words, the growth rate of the labor force was high but declined. The family planning policy implemented in 1979 caused a significant slowdown in labor growth. The growth rate of capital $G(K)$ changed in a way similar to the growth rate of labor, which goes against our common sense. Capital grew fast during the planned economy period but grew slowly after the reform and opening up, particularly after the 1990s. This is difficult to understand. However, it can be explained that the growth during the planned economy period relied more on large-scale input but was inefficient. After the reform and opening up, small-scale investment and efficiency gradually prevail.

The growth rate of labor productivity $G(Y/L)$ also shows a distinctive characteristic: it was low during the planned economy period but high after the reform and opening up. It was high in the 1960s during the planned economy period, indicating that the economy recovered from the destructive Great Leap Forward under the guidance of the central policy of "adjustment, consolidation, enrichment, and improvement". The growth rate of the capital/labor ratio $G(K/L)$ has the same tendency as the aforesaid capital growth rate. In other words, it was high during the planned economy period but low after the reform and opening up, especially after the 1990s. The growth rate of the capital/labor ratio $EKG(K/L)$ adjusted by the capital-output elasticity declined, particularly after the 1990s, which reflects the relative lack of capital and the relative labor abundance in China. Apart from some deviations in the data,[24] there may be problems of capital waste or inefficient use. In contrast to the relative lack of capital, the growth rate λ of technological progress showed significant increase, particularly after the 1090s. This shows that as China's economy develops, the original "extensive growth" model is replaced by the "intensive growth" model, which is a good thing. Finally, the contribution made by technological progress in labor productivity $\lambda/G(Y/L)$ not only changed from negative to positive but also increased. This is a good thing except for some calculation deviations.[25]

Next, the changes in China's economy and the world economy are observed. Table 1.6 shows China's share in the global population, global GDP per capita, and its growth rate from 1950 to 2010. In terms of population, China's share in the global population rose from 21.66 to 22.21 percent in 1970, and then fell to 19.41 percent in 2010. China's population grew faster than the global population, and the growth rate then declined, obviously lower than its global share in 1950. In terms of China's share of the world GDP, it was 4.50 percent in 1950. China's share changed

Table 1.6 Comparison between China and the world (1950–2010), Unit: %

Year	China's global share			Period	The world's growth rate			China's growth rate		
	Population	GDP	GDP per capita		Population	GDP	GDP per capita	Population	GDP	GDP per capita
1950	21.66	4.50	20.80	–	–	–	–	–	–	–
1960	21.95	5.32	24.23	1951–1960	1.85	4.70	2.78	1.84	6.58	4.46
1970	22.21	4.66	20.96	1961–1970	1.93	5.02	3.00	2.29	4.08	1.89
1980	22.12	5.22	23.61	1971–1980	1.85	3.83	1.94	1.75	5.18	3.20
1990	21.58	7.78	36.03	1981–1990	1.71	3.07	1.33	1.48	7.30	5.75
2001	20.94	12.29	59.23	1991–2000	1.45	2.92	1.45	1.01	7.29	6.16
2010	19.41	13.40	69.04	2001–2010	1.20	2.70	–	0.60	10.80	–

Data sources: Data on Chinese population are from the *China Statistical Yearbook* over the years and other data from Maddison (2009).

Notes:
(1) Figures before 2001 are Maddison estimates; the data for 2010 from the *World Development Indicators 2012*.
(2) It was the 1990 international dollar for years before 2001 and the PPP of the current year for 2010. GDP per capita in the column of China's global share is a percentage of the world average.

little during the planned economy period, only with a slight increase, reaching 5.22 percent in 1980. Thereafter, it gradually increased, reaching 13.40 percent in 2010. Specifically, although China's economy experienced rapid growth during the planned economy period, it did not significantly exceed the world average growth rate. After the reform and opening up, the growth of China's economy has obviously picked up speed, and its share of the world GDP has also increased rapidly. The GDP per capita refers to a proportion of the world average. In the case of China, it rose from 20.80 percent in 1950 to 69.04 percent in 2010, which is fast growth. Specifically, China's share remained below 24 percent before 1980, and there was no obvious increase. After 1990, China caught up faster in terms of GDP per capita. These can be confirmed by the growth rates shown on the right. The population grew faster than the world average and then was below the world average. The growth of GDP was slightly higher than the world average and then far exceeded the world average. The growth rate of GDP per capita also experienced this change.

1.4 Changes in industrial structure

In the course of economic development, the industrial structure will shift from the agriculture-centered state to one that centers on industry and services. Specifically, as the economy develops, labor will be transferred from primary industry to secondary industry and then to tertiary industry. This transfer, known as the Petty–Clark theorem, was discovered by the classical economist William Petty and later organized by Colin G. Clark. Table 1.7 shows that China's industrial structure in the period from 1952 to 2018 underwent tremendous changes compared with before the founding of the People's Republic of China. From the perspective

20 *Preparatory investigation*

Table 1.7 China's industrial structure, Unit: %

Year	Primary industry	Secondary industry	Tertiary industry	Total output value
1952	50.5 (83.5)	20.9 (7.4)	28.6 (9.1)	100.0
1960	23.4 (65.7)	44.5 (15.9)	32.1 (18.4)	100.0
1970	35.2 (80.8)	40.5 (10.2)	24.3 (9.0)	100.0
1980	30.2 (68.7)	48.2 (18.2)	21.6 (13.1)	100.0
1990	27.1 (60.1)	41.3 (21.4)	31.5 (18.5)	100.0
2000	15.1 (50.0)	45.9 (22.5)	39.0 (27.5)	100.0
2010	9.3 (36.7)	46.5 (28.7)	44.2 (34.6)	100.0
2018	7.2 (26.1)	40.0 (27.6)	52.2 (46.3)	100.0

Data source: China Statistical Yearbook over the years.
Notes: Outside the parentheses is the GDP structure, and inside the parentheses is the employment structure.

of output, the proportion of the primary industry in the GDP fell from 50 to 7.2 percent, the proportion of the secondary industry rose from 20.9 to 40.0 percent, and that of the tertiary industry jumped from 28.6 to 52.2 percent. This shows that China's economy showed an obvious tendency of industrialization. It can even be said that it reached the height of industrialization. The change in the proportion of the secondary industry is noteworthy. It developed ahead of time under the planned economy and reached a high level in 1960 and 1980. After the reform and opening up, it reached 46.5 percent in 2010 after adjustments. Since then, it began to decline, indicating a stage of transformation for China's industrialization.

The employment structure also exhibited this tendency. The proportion of the number of employees in the primary industry in the total employment fell from over 80 o 26.1 percent; the proportion in the secondary industry rose from about 7 to 27.6 percent; and the proportion in the tertiary industry rose from about 9 to 46.3 percent. Although the employment structure did not change as much as the output structure, this just illustrates the characteristics of each industry. The gap between the output proportion and the employment proportion in the primary sector is large because of low agricultural productivity – 26.1 percent of the labor force was needed to create 7.2 percent of the output. In contrast, 40.0 percent of output can be generated with only 27.6 percent of the labor force in the secondary sector. In the tertiary sector, 52.2 percent of output can be generated with 46.3 percent of the labor force. This comparison abundantly shows that the secondary industry has the highest productivity, followed by the tertiary industry, with the lowest productivity in the primary industry.

Table 1.8 shows the contribution made by the three industries to GDP in some years, with the tertiary industry making increasing contributions year by year. As the table shows, the contribution made by the primary sector was very low except in 1990, accounting for only 4.2 percent in 2018. The contribution made by the secondary sector rose from about 40 to about 60 percent, becoming a major contributor to GDP growth. It then declined. This reflects the Petty–Clark theorem. This is normal in the process of industrialization because the development of the

Table 1.8 Contribution made by the three industries to GDP and their pulling effect on GDP, Unit: %

Year	GDP	Primary industry	Secondary industry	Tertiary industry
Contribution to GDP				
1990	100.0	41.7	41.0	17.3
1995	100.0	9.1	64.3	26.6
2000	100.0	4.4	60.8	34.8
2005	100.0	5.6	51.1	43.3
2010	100.0	3.6	57.4	39.0
2018	100.0	4.2	36.1	59.7
Pulling effect on GDP				
1990	3.8	1.6	1.6	0.6
1995	10.9	1.0	7.0	2.9
2000	8.4	0.4	5.1	2.9
2005	11.3	0.6	5.8	4.9
2010	100.0	0.4	6.1	4.2
2018	7.3	0.3	2.4	3.9

Data source: China Statistical Yearbook 2019.

Notes:
(1) The industrial contribution ratio refers to the ratio of the increase in the added value of each industry to the increase in GDP.
(2) Industrial driver refers to the product of GDP growth rate and the contribution rate of each industry.
(3) Calculated at constant prices.

secondary sector will change in a "inverted U curve" manner as the economy develops. The tertiary sector developed rapidly, and its share rose from less than 20 to nearly 60 percent, showing the development trend of the tertiary sector. It must also be noted that the overall growth rate declined. The lower column refers to the share of the three industries in the growth rate of GDP over the years, and the sum of the three equals the growth rate of GDP. Similarly, secondary industry was the main contributor, and tertiary industry accounted for a low proportion but increasingly showed its advantages. This also reflects the Petty–Clark theorem.

The preceding discussion proves our view that the service sector is also one of the drivers of economic growth,[26] and it at least plays a greater role than agriculture, especially in the later stages of economic development. As described in Chapter 2 ("Development and Change in Agriculture"), agriculture contributes greatly to GDP in the early stage of economic development, and the industry makes a low contribution to GDP. Economic development in this stage requires capital, labor, foreign exchange, and markets. During this period, because the industry is insufficiently developed, the service industry attached to industry is relatively weak and only plays a bit role. When economic development reaches a certain extent, industry becomes the main driver of economic development, the status of agriculture declines, and the service industry plays an increasing role. As the economy further develops, the share of agriculture further declines; although industry is still important, its proportion in the economy increases slightly or even decreases, and the role of the service industry further increases.

1.5 Conclusion

This chapter introduces and discusses the overall situation of China's economic development after 1949, primarily covering three parts: the beginning of modern economic growth or economic take-off, the economic growth rate, and changes in industrial structure. As the beginning of China's economic take-off was rarely studied, analysis is conducted here, and our views are presented. In conjunction with the study of the Republic of China period, we believe that China's economy began to take off from the early 1950s after undergoing preparations or "an abortive take-off" in modern times, particularly from 1912 to 1949. After the occurrence of events such as the Great Leap Forward and the Cultural Revolution, the economy got on track since the late 1970s and early 1980s. The discussions introduce Rostow's remarks about the beginning of economic take-off in China and India and also mention the views of the Japanese scholar Makino Fumio on China's economic take-off.

With regard to the rate of economic growth, we introduce government statistics and scholars' estimates and believe that, even based on the lowest estimated growth rate, China's economic growth rate in the six decades from the 1950s to the early 21st century is second to none in the world, including Japan and later the Four Asian Tigers that had fast-growing economies after the war. At the same time, we pointed out that due to a host of negative factors, the high growth rate of China's economy did not reach the expected effect and that China is still at the upper-middle-income level without achieving the overall goal of economic development. China has a long and arduous road ahead, given constraints such as inefficient institutions, human resources, and the international environment.

How should we evaluate the economic growth or economic development as a whole after 1949? The final evaluation will be conducted in the final chapter, and only preparatory discussions are provided here. After 1949, China's economic development went through two stages: the early period (before 1978) was the planned economy period, and the later period (after 1978) was the period of reform and opening up. From the perspective of growth rate, it was lower in the early period than in the later period but not very low; it was higher than that in the vast majority of countries. The low growth rate in this period was primarily due to the level of economic development and the few resources that could be used, particularly capital equipment, funds, technology, and human resources. Because it was a period of confrontation between the East and the West, China could not obtain technologies and funds from Western countries. Moreover, due to the adoption of a seriously biased development strategy at that time, domestic resources were not utilized entirely and efficiently, and advantages were not fully exploited. In addition, because China was still a typical agrarian country at the time, the primary industry accounted for a very high proportion, the share of industry was small, and agricultural productivity was low, which seriously restricted economic growth.

Overview of China's economic development 23

After the reform and opening up, these problems were basically eliminated, at least in part and gradually. Further, the planned economy period laid the industrial foundation to some degree for subsequent development. Therefore, when China released individual initiative and introduced a wealth of advanced technologies through reform and opening up, the reserve of technology and personnel were effectively brought into play. Today, China has become the "world factory" or "world market" largely due to the reform and opening up, and, of course, the foundation laid during the planned economy period cannot be ignored. China has outperformed India, which has a similar development course, thanks in some measure to the industrial foundation laid under the planned economy.

Notes

1 Many studies have been conducted on the economic development of China in modern times and during the Republic of China period, but the views are different. Some said the economy developed while others said it stagnated. See Xu Dixin and Wu Chengming (1990, 1993), eds., Liu Foding et al. (1997), Liu Foding ed. (1999), and Rawski Thomas (2009). Based on the statistics available, we believe that China's economy developed to a certain extent during the Republic of China period, which is primarily reflected in the introduction of some emerging sectors and a trend of development featuring light industry in some cities. However, these sectors were subject to various constraints and could not drive progress as a whole. It still belongs to the natural economy dominated by the small-scale peasant economy.
2 Some countries may have higher per capita income than China, but they show no signs of development due to colonial rule. For example, according to Maddison (2009), India's GDP per capita was 584 dollars, and China's was 540 dollars in 1890; 599 dollars and 545 dollars, respectively, in 1900; 673 dollars and 552 dollars, respectively, in 1913; 728 dollars and 562 dollars, respectively, in 1929; and 668 dollars and 562 dollars, respectively, in 1938. However, because India was under colonial rule, it could not independently develop modern industries. The "dollar" here is the 1990 International Dollar based on purchasing power parity.
3 This view is from Guan Quan (2018b).
4 Rostow (2001), p. 38.
5 Ryoshin Minami and Makino Fumio (2012).
6 Ryoshin Minami (1981), p. 2.
7 Ryoshin Minami (1981), pp. 2–3.
8 Ryoshin Minami (1981), p. 8.
9 Rostow (2001), p. 4.
10 Rostow (2001), p. 6.
11 Rostow (2001), pp. 8–9.
12 Rostow (2001), pp. 39–40.
13 Rostow (2001), p. 38.
14 Rostow (2001), p. 10.
15 Regarding the controversy over Rostow's views, see Rostow (1988, 2001).
16 Rostow (2001), preface, pp. 15–16.
17 Ryoshin Minami and Makino Fumio (2012).
18 Ryoshin Minami calls the period from 1886 to when Japan's modern economic growth began to the early 20th century as "the initial form of modern economic growth" and the economic growth thereafter as "the official form of modern economic growth". Ryoshin Minami (2002), p. 6.
19 Regarding the situation and judgment of China's economic development during the Republic of China period, see Guan Quan (2018b).

24 *Preparatory investigation*

20 The original literature for this hypothesis was Gerschenkron (1962). Ryoshin Minami (1981) used this hypothesis to explain Japan's economic development.
21 See Yutaka Kosai (1981), p. 4.
22 For economic growth in developed countries, see Kuznets (1999) and Ryoshin Minami (1981).
23 See Ōkawa and Rosovsky (1973) and Ryoshin Minami (1981).
24 As the capital stock is estimated, there may be underestimation. The same problem exists in subsequent chapters on several industries.
25 Such great contribution made by technological progress is not even seen in Japan. see Ryoshin Minami (2002).
26 For the role of the service sector, see Guan Quan (2014).

Part II
Processes and characteristics

2 Development and change in agriculture

2.1 Introduction

China is a traditional agrarian country. Despite the tortuous process of industrialization, China had very developed agriculture, and it is precisely this that makes China the most populous country.[1] China's population soared from 90 million to 300 million from the beginning of the Kangxi reign (1662–1722) to the end of the Qianlong reign (1736–1795) during the Qing Dynasty. China's population at the time was close to the United States' population today. Even today, China can still be called an agrarian country in a sense. This has twofold meaning. First, China is a big agricultural country and is self-sufficient in grain, with a population accounting for one-fifth of the global population. Second, more than half of the population are farmers, although some of them are no longer engaged in agricultural production. Due to the well-known household registration system, China has more prominent work related to agriculture, rural areas, and rural residents compared with other developing countries. To put it another way, China has a high level of industrialization, and the share of industrial output in GDP is higher than that in the majority of countries, but the degree of urbanization is low (59.62 percent in 2018 according to the resident population and only 40.42 percent according to the registered urban population), even lower than that in some African countries with a lower level of development.

More importantly, despite China's rapid economic development, it will not be easy to fundamentally change this situation in the near future for a host of reasons. First, China is a country with a big population and little arable land, indicating that agriculture is more important to China compared to other countries with little arable land and a large population, such as the United States. If the production of grain and other crops cannot be ensured, China will face unimaginably and unacceptably severe difficulties. China's population may reach or exceed 1.5 billion in the coming decades, which puts higher demands on food output. There are only two ways to feed the large population. One is to increase arable land, but this is unrealistic. As urbanization deepens, arable land will decrease. The other is to increase investment in labor, fertilizers, pesticides, irrigation, machinery, etc. The greater the labor input is, the less marginal product may be under the condition of unchanged arable land. More fertilizers and pesticides are not necessarily better and may even be counterproductive. The use of machinery reduces the demand for labor force, which raises the question of how to free more rural labor from agriculture. In fact, the second path includes technological advances in both agriculture (such as irrigation) and industry (such as machinery) and, of course, biotechnology (such as seed improvement and genetically modified foods).

Second, due to a low level of urbanization in China, the surplus labor force in rural areas is not really transferred to other industries in cities. Although over 280 million farmers have become migrant workers in cities, they still occupy rural land (contracted land and land for rural housing), and the land is not used intensively. As a result, this negatively affects agricultural productivity and the economies of scale in agricultural production. Although the state has recently begun to study and implement the transfer of land contract rights, a host of problems still exist, and it is hard to thoroughly solve them in the short term. For example, should the transferred land be used for farming? If the arable land is used for other purposes, it will certainly not increase the yield of agricultural products. In another example, if the transferor reclaims the land contract right due to unemployment or other reasons, it will cause the loss of economies of scale. Therefore, this temporary land transfer mechanism is only a quick fix without solving problems in the long-term development of agriculture. That is to say, the land system or land ownership is the basis of agricultural production. It is difficult to achieve agricultural modernization unless these problems are solved.

Third, the change of farmer identity faces discrimination for a long time due to institutional and concept reasons, which harms agriculture itself and also has an adverse and far-reaching impact on social progress as a whole. The system here mainly refers to the household registration system, which divides the population into farmers and others. The farmer here is not only a profession but also an identity. Others here include all occupations except farmers, such as soldiers, workers, teachers, and doctors. The so-called institutions stem from the household registration system. Two differentiated policies and arrangements are implemented in rural and urban areas. Urban people enjoy better welfare and security benefits, whereas rural people basically rely on themselves. Urban people have better treatment than urban people in terms of housing, medical care, education, pension, etc. Urban people may not necessarily have high incomes, but they enjoy various public social services. In contrast, rural people enjoy no or insignificant services. As rural productivity is low, social accumulation is pitiful, it is difficult to meet the needs of all.

In brief, China will remain a big agricultural country for at least three decades to come, although it is also an industrial power. This is the result of China's special national circumstances and its stage of development. Therefore, it is necessary to place a higher value on agricultural issues, scientifically understand the status and role of agriculture, as well as the important of agriculture to China's economic development, and spur the development of agriculture and rural areas.

2.2 Development of agriculture

2.2.1 Changes in the status of agriculture

Table 2.1 shows several indicators of the status of agriculture in the national economy. It can be seen that the status of agriculture is declining, indicating the progress of

Development and change in agriculture 29

Table 2.1 Status of agriculture in the national economy, Unit: %

Year	Proportion of primary industry output	Proportion of rural population	Proportion of primary industry employees	Proportion of retail sales of consumer goods in rural areas	Proportion of agricultural taxes	Proportion of agricultural expenditure in fiscal expenditure	Proportion of agricultural and sideline product exports	Proportion of investment in agricultural capital construction
1952	50.5	87.5	83.5	54.6	28.0	5.3	59.3	–
1962	39.4	82.7	82.1	47.3	14.1	12.1	19.4	–
1970	35.2	82.6	80.8	53.4	11.4	7.6	36.7	–
1980	30.2	82.2	68.7	54.6	4.8	12.2	18.7	4.5
1990	27.1	78.4	60.1	55.0	3.1	10.0	16.9	1.5
2000	15.1	73.2	50.0	37.2	3.5	7.8	7.0	2.7
2014	9.2	64.1	29.5	32.0*	2.8**	9.3	2.7	3.2

Data sources: China Statistical Yearbook over the years; China Population and Employment Statistics Yearbook 2014; Ministry of Agriculture of the People's Republic of China (2009).

Note: The proportion of rural population refers to the data in 2013.
The share of retail sales of consumer goods in rural areas marked "*" refers to the data in 2013. The proportion of agricultural taxes and fees marked "**" refers to the data in 2007.

China's economy as a whole. The relative decline in the status of agriculture indicates the increase in the status of industry and services sectors, and this change symbolizes economic development. First, the proportion of output in the primary industry decreased from more than 50 percent in 1952 to less than 10 percent in 2014, a decrease of about four-fifths in more than 60 years. In other words, the agricultural output that accounted for half of China's economy now only accounts for less than one-tenth. In terms of the proportion of employees in the primary industry, it fell from 83.5 percent in 1952 to less than 30 percent in 2014, a decrease of more than 50 percentage points, although it is still far higher than the proportion of output. The comparison shows that agricultural production requires more labor compared to output, indicating low agricultural productivity. Nearly 30 percent of the labor force only creates less than 10 percent of output.

The proportion of the rural population declined from 87.5 percent in 1952 to 64.1 percent in 2014, albeit not significantly. However, this is no mean achievement because the household registration system in China largely restricts the transfer of rural population to cities. If calculated according to the permanent population, there is a reversal between urban and rural areas, with the rural and urban permanent populations in 2018 accounting for 40.4 percent and 59.6 percent, respectively. The share of retail sales of consumer goods in rural areas declined from 54.6 percent in 1952 to about 32 percent in 2008, indicating that consumption expenditure is increasingly spent on other commodities rather than on agricultural products. Because the income elasticity of food-based agricultural products is low, the income is spent more on industrial products and services rather than on agricultural products as their incomes rise.

Agricultural taxes, which had existed for thousands of years, were gradually abolished around 2004–2006. It accounted for 28 percent of the tax revenue in 1952, indicating its great importance when China was still in the initial stage of industrialization. As industrialization deepened, especially after the reform and opening up, the agricultural tax was slashed, even to a negligible extent. The proportion of agricultural expenditure in fiscal spending was relatively stable. Despite some fluctuations, it was roughly 5 to 13 percent. In a sense, it can be considered that there was no significant increase in agricultural investment. The proportion of agricultural and sideline product exports plunged from nearly 60 percent in 1952 to 2.7 percent in 2014. Over a span of more than 60 years, it changed from being the top foreign exchange earner to playing a negligible role. However, for the Chinese economy as a whole, this means the absolutely dominant role of manufactured goods exports, symbolizing the success of industrialization and economic development. Finally, the proportion of agriculture in capital investment has been low for a long time, which is a salient feature of China's economic development. During the planned economy period, there was a focus on investment in industry, especially heavy industry while agriculture was neglected. After the reform and opening up, industry and other sectors bring higher returns, and investment naturally prefers the nonagricultural sector.

2.2.2 Growth in output and input

After 1949, China's agriculture underwent difficult and tortuous development for several reasons. First, China's economy was backward at the time. The vast majority of the population lived in rural areas, and the vast majority of the labor were engaged in agricultural production, which was a small-scale peasant economy that features a small scale, low output, poor infrastructure, and a low level of mechanization. Despite great improvement, this situation is still not fundamentally changed, and China still lags far behind developed countries in this regard. Second, in terms of system, after the cooperative and collectivization movements in the 1950s, China entered a stage of collective farming under the people's commune system. This did not stimulate the farmers' initiative for production, and as a result agricultural production stagnated for a long time. It was one of the reasons that triggered China's subsequent reforms. Third, due to the slow process of industrialization and urbanization in China, much surplus labor in rural areas cannot be freed from agricultural production, and agricultural mechanization proceeds slowly. As a result, it is difficult to increase agricultural productivity. It should be noted that China's process of industrialization is not slow, but more emphasis was placed on heavy industry rather than light industry under the planned economy. Heavy industry is not as good as light industry in absorbing labor because heavy industry requires more capital equipment than labor. Fourth, in order to quickly catch up with Western developed countries during the planned economy period, the state placed a higher value on industry than on agriculture and did not preferentially allocate resources to agriculture. As a result, agriculture lagged behind industry for a long time. That is to say, China has had an insufficient understanding of agriculture for a long time, with insufficient investment and a lack of scientific and reasonable support policies.

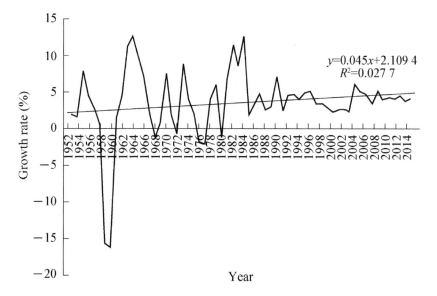

Figure 2.1 Growth rate of real added value of the primary industry

Data source: *China Statistical Yearbook* over the years.

Nevertheless, China saw rapid growth and made great strides in agriculture after 1949. Figure 2.1 shows the growth rate of the real added value of the primary industry. It shows that the growth rate fluctuated greatly in the early stage (the planned economy period) and slightly in the later stage (after reform and opening up). Particularly during the Great Leap Forward period, the primary industry declined greatly, resulting in great negative growth. Thereafter, it fluctuated largely but within a small range. In particular, negative growth occurred many times, but it was within a small range. After reform and opening up, the primary industry not only maintained high growth but also grew steadily, without drastic fluctuations. This is particularly important for the primary industry, primarily agriculture, because agricultural yield depends on the weather as well as the market. The quantity of crops sown is determined by the market situation in the preceding year. If it fluctuates frequently, the market signal will fail, which will affect farmers' sowing plans and also the market supply-and-demand relationship. Specifically, the average growth rate from 1953 to 2014 was 3.6 percent, which is very high in the case of agriculture. It is even higher than the long-term economic growth rate of developed countries.[2] In terms of stages, it was −0.7 percent from 1953 to 1962, 5.1 percent from 1963 to 1972, 3.8 percent from 1973 to 1982, 5.1 percent from 1983 to 1992, 4.1 percent from 1993 to 2002, and 4.5 percent from 2003 to 2014. The negative growth in the 1950s was clearly the result of the Great Leap Forward. Self-deceptive publicity such as a yield of over 5,000 kg per 0.06 hectare caused serious implications. It was mostly stable in other periods. Despite some fluctuations, there was overall stability. This is crucial and a matter of life and death for a populous country, especially a country with a large population and little arable land.

Table 2.2 shows several estimates of the primary sector output, the number of workers, and the growth rate of per capita output. In terms of output, the two sets of data are different mainly for the planned economy period, but the difference is not large. The trend of changes is basically the same. Both show that there was negative growth in the 1950s including the Great Leap Forward (1958–1960), although values are not high. The growth rate in the 1960s was high, although this period includes the late stage of the three years of serious hardships (1960–1962), the early stage of the Cultural Revolution, as well as the so-called period of economic adjustment (1961–1965). The growth rate in the 1970s was low, mainly due to the Cultural Revolution (1966–1976), which took up most of the time during this period. During the Cultural Revolution, vitality was lacking in agriculture and also in the industry and services sectors. All economic activities during this period were disrupted by political movements. The golden period of agricultural growth in the 1980s also saw the highest growth in history, which was obviously the result of agricultural reform. The adoption of the Household Contract Responsibility System and the disintegration of the people's communes greatly stimulated the farmers' initiative for production. Agriculture outperformed other industries in this period because the reform of other industries got off to a late start. The "ten-thousand-yuan a year household" refers to the farmers who got rich first. After the 1990s, the growth rate of agriculture declined somewhat, basically at 4 percent, which is a normal figure. It is difficult for the agricultural sector to have as high a

Development and change in agriculture 33

Table 2.2 Growth rate of primary industry, Unit: %

Period	Output		Number of employed persons		Output per capita			
	Government statistics	Hitotsubashi estimate	Government statistics	Hitotsubashi estimate	Government/ Hitotsubashi	Government/ Government	Hitotsubashi/ Hitotsubashi	Hitotsubashi/ Government
1953–1960	−1.57	−0.80	0.10	−0.89	−0.22	−0.81	0.55	−0.07
1961–1970	5.60	4.9	5.10	3.48	2.13	0.65	1.48	0.05
1971–1980	2.09	2.09	0.48	1.11	0.98	1.62	0.98	1.62
1981–1990	6.25	6.25	3.05	2.40	3.78	3.31	3.78	3.31
1991–2000	3.81	3.81	−0.75	−0.17	4.02	4.64	4.02	4.64
2001–2010	4.23	4.23	−2.50	−1.97	6.33	6.96	6.33	6.96

Sources: *China Statistical Yearbook* over the years; Ryoshin Minami and Makino Fumio (2014).

Note: The Hitotsubashi estimate refers to an estimate made by the research team at Hitotsubashi University in Japan. See Ryoshin Minami and Makino Fumio (2014) for details.

growth rate as industry has because agriculture is inferior to industry in terms of technological progress, economies of scale, and mechanization level. Moreover, China did not reach the Lewis turning point during this period. Rural areas had an abundant surplus labor force, and it was impossible to achieve large-scale agriculture and mechanized production, which is still not achieved today. Therefore, China's agriculture still has a long way to go.[3]

The growth rate of the number of employees shows an obviously different trend of changes from that of output. In the planned economy period, it has a similar basic trend with output, only with slow growth. The number of employees hardly increased in the 1950s but increased rapidly in the 1960s and slowly in the 1970s. However, the increase in the number of employees is largely the result of a swelling population because China saw an unprecedented population explosion during this period. Recognizing the negative impact of this situation, the government gradually implemented family planning policy since the 1970s. The early policy required late marriage and late childbearing. From 1979 onward, a strict family planning policy was enforced, and in particular, an urban couple could only have one child. This is the "one-child" policy.[4] The high growth rate in the 1980s may be due to the pilot agricultural reform. Agriculture had a good momentum of development, while industry and urban reform lagged. The surplus labor force in rural areas were engaged in agricultural production instead of becoming migrant workers in cities. This increase in employment also reflects the high growth of agricultural output during this period. It is the result of an increase in labor force, not driven by technological progress (or total factor productivity). After the 1990s, there was a wholly different picture, when continuous negative growth was registered. This also stands to reason. Due to the reform and development of the industrial and service sectors in cities, the demand for labor increases, and more and more rural surplus labor go to cities as migrant workers. As a result, the number of people employed in agriculture declines, while output still sees rapid growth. This is in contrast to the 1980s. In other words, output has a high growth while the input of labor decreases. This somewhat shows the positive effect of technological progress, economies of scale, and other factors of production. It also reflects that the downsized agricultural labor are what William Arthur Lewis calls persons with zero marginal productivity. In fact, capital in the factors of production also increases. The increase in capital means, to a certain extent, the wider application of mechanization.

Although there are four estimates of per capita output, they are similar. In particular, the data for the period after the reform and opening up are similar. The growth rate of per capita output basically changed in the same way as the growth rate of output, but the difference is that it was higher than the growth rate of output after the reform and opening up and lower than the growth rate of output during the planned economy period. This is, of course, reasonable. The agricultural labor during the planned economy period grew faster than after the reform and opening up, hence the opposite tendency to change. In other words, per capita output was low and then increased as a result of changes in the agricultural labor force. Of course, changes in the growth rate of per capita output are caused by the input of labor and also by technological progress, economies of scale, mechanization, operational efficiency, and other factors. From the perspective of growth rate, these factors

Development and change in agriculture 35

obviously play a very large role. These roles are at least implied by the situation that the growth rate of per capita output was low and then increased and that the growth rate of agricultural labor force was high and then decreased.

Table 2.3 somewhat shows the change in agricultural production investment. In terms of rural employees, it experienced two periods of high growth. First, in the 1960s, it is mainly the result of the high birth rate. The other occurred in the 1980s, when agricultural reforms were successful, while urban reforms had just been initiated and cities were yet to show their advantages. Agricultural labor still remained in rural areas at the time. Since the 1990s, there was a downward trend in investment in rural production, which is obviously the result of family planning policies and urban development. When a country's economy grows rapidly and further develops, the demand for labor in industrial and services sectors other than agriculture sharply increases, which is highly related to the characteristics of these two sectors. Employment in both industry and services sectors is smaller than that in agriculture in terms of absolute number and proportion, but it grows faster than in agriculture. As a result, this requires the transfer of surplus labor from agricultural labor. Due to agricultural surplus labor, the productivity level of agriculture remains unaffected even if much labor is transferred to cities.[5]

In terms of agricultural spending, it grew slowly before the 1970s and then grew rapidly and even at an extraordinary speed. This clearly shows that the government attaches increasing importance to agriculture as time goes on. Of course, there was the issue of financial resources. In the early days, little investment was made in agriculture due to the underdeveloped economy, low tax revenues, and greater emphasis on the development of industry. After the reform and opening up, as economic growth accelerated and tax revenue increased, it was possible to increase investment in agriculture. On the other hand, the government was increasingly aware of the underdeveloped agriculture and began to make compensation.

Rural electricity consumption also grew rapidly. In particular, the growth rate in the early stage was significantly higher than that in the later period, primarily because electrification was not available for China's agriculture in the early days,

Table 2.3 Partial investment in agricultural production

Period	Number of rural employees (10,000)	Agricultural expenditure (100 million yuan)	Rural electricity consumption (100 million kWh)	Consumption of fertilizers (10,000 metric tons)	Total power of agricultural machinery (10,000 kW)
1952–1962	1.56	2.95	–	64.34	364.92
1963–1970	3.16	3.26	54.94	50.83	20.68
1971–1980	1.33	20.35	23.53	26.15	58.10
1981–1990	4.86	10.54	16.33	10.41	9.47
1991–2000	0.35	30.00	18.68	6.01	8.32
2001–2013	−1.49	70.29	18.08	3.05	6.98

Data source: *China Statistical Yearbook* over the years.

36 Processes and characteristics

and there was even no data on the 1950s. The high growth in the later period was due to the fact that agricultural irrigation and mechanization required more electricity, including household electricity consumption, of course. Electrification shows the progress and development of both rural production and living. This momentum still remains strong. The amount of chemical fertilizers used was also high in the early period and low in the later period because the application of chemical fertilizers basically began in the 1950s. As it started from scratch, the growth rate was high. As chemical fertilizers become popular, the growth rate returned to a normal state. Moreover, as people gradually recognized the side effects of fertilizers, organic agriculture came back, and the momentum of growth of chemical fertilizers weakened.

This is particularly true of agricultural mechanization. There was basically no decent agricultural machinery in the 1950s. In 1952, the whole country only had 1,307 large and medium-sized tractors, which are the most important and most basic agricultural machinery, and had only 284 combine harvesters. In 1970, there were 125,000 tractors and 8,000 harvesters. The two figures reached 745,000 and 27,000 in 1980, 814,000 and 39,000 in 1990, 975,000 and 263,000 in 2000, and 4,219,900 and 2,059,200 in 2018. Both have achieved rapid growth. It is noteworthy that the number of large tractors peaked at 6,700,800 in 2017 and then declined. At the same time, the number of small tractors has been increasing, from 1.373 million in 1978 to 18.1826 million in 2018, indicating the increasingly miniaturized agricultural machinery. With the deepening urbanization and the transfer of agricultural labor in China, agricultural production will increasingly rely on mechanization, which is an irresistible trend.

2.2.3 Breakdown of growth rates

The long-term changes in the growth rate of the primary industry after 1949 have been examined. The growth accounting method is used to break down the growth rate and calculate the contribution made by various factors to economic growth. First, the rate of economic growth $G(Y)$ can be broken down into the growth rate of labor $G(L)$ and the productivity growth rate $G(Y/L)$:

$$G(Y) = G(L) + G(Y/L) \tag{2.1}$$

With the production function $Y = F(L, K, B, t)$ as the premise, $G(Y/L)$ can be broken down as follows:

$$G(Y/L) = \lambda + E_K G(K/L) + E_B G(B/L) \tag{2.2}$$

in which, K and B refer to capital and land area, respectively, and E_K and E_B refer to capital and land production elasticity, respectively. The $E_K G(K/L)$ and $E_B G(B/L)$ on the right indicate the increases in productivity caused by the increase in the capital/labor ratio, and the increase in the land/labor ratio, respectively. They refer to the contribution made by the increase in factors of production. λ represents all forms of technological progress and also the movement of production function caused by changes in product demand, etc. λ can be obtained by subtracting the increased contribution of the input from $G(Y/L)$. The results of the breakdown according to equations (2.1) and (2.2) are shown in Table 2.4. Only the 1982–2014 period is calculated due to the limited data.

The growth rate of agricultural output $G(Y)$ shows relatively flat changes. Except for the high growth in the early 1980s, it was mostly 4 to 5 percent in other periods and low in the late 1990s. This growth rate is very high as far as agriculture is concerned and even exceeded the economic growth rate of most countries. Due to the limitations of agriculture, the agricultural growth rate is generally not very high. The growth rate of the agricultural labor force $G(L)$ shows an optimistic situation. After the reform and opening up, China's agricultural labor force was reduced. Although the reduced labor contributes little to agricultural production, it contributes to other industries.[6] The growth rate of labor productivity $G(Y/L)$ is not only positive except in the late 1980s but also high, exceeding 6 percent in most periods. This is an enviable figure. The $E_K G(K/L) + E_B G(B/L)$, which is the sum of the growth rates of the capital/labor ratio, and the land/labor ratio also rose perceptibly, indicating that both capital and land contributed to the agricultural growth and labor productivity. Moreover, this contribution became more important in the late 1990s. In contrast, the advance of agricultural technology λ is unsatisfactory, indicating that agricultural technology contributed little to the growth of agricultural output and productivity. It also shows that China's agriculture still belongs to traditional agriculture and that there is still a long way to go.

2.3 Institutional changes

The development of agriculture relies on several conditions, all of which are indispensable. If any of these conditions was not met, it would lead to

Table 2.4 Growth rate of primary industry and its breakdown, Unit: %

Period	$G(Y)$	$G(L)$	$G(Y/L)$	$E_K G(K/L) + E_B G(B/L)$	λ	$\lambda/G(Y/L)$
1982–1986	7.58	0.98	6.60	−1.08	7.68	116.37
1987–1991	4.01	4.76	−0.75	−0.95	0.20	−27.13
1992–1996	4.64	−2.29	6.93	1.69	5.24	75.64
1997–2001	2.91	0.89	2.02	9.00	−6.98	−345.44
2002–2006	4.20	−2.56	6.76	4.98	1.77	26.26
2007–2014	4.18	−4.12	8.30	9.13	−0.83	−9.94

Notes:
(1) Y = GDP (1978 = 100). The data are from *Data of Gross Domestic Product of China 1952–1995* and from *China Statistical Yearbook* over the years.
(2) K = capital stock (1952 = 100); data for the 1982–1994 period from Zhang Jun and Zhang Yuan (2003); data for the 1995–2014 period are estimated based on China's total fixed asset investment on this basis.
(3) L = the number of employees; data are from *China Labor Statistical Yearbook* over the years.
(4) B = arable land area; data for 1982–1997 are from the World Bank database *World Development Indicators*; data for 1998–2014 are from *China Land and Resources Statistical Yearbook*.
(5) G = rate of change.

inefficiency or limited output. These conditions are as follows. First is land because no crop is inseparable from the land. Despite significant achievements in the latest soil-less cultivation technology, future agriculture without the land would be unimaginable. Land can be transformed to some extent. Barren land can be turned into fertile land through physical, chemical, and biological techniques, but the effect is limited and the cost high. Second is the weather. It is somewhat outdated to say that we live at the mercy of the elements, but modern technology has not fundamentally changed this situation. It is impossible to conceive an era when agricultural production is not affected by the weather. Agricultural workers are helpless in the face of natural disasters or inclement weather. Third is input of various production factors, including labor, capital equipment, and irrigation facilities. The greater these inputs are, the higher the output will be, and vice versa. Fourth is institutional factor. China's agriculture after 1949 has undergone a process of repetition in terms of the system: from individual operations to collectivization and then back to individual operations. Specifically, cooperatives were gradually introduced after 1949. Farming by individual farmers was replaced by organized production. This collectivization pattern, from elementary agricultural producers' cooperatives to advanced agricultural cooperative teams to people's communes, continued until 1983. Since the late 1970s, the Household Contract Responsibility System was implemented in some rural areas,[7] whereby farmers signed contracts with production teams to ensure how many agricultural products could be produced throughout the year. The output belonged to farmers themselves, except for the grain handed over to the state. This greatly stimulated the farmers' initiative for production. Thanks to this mechanism, China's agricultural sector was freed from inefficiency and slow going. It was officially recognized and promoted by the government and soon became popular nationwide. After a period of validation, the government recognized the superiority of this system and also decided to abolish the collective form of people's communes. The Household Contract Responsibility System, which is a system of production based on families, was adopted. Thereafter, a decentralized state of individual operation is implemented in China's agriculture.

Today, China still maintains this contract system for agriculture, but as the economy rapidly develops, there occur a host of new problems that were not encountered more than 40 years ago. It is therefore necessary to explore and study system and institutional reforms. First, China is close to depleting or has already depleted rural surplus labor. The agricultural labor gradually becomes insufficient. How to use agricultural labor more intensively and effectively becomes a problem. Second, as urbanization deepens, some farmers inevitably become urban residents, and the land contracted by these farmers must be circulated. The circulation of land poses a problem. Third, farmers with large-scale operations will emerge as a result of the circulation of land, and it is difficult to maintain this only by relying on the contract system. It will eventually raise the issue of ownership of the land, not just the right to use. Of course, many related problems remain to be solved. It should be said that the institutional reform of China's agriculture still has a long way to go.

2.3.1 From individual operations to collectivization

Like industry and other sectors, China's agricultural sector underwent a process of transformation from individual operations to collectivization and then to individual operations in terms of institutions and mode of production after 1949. The production system of China's agriculture underwent a cycle of repetition. Here is a confirmation of the first process, that is, from individual operations to collectivization. As shown in Table 2.5, the total number of farmer households in 1950 was 106 million, and the agricultural population was 461 million. By 1957, the two figures increased to 124 million and 540 million, respectively. The rural labor force jumped from 182 million in 1952 to 206 million in 1957. During this period, the collectivization movement began gradually, and the proportion of farmer households organized in different forms soared from 10.9 percent in 1950 to 97.5 percent in 1957. Almost all farmer households were organized in some forms. In particular, this proportion rose rapidly after 1954, indicating accelerated collectivization. Collectivization took different forms and progressed from primary to advanced levels. In the early days, it featured mutual aid groups and gradually transitioned to cooperatives. Cooperatives also transitioned from the primary to advanced levels. This evolution occurred primary in 1956 and 1957, when the proportion of total number of farmers admitted to cooperatives approached nearly 98 percent. This increase in total proportion was achieved through a surge in the number of advanced cooperatives.

The number of people's communes reached 26,500 in 1958 and increased thereafter, reaching 57,800 in 1961, 74,800 in 1962, and as high as 81,000 in 1963. Thereafter, it began to decrease, falling to 70,000 in 1967, fewer than 60,000 in 1968, and about 51,000 to 54,000 in 1982. The number of production brigades jumped from 518,000 in 1959 to 734,000 in 1961 and remained between 600,000 and 700,000 for a long time thereafter. The number of production teams increased from 3.29 million in 1959 to 5.643 million in 1963 and remained between 4.5 million and 6 million for a long time. It can be seen that people's communes began to develop rapidly in 1958 and reached their heyday in 1963 and 1964. It remained relatively stable thereafter, having basically achieved full coverage. The number of rural households covered by the people's communes increased from 129 million in 1958 to 183 million in 1982. In the subsequent years, people's communes should include all farmer households. During this period, the agricultural population increased from 538 million in 1958 to 836 million in 1982, and the rural labor jumped from 213 million in 1958 to 339 million in 1982.[8]

2.3.2 From collectivization to individual operations

China experienced the unusual Cultural Revolution from 1966 to 1976, which caused huge losses to the economy. Thanks to good social security, urban residents had at least access to a secured supply of food and nonstaple food although they were poor. In rural areas, people largely depended on the weather and local natural conditions for a good life. If the natural conditions were unfavorable and if all materials had to be arranged according to a fixed distribution system under the state monopoly of

Table 2.5 Development of mutual aid cooperatives for agricultural production

Item	1950	1951	1952	1953	1954	1955	1956	1957	1958
Total number of farmer households (10,000)	10,553.6	10,927.3	11,380.9	11,632.5	11,732.5	11,920.1	12,046.0	12,415.6	12,861
Agricultural population (10,000)	46,059.0	47,626.0	49,191.0	50,067.0	51,037.0	52,130.0	52,826.0	54,035.0	–
Rural labor force (10,000 people)	–	–	18,243.0	18,610.0	19,088.0	19,526.0	20,025.0	20566.0	–
Proportion of farmer households organized (%)	10.9	17.5	39.9	39.5	60.3	64.9	–	97.5	–
Number of mutual aid groups (10,000)	280.2	423.7	802.6	745	993.1	714.7	850.0	–	–
Number of households in mutual aid groups (10,000)	1,151.1	1,916.1	4,536.4	4,563.7	6,847.8	6,038.9	104.2	–	–
Number of cooperatives	19	130	3,644	15,068	114,366	633,742	756,000	789,000	741,000
Proportion of farmer households in cooperatives (%)	–	–	0.05	0.24	1.96	14.19	97.8	97.5	95.1
Proportion of farmer households in primary cooperatives (%)	–	–	0.05	0.24	1.95	14.16	8.64	1.3	–
Proportion of farmer households in advanced cooperatives (%)	–	–	–	–	0.01	0.03	89.2	96.2	–

Data source: Du Runsheng (2002), Appendix 2, pp. 763–767.

purchase and marketing, farmers had to work for collectivized production teams, and there was no opportunity to engage in individual production and management according to their own wishes. There was no surplus income. If a production team sustained a loss, production team members (or cooperative members) had no income despite one year's labor and could only borrow money from the production team in the form of loans. If a production team also had a deficit, it would borrow money from the higher-level production brigade or the people's commune. Many production teams had difficulty in maintaining operating expenses, not to mention those in the poor areas.

After the end of the Cultural Revolution, some areas began to implement the Household Contract Responsibility System, under which the production team entrusted the land to the farmer households for cultivation, and farmer households farmed the land according to their own capabilities. If it was well run, farmers could sell the remaining output on the market after handing over the prescribed amount of grain, and the income belonged to them. This led to individual operations to some extent. This contract system took several forms. As shown in Table 2.6, it was divided into five forms:[9] fixing work according to quotas, linking output quotas to each group, linking output quotas to labor, fixing farm output quotas for each household, and work contracted to households. The work contracted to households prevailed. It accounted for only 38 percent in 1981. By 1984, it basically covered all production teams.

Table 2.7 shows the changes in fixed assets in the people's commune era and its subsequent era. The fixed assets in the people's commune era were primarily owned by production teams at the primary level. Although the proportion gradually

Table 2.6 Implementation of Household Contract Responsibility System in rural areas

Year	1979	1980	1981	1982	1983	1984
Proportion of units that implement the contract system (%)	84.9	93.0	97.8	98.7	99.5	100.0
(1) Proportion of units that implement fixing work according to quotas (%)	55.7	39.0	16.5	–	–	–
(2) Proportion of units that link output quotas to each group (%)	24.9	23.6	10.8	–	–	–
(3) Proportion of units that link output quotas to labor (%)	3.2	8.6	15.8	–	–	–
(4) Proportion of units that fix farm output quotas for each household (%)	1.0	9.4	7.0	8.8	–	–
(5) Proportion of units that implement work contracted to households (%)	0.1	5.0	38.0	80.9	97.8	99.1
(6) Proportion of units that implement other systems (%)	–	7.4	9.7	–	–	–

Data source: Du Runsheng (2002), Appendix 2, pp. 773–774.

Note: The vast majority of the units here are production teams, and a few are production brigades. The proportion here refers to the proportion to all units.

Table 2.7 Changes in fixed assets of rural organizations at all levels, Unit: %

Year	People's commune era					Postpeople's commune era			
	Total fixed assets	Communes	Production brigade	Production team	Original value of fixed assets	Owned by village enterprises	Collectively operated by village groups	Owned by joint household enterprises	Self-owned by farmers
1974	100.00	9.15	16.18	74.66	–	–	–	–	–
1977	100.00	15.00	25.72	59.28	–	–	–	–	–
1980	100.00	20.52	27.24	52.25	–	–	–	–	–
1983	–	–	–	–	100.00	–	–	–	–
1987	–	–	–	–	100.00	39.85	59.74	–	40.26
1991	–	–	–	–	100.00	51.21	16.45	2.94	40.77
							8.34	2.54	37.90

Data source: Du Runsheng (2002), Appendix 2, pp. 771–772.

Note: The total for each of the two eras is 100, and it is not shown here. Due to rounding, the totals of each item are not exactly equal to 100.

decreased, they still held more than half of the share. Production brigades owned about one fourth of the fixed assets, and this figure increased slightly during the observation period. The proportion of the communes' fixed assets gradually rose from less than 10 to over 20 percent, indicating a tendency to asset concentration. In the post-people's commune era, the proportion of fixed assets collectively operated by village groups plunged from nearly 60 to less than 10 percent. These were replaced by rural enterprises, that is, township and village enterprises. In other words, the proportion of collectively owned fixed assets did not change much on the whole, only that they were transferred from original village group collectives to township and village enterprises. The part owned by the farmers remained relatively stable for a long time, with a slight decline from about 40 percent in the early period, but the decline was not large. On the whole, township and village enterprises in the post-people's commune era are a key force in terms of rural fixed assets.

2.4 The role and significance of rural industry

Like other countries, China has a rural industry that goes back a long way. It is a supplement and sideline sector for agricultural production, covering the repair of farm implements, handmade textiles and clothing processed from agricultural products as raw materials, food processing industries like rice and flour grinding, traditional handicrafts, and petty commodities. All of these originated in rural areas. In modern times, mechanical elements were added to certain extent. It was semi-automatic or improved according to mechanical principles, and production was more efficient. A more diverse and complex rural industrial system took shape, but there was no major technological progress until after 1949.

Like other sectors, the development of rural industry after 1949 can be divided into two periods: the period of planned economy and the period of reform and opening up.[10] The early period experienced complex changes, primarily under the influence of political movements and development strategies as well as their guiding ideas. The later period also underwent changes at different stages, mainly due to the system (such as ownership) and market (domestic and international). In the 1950s, it mainly concerned the changes in rural land ownership, including the transition and evolution from private ownership to collective ownership, or collectivization and people's communes, as well as the impact of the Great Leap Forward. In the early 1960s, it was the policy of "adjustment, rectification, enrichment, and improvement". The Cultural Revolution broke out in the late period. In the 1970s, commune- and brigade-run enterprises emerged and became the direct predecessor of township and village enterprises.

After the reform and opening up, China's township and village enterprises emerged and developed rapidly, making significant contributions to economic development in rural areas and even cities. First, township and village enterprises created many jobs for rural areas. At a time when China still had "surplus labor", township and village enterprises provided employment for 150 million laborers except for those farmers (about 260 million to 280 million) who worked as migrant workers in cities. Today, about 280 million people in rural areas are actually engaged in agriculture (agriculture, forestry, animal husbandry, and fisheries), accounting for 54.5 percent of the total rural employees of 520 million (in 2008).[11] In other words, most of the employees outside agriculture are employed by township and village enterprises, which are second only to agriculture in terms of job creation in rural areas. Second, it provides financial guarantee for the economic development of rural areas. In 2008, the added value of township and village enterprises was 8.4 trillion yuan, exceeding the total output value of agriculture, forestry, animal husbandry, and fishery sectors (5.8 trillion yuan). Total profits and taxes paid by township and village enterprises reached 2.1 trillion yuan and 876.5 billion yuan, respectively. These funds may not be fully used for agriculture and rural areas, but they can spur local economic development. Third, township and village enterprises lay the foundation for urbanization in rural areas. Despite their domicile in rural areas, township and village enterprises are engaged in nonagricultural products and services, and it is therefore necessary to establish an extensive commercial network and production bases. This will promote the development of transport as well as the gathering of enterprises. Gradually, large-scale areas with urban functions are formed. Many new types of towns have emerged in this way. Fourth, township and village enterprises have promoted the accumulation and development of talents from different backgrounds. Entrepreneurs, technicians, marketing staff, managers, accountants, and skilled workers are needed at the township and village enterprises. These talents are a scarce resource in rural areas. However, township and village enterprises have tempered and cultivated these talents during their development. Fifth, agricultural resources are better brought into play. Many township and village enterprises use agricultural products or related products as raw materials. Cotton, grain, fruit, timber, aquatic products, chicken, duck and fish, forest products (such as ginseng, pilose antler, Chinese herbal medicine) undergo deep processing to become industrial products with increased added value, thereby raising prices and boosting income. Sixth, many township and village enterprises export products to earn foreign exchange. Because China is a developing country and the labor cost is low, labor-intensive industries are developed, and township and village enterprises play a significant role in these industries. Export-oriented products they produce provide inexpensive, fine products for all countries and also guarantee China's import of high-grade, precision, and advanced technology in the form of foreign exchange, particularly in the 21st century.

As we know, the rural issue is not really an issue of economics, at least not entirely so, but more of a sociological issue. In the so-called "three rural issues" (issues relating to agriculture, rural areas, and rural people), agriculture belongs to an economic category, while the other two concepts are sociological issues. Therefore, when we discuss rural industry or township and village enterprises, we must observe and analyze from a sociological standpoint. Although economic study is required, economic development is part of social development after all. At the same time, sociology and economics overlap and can be complementary when it comes to some issues. The three rural issues or the rural industry (township and village enterprises) issue is such a topic.

The rural industry, or township and village enterprises in a broad sense, in China is important for economic development and economic activities and also has social significance. Due to the long-term feudal society and the impact of the household registration system in China, there is also the concept of farmer identity in addition to rural areas and agriculture, hence the three rural issues. This is not merely the field of economic research but also the field of sociological research. The discussion of the development of rural industry or township and village enterprises from a sociological viewpoint, or the impact on rural society, includes two aspects. First is whether the development of rural industry or township and village enterprises can lead to small and medium-sized cities, or new small cities centering on these enterprises. Second is how the development of these enterprises will affect rural society.

After 1949, particularly after 1958, China gradually established a strict household registration system, which divides residents into rural residents and urban residents. The two cannot be exchanged in principle. Of course, alongside the development of economy and society, especially due to the development needs of industry and cities, the practice of changing some rural residents into urban residents has been ongoing. This situation has been more prominent after the reform and opening up. Despite the existence of household registration system, this status becomes less important for the labor force. A wealth of rural laborers flock to cities alone or with their family members, becoming a population of migrant workers with Chinese characteristics. The most salient feature of this is that migrant workers do not have registered urban residency in cities and are not entitled to social security in cities. Moreover, they are divorced from agricultural production. Many young migrant workers, or second-generation migrant workers, have never been engaged in farming work since childhood. For them, the rural area is just the hometown, and being farmers is just the identity. They have lived in cities for a long time and identify more with the city, looking forward to becoming real urban residents one day. On the other hand, as the urban–rural gap and this gap widen, most young people yearn for the city. They have a city "dream". To realize this dream, they work in the city at the expense of long-term separation from their parents, wives, and children. Some succeed in becoming urban residents, and some become successful businesspeople or entrepreneurs and settle down in cities. However, the vast majority still face an uncertain identity and life.

According to the definition from an economic perspective, rural areas have diverse production and operation, such as industry and service sectors in addition to the traditional agricultural production (agriculture, forestry, animal husbandry, and fishery). As a result, a rural modern society in a sense has been formed. Small cities begin to take shape in many rural areas, with population size, industry, transport, and infrastructure. This largely depends on the development of township and village enterprises. If there were only agricultural production but no industry and services, there would be no need to build large-scale cities or towns. Farmers consume agricultural products they need and sell the surplus to cities. It is necessary to expand when agricultural product processing or other services take place in rural areas because these industries must be clustered.

What role do township and village enterprises play in this process? A key noteworthy phenomenon is the increase in the number and proportion of employees of township and village enterprises in rural areas. The absolute number increased from 30 million in 1980 to nearly 160 million in 2010, and its proportion to rural employment increased from less than 10 to nearly 38 percent. Both increased remarkably. This is important for China because China is a large country with a population of 1.39 billion, and hundreds of millions of surplus labor live in rural areas. They must be employed by nonagricultural industries, either in cities or in rural areas. If they stay in rural areas, township and village enterprises play a pivotal role in creating jobs for them in China.[12] In fact, about 280 million so-called migrant workers and their family members face a dilemma. Due to their status, migrant workers, as well as their family members, face instability in terms of social security such as education, medical care, and housing. For example, if a migrant worker gets sick in the city, they can hardly bear the high fees because medical costs at medical institutions in cities are higher than those in rural areas. The children of many migrant workers are left-behind children, who are separated from their parents for a long time. This not only harms the children's growth but also increases the living expenses and spiritual burden of migrant workers.

In addition to restrictions imposed by the household registration system, migrant workers can oftentimes only engage in simple jobs in the construction, catering, security, sanitation, and other sectors due to their educational background and limited experience. They have no choice but to return to the hometown when they are old or sick. Although township and village enterprises adopt backward production technologies, demand dangerous heavy workloads, and provide low wages, they are a key supplementary force in employing the rural surplus labor. Even if restrictions imposed by the household registration system in large cities are completely lifted, the flow of hundreds of millions of people (workers and their families) to the city would be unimaginable. Therefore, more secondary and tertiary industries in small and medium-sized cities are needed to employ rural surplus labor. Township and village enterprises can perform a greater role in small and medium-sized cities.[13]

Figure 2.2 shows the cities and villages where township and village enterprises are located from an industrial perspective. The horizontal axis represents the gap between urban and rural areas. The more it moves toward the left, the lower the level of urbanization. The more it moves to the right, the opposite applies. The vertical axis represents the level of income. In the upper right of the figure are modern industries (industry and service sectors) in cities, which have relatively high incomes. In the lower left of the figure is agriculture, which offers low incomes and has a large gap with cities. In the upper part to the right of agriculture are township and village enterprises, which have slightly higher incomes than agriculture and a slightly higher level of urbanization than rural areas. In today's China, the urban–rural gap is widening, which is not necessarily a bad thing. According to Lewis's theory on dualistic economy, in the early days of the development of the modern urban sector, the urban sector must absorb surplus labor from rural aeras. Rural areas at this time are poor, and the income is low due to labor surplus and backward

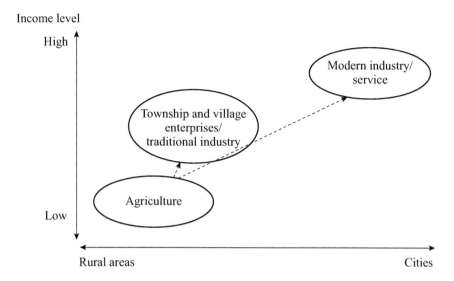

Figure 2.2 Significance and role of township and village enterprises

technology. It is what Lewis calls "survival wage", or subsistence income. As the modern urban sector further develops, there is a shortage of surplus labor for it. Therefore, the urban sector must raise wages to absorb more labor, and wages in rural areas will also rise at this time. Although wages in rural areas are not rising as fast as or as high as in the urban sector due to its gap in terms of productivity, etc., surplus labor is depleted and the economy begins to usher in a new situation. This time point is Lewis's "turning point".[14] Regarding the turning point in China, many scholars have done research, with some saying that China passed the turning point about a few years ago and others saying that it is yet to arrive.[15]

2.5 Conclusion

The development of China's agriculture has been plagued with a host of difficulties and hardships. Due to the problems inherent in Chinese society (such as the feudal landlord system) and social unrest, coupled with flow industrialization and a lack of modern economic growth before 1949, agricultural development was limited or stagnated, and farmers lived at the mercy of the weather for food. Under the planned economy after 1949, the farmers' initiative for production was seriously dampened by the people's commune system. Coupled with unfavorable policies such as price scissors for industrial and agricultural products, agricultural development was slow and of low quality. After the reform and opening up, relatively liberal agricultural policy and the dissolution of the people's communes greatly stimulated farmers' initiative for production, and agricultural production increased as never before. However, due to the institutional limitations and the backward economic development as a whole (such as slow urbanization), China's agriculture still belongs to traditional agriculture, and modern agriculture is a long distance away.

The issue of agriculture is important for any country. Even in developed countries with a small farmer population and a low share of agricultural output, agriculture is still highly valued because of the special nature of agriculture. Grain and food are indispensable for everyone, although its share in people's income is declining. Regardless of the developed economy, the fall in the Engel coefficient, or the increase in substitutes (including genetically modified foods), nothing can replace the use value of natural agricultural products. Especially for China, a country with a large population, the issue of agricultural security or food security always exists. This is a strategic issue, different from food safety in the usual sense (from the perspective of hygiene). It is no less important than other issues such as energy security, financial security, and defense security.

However, the issue of agriculture is tricky, with a full variety of factors that pull in opposite directions. In the long run, agriculture must shrink (given the proportion of output and labor) and also improve (with productivity and technology). Agricultural markets are essentially competitive and vulnerable to uncertain factors such as weather and natural disasters. If output increases, prices will fall, and farmers' income will decrease. If output decreases, we cannot cope in the event of emergencies. The situation in China is more complex. On the one hand, it is difficult to achieve economies of scale due to the constraints of the land system. On the other hand, due to the constraints imposed by the household registration system, it is difficult for farmers to really work in urban sectors, quit agriculture, and become urban residents. However, many problems are solved through development, which accumulates funds and also changes ideas. This is very important for farmers.

Notes

1 According to Malthusian Theory, there is a mutually restrictive relationship between population and (agricultural) output in an agrarian society. When agricultural yield increases, the population expands, and the population consumes more food. In this way, the increase in agricultural yield will fall, and thus the increase in population will also fall. Therefore, the population of agricultural society increases slightly. Of course, there is technological progress in agriculture, but this progress is slow. Therefore, the number of people living in a certain land area is relatively stable in the long run. China has a large population because it has a vast territory and abundant resources, and the agricultural production technology is advanced.
2 For the long-term economic growth rates of developed countries, see Kuznets (1999) and Ryoshin Minami (1981).
3 If we say the mechanized agricultural production in China is only achieved in parts of Heilongjiang and Jilin provinces, this is highly related to a small population and vast territory in these two regions as well as the conditions of the Northeast Great Plain.
4 Given the demand for labor and traditional habits in rural areas, rural residents are allowed to have a second child per couple, but there must be a certain time interval.
5 For the transfer of surplus agricultural labor, see Guan Quan (2014).
6 This is confirmed in Chapter 4, dealing with industry and services sectors. For labor mobility, see Chapter 6 of this book or Guan Quan (2014).
7 The first to explore such a system were some farmers in Xiaogang Village, Fengyang County, Anhui Province. They signed contracts at the risk of being fined or even imprisoned.

8 Appendix 2 of Du Runsheng (2002) pp. 768–770.
9 The "other" form is not certain. Five types are formal.
10 For a comprehensive study of township and village enterprises, see Guan Quan (2018c).
11 Edited by the Ministry of Agriculture of the People's Republic of China (2009).
12 A problem directly related to the issue of rural surplus labor is the so-called turning point of the economy. In other words, the rural surplus labor is absorbed by the urban sector, and the economy goes from a state of surplus labor to a state of labor shortage. Whether this has been achieved in China is still highly controversial. This is an important and complex issue that requires in-depth study.
13 The author will discuss further in other papers the question of how to absorb rural surplus labor. A brief explanation is only given here. We advocate vigorously building small and medium-sized cities because of the need to absorb surplus labor and the requirement of economic development. It is impossible to develop only large cities but not small and medium-sized cities because they are complementary. In the end, a network of cities is formed, including large cities and even megacities as well as small and medium-sized cities. This is proven by the development history of developed countries.
14 For the turning point, see Lewis (1958a, 1958b), Lewis (1989), Ryoshin Minami Minami (1973, 2008), Guan Quan (2014).
15 For the Lewis turning point in China, see Ryoshin Minami et al. (2014).

3 Industrial development and upgrading

3.1 Introduction

Like agriculture, China's industry faced a plethora of obstacles and even experienced ups and downs. Industrial development suffered many setbacks and even went the wrong way after 1949, not to mention in the period before 1949. Setbacks include not only legacy problems but also system and institutional obstacles, even mistaken policies and misconceptions. Of course, industry developed relatively smoothly compared to the agriculture and service sectors. At least, it was valued by all governments and people of insight in modern times, and many policies were favorable to industry. The agriculture and service sectors did not enjoy the attention they deserve. Moreover, the service sector was even considered dispensable for some time, and agriculture was used as a "cash dispenser".[1]

There were also cognitive and factual problems in the development of industry. Heavy industry was not developed before 1949, resulting in the extremely backward manufacturing sector. After 1949, the advance development of heavy industry slowed down the development of the light industry, and as a consequence, the people had low living standards for a long time. After the reform and opening up, this situation was put right, and China has achieved balanced development. Heavy industry is developing smoothly, and great strides have also been made in light industry.

After examining the development experience of countries around the world, we realize that whether a country can achieve economic success hinges in large measure on whether its industrialization is successful. Industrial development is at the heart of economic development. All developed countries have achieved economic development through industrialization, even for small countries such as Luxembourg, Belgium, Switzerland, and the Netherlands.[2] In this sense, China's development strategy after 1949 is correct, despite the fact that China favored industry and underestimated light industry in order to seek quick results at the beginning. Industrial development has its own laws and cannot be achieved overnight. China made wasteful efforts in this regard, and the hasty development of heavy industry caused resources waste and inefficiency. However, there are two sides to everything. Since China developed heavy industry ahead of time, the basis of heavy industry came into play when light industry was compensated. Other countries

DOI: 10.4324/9781003410393-5

have no experience in developing heavy industry. Although their light industry has developed well, their heavy industry develops slowly because heavy industry requires not only capital but also technologies. Moreover, it is far more complicated and difficult than light industry. India, for example, lags behind China in terms of heavy industry, and is therefore uncompetitive in the race to become major powers. Of course, there are also examples of the opposite. The Soviet Union or today's Russia lays particular emphasis on heavy industry and military industry, while its light industry is relatively backward. Therefore, it is not deeply involved in today's globalization.

3.2 Growth of industry

Compared with before 1949, China's industry has been significantly developed after 1949, despite many setbacks and sometimes even serious decline. Industrial development after 1949 can be divided into two periods: the planned economy period and the reform and opening up period. The early period experienced many setbacks, while the later period was smooth sailing. In addition to the weak industrial basis, there were also institutional and policy problems in the early period. In the later period, a host of problems were solved through reform and opening up. Coupled with the foundation that was laid in the early period, development was ensured.

Furthermore, industrial development after 1949 has the following noteworthy facts. First, private enterprises were turned into state-run and collective enterprises as a result of the socialist transformation of capitalist industry and commerce implemented in the 1950s. Second, the "156 major projects" with the Soviet Union aid in the 1950s laid an important foundation for industrial development. Third, the hasty program represented by the Great Leap Forward played havoc with the normal development order and caused adverse implications. Fourth, the ideas and policies of giving precedence to heavy industry over light industry disrupted the allocation of resources and led to a biased industrial structure. Fifth, China overemphasized the establishment of a complete industrial system and self-reliance and ignored the international market and international resources, causing resources waste and shortage. Sixth, due to low technology and institutional constraints, it was difficult to achieve "intensive growth". Seventh, insufficient innovation became a major bottleneck in China's industrial development. Admittedly, innovation requires long-term efforts, but in the absence of innovation, it was difficult to develop further in the fiercely competitive international environment. These problems were solved somewhat through reform, opening up economic development, but many problems still persist, primarily institutional and innovation issues.

3.2.1 Growth of output

Since 1949, industry has been the principal driver of China's economic growth, both under the planned economy and after the reform and opening up. This is important because it is difficult to industrialize and achieve economic development without

52 Processes and characteristics

rapid growth or leadership of industry. Judging from the development experience of all countries that have achieved economic development, industry without exception plays a leading role. China's industry has developed faster than those of other countries, and as a result, China becomes today's manufacturing powerhouse. Further, economic growth is the core of economic development. Without economic growth, there will be no economic development to speak of. Economic growth primarily depends on industry, especially in the early and middle stages of economic development. To put it another way, the growth of industry is an important driver of economic growth because industry has advantages such as economies of scale, technological progress, talents, innovation, and external economy, which are not available in the agriculture and service sectors.

Figure 3.1 shows the real growth rate of the added value of the secondary industry after 1949. One of its key characteristics is that it is similar to the growth rates of GDP, GDP per capita, and primary industry (Chapter 2). It roughly experienced a process of large fluctuations followed by slight fluctuations. It can be said that fluctuations in the planned economy period are greater than during the reform and opening up period. As a result, the planned economy period saw miraculously high growth, but there was also a sharp decline. Such economic growth is not steady but impulsive, unsustainable, and undesirable. In contrast, growth after the reform and opening up was relatively stable, except for fluctuations around 1989. Particularly since the 1990s, it was highly steady, which is consistent with the trend of changes in agriculture and the economy as a whole (Chapter 1).

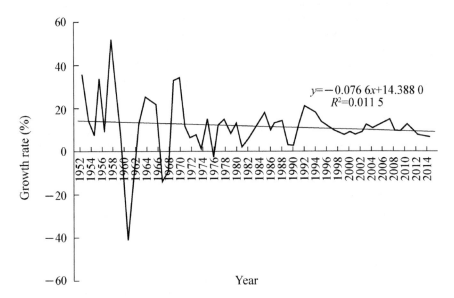

Figure 3.1 Real growth rate of added value of the secondary industry

Data source: *China Statistical Yearbook* over the years.

Another key feature is the high growth of industry. The average annual growth rate of 11 percent from 1953 to 2014 was never seen before. If divided at an interval of 10 years, the average annual growth rate was 13.3 percent from 1953 to 1962, 15.02 percent from 1963 to 1972, 8.06 percent from 1973 to 1982, 12.38 percent from 1983 to 1992, 11.93 percent from 1993 to 2002, and 10.90 percent from 2003 to 2014. Except for the period from the late Cultural Revolution to the early days of reform and opening up, the growth rate had exceeded 11 percent. This growth rate was not only more than what other countries had experienced but also exceeded that of the primary and tertiary industries. From this point of view, the driver for economic growth is none other than industry (secondary industry).

Table 3.1 shows the growth rate of the secondary industry, including output, number of employees, and output per capita. Output grew fastest in the 1950s, by more than 20 percent. On the one hand, this is due to the low industrial basis. On the other hand, it also was also attributed to the extreme impetus of the Great Leap Forward. The output growth rate was low in the 1960s to 1980s, but it did not change much. It was also high growth in the global context. Ultrafast growth occurred after the 1990s, indicating that the dividends of reform and opening up initiated by Deng Xiaoping's remarks on the tour of the South began to emerge. The growth rate of the number of employees varies according to the different statistical methods. Overall, the growth rate was high in the early and middle periods and was low or even negative in the late period or the present. According to government statistics, the negative growth in the period from 1961 to 1970 was primarily caused by a net decline in population following three years of severe hardship. There was positive growth in other periods. The high growth in the early or middle period is mainly attributed to the high growth of the population, while the low growth in the later period is caused by the gradually disappearing demographic dividends. There are four statistical methods for calculating output per capita. The results are generally close. In other words, there was low or negative growth only in the 1970s according to the majority of statistics. It was also not high in the 1980s, mainly because reform was not yet implemented or the pace of reform was modest. Neither state-owned enterprises nor collective enterprises achieved good benefits, private enterprises had not yet shown great strength, and foreign investment did not enter China on a large scale.

3.2.2 Breakdown of growth rate

Long-term changes in the growth rate of the secondary industry after 1949 have been examined. Similarly to the Chinese economy as a whole and the primary industry, the growth accounting method is used to break down the growth rate and find the contribution of various factors to economic growth. The rate of economic growth $G(Y)$ can be broken down into the growth rate of labor force $G(L)$ and the growth rate of productivity $G(Y/L)$,

$$G(Y) = G(L) + G(Y/L) \tag{3.1}$$
$$G(Y/L) = \lambda + E_K G(K/L) \tag{3.2}$$

Table 3.1 Growth rate of secondary industry, Unit: %

Period	Output – Government statistics	Output – Hitotsubashi statistics	Number of employed persons – Government statistics	Number of employed persons – Hitotsubashi statistics	Output per capita – Government/Hitotsubashi	Output per capita – Government/government	Output per capita – Hitotsubashi/Hitotsubashi	Output per capita – Hitotsubashi/government
1953–1960	23.23	21.55	27.84	−0.89	10.85	14.12	9.47	12.89
1961–1970	7.84	7.45	−0.19	3.48	9.42	7.43	8.89	6.97
1971–1980	9.22	7.25	8.39	1.11	1.14	0.89	−0.72	−0.97
1981–1990	9.62	5.12	6.13	2.4	6.92	3.43	2.51	−0.81
1991–2000	13.62	7.9	1.64	−0.17	10.99	11.84	5.33	6.28
2001–2010	11.47	14.01	3.07	−1.97	6.62	8.21	9.05	10.76

Sources: *China Statistical Yearbook* over the years; Ryoshin Minami and Makino Fumio (2014).

Note: The Hitotsubashi estimate is an estimate made by the research team of Hitotsubashi University in Japan; see Ryoshin Minami and Makino Fumio (2014) for details.

Table 3.2 Growth rate of secondary industry and its breakdown, Unit: %

Period	G (Y)	G (L)	G (K)	G (Y/L)	G (K/L)	$E_K G$ (K/L)	λ	λ/G (Y/L)
1982–1986	11.84	7.01	7.58	4.83	0.57	0.26	4.57	94.67
1987–1991	9.8	4.72	8.58	5.08	3.94	1.76	3.32	65.28
1992–1996	17.05	2.95	−0.92	14.10	−3.75	−1.68	15.79	111.92
1997–2001	9.08	0.05	−8.42	9.03	−8.42	−3.78	12.81	141.82
2002–2006	11.82	3.15	12.38	8.67	9.12	4.09	4.57	52.79
2007–2014	10.19	2.57	0.80	7.62	−1.69	−0.76	8.38	109.94

Notes:
(1) Y = GDP (1978 = 100). The data are from *Data of Gross Domestic Product of China 1952–1995* and *China Statistical Yearbook* over the years.
(2) K = capital stock (1952 = 100); data for the 1952–1994 period from Zhang Jun and Zhang Yuan (2003); data for the 1995–2014 period are estimated based on China's total fixed asset investment on this basis.
(3) L = the number of employees; data from *China Labor Statistical Yearbook* over the years.
(4) G = growth rate.

where K and L indicate capital and labor, respectively, and E_K is the productive elasticity of capital. λ represents the movement of the production function, that is, the remainder of the growth rate. The results of the breakdown based on equations (3.1) and (3.2) are shown in Table 3.2. Due to limited data, only the situation from 1982 to 2014 is calculated here.

Since the 1980s, the growth rate $G(Y)$ of secondary industry output maintained a long-term ultrahigh level, mostly around 10 percent and even more than 17 percent in some periods. This can be said to be a miracle not achieved by any other country. The growth rate of industrial labor $G(L)$ grew fast in the early period but slowly in the later period, and there was almost no growth in the late 1990s, which we believe was caused by the "wave of layoffs" as a result of the reform of state-owned enterprises. The growth rate of capital $G(K)$ changed erratically, with high growth in the early period, low or even negative growth in the middle period, and slight recovery in the later period. However, it has recently begun to decline again. The growth rate of labor productivity $G(Y/L)$ is generally high and higher in some periods (early 1990s). It has remained at a high level since the late 1990s, which is also a key basis for China's sustained rapid economic growth. The growth rate $G(K/L)$ of the capital/labor ratio was not ideal, which remained negative for half of the period, recovered somewhat in 2002–2006, and then became negative again. As mentioned earlier, data and estimates regarding China's capital stock are in doubt, primarily due to a lack of and imperfect basic information. Fortunately, the growth rate λ of technological progress has performed greatly, reaching a very high level in the 1990s; it is also not low in other periods. As a result, the contribution $\lambda/G(Y/L)$ made by technological progress to growth also demonstrates a special role.

3.3 Shifts in the model of growth

China has always faced the problem of "extensive development", particularly during the planned economy period. The so-called extensive development refers to the model of development that focuses only on expansion but ignores the role of efficiency, technological progress, and so on. The opposite is "intensive development", a model of development that values improving efficiency and technological advancement. Under the planned economy, extensive development was common due to the concept and level at that time. At that time, scale expansion was not regarded as a bad thing, as long as it could produce more products. This is highly correlated with the work and living standards at that time and is also related to a lack of a market competition mechanism. The market will cause blind competition, creating a feeling of "the bigger, the higher the sense of superiority". However, after market baptism, enterprises that blindly expand will be knocked out, while enterprises pursuing high quality will continue to develop. As China's production and living standards at that time were very low, it was not easy to satisfy people's needs, and a high-end life was out of the question.

As mentioned earlier, China gradually moved toward a planned economy since the 1950s through the "three major transformations" as well as a slew of measures such as the five-year plans. The planned economy is mainly characterized by the overall management of resources and a high level of centralization. This system has the advantage of "bringing together the resources needed to accomplish great tasks" but has the drawbacks of being inflexible and prone to the waste of resources and inefficiency. Moreover, the state strategic goal at that time was to quickly catch up with the developed countries and to establish a complete industrial system as soon as possible. As a result, people pursued fast results, expanded scale, craved for things big and foreign, acted recklessly, and proceeded blindly without regard to science or economic laws. It resulted in redundant development and low-level circulation. Considering that the aforesaid "three-line construction" and other military and strategic goal-led projects did not regard economic benefits and efficiency as the top goals, many investments did not achieve economic benefits. Coupled with the development strategy of prioritizing heavy industry, a top-heavy industrial structure was formed. There was more heavy industry but inadequate light industry, and the heavy industry ran below capacity while there was short supply in light industry.

Figure 3.2 shows the relationship between the original value of fixed assets per capita and the net output value per capita in industry. It is theoretically similar to the production function. As per capita capital increased, per capita output showed an upward trend. Generally, this trend follows the law of diminishing returns, but it is not always the case. Some sectors (generally in industry) have the characteristics of increasing returns. Shown here are the changes from 1952 to 1978, which are consistent with the theory on the whole. Some changes in the middle are normal. For example, in 1961 and 1962, there was a high increase in capital per capita but a low output per capita. This period, also known as the adjustment period, aimed to put right the Great Leap Forward and the three-year difficult period. In 1963, it began to rebound and get on track. Furthermore, the changes during the Cultural Revolution were interesting, with no obvious progress for about a decade and with ups and downs. It fell to a low level in 1976, began to bottom out in 1977, and fared better in 1978. On the whole, it went well in the 1950s, despite the Great

Industrial development and upgrading 57

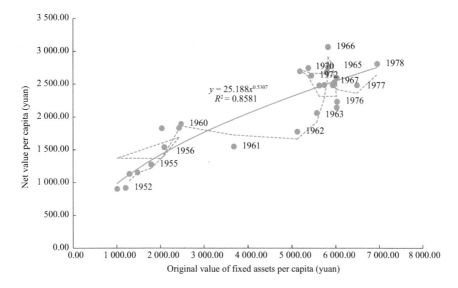

Figure 3.2 Approximate production function of industry (net value per capita)

Data sources: China's Labor Wage Statistics: 1949–1985; China's Statistics on Industrial Economy: 1949–1984; China's Statistics on Fixed Asset Investment: 1950–1985.

Leap Forward in the later period. In the 1960s, there were large fluctuations due to adjustment and the Cultural Revolution. In particular, the outbreak of the Cultural Revolution played havoc with development. The early 1970s played out still in the throes of the Cultural Revolution but stably without major ups and downs. After the end of the Cultural Revolution in the late 1970s, the economy began to get on track.

Figure 3.3 shows the production function in a different way based on the same data. The horizontal axis represents the labor coefficient (number of employees/net output value), and the vertical axis represents the capital coefficient (original value of fixed assets/net output value). The labor coefficient indicates the amount of labor contained per unit of output, and the capital coefficient indicates the capital stock contained per unit of output. The curve formed by the two is equivalent to the isoquant curve in the production function. These two indicators mirror the production efficiency, or the amount of input in the output. The less the input, the higher the efficiency. The more the input, the more inefficient it is. Therefore, the lower, the better. In the figure, the closer to the far point, the better. It is clear from the figure that China moved from labor-intensive to capital-intensive in the 1950s, with a certain degree of technological progress (movement toward the origin). The changes after the 1960s were erratic, without obvious progress. It shows the characteristics of the Cultural Revolution, which was a time of turmoil. For example, it was closer to the origin in 1966 than in 1977, indicating that more capital was used in 1977 but that productivity was not higher than in 1966.

The "extensive growth" model improved after the reform and opening up, especially with the emergence of private enterprises and the self-employed

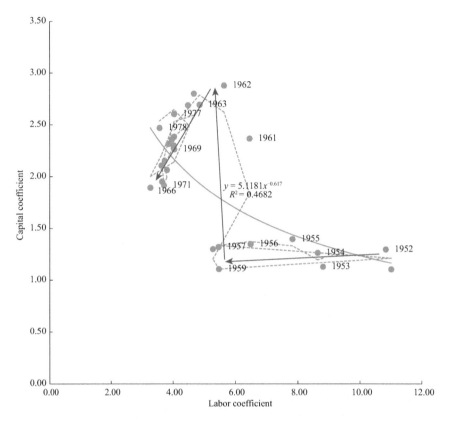

Figure 3.3 Labor coefficient and capital coefficient in industry (net output value)

Data source: China's Labor Wage Statistics: 1949–1985; China's Statistics on Industrial Economy: 1949–1984; China's Statistics on Fixed Asset Investment: 1950–1985.

who pursue maximum profits and maintain high efficiency. They faced pressure from state-owned and foreign-owned enterprises, as well as competition from peers in the private sector. State-owned enterprises gradually adopted intensive development after various reforms, but there were still weaknesses. These are mainly manifested in two areas. First, although state-owned enterprises were reformed, their basic nature remains unchanged. The consciousness of relying on the state still persists. Therefore, they are not as obsessive as private enterprises in the pursuit of maximum profits. Second, because the market economy has a short history in China, many enterprises did not fully realize the cruelty of the market. In particular, because state-owned enterprises enjoy preferential protection by the state, they lack a sense of market competition. Of course, China has gradually moved toward a market economy, even though state-owned enterprises operate under the watchful eye of the people and face intense competitive pressure. Therefore, they must pursue a model of intensive development.

Industrial development and upgrading 59

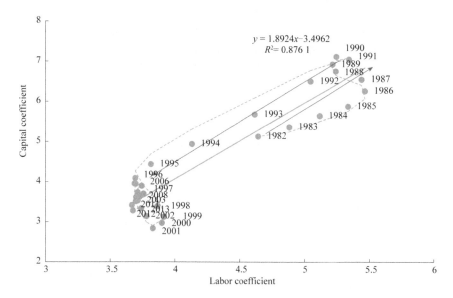

Figure 3.4 Labor coefficient and capital coefficient in secondary industry (1982–2013)

Data source: *China Industry Economy Statistical Yearbook* over the years.

Figure 3.4 shows the relationship between the labor coefficient and the capital coefficient of the secondary industry after the reform and opening up in the same way used in the previous section. The situation shown in the figure is different from that during the planned economy period in the previous section because there was no obvious shift from labor-intensive to capital-intensive. Instead, there was a movement toward the origin along an angle close to the 45-degree line. This is often regarded as a "learning effect" or "experience effect", which is similar to "learning by doing".[3] It refers to the occurrence of neutral technological advances, as manifested in the movement along the 45-degree line toward the origin in the figure. It means the accumulation of experience at work and learning effect, usually little technological progress. The figure shows neutral technological advances in general, but sometimes there was movement in the opposite direction. This was the case for the decade from 1982 to 1991, when regression occurred. In other words, the input of labor and capital increased while output remained unchanged, which means inefficiency because of greater input than output. We believe that in addition to the flawed data, this phenomenon possibly occurred because the reform and opening up was just initiated, and there were tentative steps toward a market economy. Many enterprises increased investment in a wait-and-see fashion, hoping to achieve higher output. Therefore, the possibility of "extensive growth" cannot be ruled out. The situation changed perceptibly after 1992, when the curve moved toward the origin almost in a linear fashion. Neutral technological progress was achieved around 1996. Thereafter, due to the reform of state-owned enterprises and other reasons, there was stagnation or a certain degree of technological advance.

60 *Processes and characteristics*

In short, there was no obvious technological advance in the secondary industry in the early days of the reform and opening up (the 1980s), but the second wave of reform (after 1992) led to perceptible neutral technological progress. However, in the late 1990s and after 2000, there was stagnation, and the pace of technological progress was small.

3.4 Structural changes

As an economy grows, the internal structure of industry also changes, including the relationship between light and heavy industries or between capital goods and consumer goods. Generally speaking, an agrarian country starts with light industry when developing industry. The light industry mainly includes daily necessities such as textiles and food. As the economy develops, production technology is improved, and capital is accumulated, and it is gradually possible to produce more complex industrial products or capital goods, such as machinery and equipment. However, the situation in China is somewhat different because the development speed and scale of the heavy industry far exceed those in other countries.

Figure 3.5 shows two structural changes: the relationship between heavy industry and light industry and the relationship between the state sector of the economy and other sectors of the economy. The proportion of heavy industry soared from 26.4 percent in 1949 to 66.6 percent in 1960. Since then, the proportion of heavy

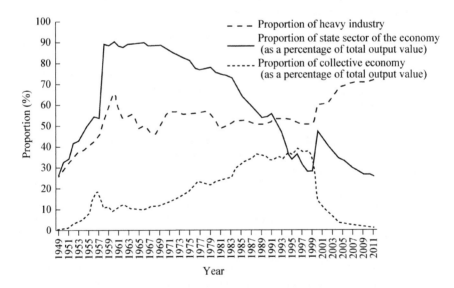

Figure 3.5 Proportions of heavy industry, state sector of the economy, and collective economic operations

Data sources: *China Statistical Yearbook* over the years; *China Industry Economy Statistical Yearbook* over the years.

industry has remained basically around 50 percent until the end of the 20th century. In the 21st century, the proportion of heavy industry has increased rapidly again, maintaining an unprecedented high of about 70 percent since 2006. In this regard, it is very high compared to the rest of the world.[4]

We have reason to believe that the proportion of China's heavy industry will remain at a high level in the coming period, for the following reasons. First, China is still in the middle of industrialization, when heavy industry plays a role. This creates conditions for the development of heavy industry from the perspective of both demand and supply. From the perspective of demand, China is in the course of urbanization, which requires construction of housing, transport, infrastructure, etc. Therefore, heavy industrial products such as steel, cement, metal, timber, glass, and chemical materials are needed. From the supply viewpoint, China has built a world-class heavy industrial system and can produce anything from screws to aircraft carriers. Second, China's industrial production not only serves the domestic market but also serves the world. This situation will not change in the short term because Chinese products are competitively priced and of good quality, and there are few foreign substitutes in the world. Countries that are closer to China, such as other members of the BRICS, have weaknesses and cannot replace China. Russia is very strong in heavy industry, but it is limited to the military and large-scale equipment industry. China's equipment industry is also developing at a fast clip, and is comparable to that of Russia. Brazil's industrial system leaves something to be desired, and many of its industrial products are not globally competitive. India's manufacturing industry is low and cannot compete with China's. South Africa is a highly industrialized country in Africa, with many industrial categories, but it is difficult for it to become an industrial power due to its incomplete system and inefficiency. However, the exceptional state of heavy industry will gradually return to a reasonable level as China gains a better understanding of the environment and resources, and problems such as overcapacity are resolved.

Another structural change shows Chinese characteristics, namely the change in the proportion of the state sector of the economy and collective economy, which is an interesting phenomenon. Since 1953, China conducted the socialist transformation of capitalist industry and commerce and transformed the state capital and private capital during the Republic of China period into the state sector or collective economy through approaches such as public–private partnerships. This transformation led to an economic pattern for a long time afterward, which continued until after the reform and opening up. An interesting change is that the proportion of the state sector of the economy hit a high of 90 percent during the Great Leap Forward. Together with the collective economy, it covered almost all of China's industry. Intriguingly, the share of the state sector declined thereafter, while the share of the collective economy rose. The two were on a par in the 1990s. In the 21st century, both declined rapidly in number and proportion, and reached the current low levels. The collective economy is almost negligible, and the state sector still occupies a large chunk. It is noteworthy that the decline in the share of the state sector did not begin after the reform and opening up but rather during the Cultural Revolution. We believe that this is due to the development of urban neighborhood enterprises[5] and the development of rural commune and brigade-run enterprises (later township and village enterprises). In other words, the state sector did not further expand since the Cultural Revolution but developed in the form of a collective economy.

China has always faced the problem of extensive development. "Extensive development" refers to the model of development that focuses only on scale expansion but ignores the role of efficiency, technological progress, etc. The opposite is the model of intensive development that focuses on the role of efficiency, technological progress, etc. Under the planned economy, extensive development was common due to the concept and level at that time. At that time, scale expansion was not regarded as a bad thing, as long as it could produce more products. This is highly correlated with the work and living standards at that time and is also related to the lack of a market competition mechanism. The market will lead to blind competition, creating a feeling of "the bigger, the higher the sense of superiority". However, after a period of time, enterprises that blindly expand will be knocked out, while enterprises pursuing high quality will carry on. As China's production and living standards at that time were very low, it was not easy to satisfy people's needs, and a high-end life was out of the question.

The "extensive growth" model improved after the reform and opening up, especially with the emergence of private enterprises and the self-employed, who pursue maximum profits and maintain high efficiency. They faced pressure from state-owned enterprises and foreign-owned enterprises, as well as competition from peers in the private sector. State-owned enterprises gradually adopted intensive development after various reforms, but there were still weaknesses. These are mainly manifested in two areas: First, although state-owned enterprises were reformed, their basic nature remains unchanged. The consciousness of relying on the state still persists. Therefore, they are not as obsessive as private enterprises in the pursuit of maximum profits. Second, because the market economy has a short history in China, many enterprises did not fully realize the cruelty of the market. In particular, because state-owned enterprises enjoyed preferential protection from the state to begin with, they lacked a sense of market competition. Of course, China has gradually moved toward a market economy, and even state-owned enterprises operate under the watchful eye of the people and face intense competitive pressure. Therefore, they must pursue a model of intensive development.

3.5 Institutional changes

The institutional changes in industry, as in agriculture, went through a process from decentralization to concentration and then to decentralization again. The socialist transformation of capitalist industry and commerce was conducted after 1953 and was written into the *Constitution of the People's Republic of China* in 1954. Article 10 of the *Constitution* stipulates:

> The state adopts a policy of utilizing, restricting and transforming capitalist industry and commerce. Through the administration of the government bodies, the leadership of the state sector as well as supervision by the workers, the state leverages the positive role of capitalist industry and commerce in terms of the country's

stability and our people's wellbeing, limits their negative effects, encourages and guides them to become state-capitalist economy in various forms, and gradually replaces capitalist ownership with ownership by the whole people.[6]

This was the period when the First Five-Year Plan was formulated. The First Five-Year Plan stipulates: "The first step taken by the state to transform capitalist industry is to transform capitalism into state capitalism in different forms. The second step is to transform state capitalism into socialism".[7] Therefore, a key task during the First Five-Year Plan period was how to realize the socialist transformation of capitalist industry and commerce.

After several years of transformation, the proportion of socialist industry in the gross value of industrial output rose from 34.7 percent in 1949 to 67.5 percent in 1956.[8] This reached its peak during the Great Leap Forward period and then gradually returned to a reasonable level. Instead of increasing the proportion of the state sector, it took the form of collective economy, which helped to reduce the burden on the state and gave flexibility to local governments because the collective economy was locally operated, including "enterprises under the administration of district authorities or higher levels", "enterprises under the administration of neighborhood committees or communes", as well as commune- and brigade-run enterprises (later township and village enterprises).

Table 3.3 show changes in the share of several types of economy in gross output value between 1949 and 1980. From 1949 to 1957, the share of enterprises owned by the whole people rose from 26.2 to 53.8 percent, the share of collective enterprises rose from 0.5 to 19 percent, the share of joint state–private enterprises rose from 1.6 to 26.3 percent, the share of private enterprises plunged from 48.70 to less than 0.10 percent, and the share of the self-employed declined from 23 to

Table 3.3 Proportion of various types of economy in gross value of industrial output, Unit: %

Year	Ownership by the whole people	Collective ownership	Public-private partnership	Private	Self-employed people
1949	26.2	0.5	1.6	48.70	23.0
1952	41.5	3.3	4.0	30.60	20.6
1955	51.3	7.6	13.1	13.20	14.8
1956	54.5	17.1	27.2	0.04	1.2
1957	53.8	19.0	26.3	0.10	0.8
1958	89.2	10.8	–	–	–
1960	90.6	9.4	–	–	–
1970	87.6	12.4	–	–	–
1980	76.0	23.5	–	–	–

Sources: Chinese Academy of Social Sciences and Central Archives (1998), p. 798; *China Statistical Yearbook* over the years.

Notes:
(1) The total output value is 100 and "other" for some years. It is not shown here.
(2) Handicrafts are included in the data.

0.8 percent. The share of the latter two in 1957 was almost negligible, indicating that this transformation had a perceptible effect. As a result of transformation, the economic structure featuring private enterprises and self-employed people was transformed into one that features ownership by the whole people: collective and public–private partnership. From 1958 to 1980, there was the ownership by the whole people and collective ownership, while other forms almost disappeared. It is a manifestation of the thorough transformation.

Table 3.4 show the same situation but excluding handicrafts. It shows the proportion of gross value of industrial output, the number of enterprises, and the number of workers. From 1949 to 1957, the proportion of the gross output value of state-run enterprises rose from 34.2 to 64.8 percent; the number of enterprises jumped from 6.37 to 32.82 percent, an increase of more than 4 times; the number of employees rose from 42.33 to 65.73 percent, up by about 55 percent. Cooperative-run enterprises were basically of a collective nature and were not prominent in this period. Except for a somewhat high proportion of the number of enterprises, the proportions of gross industrial output value and the number of workers were relatively low. This is slightly different from what was just described, primarily because the handicraft industry was excluded here. Handicraft industry generally takes the form of collectives or cooperatives. The number of joint ventures rose from a negligible level to accounting for about one-third, and the number of units was more than half. Later, most of these joint state–private enterprises became

Table 3.4 Changes in the proportion of enterprises in industry, Unit: %

Year	State-run	Cooperative-run	Public–private partnership	Private
Gross industrial output value				
1949	34.2	0.5	2.0	63.3
1952	52.8	3.2	5.0	39.0
1955	62.9	4.8	16.1	16.2
1956	65.5	2.0	32.5	0.1
1957	64.8	3.4	31.7	0.1
Number of enterprises				
1952	6.37	3.68	0.59	89.35
1955	12.11	14.57	2.54	70.78
1956	26.75	16.76	55.06	1.43
1957	32.82	14.43	51.04	1.71
Number of employees				
1949	42.33	0.49	3.43	53.74
1952	52.84	3.38	4.71	39.06
1955	59.91	5.09	13.11	21.88
1956	63.85	3.48	32.49	0.19
1957	65.73	3.79	30.31	0.16

Data source: Chinese Academy of Social Sciences and Central Archives, ed. (1998), pp. 799–800.
Note: The data do not include handicraft industry.

collective enterprises. Corresponding to these changes are private enterprises, which were in the overwhelming majority at the beginning but were reduced to almost zero. In particular, the proportion of the number of enterprises plunged from nearly 90 to 1.71 percent.

This situation continued until after the reform and opening up, that is, after the 1980s. Reforms began to take place in all industries to streamline administration and institute decentralization and to introduce all forms of ownership. To date, major changes have taken place in the ownership relations of the economy, and there are mainly four patterns: state sector, shareholding, private sector, and foreign capital (including overseas Chinese capital). Table 3.5 shows the overview of industrial enterprises under all forms of ownership in 2015. China's Hong Kong, Macao, and Taiwan enterprises and foreign-funded enterprises account for about one-fifth of all enterprises, accounting for 13.8 percent of the number of enterprises, 22.2 percent of the output value, 19.6 percent of the total assets, 24 percent of the total profits, and 24.1 percent of employees. In contrast, the proportion of state-owned enterprises has decreased to a very low level, and there is little change in state-owned enterprises and collective enterprises because the proportion of collective enterprises is very low, and this is one of the outcomes of reform. Relative to the decreasing proportion of state-owned enterprises is the high proportion of limited liability companies and private enterprises. Limited liability companies account for 28.5 percent of enterprises in mainland China as a whole. Except in terms of total assets, private enterprises account for nearly half or more than half of enterprises in mainland China, and the number of private enterprises is up to 65.5 percent.

China's economy featuring industry faced a host of difficulties in the later period of the Cultural Revolution. Due to a lack of market mechanism, state-owned enterprises and collective enterprises that were "big and all-embracing, or small and all-inclusive" sustained large-scale losses and were seriously overstaffed. Good performance and bad performance were treated alike, there was a lack of competition awareness, and slow going was widespread. Under such circumstances, the central government decided to initiate reform and opening up. Introducing competition mechanism, importing advanced technologies, improving corporate competitiveness, and enhancing product quality became the primary tasks. In short, state-owned enterprises achieved a quantum leap as a result of reforms, such as reducing staff for greater efficiency, implementing the system of overall responsibility by factory managers, taking responsibility for profits and losses, invigorating large enterprises while relaxing control over small ones, enterprise restructuring, and the shareholding system. Enterprises were much smaller in number but became significantly more competitive.

However, as China's market economy was still immature, many factors impeded the development of the market economy. Well functioning private enterprises were lacking, the technical level and competitiveness of private enterprises were low, and the private economy needed to be further improved. These can be seen in Figure 3.6, which shows the relationship between per capita fixed assets *(K/L)* and per capita output *(Y/L)* of enterprises divided by the type of ownership in 2011. It can also be seen as an approximate production function, although no value added

Table 3.5 Basic situation of industrial enterprises by forms of ownership (2015)

Item	Number of enterprises (%)	Output value (100 million yuan, %)	Total assets (100 million yuan, %)	Total profits (100 million yuan, %)	Number of employees (10,000, %)
Total	38,3148 (100.0)	1,104,026.70 (100.0)	1,023,398.1 (100.0)	66,187.1 (100.0)	9,775.0 (100.0)
Enterprises in mainland China	330,390 (86.2)	858,603.80 (77.8)	822,095.4 (80.3)	50,281.3 (76.0)	7,419.6 (72.3)
State-owned enterprises	3,234 (1.0)	43,594.48 (5.1)	71,514.9 (8.7)	2,107.7 (4.2)	296.3 (4.0)
Collective enterprises	2637 (0.8)	6,582.79 (0.8)	5,092.5 (0.6)	1,499.4 (3.0)	162.8 (2.2)
Joint-equity cooperative enterprises	1,136 (0.3)	1,470.55 (0.2)	940.3 (0.1)	108.9 (0.2)	15.6 (0.2)
Limited liability companies	94,299 (28.5)	314,906.09 (36.7)	374,094.9 (45.5)	16,712.5 (33.2)	2,754.1 (37.1)
Companies limited by shares	11,061 (3.4)	97,332.58 (11.3)	139,031.4 (16.9)	6,447.7 (12.8)	793.4 (10.7)
Private enterprises	216,506 (65.5)	391,618.21 (45.6)	229,006.5 (27.9)	24,249.7 (48.2)	3,464.0 (46.7)
Other businesses	1,370 (0.4)	2,817.76 (0.3)	2,224.9 (0.3)	134.3 (0.3)	26.7 (0.4)
China's Hong Kong, Macao, and Taiwan enterprises	24,488 (6.4)	96,995.39 (8.8)	83,244.0 (8.1)	5,948.3 (9.0)	1,171.2 (12.0)
Foreign-funded enterprises	28,270 (7.4)	148,427.55 (13.4)	118,058.7 (11.5)	9,957.5 (15.0)	1,184.2 (12.1)

Data source: China Industry Statistical Yearbook 2016.

Note: Real figures are outside the parentheses, and the proportion are inside the parentheses. The types of enterprises also include jointly run enterprises, which are not listed here due to their low quantity and proportion. The proportion of enterprise in mainland China, China's Hong Kong, Macao, and Taiwan enterprises, and foreign-funded enterprises is 100. The proportion of various types of enterprises among enterprises in mainland China is 100.

is used here (because the data on cost are unclear). It can be seen that the per capita fixed assets of central state-owned enterprises are far higher than those of other types of enterprises, and the per capita output value is also high. Therefore, they are in the upper right corner of the production function. In contrast, the per capita fixed assets and per capita output value of private enterprises are low, and therefore they are in the lower left corner. It is noteworthy that the per capita fixed assets of Sino-foreign joint ventures are not high, but their per capita output value is very high. Therefore, it is far above the average production function and is placed above. Most types of enterprises basically center around the production function. State-owned enterprises, wholly state-owned enterprises, etc. are strong and are placed on the right. China's Hong Kong, Macao, and Taiwan enterprises, collective enterprises, etc. are relatively weak and are placed on the left.

However, from the perspective of efficiency, this situation is not necessarily tenable. Figure 3.7 shows the relationship between the total asset's contribution ratio and the ratio of profits to cost of enterprises divided by the forms of ownership. It is inconsistent with what Figure 3.6 describes. As Figure 3.6 shows, state-owned enterprises, especially central state-owned enterprises, hold a distinct advantage, while private enterprises and collective enterprises are in a weak position. However, from the perspective of efficiency, it is wholly different. In the upper right

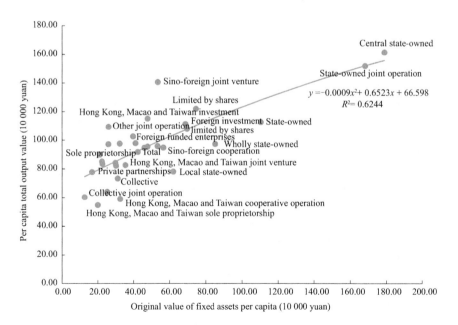

Figure 3.6 Relationship between per capita fixed assets and per capita gross output value of industrial enterprises (2011)

Data source: *China Industry Economy Statistical Yearbook 2012*.

68 *Processes and characteristics*

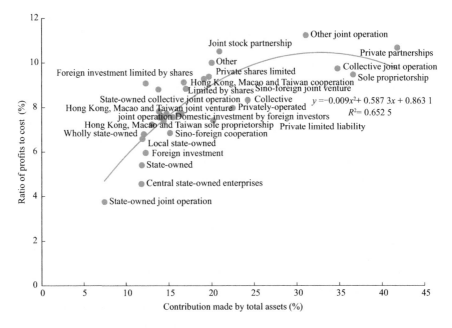

Figure 3.7 Relationship between the total asset's contribution rate and the ratio of profits to cost of industrial enterprises (2011)

Data source: *China Industry Economy Statistical Yearbook 2012*.

corner are not state-owned enterprises but joint-equity cooperative enterprises, collective enterprises, and other non-state-owned enterprises. State-owned enterprises, particularly central state-owned enterprises, are in the lower left, which shows the lowest efficiency. This is in sharp contrast with the preceding figure.[9]

3.6 Conclusion

The path of China's industrial development is arduous and tortuous. After overcoming many setbacks, it has finally gotten back on the right track and has made great strides. China's industrial development or industrialization represents in large measure the development and progress of China's economy. China's progress from being a poor and weak agricultural country that was bullied by imperialist countries to today's "world factory" can be said to be a miracle because China is not the country with the best development potential, nor does it have an advantage over other similar countries from many perspectives.

First, China suffered more hardships than other countries. Some countries may have been colonized by Western powers for a long time, but they may not have been mired in prolonged wars, which may be more damaging than colonial rule. Second, China has a large population and a weak economy and doesn't necessarily hold an advantage over other countries in terms of resources. India's land area is merely about one-third of China's, but it has no less cultivated land than China. Third, China's path of industrialization is marked by radical changes primarily as a result of the government's development strategy and line, including both correct decisions and gross mistakes. Although other developing countries have adopted different policies such as nationalization and privatization, they have not experienced an inverted U curve – from nationalization and collectivization to privatization and market-oriented operations – as China experienced.

Some may say that since China is a large country in terms of population, territory, and development history, it is bound to make industrial development a success. In fact, similar countries such as India, Brazil, and Russia also have their respective advantages, and it is hard to say that they will achieve success by relying on certain favorable conditions. Brazil has better advantages, with a small population, more resources, a peaceful external environment, and being far away from disputed zones, but Brazil lacks the conditions to become the "world factory", at least for the time being. Russia has a small population, a vast territory, and abundant resources, as well as a good foundation for the development of industry, but today's Russia has comparative advantages only in the military industry and is not competitive in most other fields. After being ruled by the British for many years, India has a larger English-speaking population than these other countries, including China, and its institutions and system are more in line with those of Western countries, but India has a weak industrial base, and it is competitive in only some fields (such as software and pharmaceuticals).

Nevertheless, China still lags far behind the world's advanced level in terms of industrial development. Essentially, more efforts must be made to improve systems and mechanisms. For example, there is a waste of resources and an inability to give full play to human resources. The education is seriously exam-oriented, and there is a lack of heuristic education that encourages creativity. As a result, young people lack personality and independence. Talents are used based on blind decision making, and it is difficult to bring into play personality and creativity.

Notes

1 Of course, this statement is only symbolic. The relationship between agriculture and industry will be discussed later. On this issue, see Katsuji Nakagane (1992), Li Wei (1993), and Yuan Tangjun (2015).
2 This refers to developed countries rather than high-income countries because some countries, such as oil-producing countries in the Middle East, obtain handsome returns through certain means, such as the export of resources. However, those countries will eventually be in trouble due to the depleted resources. Of course, it would be a different matter if they could use their resources to industrialize.
3 For the types of technological progress, see Ara Kenjirō (1969). For Hicks-neutral technical progress, see Hayami Yujiro (1995).
4 Japan and South Korea have also reached this level.
5 Regarding neighborhood enterprises, these are little known and rarely studied because it is the product of a special period, and statistics on them are scarce. We know that there were collective enterprises in cities in the planned economy period. Collective enterprises were divided into large collectives and small collectives. Collective enterprises usually

mentioned are mostly large collectives, and small collectives are rarely mentioned. These were mainly enterprises run by housewives who were organized by subdistrict offices and some young people who did not go to rural areas for physical and family reasons and who stayed in cities during the Cultural Revolution period. Also, school-run factories were opened by primary and secondary schools to allow students to engage in social practice, and one of the goals was to create jobs for their children. Most of these enterprises were dissolved or transformed into private enterprises after the reform and opening up.
6 See *Constitution of the People's Republic of China* of 1954.
7 *First Five-Year Plan of the People's Republic of China for the Development of the National Economy (1953–1957)*, p. 74.
8 National Bureau of Statistics (1959), p. 32.
9 However, there is also a puzzling phenomenon: foreign-funded companies are in the lower left.

4 Development and significance of the service industry

4.1 Introduction

Compared with agriculture and industry, China's service sector has always been weak for at least two reasons: First, the definition, scope, statistics, and other aspects of the service sector are unclear compared to agriculture and industry because these constantly change according to economic development.[1] Second, after 1949, China's economy and statistical data were defined according to Soviet rules based on material output. It was considered that the service sector did not create economic value, and there was no concept of the service industry, except industry and agriculture.[2] In fact, it is not that there was no service sector but rather that there was no such definition. Such thinking significantly hampered the development of the service sector.

In addition to the impact of such thinking and system, the changes in the service industry itself are noteworthy. As the economy develops, the scope of the service industry is expanding, covering emerging education, medical, consulting, government, finance, social services, etc. in addition to traditional business, catering, hairdressing, bathing, pawnshops, and so on. Some of these industries were completely new to China at the time, such as finance, insurance, law, consulting, logistics, warehousing, intermediary, R&D and design, accounting, human resources, and after-sales service in the producer services sector. These industries emerge as the deep processing industry develops. The more processing links there are in the manufacturing sector, the greater the demand for and the faster the development of the service industry. The demand for the service industry grows as the scale of enterprises expands. China is in the upgrading stage of industrialization. In addition to simple processing industries, a more complex and difficult manufacturing sector is being vigorously developed, which requires more support from the producer service industry.

The development of the service sector itself is a topic worth studying. According to the experience of developed countries in development, as the economy develops, the scope of the service industry is expanding in all countries. Whether this is a general law deserves further study because it involves the following issues. First, what is the boundary of the service industry? In other words, which industries belong to the service industry? In fact, new industries are emerging, such as online transactions. Second, does the development of the service industry depend on itself or on other industries? At least part of the service industry depends on the manufacturing sector, such as the producer service industry. Third, as the economy becomes further service-oriented, its productivity declining or its development remains stagnant. The economic growth of some countries is also declines. This is known as the cost disease of the service industry.[3] What should be done to solve these problems?

4.2 Growth in the service sector

4.2.1 Growth in output

The service sector has been developing slowly for a long time for a host of reasons compared to agriculture and industry. The service sector did not develop rapidly and soundly until after the reform and opening up, especially since the 1990s, when people began to better understand the service sector and to align with the world in the service sector. Previously, under the influence of Soviet economic theory and practice, China mistakenly believed that the service sector did not create value. At the same time, under the planned economy, the role and function of the service sector did not receive due attention. What seems like typical service industries today were at the time either subordinate to certain industries (such as education, healthcare, post & telecommunications, literature and art, tourism, and community services) or non-existent (such as finance, insurance, securities, consulting, real estate, and logistics).

Figure 4.1 shows the real growth rate of the added value of the tertiary sector after 1949. In general, similar to the primary industry and the secondary industry,

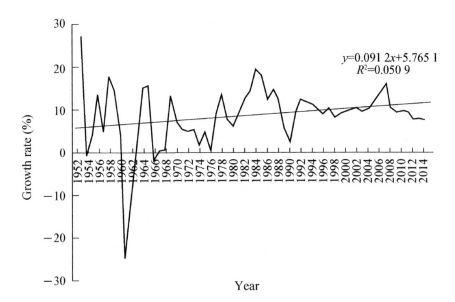

Figure 4.1 Real growth rate of added value of tertiary industry

Data source: *China Statistical Yearbook* over the years.

the tertiary industry had great fluctuations in added value under the planned economy but little fluctuations after the reform and opening up. This shows that the political events during the planned economy period led to economic fluctuations, such as the Great Leap Forward and the Cultural Revolution, which played havoc with economic activities. After the reform and opening up, the growth rate of the added value of the tertiary industry is both stable and very high, which greatly facilitated the development of the tertiary sector and also promoted the development of China's economy as a whole. Specifically, the growth of the tertiary industry in more than 60 years from 1953 to 2014 was up to 8.7 percent, which is rare in the world, particularly for China, which did not regard the service industry/tertiary industry as an economic sector. The growth rate of the added value of the tertiary industry under the planned economy was not as high as that after the reform, and opening up but was not low: 5.3 percent from 1953 to 1962, 6.6 percent from 1963 to 1972, 7.3 percent from 1973 to 1982, 12.13 percent from 1983 to 1992, 10.14 percent from 1993 to 2002, and 9.90 percent from 2003 to 2014. It can be seen that the tertiary industry made great progress after the reform and opening up, which largely made the compensation.

Table 4.1 shows the growth rates of output, number of employees, and output per capita in the tertiary sector. In addition to government statistics, there are estimates made by Hitotsubashi University regarding the latter two. In terms of output, the 1960s and 1970s were a period of slow growth in the tertiary industry, with as low as 2.04 percent in the 1960s and 6.05 percent in the 1970s, which was only relatively low compared with other periods. This reflects the status of the most strictly planned economy, especially in the 1960s, when people were conservative, and there were no conditions amenable to developing the service industry.

The reasons for the high growth of the tertiary industry in the 1950s are twofold. First, the economy was still in a period of recovery and adjustment in the early period, and the socialist transformation of capitalist industry and commerce was launched. The transformation, which was completed in 1956, greatly stimulated motivation,

Table 4.1 Growth rate of tertiary industry, Unit: %

Period	Output growth rate	Growth rate of employees		Growth rate of output per capita	
	Government statistics	Government statistics	Hitotsubashi estimate	Government statistics	Hitotsubashi estimate
1953–1960	10.74	14.36	6.91	−0.61	4.37
1961–1970	2.04	−3.15	−2.03	5.85	3.93
1971–1980	6.05	5.80	6.22	0.28	−0.13
1981–1990	12.33	8.15	4.88	4.09	7.10
1991–2000	10.20	5.20	4.80	4.81	5.26
2001–2010	11.23	2.89	4.86	8.13	6.10

Data source: China Statistical Yearbook over the years; Ryoshin Minami and Makino Fumio (2014).

Note: The Hitotsubashi estimate is an estimate made by the research team at Hitotsubashi University in Japan. See Ryoshin Minami and Makino Fumio (2014) for details.

which was at least the case at the time, although it may be somewhat obsolete from today's perspective. The reasons for the high growth of the tertiary industry after the 1980s are clear because it is linked to the primary and secondary industries, and the overall economic growth was high. It is obviously the effect of reform and opening up.

Both statistics (estimates) on the growth rate of the number of employees show negative growth in the 1960s, indicating that the development of the service industry was the worst during this period. Negative growth means that the number of employees in the tertiary sector decreased. If there is no change in the primary sector, the increase in the number of employees flows to the secondary sector. The high growth of the number of employees is the same as that of output, which should be decided by the economic basis at that time. In other words, the market economy played a role at that time. Because it was still the planned economy in the 1970s, there was little room for the development of the service industry, but people began to realize the importance of the service industry. The service industry developed to some extent in both urban and rural areas.

High growth in the 1980s was an inevitable trend because the right to individual operations was available in both urban and rural areas, and many people began to engage in wholesaling and retailing small commodities as well as in domestic trade, including services in cities like hairdressing, accommodation, catering, and bathing. The decline in the growth of the number of employees according to government statistics should be due to the absorption of abundant labor – especially rural surplus labor – in the 1990s by industrial development. Thanks to low labor costs, the export processing industry had comparative advantages during opening up. It can be said that the four decades after the 1980s are the optimal time for the development of China's manufacturing sector or industry. As labor costs rise and the service industry rapidly develops (high growth in output) in China, the number of employed persons in the service industry will keep rising.

There are some discrepancies between the two estimates regarding output per capita, particularly in the 1950s. Government statistics are negative, while Hitotsubashi estimates are not only positive but also high, possibly due to different sources of data and concepts. The high growth rate of output per capita in the 1960s is meaningful, although the growth rates of output and the number of employees are not high and even are negative, indicating that labor productivity increased during this period. It was a case of "few people doing more work". In contrast, in the 1970s, both output and the number of employees increased significantly, but output per capita was low or even negative. This shows that because the number of employees in the service industry in this period increased significantly but the output increased slightly, output per capita declined. It was a case of "more people doing less work". This disappeared after the reform and opening up. After the 1980s, both estimates indicated a high growth rate, showing the effective market function in resource allocation.

4.2.2 Breakdown of growth rates

The long-term growth rate of the tertiary industry after 1949 has been observed. Similarly to China's economy as a whole and to the primary and secondary industries, the growth accounting method is used to break down the growth rate and calculate the contribution made by various factors to economic growth. The rate of economic growth $G(Y)$ can be broken down into the growth rate of labor $G(L)$ and the productivity growth rate $G(Y/L)$:

$$G(Y) = G(L) + G(Y/L) \tag{4.1}$$
$$G(Y/L) = \lambda + E_K G(K/L) \tag{4.2}$$

where K and L indicate capital and labor, respectively, and E_K is the productive elasticity of capital. λ represents the movement of production function, or the remainder of the growth rate. The results of a breakdown based on equations (4.1) and (4.2) are shown in Table 4.2. Due to limited data, only the situation from 1982 to 2014 is calculated here.

The growth rate $G(Y)$ of output in the tertiary industry is generally far higher than that of the primary industry, and it is no less than that of the secondary industry. It has maintained a high growth rate for almost all periods. The growth rate $G(L)$ of labor exhibited a downward trend, which remained high until the mid-1990s and has since fallen to a low level. In other words, the labor or employment in the tertiary industry did not increase so much and so fast, which is somewhat beyond expectation. The number of jobs in this sector should have grown faster as a result of China's greater efforts for reform and opening up during this period, as well as the rapid development of the service sector. The growth rate $G(K)$ of capital in the tertiary sector fell from a high level to a low level, although not as low as in the secondary sector. The growth rate $G(Y/L)$ of labor productivity showed the opposite situation, increasing from a low to a high level, and remaining high for a long time since the late 1990s. The growth rate $G(K/L)$ of the capital/labor ratio increased from a low to a high level and then declined or was even negative, which

Table 4.2 Growth rate of tertiary industry and its breakdown, Unit: %

Period	$G(Y)$	$G(L)$	$G(K)$	$G(Y/L)$	$G(K/L)$	$E_K G(K/L)$	λ	$\lambda/G(Y/L)$
1982–1986	15.49	8.30	10.08	7.20	1.81	0.81	6.39	88.74
1987–1991	9.15	7.18	8.21	1.97	1.37	0.61	1.36	68.92
1992–1996	11.12	7.70	12.62	3.42	4.60	2.06	1.36	39.73
1997–2001	9.60	2.38	5.02	7.22	2.58	1.16	6.06	83.95
2002–2006	11.30	3.67	−4.79	7.63	−8.17	−3.66	11.30	148.00
2007–2014	9.90	3.34	2.66	6.56	−0.63	−0.28	6.84	104.29

Notes:
(1) Y = GDP (1978 = 100). The data are from *Data of Gross Domestic Product of China 1952–1995* and *China Statistical Yearbook* over the years.
(2) K = capital stock (1952 = 100); data for the 1982–1994 period are from Zhang Jun and Zhang Yuan (2003); data for the 1995–2014 period are estimated based on China's total fixed asset investment on this basis.
(3) L = the number of employees; data are from *China Labor Statistical Yearbook* over the years.
(4) G = rate of change.

is similar to that of the secondary industry, but the reasons are unclear. However, the growth rate λ of the technological progress rate showed a different situation, increasing from a low to a high or even a very high level, and its contribution to output growth was also quite high.

4.3 Structural changes

As we know, due to the complex definition and connotations, the service sector is diversified, including traditional business and catering, as well as modern finance, real estate, and transport. Some changes and evolution have taken place in the process. The traditional service sectors have not completely declined but have been transformed and can still exist in the process of industrialization and postindustrialization because these industries directly serve consumers. As the economy develops and per capita income increases, the demand for these services is growing. For example, traditional commerce may take the form of small-scale stores. Large shopping malls and supermarkets emerge in modern society, and there are a wealth of scattered points of sale. As large stores cannot meet the needs of everyone, small stores are indispensable. The same is true of the catering sector. Traditionally, there were only small restaurants. In modern society, there are both small and large restaurants, which cater to different groups of customers with different needs. As people's incomes increase, services that were previously luxury are now commonplace.

The modern service industry emerges alongside further industrialization, including education, medical care, finance, consulting, accounting, real estate, transport, and so on. For example, education was an advanced service that was acceptable to the rich and to those who fulfilled the conditions in premodern times. It was generally tailored to private individuals, such as private schools or tutors. In modern times, education became a service that is accepted by and acceptable to the general public and that has become a must-have in many countries. For example, compulsory education is an obligation, not a luxury. The transport industry basically did not exist in traditional times. Even if it existed, it was short-distance transport, because long-distance transport was impossible without the means of transport and equipment. In modern times, transport has become a basic means of improving the efficiency of economic activity. The transport of goods or people, short-distance transport or long-distance transport, and even international transport have become commonplace.

The same goes for medical treatment. It also existed in premodern societies, but it was generally individual behavior, such as private clinics or physicians trained in herbal medicine or even family behavior. They were not involved in market activities or at most played a role within a small range, such as acquaintance introduction. Both forms exist in modern times: on the one hand, there are still a wealth of private doctors and private clinics. On the other hand, there are many large hospitals equipped with modern medical facilities. Both are forms of market behavior, a key feature of which is that everyone is treated equally. Consulting, accounting and other sectors did not exist in premodern times. Even if they existed, they could not be called industries, but they are indispensable in modern society. Tourism was unimaginable in premodern times. It was only available for some individuals or the literati as cultivated pleasures, but it was not something that ordinary people could enjoy. It was therefore not an industry. In modern times, tourism has become a popular activity and is by no means the privilege of the few. More importantly, it has become an industry.

Table 4.3 enumerates the proportion of some sectors in the service industry. It can be seen that, except for the "Others" that accounted for about 30 percent, the wholesale and retail trade (i.e., commerce) had the largest proportion in the early 1950s but has recently plunged, accounting for only about 18 percent. The proportion of transport, warehousing, postal services, etc. has declined, while the proportion of finance and real estate has increased. In other words, the proportion of business as a traditional service sector has declined, while modern industries such as finance and real estate have developed at a fast clip. The "Others" category includes information transmission, computer services and software, leasing and business services, scientific research, technical services and geological survey, water conservancy, environment and public facilities management, resident services and other services, education, health, social security and social welfare, culture, sports and recreation, as well as administrative institutions.

Table 4.5 shows the proportions of the sources and distribution of aggregate purchasing power in the planned economy period. It reflects the social value creation. In other words, the goods produced must eventually be absorbed by organizations or individuals to realize their value. According to the table, the largest proportion is the income from the sale of products by farmers, or the income that farmers receive through the market. Although there was no open market at that time, it was realized through production organizations such as production teams. It is followed by the wages of employees in units owned by the people as a whole, as well as units under collective ownership. The combined proportions of the two are roughly

Table 4.3 Composition of output value of the tertiary industry, Unit: %

Year	Transport, warehousing, and postal	Wholesale and retail	Accommodation and catering	Finance	Real estate	Others
1952	14.9	41.3	–	5.7	7.2	30.9
1960	22.2	28.4	–	13.0	3.8	32.5
1970	18.3	32.5	–	10.4	6.2	32.5
1980	21.7	19.7	4.8	7.6	9.8	36.3
1990	19.8	21.5	5.1	17.3	11.2	25.0
2000	15.9	21.1	5.5	10.6	10.7	36.2
2010	8.6	17.9	3.4	14.7	12.7	41.8
2018	8.6	17.9	3.4	14.7	12.7	41.8

Sources: Data for years before 1980 are from the Department of National Economic Accounting of the National Bureau of Statistics (1997), and data for years after 1980 are from *China Statistical Yearbook 2019*.

Note: Classifications were different before and after 1980.

Table 4.4 Sources and distribution of aggregate purchasing power in the planned economy period, Unit: %

Year	Wages of employees in organizations owned by the whole people	Wages of employees in organizations under collective ownership	Income of other professions	Farmers' income from sales of products	Farmers' labor income	Residents' income from government finances	Net increase in agricultural loans and advance payments for future purchases of banks and credit unions	Residents' other monetary income	Currency of urban groups for purchase of consumer goods
1952	19.71	15.63	3.01	42.44	1.84	1.40	0.50	8.24	7.24
1960	32.45	7.51	1.99	29.72	4.61	4.98	2.16	7.30	9.28
1965	29.80	8.74	2.93	38.77	3.29	3.33	0.82	6.12	6.20
1970	29.32	8.66	2.98	37.15	4.47	2.23	0.16	9.11	5.93
1975	27.37	8.90	2.38	34.41	5.20	3.14	0.66	9.99	7.95
1980	24.76	8.16	1.68	35.21	7.36	2.53	1.44	12.29	6.35
1985	18.86	8.35	1.09	38.17	9.14	1.67	0.37	15.49	6.48

Data source: Department of Trade Material Statistics, National Bureau of Statistics, (1990), pp. 35–36.

Note: The total of the items is 100.

Table 4.5 Proportion of private commerce and transport, Unit: %

Year	Commerce			Transport		
	Socialist	State capitalist and cooperative	Private	State-run	Public–private partnership	Private
1949	–	–	–	85.5	–	11.5
1950	14.9	0.1	85.0	95.3	–	4.7
1951	24.4	0.1	75.5	94.7	–	5.3
1952	42.6	0.2	57.2	95.8	0.7	3.5
1953	49.7	0.4	49.9	95.8	1.3	2.9
1954	69.0	5.4	25.6	95.3	3.1	1.6
1955	67.6	14.6	17.8	94.8	4.6	0.6
1956	68.3	27.5	4.2	99.3	0.7	–
1957	65.7	31.6	2.7	99.7	0.3	–

Data source: National Bureau of Statistics (1959), pp. 34–35.

Note: The figures refer to the retail sales of commodities and the turnover of goods of commercial enterprises, which are 100.

about the same as the income of farmers from the sale of products. In other words, the total income of urban residents is roughly the same as the total income of rural residents. However, it should be noted that the number of farmers at that time was far greater than that of urban residents and that the real income level of urban residents was higher than that of rural residents. Other monetary income of residents also accounted for a large proportion, indicating the existence of income other than wages, although few people had such income. The currency of urban groups for the purchase of consumer goods also accounts for a certain proportion, reflecting collective consumption. For example, various types of organizations need to purchase commodities needed by the collective, and some organizations purchase commodities and distribute them to employees. It is noteworthy that the farmers' income from labor service has increased from a negligible proportion in the early days to a large proportion in the later period, showing the increase in the farmers' personal income after the reform and opening up.

4.4 Institutional changes

Through the introduction in the previous two chapters, we have learned that private enterprises and the self-employed in agriculture, industry, and service sectors were transformed into two forms of collective and state ownership seven or eight years after 1949 through agricultural cooperation and the socialist transformation of capitalist industry and commerce. Because the positioning and connotations of the service sector were not very clear at that time, the discussion has certain limitations. Nevertheless, certain data analysis reveals the general situation of institutional changes at that time.

Table 4.5 shows the socialist transformation of private commerce and transport sectors. In terms of commerce, the socialist sector accounted for only about 15 percent in 1950, while the private sector accounted for 85 percent, indicating that commercial services in China at that time were primarily provided by private individuals. Through socialist transformation, this proportion was gradually reversed. By 1957, the private sector was almost negligible, the socialist sector accounted for about two-thirds, and the state capitalist and cooperative sector also accounted for about 30 percent. Individual and private commerce was gradually replaced by collective and state commerce. The transport industry was different from the commerce industry because the state sector was overwhelmingly dominant from the outset, with the public–private partnership and the private sector accounting for only a small proportion. This is highly linked to the characteristics of this industry, which is capital-intensive. Coupled with its importance in other areas (as infrastructure, with the characteristics of the public sector of the economy), state operation is almost inevitable in this industry.

The number of workers in the transport and post & telecommunications sectors is further examined. Table 4.6 also shows the effect of institutional changes

Table 4.6 Number of employees in various sectors of the service industry, Unit: 10,000 people (%)

Year	Total	State-run	Public–private partnership	Cooperative-run	Private
Transport and postal & telecommunications					
1949	64.2	49.2 (76.6)	–	–	15.0 (23.4)
1950	78.9	47.6 (60.3)	0.1	–	31.2 (39.6)
1951	89.8	56.5 (62.9)	0.1	–	33.2 (37.0)
1952	112.9	76.7 (67.9)	0.9	–	35.3 (31.3)
1953	124.7	88.2 (70.7)	1.1	–	35.4 (28.4)
1954	140.5	102.7 (73.1)	2.4	–	35.4 (25.2)
1955	148.1	111.1 (75.0)	3.7	0.1	33.2 (22.4)
1956	156.4	145.5 (93.0)	5.3	4.2	1.4 (0.9)
1957	166.5	154.2 (92.6)	5.1	6.7	0.5 (0.3)
Business and catering					
1949	125.6	9.0 (7.2)	–	7.3 (5.8)	109.3 (87.0)
1950	152.5	23.2 (15.2)	–	20.4 (13.4)	108.9 (71.4)
1951	208.6	33.5 (16.1)	–	40.5 (19.4)	134.6 (64.5)
1952	292.3	71.9 (24.6)	–	90.3 (30.9)	130.1 (44.5)
1953	296.5	79.2 (26.7)	–	105.8 (35.7)	111.5 (37.6)
1954	330.9	107.6 (32.5)	–	146.9 (44.4)	76.4 (23.1)
1955	340.6	147.8 (43.4)	7.5 (2.2)	128.8 (37.8)	56.5 (16.6)
1956	494.3	227.4 (46.0)	107.7 (21.8)	159.2 (32.2)	0.0 (0.0)
1957	488.7	235.1 (48.1)	108.0 (22.1)	145.1 (29.7)	0.5 (0.1)

Data source: Department of Social Statistics, National Bureau of Statistics (1987), p. 83.

Note: The figures outside the parentheses refer to the number of people, and those in parentheses refer to the proportion. The total is 100. Only the proportions of the state and private sectors are indicated here.

during this period. Originally, these two sectors were overwhelmingly dominated by the state. As the number of workers in the private sector between 1950 and 1955 shows, the private sector accounted for about one-third and about one-quarter in some years, but it plunged to almost negligible levels in 1956 and 1957. The state sector originally had accounted for two-thirds but rose to more than 92 percent in 1956 and 1957, indicating absolute monopoly. This shows that public–private partnership mainly began in 1956 and was completed in 1957, as evidenced by other sectors, including agriculture and industry. Public–private partnership and cooperative operations also accounted for a small proportion, although a certain share was maintained. At the same time, this situation shows that the so-called socialist transformation of capitalist industry and commerce was primarily targeted at the private sector, and public–private partnerships and cooperative operations were retained to some degree.

The number of employees in the commerce and catering sectors is completely different from that in the aforesaid transport and post & telecommunications sectors. Before the socialist transformation, the private sector had an overwhelming advantage. Then it fell from a high of 87.0 percent, and this decline accelerated from 1952 and still maintained a certain share in 1955. However, it suddenly reached the level of disappearance in 1956 and 1957, while the state sector gradually rose from a small proportion (7.2 percent) to nearly 50 percent. Cooperative-run operations also increased significantly, from less than 6 to 44.4 percent in 1954. Although it later declined (mainly due to the increase in the state sector), it also accounted for nearly 30 percent. Public–private partnerships emerged late but had a significant proportion, accounting for about 22 percent in 1956 and 1957. It can be concluded from Table 4.7 that socialist transformation is mainly targeted at the private sector.

Table 4.7 shows the number of employees in the financial sector, which is very different from the commerce sector. The state sector has long occupied an absolute advantage, holding the entire share from the outset. Later, public–private partnerships emerged, accounting for about 4 percent. This is a special

Table 4.7 Number of employees in the financial sector, Unit: 10,000 people (%)

Year	Total	State-run	Public–private partnership
1949	4.5	4.5 (100.0)	–
1950	9.8	9.8 (100.0)	–
1951	24.9	24.9 (100.0)	–
1952	34.4	33.6 (97.7)	0.8 (2.3)
1953	37.7	36.9 (97.9)	0.8 (2.1)
1954	36.7	36.0 (97.1)	0.7 (1.9)
1955	35.7	34.1 (95.5)	1.6 (4.5)
1956	37.3	35.7 (95.7)	1.6 (4.3)
1957	36.2	34.6 (95.6)	1.6 (4.4)

Data source: Department of Social Statistics, National Bureau of Statistics (1987), p. 83.

Note: The figures in parentheses are the proportion, and the total is 100.

situation, which is due to the special nature of the financial sector in rural areas. A key feature of rural areas is their being fragmented and scattered, not only geographically but also in terms of funds. As a result, the adoption of appropriate public–private partnerships is more in line with the reality in rural areas. Of course, since the financial industry gradually became an appendage of the fiscal department even in cities at that time, there was no real financial market. Therefore, state-run finance was only a formality, and there was no real financial business to speak of.

Next is the examination of the long-term changes in the proportion of total retail sales of consumer goods for various economic types. Table 4.8 shows the long-term changes. Two changes occurred from 1952 to 1998. First, private businesses and other sectors of the economy were transformed into the state sector and collective economy as a result of socialist transformation. The second was the transformation from state sector and collective economy to private businesses and other sectors of the economy after the reform and opening up. In other words, China's economy has experienced a cycle from decentralization to concentration and then to decentralization. Specifically, in 1952, private businesses and other sectors of the economy together accounted for about two-thirds of the total, while the state sector and collective economy accounted for about one-third. In 1958, following the socialist transformation, the state sector and collective economy accounted for an overwhelming 87.44 percent, while private businesses and other sectors of the economy accounted for only a meager 3.23 percent. This structure continued until the 1980s, when the state sector and the collective economy were evenly matched, with the state sector having a slight majority. After 1985, this situation began to change, with private businesses and other sectors of the economy gradually increasing, and the state sector and collective economy declining. In 1998, private businesses and other sectors of the economy together accounted for over 60 percent, while the state sector and collective economy accounted for only 37.22 percent. However, not much changed in 1990, indicating that this reform was mainly conducted in the 1990s.

Table 4.8 Total retail sales of consumer goods by economic types, Unit: %

Year	State-owned	Collective	Joint ventures	Private	Other
1952	16.26	18.17	0.62	60.91	4.26
1958	74.45	12.99	10.78	1.84	1.39
1965	53.04	43.16	–	1.86	1.94
1975	55.72	42.17	–	0.14	1.97
1980	51.43	44.62	0.02	0.70	3.22
1985	40.42	37.17	0.29	15.35	6.76
1990	39.59	31.70	0.48	18.91	9.32
1998	20.65	16.57	0.56	37.05	25.16

Data source: National Bureau of Statistics (1999), p. 57.

Note: The total retail sales of products is 100.

4.5 Conclusion

China's service sector got off to a late start and developed slowly, as a result of a poor understanding of the service sector and the advanced industrialization strategy. The former was influenced by Soviet economic theory, which was of the view that only agriculture and industry created value and that the service sector was not a productive sector. The latter was influenced by economic development strategies and thinking, which led to the development of industry, especially heavy industry, ahead of time while belittling agriculture, light industry, and service sector. This lasted a long time, and the importance of the service sector was not recognized until recently, and this has promoted the development of this sector.

Although China's service sector got off to a late start and experienced large fluctuations, the development in recent years has been rapid, and its future development will make compensation in this regard. The reasons for this are as follows. First, there are more opportunities in this sector due to its inadequate development in the past. Some sectors (such as warehousing, consulting, training, and express delivery) that were not fully recognized in the past have now mushroomed. Second, as China's industrialization reaches a stage when more service sectors are needed, the service sector is bound to see rapid development. In the past, the industrial system referred to simple processing and production. Today, an integrated situation has been formed. That is to say, the industry has richer connotation, higher demands, and better coherence. For example, creativity, ordering, design, modeling, processing, assembly, supporting facilities, sales, after-sales service, and other aspects are more closely linked and diverse. Third, China's industry did not require so many service sectors due to institutional limitations. As marketization deepens, this situation will radically change. Before the reform and opening up or when corporate reform was conducted in the 1980s and 1990s, China's enterprises were mostly characterized as being "large and all-inclusive, and small and all-inclusive", which reduced much work that should have been performed by the market. For example, enterprises had canteens, kindergartens, elementary schools, and logistics departments. Through reforms, these sectors have been separated, which is not only a relief for enterprises but also spawns more service sectors.

Although China's service sector has made great strides in recent years, it is still in its infancy, with large room for development in both scale and standards and also many problems. Similar to industry, China's service sector tends to pursue quantity and scale during its development, while ignoring quality and standards. Moreover, vicious competition and excessive competition often exist in the intense market competition, and this is more serious than in other sectors because the service sector is generally more competitive, and economies of scale are not easily manifested. Furthermore, because China's market economy has a short history and there is a lack of experience, people lack a full understanding of market rules and laws and even ignore laws and regulations, resulting in inappropriate competition.

Nevertheless, China's service sector has great potential for development and has bright prospects because China's economy has tremendous potential for development. In particular, industry and manufacturing are still the leading sectors of

China's economy. With the upgrading of industry, the service sector will also move with the times. At the same time, some service sectors, such as medical care, education, accounting, design, and consulting, have considerable potential of development. However, we must also learn from the cautionary tale of the cost diseases of the service sector that has occurred in developed countries, and we must take precautions to prevent economic downturn.

Notes

1 For changes in the positioning and understanding of the service sector, see Jansson (2013), Delaunay and Gadrey (2011), and Guan Quan (2014).
2 Before the reform and opening up, common occupations were workers, peasants, soldiers, students, and businesspeople. If the service industry was mentioned, it meant commerce. It is a fact that, although the wages varied slightly from industry to industry, the wages of business employees were relatively low.
3 For the cost disease of the service sector, see Baumol (1967), Jansson (2013), and Guan Quan (2014).

5 Demographic changes and labor supply

5.1 Introduction

Speaking of China's population, the first thing that springs to mind is that China is the world's most populous country, which has brought unlimited benefits as well as endless troubles to China. The advantage is that there is strength in numbers. Even though an individual person's strength is limited or the income is in consequential, the numbers can add up, and there is a synergy effect. In 2019, China's GDP per capita exceeded US$10,000, which is only a medium level in the world, but it adds up considerably in a country with a population of 1.4 billion, making China the second largest country in the world. Furthermore, according to the principle of probability, there should be more geniuses in China, a country with a large population. China's ability to make brilliant achievements in history is a manifestation of this advantage.[1] On the other hand, although China is the world's second largest economy, its GDP per capita ranks only a little above 60th, which has a troublesome side. Many more problems are facing China that other countries with a small population cannot experience or understand. For example, our family planning policy is a last resort, and countries with a small population do not need such a policy. However, this is not absolute because a population must have living space. If the land area is small, even a country with a small population seems crowded. In addition, the size of China's population is not only a domestic issue but also a global issue because it can affect the world's resources and markets.

When it comes to the relationship between economic development and population growth, this ancient country that has witnessed vicissitudes has "a big population and a weak economy". Then what is the relationship between the two? Is it because a large population consumes more output and lowers living standards or because more people are born because of low productivity? Of course, chance cannot be excluded, and there is no necessary connection between the two, but this is unlikely. In fact, the former and the latter are actually two sides of the same coin. According to the theory of demographic transition, in the traditional era with low productivity and the early stage of economic development, the birth rate and death rate are high because of outdated views and poor medical services. This period is equivalent to the Malthusian trap. People need more labor in order to survive, but due to the limited productivity, a larger population cannot be fed, and therefore the

DOI: 10.4324/9781003410393-7

population will decline. When productivity increases or new land is developed, the population increases, but the living standards remain low. This not only is a characteristic of China's traditional era but also is a true portrayal of all countries.

Compared with other countries, the relationship between China's economic development and population growth as well as demographic transition is special. First, when China began to achieve modern economic growth, it had a population of 600 million to 1 billion people.[2] The "large population and a weak economy" was put forward during this period. India is most similar to China in this regard because the two countries are not only populous countries but also close in terms of the beginning of modern economic growth or the level of economic development. According to comparable data from the World Bank, the GDP per capita of China and India was US$90 and US$84, respectively, in 1960, US$113 and US$115, respectively, in 1970, US$195 and US$272, respectively, in 1980, and US$318, and US$375, respectively in 1990.[3] India began to lag behind China from the 1990s.

Second, due to the existence of the first particularity, the fruits of China's economic development had been largely consumed by population growth for a long time. As a result, China had to adopt a rigid "family planning" policy, a unique policy that limits population growth that other countries do not have. This unique policy has received mixed reviews worldwide. In the more than 30 years after this policy was implemented, China's economy has seen rapid growth, and people's living standards have been considerably improved. There are now complex and contradictory changes in views on this policy. Some say that the "family planning" policy should be abolished, believing that the only-child issue is serious and will even negatively impact the next two generations and the development of China's economy. Others oppose the abolition of this policy, arguing that China's economic development is not high and that the limited arable land cannot feed a larger population. Given the gradual disappearance of the demographic dividends, the government has decided to relax the restrictions and allow each couple to have two children.

Third – closely associated with the first two particularities – although China is a country with a big population, it is a pioneering achievement for China to achieve fast economic growth. However, neither the experience of various countries in economic development nor economic theories can prove that a populous country like China can achieve such rapid growth. Although the United States has a population of over 300 million, it is different from China in at least two respects. First, when the United States began to achieve modern economic growth (in the mid-19th century), it had a population of less than 100 million. Although it was also a populous country at the time, it was not on a par with India and China in terms of population size. Second, on the whole, the United States is a sparsely populated country with a vast territory, and the human/land ratio is low. It does not face the demographic pressure that China and India do and even needs to supplement the population shortage by attracting immigrants. Japan, a country with a large population and little land, is comparable in this sense, although its absolute population cannot be compared with that of China and India. Of course, economic development is driven by a slew of factors, and it is by no means determined by the population alone, but population is one of the most basic factors after all.

5.2 Population increase

The overview of China's population after 1949 is roughly as follows: 550 million in 1950, over 600 million in 1954, over 700 million in 1964, over 800 million in 1969, over 900 million in 1974, over 1 billion in 1981, over 1.1 billion in 1988, over 1.2 billion in 1995, over 1.3 billion in 2005, and 1.37 billion in 2015.[4] It can be seen that it took 10 years to increase from 600 million to 700 million, only 5 years from 700 million to 800 million, 5 years from 800 million to 900 million, 7 years from 900 million to 1 billion, 7 years from 1 billion to 1.1 billion, 7 years from 1.1 billion to 1.2 billion, and 10 years from 1.2 billion to 1.3 billion. A law can be observed: the population grew slowly and then rapidly, before slowing down again. According to the laws of nature, there should be a process of accelerated growth. That is to say, as the population base expands, the time for each increase of 100 million people should be increasingly shortened. However, this is not the case. Except for the initial period, the population increase of each 100 million took 5 years, 7 years, and then 10 years.

Table 5.1 shows the changes in China's population after 1949, from about 540 million to nearly 1.4 billion in 2018. It experienced two stages of relatively fast growth and relatively slow growth. Either type of statistics shows an increase of about 440 million in the 30 years from 1949/1950 to 1980 and an increase of about 360 million in the 30 years from 1980 to 2010. The durations of time in the two periods were similar, while the population increases were very different, especially when the base effect was taken into account. In other words, the population in 1949 and 1950 was only 540 million and was then close to 1 billion in 1980. If the growth rate of the first 30 years was followed, the population should double or nearly double in the next 30 years, approaching 2 billion, but this is not the case in reality. This is attributed to the family planning policy that has been in place since 1979. It is also related to the laws of economic development and demographic transition.

Table 5.1 China's population after 1949, Unit: 10,000 people

Year	Government statistics	Maddison estimate	Hitotsubashi estimate
1949	54,167	54,394.1	–
1950	55,196	54,681.5	55,900
1960	66,207	66,707.0	67,018
1970	82,992	81,831.5	81,523
1980	98,705	98,123.5	98,020
1990	114,333	113,518.5	113,439
2000	126,743	126,264.5	126,483
2010/2008	134,091	132,685.6	133,922
2018	139,538	–	–

Data source: Government statistics from the *China Statistical Yearbook* over the years, Maddison estimate from Maddison (2008) and Maddison (2009); Hitotsubashi estimates from Ryoshin Minami and Makino Fumio (2014).

Note: Maddison data for 2010 refers to 2008.

88 Processes and characteristics

What is the relationship between population growth and economic growth during this period? Simply put, the population grew fast (about 2.7 percent), and the economy grew slowly (about 6.5 percent) in the first 30 years. In the subsequent 30 years, the opposite was true, with slow population growth (about 1.2 percent) and rapid economic growth (about 9.7 percent). The meaning of this phenomenon is self-evident. The early economic growth is both the wealth created by a large population and the product of consumption by a large population. In other words, more labor leads to corresponding economic growth, and the achievements of economic growth are consumed by a bigger population, resulting in little increase in per capita income or living standards. Moreover, this growth relied more on factor inputs than on increased productivity. Economic growth in the latest 30 years or so was not the result of a larger population and labor (though this is also a factor) but the result of technological advance or efficiency gains. A low population/labor force growth and high economic growth inevitably lead to an improvement in living standards.

5.3 Demographic transition

Figure 5.1 shows the process of demographic transition after 1949, which shows three distinct characteristics.[5] First, from 1958 to 1961, there was an abnormal state, or a sudden decline in the birth rate, which was 35 to 37 percent, while the

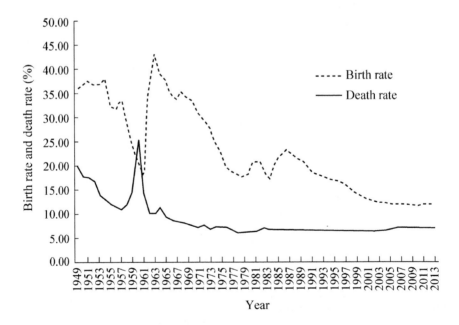

Figure 5.1 Demographic transition in China

Data source: *China Statistical Yearbook* over the years.

figures fell to 20 and 18 percent, respectively, in 1960 and 1961. In contrast, the death rate rose sharply. It should be 10 to 11 percent. It reached 14 percent in 1959 and 1961 and was up to 25 percent in 1960. As a result, the natural rate of growth was also abnormal, reaching 10.19 percent in 1959, −4.57 percent in 1960, and 3.78 percent in 1961. The population growth was negative in 1960. The total population was 672 million in 1959, 662 million in 1960, and 659 million in 1961. The absolute population decreased by more than 13 million in 2 years. It is generally believed that the reasons are twofold. First, it was caused by 3 years of severe hardship. Second, the Great Leap Forward and the people's commune movement led to a decline in productivity and a rise in mortality.

The second feature is that China's birth rate has fallen rapidly compared to other developing countries at the same level, resulting in a natural rate of growth close to that of developed countries. This was apparently caused by the family planning policy. The birth rate has been declining since the 1980s from its peak in 1963 (43.37 percent). More importantly, China saw a rapid transition from a typical demographic structure of a developing country to a demographic structure of a developed country, which is unprecedented.

The third feature is that the population increase was encouraged in the early period, which led to a serious population explosion from 1949 to the 1970s. The birth rate was grossly separated from the mortality rate, and the natural rate of growth even peaked at 33.33 percent (1963). This situation was only seen in developing countries.

5.4 Age structure

The age structure and dependency ratio for China's population are examined next. Table 5.2 shows the proportions of the working-age population and the non-working-age population as well as the child dependency ratio and the elder dependency ratio from 1960 to 2018. First of all, the age structure of China's population has changed significantly over 60 years. The proportion of the population aged zero to

Table 5.2 Age structure and dependency ratio of China's population, Unit: %

Year	Zero to 14 years	15 to 64 years	Over 65 years	Total dependency ratio	Child dependency ratio	Elder dependency ratio
1960	35.9	59.7	4.4	67.5	60.2	7.3
1970	33.6	61.5	4.9	62.6	54.6	8.0
1980	33.6	61.5	4.9	62.6	54.6	8.0
1990	27.7	66.7	5.6	49.8	41.5	8.3
2000	22.9	70.1	7.0	42.6	32.6	9.9
2010	16.6	74.5	8.9	34.2	22.3	11.9
2018	16.9	71.2	11.9	40.0	23.7	16.8

Data source: *China Statistical Yearbook* over the years.

14 years fell from 35.9 to less than 17 percent. This is a highly extreme situation, which is not seen in any other country in the world. It is clearly not the result of natural development. According to the data from the World Bank's *World Development Indicators 2010*,[6] the world average proportion of the population in the same age bracket is 27 percent. This figure was 39 percent for low-income countries, 32 percent for low- and middle-income countries, 22 percent for middle- and high-income countries, and 17 percent for high-income countries. China is equivalent to high-income countries in this regard. In terms of the proportion of the working-age population aged 15 to 64 years, the figure for China rose from 59.7 to 71.2 percent (up to 74.5 percent in 2010). With reference to the statistics from the World Bank, the world average proportion of the population in the same age bracket in 2010 was 66 percent. This figure was 57 percent for low-income countries, 63 percent for low and middle income countries, 70 percent for middle- and high-income countries, and 67 percent for high-income countries. It is roughly in an inverted U curve. China was at the highest level, and only a few countries in the world exceeded this level. Finally, the proportion of people aged over 65 years in China rose from less than 4.4 to 11.9 percent. The world average proportion of the population in the same age bracket was 8 percent in 2010. This figure was 4 percent for low-income countries, 5 percent for low- and middle-income countries, 8 percent for middle- and high-income countries, and 16 percent for high-income countries. China's corresponding population was far larger than the average of middle- and high-income countries, and this obviously exceeded its level of development.

Directly associated with this is the dependency ratio. The child dependency ratio dropped from 60.2 to 23.7 percent, almost to one third of the original figure. Conversely, the elder dependency ratio jumped from 7.3 to 16.8 percent. Referring to World Bank statistics, the world average of the child dependency ratio in 2010 was 41 percent, close to China's level in 1990. The same figure was 69 percent for low-income countries, 51 percent for low- and middle-income countries, 31 percent for middle- and high-income countries, and 26 percent for high-income countries. China's child dependency ratio in 2018 was lower than that of high-income countries. The world average of the elder dependency ratio in 2010 was 12 percent, similar to that in China. The same figure was 6 percent for low-income countries; 8 percent for low- and middle-income countries, which was China's level in the 1970s and 1980s; 11 percent for middle- and high-income countries, well below China's level in 2018; and 23 percent for high-income countries. China's total dependency ratio in 1980 was equivalent to Japan's level in the mid-1920s, and China's level in 2000 was equivalent to Japan's level in 1990. In 2018, China reached a low level that Japan had not experienced. Japan's dependency ratio rose from 57.8 percent in 1867, before the Meiji Restoration, to 71.6 percent in 1920, and then began to decline. It showed an inverted U curve, which is somewhat different from that of China.[7]

In general, the age structure of China's population differs from that of many countries for two reasons. First, China has put in place a strict family planning policy, which has achieved in a short time a fertility level that takes a long time to achieve in other countries. Specifically, the birth rate declines to the level of developed countries. Second, China implemented the family planning policy as it initiated reform and opening up and achieved rapid economic growth. The combination of the two has an amplification effect. Rapid economic growth leads to higher incomes, which can prolong life expectancy and reduce the birth rate.

5.5 Population policy

Economic development and social stability were achieved after 1949, and it was mistakenly believed that there was strength in numbers. China gave precedence to the quantity rather than quality of the population, and only focused on the productivity of the people without recognizing consumption. As a result, the population burgeoned. China's population increased from 542 million in 1949 to 975 million in 1979, an increase of 433 million in 30 years, with an average annual growth rate of 1.98 percent, which is a high growth rate in terms of world averages. Thereafter, the growth rate has gradually declined. The world average growth rate was 1.8 percent from 1970 to 1980, 1.7 percent from 1980 to 1993, 1.4 percent from 1990 to 2003, 1.2 percent from 2000 to 2010, and 0.99 percent from 2010 to 2020. However, low-income countries maintained a long-term growth rate of 2.0 to 2.1 percent, with basically no change. In high-income countries, it fell from 0.8 to 0.4 percent.[8] It can be seen that the growth rate of China's population during this period was close to that of low-income countries but far higher than that of high-income countries.

Under such circumstances, the Chinese government has been experimenting with family planning policies since the 1970s. At that time, it adopted loose policy such as encouraging late marriage and late childbearing and keeping a certain interval between the first and second births, instead of a one-size-fits-all policy for birth restriction. In 1979, a stricter population control policy was introduced, such as putting forward the slogan of "one child by a couple", strictly restricting urban residents from having two children and allowing rural residents to have two children but basically not restricting births for ethnic minorities. Thereafter, China entered the era of family planning, except for ethnic minorities and the rural registered population, as well as under certain special circumstances.[9] This biased family planning policy is mainly targeted at urban residents, while rural residents were also subject to certain restrictions. This policy directly led to a reduction in the birth rate and in the number of new births. As a result, the growth rate of China's population has declined rapidly, and the absolute population has grown slowly. This far exceeds the stage of economic development and has also given rise to a host of problems and controversies. In the 36 years from 1979 to 2015, the population increased to 1.375 billion, an increase of about 390 million, with an annual growth rate of 0.99 percent, which is significantly lower than the previous period and close to that of high-income countries from 1970 to 1980. It can be seen that the effect of the family planning policy is very obvious.

The problems caused by this biased family planning policy are also prominent.[10] To begin with, the rural population grew faster than the urban population due to the large rural population base and the small urban population base at that time, coupled with the fact that most urban couples could only have one child while some rural couples could have two children. According to the law of normal birth, the birth rate of the urban population is usually lower than that of rural areas as a result of the influence of schooling and other factors. This situation intensified following the implementation of biased family planning, although the number of new births decreased. Even in 2017, China's annual population of new births was nearly 18 million, and, according to household registration statistics, the population born in rural areas was in the majority, estimated at more than 12 million. This figure for that time can be imagined from this. According to household registration statistics, China's urbanization rate is 36 percent, compared with 17 percent in 1980, with an urban population of 168 million and a rural population of 819 million (a total population of 987 million). Moreover, as a result of the strict family planning policy implemented in cities and the loose family planning policy in rural areas, the children born in cities become spoiled "little emperors", while the rural children go to cities to serve as second- and third-generation migrant workers. This causes the class isolation among the young generation to the prejudice of the growth and development of young people.

The Fifth Plenary Session of the 18th CPC Central Committee held in October 2015 put forward a slew of new policies, including "fully implementing the policy that allows one couple to have two children, and taking active steps to deal with the aging of the population". This represents a significant shift in family planning policy that has been in place for more than 30 years, despite the somewhat relaxed birth restrictions before that time. In 2013, it was decided to issue a new policy that allows one couple to have two children if either of the couple is an only child. The new policy, if implemented, will change the family and social structure that has been formed over more than 30 years and will also affect the interests of individuals and the country in many areas. As China's economy reaches a medium level and still further develops, the roles of population and family planning policies have changed. The new policy will assist in China's economic development. Of course, it also needs the support of other factors, such as education and social security mechanism, as well as better science and technology. We believe that the universal two-child policy will have the sociological and economic effects in the following eight areas: (1) an increase in the absolute number of the population, (2) a change in the age structure of the population, (3) an increase in the number of urban residents, (4) an increased burden of bringing up children, (5) a change in the household consumption structure, (6) a further development of the education industry, (7) an eased burden of eldercare, and (8) a decrease in the number of families that have lost the only child.[11]

5.6 Labor supply

Figure 5.2 shows the growth rate of several indicators representing the labor supply, including the population of people aged above 15 years, the labor force, and the number of employed persons. These show changes in several stages. First, the three years of severe hardship following the Great Leap Forward led to severe negative growth, including a decline in the total population. This was a special circumstance. Second,

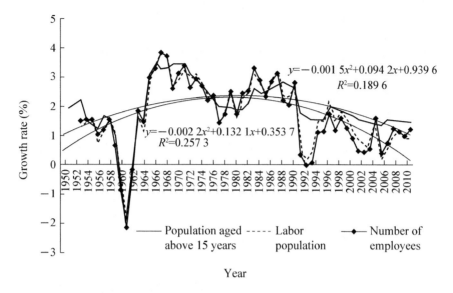

Figure 5.2 Growth rate of labor supply
Data source: Ryoshin Minami and Makino Fumio (2014), pp. 363–366.

the three indicators were basically linked, with some deviations in individual periods, especially after the 1990s. Third, all three indicators showed a high growth rate from the beginning of the Cultural Revolution to around 1990, indicating that China's labor supply was sufficient during this period. The growth rate of the population of people aged above 15 years did not decline significantly in the early 1990s, but there was very low growth in the labor force and the number of employees. The reasons are unclear. It was possibly caused by the wave of people setting up businesses and policies such as early retirement and layoffs as a result of corporate reforms. It might also be related to the rapid development of higher education sector. More school-age young people went to school rather than work, and the labor force and the number of employed persons were reduced. This tendency was more pronounced after the increased enrollment by Chinese universities in 1998. The increase in the enrollment rate also complemented industrialization and economic development. The increase in income enabled more families to send their children to schools.

If the growth rate of the three indicators is studied by stages, it was 1.0 to 1.4 percent in the 1950s, 2.04 to 2.12 percent in the 1960s, 2.39 to 2.47 percent in the 1970s, 2.51 to 2.66 percent in the 1980s, 0.94 to 1.72 percent in the 1990s, and 0.82 to 1.47 percent after 2000. In other words, all three indicators showed an inverted U curve change – it was low in the 50s, remained high until 1990, and then began to decline. This is clearly related to changes in the population growth, demographic transition, and, to a greater extent, economic growth.[12]

Table 5.3 shows the proportion of the population of people aged above 15 and the labor participation rate. In general, it shows the increasing proportion of the

Table 5.3 Population of people aged above 15 years, labor force, employed persons, the unemployed

Year	Population of people aged above 15			Labor population				Employees			Jobless people	
	Real number (10,000 people)	Proportion in total population (%)	Growth rate (%)	Real number (10,000 people)	Labor participation rate (%)	Growth rate (%)	Real number (10,000 people)	Growth rate (%)	Real number (10,000 people)	Unemployment rate (%)
1952	37,058	63.72	–	30,158	81.38	–	29,739	–	419	1.39
1960	40,941	61.09	1.26	32,671	79.80	1.01	32,279	1.03	392	1.2
1970	50,440	61.91	2.12	39,911	79.08	2.04	39,539	2.07	372	0.93
1980	64,373	65.78	2.47	50,537	78.38	2.39	50,044	2.39	493	0.98
1990	82,459	72.39	2.51	65,658	79.95	2.65	65,083	2.66	574	0.87
2000	97,828	77.15	1.72	74,113	75.95	1.22	71,473	0.94	2,641	3.56
2010	11,3154	84.49	1.47	80,398	71.05	0.82	78,096	0.89	2,302	2.86

Data source: Ryoshin Minami and Makino Fumio (2014), p. 368.

Note: The proportion of the population of people aged above 15 years = population of people aged above 15 years ÷ the total population × 100 percent. Labor participation rate = labor force ÷ the population of people aged above 15 years × 100 percent. The range of growth rate is as follows: 1952–1960, 1961–1970, 1971–1980, 1981–1990, 1991–2000, and 2001–2010.

population of people aged above 15 years and the declining labor participation rate. The reason for the former is the population aging and the decline in the birth rate, particularly the impact of the family planning policy after 1980 and the obvious tendency of population aging after 2000. The decline in the labor participation rate was primarily caused by the development of higher education and the rise in the enrollment rate. The enrollment rate increased primarily as a result of the declining demand for labor caused by economic development, especially household labor in rural areas. Of course, the difference between men and women is very large, with a significantly higher labor participation rate for men than for women, indicating that some women opt for housework, while men go to work more customarily.

5.7 Conclusion

This chapter discusses China's population growth and demographic transition as well as several issues concerning China's population and economic development, such as population policy. It shows some distinctive characteristics of issues on China's population compared to other countries and gives a better insight into the relationship between population and economic development. "A large population and a weak economy" sets China apart from other countries. As an ancient power, China has always been beset by the population issue. The government is torn between allowing the population to grow unchecked and imposing some restrictions. This prominent feature of China gave rise to the family planning policy, which has been debated for a long time, and this debate will continue for a long time to come. Due to the family planning policy, China's demographic transition has caused many explicit and implicit problems. This policy is associated with the excessively rapid demographic transition, the premature aging of the population, the low level of social security, the excessive urban–rural population gap, etc.

As the economy develops and income rises, a new trend has emerged in recent years: having more children than the family planning policy stipulated among some high-income groups. As society enters the era of pluralism, there is a serious conflict between people's views and the government's administrative system, particularly regarding the issue of fertility. There is a paradox in this regard. Having more children not only may bring hope to the poor by creating wealth for the family but may also have a more profound significance. If a child is admitted to a university and works in a city after graduation, he will become an urban resident. Ordinary urban dwellers can support only one child on their income. Even if the government allows the birth of a second child, many people will not do so. Of course, the high-income urban dwellers will opt to have a second child because having only one child carries great risk. For the rich, it is believed that an only child is lonely and that there is no one to inherit the family business. As a result, they would rather risk having a second child or more. Furthermore, there is still a serious flaw in the current policy: it is strict with public servants, who can often pay fines for having more children than the family planning policy stipulated, but not the others. This is totally unfair and has an adverse demonstration effect. However, this situation is beginning to change. The government has introduced a universal two-child policy that allows urban youth of an appropriate age to have a second child. This will have a significant impact on the economy as a whole and on every family, and we speak positively of this policy. Interestingly, after this policy was implemented, the number of newborns does not increase, as expected, but instead decreased. This is a sociological problem.

This chapter also examines the situation of the labor supply, which is related to the level of economic development in addition to being directly related to demographic changes. In an underdeveloped economy, people can only engage in agricultural production, and few people engage in industry and commerce. As the economy develops, various new occupations keep emerging, and the proportion of employees has changed significantly; the proportion of the population of people aged above 15 years and the labor participation rate also changes. China is in the middle of economic development and industrialization, and these indicators are consistent with this stage.

Notes

1 On this point, see Lin Yifu (1992).
2 For the time of modern economic growth, see Chapter 1 of this book or Guan Quan (2014, 2019b).
3 World Bank database.
4 *China Statistical Yearbook* over the years.
5 For the theory of demographic transition and the situation by country, see Guan Quan (2014).
6 For more information on the age of the population in various countries, see Guan Quan (2014).
7 Yano-Tsuneta Kinenkai (2000); Ryoshin Minami (1981).
8 World Bank, *World Development Report*, *World Development Indicators* for each year.
9 For example, if the first child has a severe illness or is mentally retarded.
10 Guan Quan (2014) conducted an analysis of this policy from the perspective of economic theory.
11 For this issue, see Guan Quan (2016).
12 The same goes for Japan's postwar experience, see Ryoshin Minami (2002).

6 Urbanization and labor mobility

6.1 Introduction

China's urbanization and labor mobility issues are important because China's urbanization rate should be far higher than it is by industrialization standards. In other words, China's urbanization seriously lags behind industrialization. Of course, there is no single standard in this regard, and the level of industrialization (proportion of the secondary industry) is not necessarily exactly consistent with the degree of urbanization (proportion of the urban population). However, it is still possible to make a rough judgment based on the experience of foreign countries because the so-called industrialization refers to the increase in the proportion of industry. Industry usually concentrates resources for better efficiency and has obvious accumulation effect and scale effect. Cities and even urban agglomerations are formed as a result of the concentration of industrial enterprises. Historically, many cities have been established on the basis of industry. Even before the Industrial Revolution, most of cities were dominated by industry (handicrafts), and some were also supported by commerce, with the exception of a few cities. Agriculture cannot lead to the formation of cities; only commerce and industry can. It is difficult to form cities through commerce alone, except for a few ports, metropolises, and trade centers. In modern times, many commercial or other services sectors are formed based on industry, such as producer services. This is different from that before industrialization. The city itself is not large in the commercial era, and handicrafts and commerce are enough to support the development and expansion of the city.

Nevertheless, China may see a period of rapid urban development in the future because in view of the high degree of industrialization, there is no reason against the formation of more and larger cities. In fact, China has many megacities, some of which have become the world's major cities. Typical cities are so-called "first-tier cities" such as Beijing, Shanghai, Guangzhou, and Shenzhen. However, there is a characteristic that sets Chinese cities apart from cities in other countries: residents who live in these cities every day are not necessarily the registered residents of these cities. Many people do not have registered urban residency in these cities, and they may return to their hometowns at a certain time. This involves the issue of labor mobility examined in this chapter.

DOI: 10.4324/9781003410393-8

According to economic theory, the efficient flow of factors of production helps improve efficiency, and it is very similar to the circulation of currency in this regard. Specifically, the efficient allocation of land, capital, and labor is highly important. Capital will seek the industries or regions with the highest profit margins, and the labor force will also go to the industries and regions offering the highest wages. The most salient feature of China and the world's largest migrant workforce is the group known as "migrant workers" who move from rural areas to cities in search of work. The majority of them work in labor-intensive industries in cities, such as catering, accommodation, commerce, construction, security, express delivery, cleaning, canteens, housekeeping, and other sectors. Many also work in small factories. In addition to being labor-intensive, these industries are seasonal and may be more suited to them because they sometimes need to return to their hometowns to engage in agriculture and look after family members, such as wives, children, and parents. However, the most important reasons are the restrictions imposed by the household registration system, as well as the various benefits attached to the household registration system.

6.2 Urbanization and labor mobility

6.2.1 Urbanization

China's urbanization level was low in the early 1950s but has gradually increased since then. The urbanization rate rose from 10.64 percent in 1949 to 19.75 percent in 1960, decreased to 17.38 percent in 1970, increased to 19.39 percent in 1980 in the early days of reform and opening up, reached the level of 1960 and then stagnated for 20 years. Thereafter, it began to rise, reaching 26.41 percent in 1990, 36.22 percent in 2000, and 54.8 percent in 2014.[1] However, the data were perfect until the 1980s and have since gradually altered, that is, in the distinction between the registered population and the permanent population. The current statistical standard refers to the permanent population, that is, including floating population. If the statistics on registered population are used, the urbanization rate in 2013 was only about 36 percent (see Figure 6.1). The reason for this is obviously the extensive labor mobility after the reform and opening up, particularly the migrant workers who have worked and lived in cities for a long time, while they are still registered as rural residents (farmer households). According to the current statistical caliber of the permanent population (those who have lived in a certain place for more than half a year), these migrant workers become urban residents. In other words, these migrant workers have two identities: household registration status (rural residents) and permanent residence status (urban residents). This is a key feature that distinguishes China from other countries today.

After 1949, China's urbanization has advanced slowly for a long time. The urbanization process has lagged far behind industrialization, particularly from the full implementation of the household registration management system in 1958 until the reform and opening up. This is an issue deserving serious study, and it is also a subject that is not sufficiently researched. Rapidly developing industry

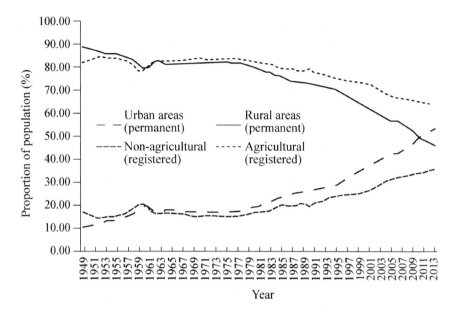

Figure 6.1 Urbanization in China (1949–2013)

Data source: *China Statistical Yearbook* and *China Population & Employment Statistics Yearbook* over the years.

on the condition of limited resources and catching up with developed countries in Europe and the United States became a big wish of Chinese policymakers at that time. It was also a last resort. In the early 1950s, China was faced with a situation in which everything remained to be done, and its economic development lagged far behind that of developed countries. Only by concentrating resources could it achieve greater success. Therefore, only a small number of people could be allowed to live in cities to ensure industrial development, while the majority of people lived in rural areas to provide support for industrialization, including food, raw materials, capital, foreign exchange, and labor.[2] In order to achieve this vision, the urban population was strictly restricted to prevent too many people from flocking to cities and forming slums.[3]

Another reason is China's rapid population growth and food shortage. Given the need for productivity and way of thinking at that time, only by allowing more labor to engage in agricultural production could China provide enough food and other agricultural products. To put it another way, the administrators and decision makers at that time were ignorant about the law of diminishing marginal returns. They only emphasized strength in numbers but overlooked the basic law of economic activities. Of course, the inefficiency of the planned economy and the slow economic growth also caused employment difficulties in cities. Even the urban residents had difficulty in finding jobs, not to mention allowing urban residency to migrant workers. Since the 1960s, a large number of urban residents went to rural areas through the form of "transfer of cadres to the countryside" and other forms,[4] becoming rural residents. Especially during the Cultural Revolution, tens of millions of urban middle school graduates "went and worked in the countryside and mountainous areas" to alleviate the pressure of urban employment.[5]

6.2.2 Labor migration

The issue of population and labor migration can be discussed based on two stages – before and after the reform and opening up – because these two periods show completely different characteristics. Before the reform and opening up, the population and labor migration were mainly conducted in accordance with the national strategy and policies, and the results were also unique. According to statistics, during this period, the population primarily flowed from the developed areas to the backward areas, which obviously went against the laws of economy from the standpoint of today's economic development, but this is a fact at that time.

In general, three large-scale population and labor migrations occurred between 1955 and 1980: the late 1950s, 1961–1961, and 1968–1970. A key feature was that the population outflow exceeded the inflow, which was the case for 19 provinces/autonomous regions/municipalities, such as Beijing, Tianjin, Shanghai, Hebei, Inner Mongolia, Liaoning, Jilin, Jiangsu, and Zhejiang. The three municipalities directly under the central government were the most prominent, particularly Shanghai, which had a net migration ratio of −62.08 percent in 1955, −2.71 percent in 1960, −4.11 percent in 1965, −28.84 percent in 1970, −0.47 percent in 1975, and 6.73 percent in 1980.[6] The population outflow of the three municipalities exceeded the inflow, primarily as a result of the large number of skilled personnel and professionals going to support the inland remote provinces. The same phenomenon is also observed in some developed provinces other than the three municipalities, such as Liaoning, Shandong, Hebei, Zhejiang, and Jiangsu. The other nine provinces/autonomous regions/municipalities are characterized by the population inflow exceeding the outflow, including Heilongjiang, Qinghai, Ningxia, Xinjiang, Jiangxi, Fujian, Guangxi, and Sichuan. For example, to develop the "Great Northern Wilderness" in Heilongjiang, a wealth of young intellectuals rushed to Heilongjiang and turned the wilderness into a "Northern Grain Warehouse". A similar situation occurred in Xinjiang, where there is still a paramilitary unit of the Xinjiang Production and Construction Corps, which operates independently. It is a special corps that is engaged in both production and training. It develops and also defends the frontier. In the case of Yunnan, Guizhou, Sichuan, Shaanxi, and other regions, a large number of engineering and technical personnel as well as experts were mobilized from developed coastal areas to primarily assist in the "three-line construction". This adjusted the country's economic and geographical distribution and also prepared for the outbreak of hostilities.[7]

China's urban population was 57.65 million in 1949 and soared to 382.44 million in 1985. In addition to the natural increase in population during this period, the remaining 260 million people were increased mainly through the following channels: (1) the expansion of urban areas, (2) new construction of towns, and

(3) migration from rural areas. Of these, the migration from rural areas accounted for the largest proportion. The reasons for the migration during this period are as follows: accompanying migration, job transfer, recruitment and substitution, marriage-related migration, foster care, job assignment, demobilization, return of educated youths to cities, schooling and training, migrant workers and businesspeople, implementation of policies, and retirement. These reasons are summed up by some as economic reasons, social reasons, policy reasons, and schooling reasons.[8]

The labor mobility after the reform and opening up shows different characteristics compared with before. First, following the implementation of the rural land contract policy and the disintegration of people's communes, a wealth of surplus labor emerged in rural areas, and the farmers who were bound to the people's communes and production teams under the planned economy had the opportunity to work as migrant workers. As a result, more and more craftsmen appeared in cities, such as shoemakers, bathing rubdown workers, nannies, carpenters and masons, and tailors. There were few job opportunities in the early days of the reform in the 1980s, and the trailblazers were those craftsmen with skills, as well as some who did odd jobs and businesspeople. Second, as urban reform and the urban construction advanced, a large number of rural laborers are involved in urban construction, especially in the fields of construction, catering, sanitation, security, housekeeping, and small business under individual ownership. Migrant workers have gradually become an indispensable force in large cities and emerging small and medium-sized cities in coastal areas. Third, in addition to migrant workers, many migrants move from city to city. Most of them are from relatively backward regions and migrate from northwest to southeast or from north to south. The most representative are special economic zones, which were previously not large cities. Shenzhen has evolved from a small county town into a first-tier city that is on a par with Beijing, Shanghai, and Guangzhou, with a population of over 10 million, mostly a floating population. Of course, migration and labor mobility after the reform and opening up have a traditional aspect, such as marriage-related migration, work-related migration, and demobilization, but there are no forms specific to the planned economy period.

The largest group of people for migration and labor mobility in China today is that of the "migrant workers". According to the National Bureau of Statistics, there were over 280 million migrant workers in 2017.[9] This situation has attracted much attention in China, because it involves many issues and deserves serious study.[10] First, the fact that these migrant workers can leave rural areas for the city means that agricultural production can be conducted without them. They are what Lewis calls zero marginal productivity (ZMP) workers. In other words, there is a surplus labor in rural areas, and they can choose other occupations or work. Second, the presence of migrant workers does not put employment pressure on cities because China's urban unemployment rate is low.[11] According to economic theory and market principles, the labor market has a balance between supply and demand. Since there is a lack of labor in cities, migrant workers can fill this gap. Migrant workers, in a sense, have become the pillar of China's urban construction and industry as well as service sectors. Third, the term "migrant worker" is used because they are

102 *Processes and characteristics*

not urban dwellers, and they have to return to their hometowns at a certain age or for other reasons. This is a significant feature of China, which is caused by the barrier imposed by the household registration system. Fourth, this situation has given rise to a host of problems in transport, accommodation, education, medical care, etc. Migrant workers generally go home for the Spring Festival; they usually need medical services; there is the problem of schooling for children; their left-behind parents, wives, or children must be cared for. Fifth, although it has been previously said that their departure does not affect agricultural production, there are problems of inadequate young and strong labor as well as a lack of technological innovation capabilities because only the elderly, women, and children are left in the rural areas. If these vulnerable people (left-behind children and women) are counted, there is a huge risk hazard to both rural society and agricultural production.

6.3 Economic analysis of the household registration system and family planning policy

China's household registration system and family planning policy have been discussed in Chapter 5, and only theoretical discussions are given here. Through the previous observations and analysis, we know the main characteristics and reasons for China's rural labor mobility: economic gap and social, institutional, and human factors. In order to comprehend this unique system and mechanism in China, the famous Todaro model (or Harris–Todaro model) is used to analyze the unique aspect of rural labor mobility in China.[12] The analysis is performed in two parts: the household registration system and family planning policy.

As shown in Figure 6.2, the Todaro model supposes that an economy only has two sectors: urban manufacturing and rural agriculture. On the premise of wages determined in the neoclassical free market and full employment, equilibrium wages will be set at point E, when agriculture and manufacturing employ all labor. However, it is supposed that wages in the urban sector are determined by the rules and are significantly higher than the equilibrium wages, as at W_{M1}. It is further assumed that there is no unemployment, only the labor force of $O_M L_{M1}$ work in cities, and that the remaining is employed in the agricultural sector and receive wages $O_A W_A^{**}$, which is lower than the original market wage $O_A W_A^{*}$, resulting in the real wage gap $W_{M1} - W_A^{**}$ between urban and rural areas. Although there are few jobs in cities, many rural residents will come out to try their luck in job hunting as long as they can move freely. If the ratio of manufacturing employment L_{M1} to the total urban labor force L_{US} means the opportunity of the rural labor force to find a job in the city, then the equation

$$W_A = \frac{L_{M1}}{L_{US}} (\overline{W}_{M1}) \tag{6.1}$$

represents the probability of successful job hunting in the city. It is also a necessary condition for the equivalence between the revenue of the agricultural sector and the expected urban income.

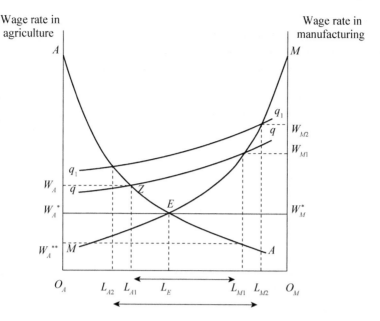

Figure 6.2 Todaro model under the household registration system
Data source: Guan Quan (2014), p. 173.

In Figure 6.2, Michael P. Todaro uses the curve qq to represent the trajectory linking urban and agricultural wages, and point Z, representing the unemployment equilibrium, appears. In this regard, the real urban–rural wage gap is $W_{M1}-W_A$, the labor force $O_A L_{A1}$ remains in rural areas, and the labor force $O_M L_{M1}$ works in the urban modern sector and receives wages W_{M1}. The rest of the labor force, which is $O_M L_{A1} - O_M L_{M1}$, is either jobless or engaged in low-income informal sector.

That is a basic explanation of the Todaro model. Two points must be clarified. First, Todaro's so-called unemployment equilibrium, or the existence of the employment issue in the informal sector, is very common in China. This is linked to the second point and deserves further analysis. Some jobless, as described by Todaro, are those who can't find regular jobs in the city. Others are different – they work in the relatively formal sector, but they are not "regular employees" in the formal sector. Instead, they are temporary workers or contract workers, who may be dismissed at any time. The second point is the focus of this book. It is the existence of the household registration system, which increases the existing institutional barrier between urban and rural areas. China's household registration system is an obstacle to rural labor who could work in the urban formal sector, and this increases the number of people employed in the informal sector, as represented by the curve $q_1 q_1$, which is higher than the Todaro model in the figure. In other words, the wage gap between China's urban and rural sectors is larger, and more people work in the informal sector.

104 Processes and characteristics

Figure 6.3 further shows another institutional policy that hampers rural labor mobility: the family planning policy. As mentioned earlier, according to the family planning policy, which was put in place since 1979, an urban couple can only have one child, and a rural couple can have two children. This leads to two problems. First, the natural increase in the urban population, which is already small, slows down, while the large rural population further increases significantly. As a result, China's urbanization lags far behind the level of industrialization and is even lower than that in other countries at similar stages of development.[13] Second, the rural areas are relatively poor, are short of medical services and supplies, and have a low level of education and social development. As most children are born in rural areas, these factors have an adverse impact on their physical growth. More importantly, if urbanization is an inevitable trend, these young workers who grow up in rural areas will go to the cities to work, but they cannot obtain registered urban residency, which swells the number of employed persons in China's informal sector.

Figure 6.3 shows that the difference between the new rural labor force and the new urban labor force can be expressed as an increase in the labor supply in the rural sector, such as $OA_2 - OA_1$ on the condition that the new young urban labor force is ignored.[14] Assuming that all the new rural labor force goes to cities in search of work, this increases employment in the informal sector, that is, the elongation of the qq curve or the q_1q_1 curve and wage reduction under China's current

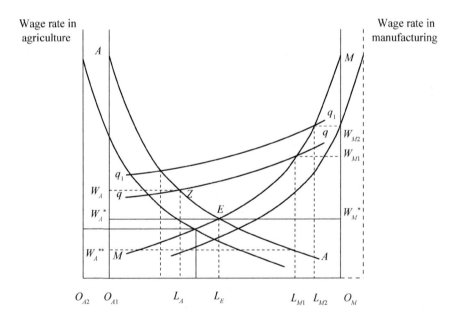

Figure 6.3 Todaro model under the dual roles of household registration system and family planning policy

Data source: Improvements based on Guan Quan (2014).

institutional arrangements. The dotted line on the right side of the figure shows the recent relaxation of the one-child policy. It is the change after urban residents are allowed to have two children. This corresponds to an absolute increase in the urban population, which aids the employment of urban residents and the reduction of the rural surplus labor employed in cities. Of course, this cannot solve the problem of household registration for many rural surplus laborers but only eases the labor supply in cities.

6.4 Lewis turning point

The American economist W. Arthur Lewis advanced the dual economy model in the 1950s, thinking that in the early days of economic development in developing countries, there is a dual economy structure. In other words, there are two disconnected sectors: the subsistence sector that produces in the traditional mode of production and the capitalist sector that produces in the modern mode of production. Due to the law of diminishing marginal productivity, the marginal productivity of labor in agriculture is low or even zero as the number of laborers increases, resulting in many surplus laborers in the agricultural sector. By this time, if the industrial sector can offer a set wage slightly higher than what is needed for minimum subsistence in rural areas, a wealth of labor will be attracted to the industrial sector. Since the labor supply is unlimited based on a set wage level, the industrial sector passively raises wages and continues to absorb rural labor until the industrial and agricultural sectors have the same marginal productivity and the surplus labor in rural areas is fully absorbed. As a result, the dual structure becomes a unitary structure, and developing countries move toward industrialization and urbanization. This point in time when the rural surplus labor force is fully absorbed is the Lewis turning point. John C. H. Fei and Gustav Ranis revised and developed the labor transfer model and proposed the Ranis–Fei model that features the analysis of surplus labor transfer from agriculture and focuses on technological changes. He pointed out the importance of the balanced growth of industry and agriculture in the dual economy stage.[15]

In terms of empirical analysis, Japanese economist Ryoshin Minami performed an empirical analysis of the issues of labor mobility and turning point based on the experience of the Japanese economy. Six criteria were selected to empirically validate the issue of turning point in the Japanese economy by comparing the differences between unskilled workers and skilled workers and between noncapitalist sector and capitalist sector, as well as the change tendency. First of all, the production function is used to calculate the labor elasticity of the noncapitalist sector. Second, the real wages of labor in the noncapitalist sector are compared to the marginal productivity to calculate whether and when there is a turning point in the Japanese economy. Finally, through empirical testing, he concluded that the Japanese economy had a turning point around 1960, and this becomes a final conclusion in Japan.[16]

There are also research findings on countries and regions such as South Korea in addition to Japan.[17] This is obviously an issue that East Asia must face in the course of development. That is to say, this problem mainly arises in countries and regions with a large resource of rural surplus labor. East Asia and South Asia are typical countries and regions with abundant or even surplus population and labor force, while Central Asia, Africa, and other regions do not necessarily have a severe labor surplus, or at least they are not typical. The problems of development and poverty there are not surplus labor but low productivity or a lack of industrialization and economic development, as well as noneconomic factors such as political changes and religion.

China has experienced over 40 years of rapid economic growth since the launch of the reform and opening up. The proportions of the three industries have changed remarkably, and new changes have also occurred in urban and rural areas. Coupled with China's special national circumstances (such as the household registration system), the issue of the turning point in China is more complex and uncertain compared to other countries, and it is difficult to make accurate judgment. Since the beginning of the 21st century, the turning point of China's economy has come under greater discussion, and there are naturally different views and judgments. There are primarily two views. One view holds that China's economy had the turning point around 2008 to 2010, and some even advocate that the turning point occurred in 2004. Another view is that China has yet to experience the turning point.[18]

On the issue of the turning point in China's economy, Japanese scholar Ryoshin Minami raised the following issues worth consideration.[19] First, Lewis's view on surplus labor discussed in China is different. Second, the question of whether Lewis's theory of dual economy is appropriate for China. The view on dual economy put forward by Lewis refers to the capitalist and noncapitalist sectors, which usually represent the urban sector and agriculture, respectively. However, there are many state-owned enterprises in Chinese cities. Despite the possession of advanced technology and equipment, they do not operate in accordance with the laws of the market economy. Which sector should rural township and village enterprises belong to? Third, it remains to be seen whether the shortage of urban labor in China is caused by the rapidly growing labor demand as a result of the development of urban sector or by the rapid reduction in rural labor supply. Fourth, it is uncertain whether the recent changes in the labor market are short-term or long-term. Fifth, China's deteriorating income distribution contradicts the economy's turning point. In other words, the economic turning point should not coincide with the widening income distribution gap.

As China's economy rapidly develops, the turning point seems to appear in some regions (the shortage of migrant workers). This is understood in two different ways. The first view is that China has reached a turning point and that there is a shift from a labor surplus economy to a labor shortage economy. The other view is that China's economy is far from reaching a turning point and that the current situation is an illusion or a temporary phenomenon. This debate is expected to continue for some time to come. We have no agenda in this debate; we just want to learn from Japan's experience in reaching a turning point and make suggestions for China to reach its turning point.[20]

Japan reached the turning point in the process of rapid economic growth primarily thanks to the dual structure of the secondary industry. In other words, large enterprises and small and medium-sized enterprises develop rapidly and simultaneously. The development of the secondary industry is a major generator of jobs, and this type of development mainly lies in small and medium-sized enterprises. In fact, the rapid growth of China's secondary sector since the reform and opening up has also benefited greatly from the development of small and medium-sized enterprises. Why hasn't China reached the turning point in this process? This question deserves further research. We believe that China's special national circumstances and systems, as well as its policies and strategies, have led to a situation in which China's economy grows rapidly but the surplus labor is not sufficiently absorbed. For example, the household registration system is a significant obstacle to the real transfer of rural surplus labor to cities. Surplus laborers can work in cities only as farmers. This imbalanced situation is not seen in other countries. Moreover, China's mode of economic growth is generally export-oriented, while the economic development of hinterland areas is ignored. This creates many opportunities for foreign investment without bringing more benefits to the local economy. As foreign-funded enterprises are inclined to be capital- and technology-intensive, they perform worse than local enterprises when it comes to employ surplus labor. In addition, during the period of reform and opening up, China's state-owned enterprises and collective enterprises face stiff market competition and have no choice but to make many layoffs, thereby imposing many constraints on the employment of rural surplus labor by these enterprises.

China still has not reached the turning point possibly because of what has just been discussed and other factors (such as different starting conditions for economic development). In order to achieve the turning point early, the preceding disadvantages should be addressed. For example, the current household registration system can be gradually removed, so that more rural surplus laborers can become registered urban residents. In addition, a development strategy that excessively relies on an export-oriented economy is not the best option. It is necessary to make adjustment and focus on the effective allocation of domestic resources as well as the development of labor-intensive industries. For example, small and medium-sized enterprises, especially those in rural areas, should be given policy support and preferential treatment; appropriate subsidies need to be given to enterprises that can hire surplus labor; preferential treatment must be given to enterprises that invest in areas with abundant surplus labor in central and western regions. Private enterprises should be given more support in terms of economic policies, government power should be decentralized, and state-owned enterprises should be further reformed.

6.5 Conclusion

China's urbanization and labor (population) mobility were discussed. It shows the universal and particular nature of China compared with other countries. In terms of universality, urbanization will appear as long as modern economic growth begins, and this is objective law, independent of human will. Modern economic growth or economic development must be realized through industrialization, which must be underpinned by urbanization or which inevitably leads to urbanization. Furthermore, urbanization requires a wealth of laborers, mostly from rural areas. Before industrialization, the vast majority of the population and labor force live in rural areas and engage in agricultural production. As a result, there is a wave of migration from rural areas to cities. This wave of migration will eventually lead past the turning point, as put forward by Lewis. China is also moving toward this threshold. Some think that China has already reached this turning point.

Speaking of particularity, China is a country that is different in many areas when viewed according to the standards of the developed countries, such as its vast territory and large population. China has exhibited a distinctive personality in terms of both labor mobility and the turning point. First, there was practically no market-oriented labor mobility under the planned economy, except mobilization based on government policies and strategies. Second, contrary to the planned economy period, a spectacular wave of migrant workers was observed after the reform and opening up. Some 280 million farmers left rural areas on their own or with their family members for cities and returned to their hometowns for the Spring Festival. Third, China's labor mobility is not only large scale but also unstable because this floating population of laborers basically cannot stay in cities as registered urban residents due to the household registration system. This gives rise to a host of problems that are difficult to solve in reality.

Notes

1 *China Statistical Yearbook* over the years.
2 For the contribution made by agriculture to economic development in early years, see Guan Quan (2014).
3 Slums emerge in many developing countries, such as the Philippines and India, as a result of slow industrialization and the influx of rural labor into cities.
4 Some of them were intellectuals, as well as those who had made political mistakes, and who had perpetrated crimes in cities.
5 According to statistics, from 1962 to 1979, a total of 17.76 million educated young people went to the mountainous and rural areas. *Statistics of Labor Wages in China: 1949–1985*, p. 110.
6 Department of Population and Statistics of National Bureau of Statistics, Third Bureau of Ministry of Public Security (1988).
7 Regarding the "third-line construction", it is generally believed that it was first implemented in 1965. A large-scale infrastructure construction covering national defense, science and technology, industry, and transport was conducted in 13 regions in western China, guided by the idea of war preparedness. It began in the context of deteriorating China–Soviet Union relations and U.S. harassment along China's southeastern coastal areas. The third-line construction is another large-scale industrial migration in China's economic history, with a scale comparable to that of industrial migration from coastal areas to the hinterland during the War of Resistance against Japanese Aggression. Due to the remote location of construction sites, it was difficult to form an advantage after the reform and opening up, causing difficulties to the operation of enterprises. Such construction is wasteful and inefficient in peacetime.
8 Yang Zihui, ed. (1996) p. 1647.
9 *The Economic Observer*, April 29, 2019.
10 Guan Quan (2014) introduces the literature on China's labor mobility in recent years.

11 There are two statistical calibers on China's unemployment. One is the registered unemployment rate in cities, which is around 4 percent throughout the year, and 3.6 percent in 2019. The other is a new statistic released in 2018: the urban surveyed unemployment rate, which is generally one percentage point higher than the registered unemployment rate in cities.
12 For a prototype of the Todaro model, see Todaro (1969) and Harris and Todaro (1969). The content here comes from Guan Quan (2014, 2018a).
13 For this, see Guan Quan (2014, 2018a).
14 The total number of new births in the country minus the number of new births in cities equals the number of new births in rural areas.
15 For a prototype of Lewis's theory, see Lewis (1955, 1958a); for the Ranis–Fei Model, see Fei and Ranis (1964); for an introduction to related theories, see Guan Quan (2014).
16 For Ryoshin Minami's study of the Lewis turning point, see Ryoshin Minami (1970, 1973). The six criteria are: (1) the relationship of size between wages and marginal productive forces in noncapitalist sectors; (2) the correlation between wages and marginal productive forces in noncapitalist sectors; (3) changes in real wages in noncapitalist sectors; (4) changes in the difference between real wages between unskilled and skilled labor; (5) changes in marginal productivity in noncapitalist sectors; and (6) elasticity in labor supply.
17 For the turning point in South Korea, see Bai Moo-ki (1982) and Kim Changnam (2014).
18 The issue of turning point in China's economy has been extensively discussed, and opinions vary greatly. Cai Fang et al. argue that China began to see a turning point in 2004, see Cai Fang (2012). Ryoshin Minami et al. believe that China is yet to see a turning point, but it is close, see Ryoshin Minami and Ma Xinxin (2014).
19 The content here comes from the Chinese edition of Ryoshin Minami (2008).
20 Guan Quan (2010) compares the relationship between economic growth and employment in China and Japan.

7 Income distribution and poverty issues

7.1 Introduction

Economic development in any country is intended to benefit the people, boost income, and generate wealth. Of course, there are other purposes, such as political stability, social harmony, and international reputation. However, these goals must be underpinned by an economic base. Political stability without economic development is unreliable, and it is difficult to maintain long-term social harmony. The same goes for China. As the economy develops, the income and living standards of Chinese people are increasing, which is an indisputable fact. Since the reform and opening up were initiated in the late 1970s, China's economy has grown significantly, and the per capita income has also increased rapidly because there has been no rapid population growth during this period.

However, the rapid development of the economy is not everything. It also involves the use and distribution of development achievements. This leads to two issues. First, can the economic gains can be better distributed to more workers and populace, which involves the issue of functional distribution?[1] The second is the issue of scale distribution, such as which groups of people have more gains, which groups of people have less, or what is the income gap between them. Like other countries, China also faces the problem of income distribution. That is to say, income distribution will expand from a low to a high level for a long time to come. If the problem of income distribution is not properly solved, it will impede the realization of social stability and the goal of prosperity for all.

Finally, the goal of economic development is to make everyone rich, but there will always be some people who are left behind, resulting in poverty. The developed countries have basically solved this problem. Despite the existence of a small number of poor people, they do not threaten the stability of society thanks to the mature social security and relief mechanisms and other assistance (such as church and individual donations). However, developing countries were originally poor. The less developed the country is, the more poor people there are. Underdeveloped countries are unable to provide help and support. As a result, poverty is a thorny problem for developing countries. China has made impressive achievements in eradicating poverty through rapid economic growth and the concerted efforts of the government and the private sector, but a raft of problems persists. According

DOI: 10.4324/9781003410393-9

to statistics released by the government, 16.6 million lived in poverty in 2018 in China under the 2010 standards, for a poverty rate of 1.7 percent.[2] This poverty has been eliminated by 2020.

7.2 Income distribution

Usually, people divide China's economic development after 1949 into two periods: planned economy and reform and opening up because the two periods show different characteristics in many areas, and the issue of income distribution also follows this logic. First of all, Chinese people were divided into rural residents and urban residents during the planned economy period. Since 1958, the rural residents lived under the system of the people's communes, and every farmer belonged to a certain production brigade and a production squad of a certain commune. Remuneration for work was determined by attendance. One-day attendance earned several workpoints. Usually, there were 10 workpoints for adult male laborers, 8 for females, and 6 for juvenile laborers. At the end of the year, the production team calculated the monetary value of each workpoint based on the attendance in the year, and then calculated the full remuneration of a farmer (then called a commune member) based on the number of days when each laborer went to work.

Due to the special nature of agricultural production, dividends could be shared once a year. Because farmers usually had no income, they only received dividends once a year. As a result, the everyday expenses had to be arranged according to the year-end income. In the event of urgent need because of wedding and funeral, house construction or renovation, critical illness, schooling for children, etc., and there were no savings, they could only borrow money from relatives and friends or from the production team and repay borrowings at the end of the year. However, as all people had generally the same living standards at that time, the relatives and friends also had no savings. As a result, farmers could only borrow from the production team. The production team might also have little savings because there was a poor harvest or because the production team also had to make investment, such as repairing houses, buying large livestock, and paying off arrears owed by the production team to the higher-level production brigade.

In a word, farmers had similar standards of living during this period. There were only the gaps among regions but rarely a gap between individuals or families. Due to poor natural conditions and low productivity, some areas became poor counties, but there were only slight differences among individuals or families living in the same area. For example, some families had more adult labor who had high attendance, and therefore there was less burden. Other families might have heavier burden because there were more women or patients, or they met certain troubles.

There was also no big income gap for urban households. The vast majority of urban residents worked at state-owned enterprises (or state-run enterprises at the time), collective enterprises, government bodies, and public institutions. The employment structure was simple. There were no self-employed people or private entrepreneurs, joint-stock companies, limited liability companies, not to mention foreign-funded enterprises. There was little income gap regardless of the type of employer. There was a small wage gap between state-run enterprises and collective enterprises, along with a certain gap for different industries and types of work. Wages or subsidies were generally higher in electricity, geological exploration, field operations, outdoor work, and other sectors. Wages were lower in commercial and service sectors (such as bathing and hairdressing). There was also a certain gap from region to region, with low wages in Beijing, slightly higher wages in Shanghai, high wages in Xinjiang, and relatively low wages in Sichuan, Guizhou, and other regions.

Under the planned economy, China's wage standards were formulated in 1956,[3] and the wages of workers were divided into eight levels. In the northern region represented by North China and Northeast China, the minimum wage for level 1 workers was about 32 yuan per month, and more than 100 yuan for level 8 workers. Nevertheless, the difference between the two is only about 2 times. Wages for cadres (now public servants) were divided into 24 levels. Contrary to the standards for workers, the smaller the number, the higher the level for cadres. The wage for the lowest level 24 was about 38 yuan, and the wage for the highest level was about 600 yuan. Despite the large difference, the higher the level, the fewer the number of people. According to the common understanding, cadres at level 13 or above are called "senior cadres", most of whom fought in wars and contributed to the cause of liberation in China. Intellectuals belonged to another category and were divided into 18 levels according to technical titles. The wage for the highest level (level 1) professors (few in number, several in even first-class universities) was about 300 yuan, which was equivalent to the wage of provincial or ministerial-level cadres. The wages were about 56 yuan for university graduates and about 38 yuan for graduates of secondary specialized or technical schools. Another issue is that those with high wages tended to have more children and less per capita income. Due to a lack of family planning policy at that time, traditional concepts (for bringing up sons to provide for one's old age or for family prosperity) affected the family structure and the actual living standards. Even poor workers and farmers had many children, further aggravating poverty.

For the study of the income gap, the Gini coefficient is often used as an indicator. No Gini coefficient is applicable to the income gap during China's planned economy period, but many people have calculated the Gini coefficient for the reform and opening up period. A brief introduction is given here.[4] A study on the Gini coefficient from 1978 to 2009 shows that the Gini coefficient was 0.21 for rural residents in China and 0.16 for urban residents in 1978; 0.31 and 0.23 in 1990, respectively; 0.35 and 0.32 in 2000, respectively; 0.39 and 0.34 in 2009, respectively.[5]

Three tendencies can be observed from this. First, a significant increase was observed in both rural and urban areas, but according to the experience of other countries, this income gap is not very large, or at least there is no serious inequality. Second, the income gap was greater among rural residents than among urban residents, and this is consistent with what we discuss next using other indicators. Why is the income gap among rural residents greater than that of urban residents? According to the laws of economic development, as the economy develops, the degree of inequality in income distribution will exhibit an inverted U curve, that is, changing from equality to inequality and then again to equality.[6] When the economic growth was faster in cities than in rural areas, why was the income distribution more equal in cities? A full explanation of this question requires further analysis. A rough explanation will be made here.

To begin with, urban residents enjoy better social security than rural residents, such as with the subsistence allowance system. Low-income households enjoy the basic living allowance from the local government. In comparison, rural residents do not enjoy such treatment. Although the system is gradually applied to more areas, it is still very fragile. Second, if the vast majority of rural residents rely on agricultural production for income, and they receive arable land according to the number of family members, it will be difficult to widen the income gap. There will be no difference in productivity for similar land, even with the use of more fertilizers or labor. Of course, this situation has changed as a result of more farmers going to cities to work. Some land has been intensively developed, that is, land transfer. Some farmers who remain in rural areas can rent the land of migrant workers for large-scale operation, which generates more benefits. Finally, rural residents can go into business, including setting up businesses, acting as drivers, or operating shops. These bring them higher income than agricultural production. They stand out among the relatively poor farmers, but this is common in cities. There are many businesspeople and high-income people in cities. As a result, the income gap is not large in cities, although the income of urban residents is far higher than that of rural residents in absolute terms.

Third, the aforesaid Gini coefficient is lower than what we usually think. Studies by other scholars show that China's Gini coefficient is between 0.45 and 0.48, or higher.[7] Scholars have been at odds over China's Gini coefficient or whether it accurately reflects China's current real income status. This involves many issues, such as whether the sample size and region as well as the selection of populations are appropriate, whether the calculation methods are reasonable, and whether scholars exhibit certain tendencies. This is due to the large difference between academic and official figures and people's perception.

China's wage system was flawed in the early days of reform and opening up, and it was unclear which industry and which level should have how much income. More important is the so-called gray income. Some people who held power and resources do not have high nominal wage income but in fact have many opportunities to get involved in investment or take bribes. Moreover, Chinese people are fond of equalitarianism and have long been accustomed to equality. They are unwilling to accept a large gap. This mentality is both rational and irrational. It is rational because people in any country will share this mentality, which is not unique to China. Too large an income gap indeed has a negative impact on society. It is irrational because Chinese people have not yet been accustomed to the market economy, which has the nature of widening the income gap. The advantage of the market is that everyone can freely use their ability to obtain gains, but there are differences among people, and the ability varies from person to person. As a result, the gains are different.

114 *Processes and characteristics*

Next, we examine the issue of income gap from another perspective. Table 7.1 shows the income and expenses of urban and rural residents as well as the differences between the two (savings), etc. The following two situations can be observed. First, per capita income and expenditure in both rural and urban areas increased rapidly. Although expenditures also grew rapidly, surplus gradually increased and the savings rate began to rise. The personal savings rate for rural residents increased from 15.2 percent in 1980 to 29.1 percent in 2018, and that of urban residents increased from 13.7 to 41.4 percent. It is noteworthy that the savings rate of urban residents was lower than that of rural residents for some time during the planned economy period, and this remained so for a long time after the reform and opening up. This may be associated with the social security system, which gives subsistence allowances to urban residents,[8] while rural residents do not enjoy such institutional support and must rely on savings as a precaution. Second, the urban–rural gap still exists, with a tendency to widen. The income gap between urban and rural residents rose from 2.2 times in 1990 to 3.2 times in 2010.[9] On the one hand, there is the gap in terms of absolute income. Although urban residents make large expenditures, the huge gap in absolute income leads to a large gap between urban and rural residents. On the other hand, the difference between income and spending leads to a difference in the savings rate for urban and rural residents. The difference in the savings rate also reflects the difference in terms of risk resistance, asset investment, and so on.

Next is the examination of the relationship between income and expenditure of urban as well as rural residents according to income levels. Table 7.2 shows the

Table 7.1 Income and expenditure of urban as well as rural residents, Unit: yuan (%)

	1980	1990	2000	2010	2018
Rural households					
(1) Per capita net income (yuan)	191.3	686.3	2,253.4	5,919.0	13,912.8
(2) Per capita consumption expenditure (yuan)	162.2	584.6	1,670.1	4,381.8	9,862.0
(3) Personal savings rate (%)	15.2	14.8	25.9	26.0	29.1
Engel coefficient (%)	61.8	58.8	49.1	41.1	32.7
Urban households					
(1) Per capita disposable income (yuan)	477.6	1,510.2	6,280.0	19,109.4	36,316.2
(2) Per capita consumption expenditure (yuan)	412.4	1,278.9	4,998.0	13,471.5	21,287.1
(3) Personal savings rate (%)	13.7	15.3	20.4	29.5	41.4
Engel coefficient (%)	56.9	54.2	39.4	35.7	33.4
The urban–rural gap in income (times)	2.5	2.2	2.8	3.2	2.6

Data source: *China Statistical Yearbook* over the years.

Note: (3) Personal savings rate = [(1) − (2)] ÷ (1) × 100 percent.

Table 7.2 Basic situation of urban residents by income grade, Unit: yuan (%)

	Total average	Lowest	Low	Below-middle	Middle	Above middle	High	Highest
1985								
(1) Disposable income (yuan)	752.40	437.40	546.72	632.88	737.28	861.96	1,012.32	1,276.20
(2) Living expenses (yuan)	732.24	455.64	551.28	626.88	724.20	830.28	963.24	1,162.92
(3) Personal savings rate (%)	2.68	−4.17	−0.84	0.95	1.78	3.68	4.85	8.88
1990								
(1) Disposable income (yuan)	1,387.27	761.16	968.64	1,144.44	1,351.68	1,598.28	1,889.52	2,447.92
(2) Living expenses (yuan)	1,278.89	782.28	960.72	1,097.76	1,275.12	1,456.68	1,685.28	2,039.76
(3) Personal savings rate (%)	7.82	−2.78	0.82	4.08	5.67	8.86	10.81	16.68
1995								
(1) Disposable income (yuan)	3,892.94	1,923.80	2,505.68	3,040.90	3,698.41	4,512.20	5,503.67	7,537.98
(2) Living expenses (yuan)	3,537.57	2,060.96	2,516.22	2,934.16	3,446.12	4,045.52	4,665.91	6,033.10
(3) Personal savings rate (%)	9.13	−7.13	−0.42	3.51	6.83	10.35	15.23	19.97
2000								
(1) Disposable income (yuan)	6,279.98	2,653.02	3,633.51	4,623.54	5,897.92	7,487.37	9,434.21	1,3311.02
(2) Living expenses (yuan)	4,998	2,540.13	3,274.93	3,947.91	4,794.56	5,894.92	7,102.33	9,250.63
(3) Personal savings rate (%)	20.42	4.26	9.87	14.62	18.71	21.27	24.72	30.51
2005								
(1) Disposable income (yuan)	10,493.03	3,134.88	4,885.32	6,710.58	9,190.05	12,603.37	17,202.93	28,773.11
(2) Living expenses (yuan)	7,942.88	3,111.47	4,295.35	5,574.32	7,308.06	9,410.77	12,102.51	19,153.73
(3) Personal savings rate (%)	24.31	0.75	12.08	16.94	20.48	25.34	29.65	33.44
2011								
(1) Disposable income (yuan)	21,809.78	6,876.09	10,672.02	14,498.26	19,544.94	26,419.99	35,579.24	58,841.87
(2) Living expenses (yuan)	15,160.89	6,431.85	8,509.32	10,872.83	14,028.17	18,160.91	23,906.21	35,183.64
(3) Personal savings rate (%)	30.49	6.46	20.27	25.01	28.23	31.26	32.81	40.21

Data source: China Statistical Yearbook over the years.

Note: (3) Personal savings rate = [(1) − (2)] ÷ (1) × 100 percent.

income and expenditure as well as savings rates of urban residents divided into 7 grades for several years in the 1985–2011 period. The following situations are shown here. First, the gap between the lowest and highest incomes was 1.92 times in 1985, 2.22 times in 1990, 2.92 times in 1995, 4.02 times in 2000, 8.18 times in 2005, and 7.56 times in 2011. In general, it shows a gradual upward trend, which deserves close study. Second, from the perspective of the savings rate, the savings rates of the lowest-income households and low-income households from 1985 to 1995 were negative (low-income households had a savings rate of 0.82 percent in 1990). In other words, they lived beyond their income and had either to borrow money or to resort to savings (most likely no deposits), or they depended on government subsidies. In 1985, the savings rates of low- and middle-income households were fragile, with almost no savings. Even upper-middle-income and high-income households had little savings. It can be seen that urban households lived on a tight income even in the early days of reform and opening up, but this situation has greatly improved as the economy develops and the reform and opening up effect deepens. By 2000, households with all income levels had surpluses, and most households had high savings rates, although the savings rate of the lowest-income households was low. Life was hard for the lowest-income households in 2005, but the savings rate for most households rose, and this situation further improved in 2001.

Figure 7.1 shows the distribution of the number of urban worker households grouped by monthly income in 1964 and 1981. It is clear that the distribution in

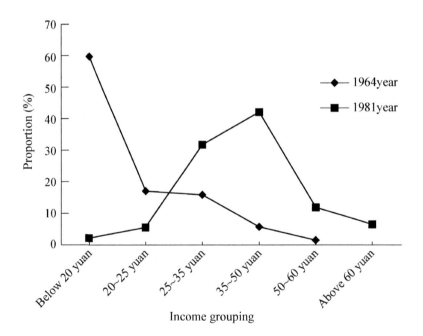

Figure 7.1 Distribution of the proportion of urban worker households grouped by monthly income in China (1964 and 1981)

Data source: China Statistical Yearbook 1984.

Income distribution and poverty issues 117

1981 was close to the normal distribution, while the distribution in 1964 was closer to the *F*-distribution. In 1964, more people belonged to the low-income group, accounting for nearly 60 percent. In other words, more than half of the people had a monthly income of less than 20 yuan. If the 17 percent with a monthly income of 20 to 25 yuan and the 16 percent with a monthly income of 25 to 30 yuan are added, they account for more than 90 percent. However, in fact, according to the price level at that time, an average monthly income of 20 yuan ensured adequate food and clothing; a monthly income of 25 to 30 yuan meant moderate prosperity. This situation was different in 1981, when nearly 32 percent of the people belonged to the 25–30 yuan income group, and 42 percent belonged to the 35–50 yuan income group. The two groups accounted for the majority, reaching 74 percent. It shows that people's income increased significantly even in the early days of reform and opening up. From the perspective of income distribution alone without considering the factor of rising prices, more people had a middle-level income, which is a more ideal situation in a sense.

However, this situation was soon altered by new changes. Figure 7.2 shows the distribution of the proportion of urban resident households grouped by income in 1986 and 1990. Compared with the previous figure, only the income level of groups is different. Due to the influence of factors such as income levels and rising prices, it is difficult to accurately measure the real situation of people with various

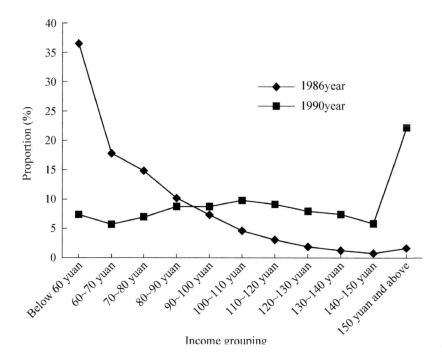

Figure 7.2 Distribution of the proportion of urban resident households grouped by monthly income in China (1986 and 1990)

Data source: *China Statistical Yearbook 1991*.

incomes using the original measurement scale. The scale here is obviously higher. According to the new scale, the people with a monthly income of less than 60 yuan in 1986 accounted for 36 percent, but this proportion gradually decreased as the income increased, showing a smooth downward trend and an even distribution. There were not many rich people at that time according to this measurement scale. However, it was different in 1990. According to the same scale, the various groups with a monthly income of less than 150 yuan were generally evenly distributed, indicating that the number of people with a monthly income above 150 yuan increased sharply, accounting for 22 percent. This shows that many Chinese people became affluent in just a few years, and, of course, the price factor must also be considered.

Table 7.3 shows the basic situation of rural households grouped by income in 2011. It shows differences after comparison with cities. First of all, low-income households had a large gap between revenue and expenditure, resulting in large negative savings, reaching −65.59 percent. This indicates that such households needed the support and assistance of the state or collectives. Second, the savings rate of high-income earners is even higher than that of the highest-income households in cities, although the absolute value of income and expenditure is lower than that of the highest-income urban households. This shows that the spending level in rural areas is not high. Given proper income, there will be more surplus. The absolute value of high income in rural areas is only equivalent to the middle income in urban areas. This can be seen from the middle-level and upper-middle savings rates. The absolute value of the two income levels is lower than the "minimum" and "low" income levels of urban households, but the rural savings rate is higher than that of the two groups. Overall, these figures show that the income gap is greater in rural areas than in cities.

Further, we observe the income distribution for rural residents over the years. Data on the distribution for rural areas are only available for 1980 and subsequent years. Figure 7.3 shows the distribution of the proportion of rural households grouped by income in 1980, 1985, and 1990. It can be seen that there was a progressive process from 1980 to 1990 according to grouping based on the current

Table 7.3 Basic situation of rural households by income level (2011), Unit: yuan (%)

	Total average	Low income	Below middle income	Middle income	Above middle income	High income
(1) Per capita net income (yuan)	6,977.30	2,000.51	4,255.75	6,207.68	8,893.59	16,783.06
(2) Per capita consumption expenditure (yuan)	5,221.10	3,312.59	3,962.29	4,817.91	6,002.88	9,149.57
(3) Personal savings rate (%)	25.20	−65.59	6.90	22.39	32.51	45.49

Data source: China Statistical Yearbook 2012.

Note: (3) Personal savings rate = [(1) − (2)] ÷ (1) × 100 percent.

Income distribution and poverty issues 119

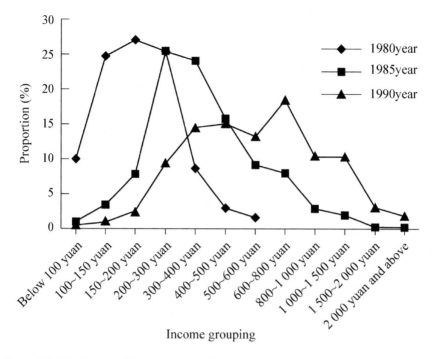

Figure 7.3 Distribution of the proportion of rural households in China grouped by income (1980, 1985, and 1990)

Data source: *China Statistical Yearbook 1991*.

income levels. That is to say, thanks to the economic development as well as the reform and opening up, people's incomes have increased significantly. Therefore, households are grouped according to the fixed income levels. In 1980, the annual per capita income of most families was generally concentrated in the 100–150 yuan level (24.7 percent), 150–200 yuan level (27.1 percent), and 200–300 yuan level (25.3 percent). The three groups together account for 77.1 percent of the total. In 1985, the corresponding figures were 200 to 300 yuan (25.6 percent), 300 to 400 yuan (24.0 percent), and 400 to 500 yuan (15.9 percent), and the three groups account for 65.5 percent of the total. By 1990, this trend intensified, and there was dispersed distribution. In other words, the groups were more evenly distributed. The highest proportion had the income of 600 to 800 yuan (18.56 percent), followed by 400 to 500 yuan (15.11 percent) and 300 to 400 yuan (14.44 percent), 500 to 600 yuan (13.26 percent), 800 to 1,000 yuan (10.45 percent), and 1,000 to 1,500 yuan (10.31 percent). Overall, it leaned toward high income.

As the economy develops, people's income increases, and the groupings must be adjusted. Figure 7.4 shows the distribution of the new groupings based on income levels in 1995, 2000, and 2005. This shows a different picture. In other words, the distribution in the decade from 1995 to 2005 is basically the same, exhibiting a

120 *Processes and characteristics*

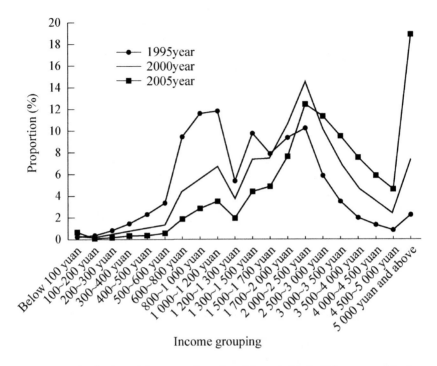

Figure 7.4 Distribution of the proportion of rural households in China grouped by income (1995, 2000, and 2005)

Data source: *China Statistical Yearbook* 2006.

similar tendency. First, it may also be due to excessively detailed grouping. Overall, the proportion of all groups is relatively average. In 1995, the proportion of the 600–800 yuan group and the 2,000–2,500 yuan group was about 10 percent, and these groups together accounted for more than 75 percent of the total. In 2000, the situation changed somewhat, and the proportion of about 10 percent was concentrated in the 1,700–2,000 yuan group and the 2,500–3,000 yuan group, which together accounted for only 35 percent. The situation in 2005 was similar to that in 2000, and it was concentrated in the 2,000–2,500 yuan group and the 3,000–500 yuan group, which together accounted for 33 percent of the total. It is also noteworthy that as the economy further developed, the proportion of the highest-income households increased. The proportion of the number of households with an income above 5,000 yuan in 1995 was only 2.26 percent, increased to 7.45 percent in 2000, reached 18.96 percent in 2005, and was up to 52.41 percent in 2010 (not shown in the figure due to the large deviations). In other words, this grouping of absolute income levels cannot accurately reflect the real situation as the economy develops and the income increases. As a result, grouping is made according to higher income levels.

Figure 7.5 shows the distribution of households grouped by new income levels. The grouping in the figure is different from the previous one, with the lowest

Income distribution and poverty issues 121

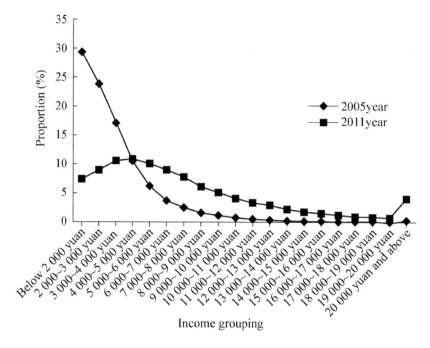

Figure 7.5 Distribution of the proportion of rural households in China grouped by income (2005 and 2011)

Data source: *China Statistical Yearbook 2012*.

income below 2,000 yuan instead of below 100 yuan. Therefore, the distribution is wholly different. It may be because this grouping method is too advanced, and many households were concentrated at a low level. In 2005, the number of households with an income below 2,000 yuan accounted for 29.43 percent, the 2,000–3,000 yuan group accounted for 23.91 percent, the 3,000–4,000 yuan group accounted for 17.12 percent, and the 4,000–5,000 yuan group accounted for 10.57 percent. These groups together accounted for 81 percent of the total. The situation changed in 2011. Although most households were still concentrated in a few low-income groups, they were more dispersed, and their proportions were not very high. The 2,000–3,000 yuan group, 3,000–4,000 yuan group, 4,000–5,000 yuan group, 5,000–6,000 yuan group, and 6,000–7,000 group accounted for 9 to 10 percent respectively, and they together accounted for less than 50 percent of the total.

7.3 Poverty issue

Like other developing countries, China also faces the thorny problem of poverty. Due to low productivity, many people live below the poverty line and are in need of government and social aid. As poor countries lack the resources and capacity to provide such aid, a vicious circle will be formed. China may have been under this situation at least before 1949, when there were a large number of poor people, and the government and society were unable to provide relief. The disparaging term "sick man of East Asia" was also related to this. Because of poverty, people had no access to the basic nutrition needed for survival, and some vices (such as opium smoking) seriously damaged people's health, aggravating poverty.

After 1949, the government stepped up efforts to promote economic development and did a lot of work to improve the people's living standards, but this goal fell through for a host of reasons during the planned economy period. Despite a high rate of economic growth, the people's living standards were not improved, and there were a huge number of poor people. Due to a lack of data on the poor population during this period, it is difficult for us to make accurate estimates. It can only be inferred from the situation after the reform and opening up. A simple calculation follows. Table 7.4 shows the number and proportion of poor rural residents in China from 1978 to 2018. It can be seen that, as the economy developed, the poverty line was raised year by year, while the poor population dwindled year by year, and the incidence of poverty also decreased. However, there is an issue of standards. According to China's own poverty line, the incidence of poverty indeed decreased year by year. However, according to the conversion (2,300 yuan in 2010) from the World Bank standard (consumption of US$1.25 per person per day), the number of poor people increased significantly compared to those under the previous statistical standards. It is gradually decreasing now.

Based on these figures, the figures for the years before 1978 should not be less than that in 1978, even according to the standards set by China itself. In other words, the incidence of poverty was not less than 30.7 percent, and the number

Table 7.4 Rural poverty in China

Year	Standard in 1978		Standard in 2008		Standard in 2010	
	Poor people (10,000 people)	Incidence of poverty (%)	Poor people (10,000 people)	Incidence of poverty (%)	Poor people (10,000 people)	Incidence of poverty (%)
1978	25,000	30.7	–	–	77,039	97.5
1980	22,000	26.8	–	–	76,542	96.5
1985	12,500	14.8	–	–	66,101	78.3
1990	8,500	9.4	–	–	65,849	73.5
1995	6,540	7.1	–	–	55,463	60.5
2000	3,209	3.5	9,422	10.2	46,224	49.8
2005	2,365	2.5	6,432	6.8	28,662	30.2
2010	–	–	2,688	2.8	16,567	17.2
2018	–	–	–	–	1660	1.7

Data source: China Statistical Yearbook 2019.

Note: The standards 1978 and 2008 were set according to China's reality, and the standards 2010 were set according to the World Bank's poverty standards. The standard 2010 for poverty is 2,300 yuan per person per year (price in 2010).

Table 7.5 Income and expenditure of urban households in financial difficulties in China

Item	1985	1990	1995	2000	2005	2011
Disposable income (yuan)	394.80	688.97	1,975.84	2,325.05	2,495.75	5,398.17
Consumption expenditure (yuan)	417.96	724.80	1,904.41	2,320.36	2,656.41	5,575.56
Savings rate (%)	−5.87	−5.20	3.62	0.21	−6.44	−3.29

Data source: *China Statistical Yearbook* over the years.

of poor people was 250 million. However, since the population increased from 520 million in 1949 to 960 million in 1978, the proportion of 30.7 percent is preferable. However, is this proportion fixed? Obviously not, because although the people's living standards did not improve significantly during this period, the rate of economic growth was relatively high, and the various welfare systems further improved. Therefore, it should be said that the earlier the period, the higher the incidence of poverty, at least no less than 30 percent or perhaps up to 40 to 50 percent. The discussion here refers to the issue of rural poverty. Given that China's urbanization rate was very low at that time (less than 20 percent in 1980), it was actually a nationwide issue, and there were also many poor people in cities.

There are no complete statistics on the number of poor people and the incidence of poverty in towns and cities, except the data on the living standard of such households. Table 7.5 shows the income and expenditure of urban households in financial difficulties from 1985 to 2011. These figures can be compared with other income levels described in Table 7.4. As the simply calculated savings rate shows, the urban poor households were financially distressed. With the exception of slight surpluses in 1995 and 2000, households lived beyond their income in other years, or they were in need of relief from others or government.

7.4 Conclusion

The chapter discussed the issue of income during China's economic development, including the increase and distribution of income as well as poverty. It is learned that China has similarities and differences with other countries in these respects. In terms of similarity, they have all experienced a process of income increases, as well as a process of very equal income distribution to unequal distribution, and have faced the issue of poverty. In terms of difference, China has its own characteristics in these processes, which are related to the system and institutions. Although the rate of economic growth was not low during the planned economy period, the people's living standards did not improve much. On the one hand, this was consumed by the rapid population growth. On the other hand, in order to "catch up with Britain and the United States" in terms of system and policy, savings and investment were made instead of consumption. As a result, a relatively complete industrial system was put in place, but living standards were constrained. Because the reform and opening up stimulated the people's initiative, the rate of economic growth increased, population growth was checked by family planning, income levels were not suppressed, and per capita income rose in an unprecedented way.

The issue of income distribution remained the same. Under the planned economy, people's income levels were very close due to the practice of egalitarianism. In the absence of flexible market mechanisms, the economic activities of individuals were restricted, and they were not allowed to conduct business activities outside the system. Almost all people could engage in the prescribed work within the system. There was the so-called crime of speculation at that time. Any individual who did not allocate materials through the system of controlled procurement and distribution would be held accountable and convicted. After the reform and opening up, economic organizations of all descriptions began to emerge. Under the role of the market mechanism, the government encouraged some people to get rich first. As a result, people had the opportunity to give full play to their strengths. "A household with an annual income of 10,000 yuan", rich people, etc. emerged. Many people still worked within the traditional system or for the rich, and different classes emerged. As a result, the income distribution gap gradually widened. The problem of income distribution has become a serious social issue for China. Efforts should be made to prevent China from falling into the "income gap dilemma" experienced by some Latin American countries.[10]

Notes

1 Functional distribution refers to the internal distribution mechanism of enterprises, that is, how the new value added of an enterprise in the current year is distributed according to the owners of capital and labor.
2 In 2012, the government first published the number of poor people in China using World Bank standards. Previously, it used China's own standards.
3 For the wage system in the planned economy period, see Yao Shuben (1986).
4 Some also calculated the Gini coefficient for 1952–2010 based on official data; see Song Xiaowu et al. (2013). According to their calculations, the Gini coefficient was 0.224 in 1952 but rose to 0.414 in 2010. The Gini coefficient was relatively low during the planned economy period, but it rose briefly in the 1950s and remained relatively stable until the reform and opening up. There was an obvious upward trend after the reform and opening up.
5 Zhang Dongsheng (2010). According to another series of studies, the Gini coefficients of rural residents and urban residents were 0.21 and 0.16 in 1978, 0.29 and 0.23 in 1990, 0.36 and 0.34 in 2000, and 0.41 and 0.39 in 2005, respectively. See Zhou Yunbo and Qin Yan (2008).
6 As this theory was advanced by Kuznets, it was named the "Kuznets's inverted U" hypothesis.
7 World Bank experts calculated that the Gini coefficient reached 0.47 in 2001, see Cai Fang et al. (2006). The Gini coefficients calculated by Li Shi et al. (2013) were 0.46 and 0.49 in 2002 and 2007, respectively. Li Shi and Luo Chuliang, et al. (2014) also produced similar calculation results. According to *China Statistical Yearbook 2019*, it was 0.468 in 2018. According to *China Household Finance Survey Report* released by the Survey and Research Center for China Household Finance of Southwestern University of Finance and Economics, China's Gini coefficient in 2010 reached 0.61, see Gan Li et al. (2012). For the debate over income distribution or the Gini coefficient in China, see Song Xiaowu et al. (2013).

8 For example, the minimum standard of living in Shenyang was 8 yuan per person per month during the planned economy period, and subsistence allowances applied to a household with a living standard below this level.
9 This gap declined in 2018, but it was not stable. This illustrates a trend of changes in income distribution – rising from a low to high level and then falling to a low level. However, this trend is not certain because China's economy is still developing.
10 We tentatively use this term. A country has a large income gap for a long time, which impedes economic development. This is also one of the reasons for the middle-income trap.

8 Price changes and citizens' lives

8.1 Introduction

Prices are a signal of economic activities. The trends of economic activity, as well as the reasons behind them, can be observed through prices. As microeconomics is also called price theory, it implies the importance of prices in a market economy. Prices are an overall embodiment of market activities. Changes in the supply and demand for production and services are reflected in prices as long as there is a competitive market or there is no obvious distortion (such as monopoly), whatever the reasons. In terms of the scope discussed herein, prices rise as the economy develops and grows for at least the following reasons. First, an economy does not grow or develop in a straight line but is accompanied by volatility or business cycles. When the economy remains strong, the effective demand increases, and prices rise accordingly. When the economy is bad, prices fall because of insufficient demand. Second, the cost of production affects price volatility. If wages rise and even surpass labor productivity, the cost of labor per unit will rise, resulting in price rises. Third, the amount of money supply causes price changes. If the money supply increases significantly, the currency value decreases or the purchasing power of the base currency decreases, constituting substantial inflation. If the money supply decreases, the currency value rises, and the purchasing power of the base currency rises, which can easily lead to price austerity.

The chapter also discusses changes in the living standards. Economic development aims to improve people's living standards. If people's living standards are improved, it can be said to be economic development to a great extent. Conversely, if the rate of economic growth is high, but the living standards do not improve significantly, this economic growth is dubious or at least problematic. For example, the national economy usually grows during a war because a large number of weapons are needed. There must be growth as far as GDP is concerned. Moreover, people would work harder out of patriotism during a war and often generate more wealth. However, such wealth is not consumer goods but a necessity for wars. As a result, people's living standards cannot be improved. In another example, China's economy also grew rapidly during the planned economy period. Although it was outperformed by the reform and opening up period, the fruits of economic growth were rarely manifested in people's living standards but were more used for

DOI: 10.4324/9781003410393-10

investment (such as building factories, mines, and railways). Although a relatively complete industrial system established through investment laid the foundation for subsequent development, the living standards for that generation did not improve much. Besides, owing to the institutional problems at the time, much investment was inefficient or even wasteful.

8.2 Changes in prices

China's price changes after 1949 can be divided into two periods: one is the planned economy period from 1949 to 1978, and the other is the period from the beginning of the reform and opening up in 1978 to the present. Compared with other areas, the price issue shows huge differences between the two periods more clearly. A key feature of the planned economy period is the price control, or controlled procurement and distribution. Products or commodities were not priced according to market principles but were priced according to the prior arrangement of production (supply) and consumption (demand). Costs were also considered, of course. The prices of some scarce commodities, such as industrial products, were higher, while the prices of commodities in abundant supply were lower, such as agricultural products. As China's industrialization progressed slowly, it lacked both technology and talents, and some products could not even be produced. China is traditionally an agricultural country. Despite the relatively backward agricultural technology, there is no problem with basic production. Moreover, China has gained rich experience and mastered most production techniques. Despite a lack of significant increase in prices in the planned economy period, it still rose slightly. The level of prices depends on many factors, such as money supply, policy adjustments, international economic and trade relations, etc. in addition to production costs and technical levels.

Table 8.1 shows the retail price index for goods in urban and rural areas. Through comparison, it is found that the prices of three types of products were lower in cities than in rural areas: food, clothing, and daily necessities. As these three types account for a large proportion, they affect their respective averages. This is because people's living standards at that time were relatively low, and daily consumption basically referred to food and clothing. People mostly bought daily necessities, while higher-level cultural and recreational services as well as other goods and services were rarely purchased. The question is why were the prices of the aforesaid three types of goods lower in cities than in rural areas? If both clothing and daily necessities were industrial products, it is easy to understand because the prices of industrial products were relatively high at that time due to the low productivity, coupled with a large population and a short supply.

Why were the prices of food lower in cities than in rural areas? As rural areas have advantage in terms of food, it should have been cheaper in rural areas. This requires studying the policy orientation at that time, which is usually called the controlled procurement and distribution policy. Under the planned economy, it was necessary to include all varieties of commodities in the plan, including, of course, grain, in order to allocate resources according to plan. Moreover, due to the strategy of catching up with the developed countries, it was necessary to concentrate

128 *Processes and characteristics*

Table 8.1 Retail price index of commodities grouped by urban and rural areas (1980 = 100)

Year	National average	Food	Clothing	Daily necessities	Cultural and recreational products	Pharmaceuticals	Fuels
Cities							
1950	56.1	48.6	84.0	75.5	113.6	193.1	67.7
1960	73.6	66.2	100.1	94.3	108.8	152.1	96.4
1970	79.2	82.1	101.0	97.6	102.0	97.7	100.7
1980	100.0	100.0	100.0	100.0	100.0	100.0	100.0
1990	202.2	223.7	153.9	150.4	126.9	201.2	173.7
2000	353.8	493.3	277.9	219.3	142.7	374.9	624.3
Rural areas							
1950	67.1	60.2	93.4	78.0	113.8	129.7	61.9
1960	84.5	81.1	100.0	93.8	106.4	143.2	105.9
1970	91.2	90.0	100.7	97.8	102.5	97.4	103.3
1980	100.0	100.0	100.0	100.0	100.0	100.0	100.0
1990	182.1	208.7	145.0	157.7	122.9	187.0	193.4
2000	360.3	366.4	200.6	235.7	172.1	349.8	515.3

Data source: Ryoshin Minami and Makino Fumio (2014), pp. 434–435.

superior forces for greater effect. It was to ensure the basic livelihood of the urban residents because industry was mainly located in cities, and it was necessary to give better treatment to urban residents. Since the low wage policy was implemented at that time, the standard of living of the urban residents was low. The lives of workers would be insecure without the support for basic means of subsistence. Therefore, the prices of agricultural products were artificially depressed, which led to the so-called scissors movement of prices.[1]

The price indexes of agricultural and industrial products are examined next. We first take a look at the agricultural product purchase price index (see Table 8.2). Under the planned economy, the procurement price index of agricultural products was relatively low as a whole, and the mean value rose from 35.2 in 1950 to 100.0 in 1980. Agricultural by-products were the lowest, followed by industrial oils, vegetables and condiments, medicinal materials, food as well as livestock products, bamboo and timber, fruit, aquatic products, silkworms and cash crops. Agricultural by-products usually include diverse plant fibers such as rice husks and fruit shells, and animal by-products such as feathers and bones. These products can be processed as industrial raw materials, similar to industrial oils and medicinal materials. The cheap vegetables, food, etc. are easier to understand because these products are the daily necessities for urban residents. On the one hand, despite the low technological level of agricultural production, the proportion of the agricultural population and the labor force was large, and these products could be provided. On the other hand, it was also necessary to lower prices through policy to ensure that the urban residents with low wages had decent living standards. Other agricultural products, such as fruits and aquatic products, were luxuries at that time, and more land was used to produce grain. There was no room for the development of these

Table 8.2 Agricultural product procurement price index (1980 = 100)

Year	Average	Food	Cash crop	Bamboo and timber	Industrial oils	Livestock products
1950	35.2	36.8	47.4	43.3	31.3	39.1
1960	55.3	55.8	63.5	51.9	53.4	63.6
1970	68.6	81.3	73.5	64.8	67.2	75.8
1980	100.0	100.0	100.0	100.0	100.0	100.0
1990	209.5	309.1	204.6	367.1	130.5	232.2
2000	312.9	488.5	321.7	501.6	134.7	368.1

Year	Silkworm	Fruits	Vegetables and condiments	Medicinal materials	Agricultural and sideline products	Aquatic products
1950	46.5	45.4	33.0	35.8	26.6	46.4
1960	69.8	83.7	93.6	102.8	77.2	74.3
1970	79.6	78.7	78.4	104.0	82.2	78.4
1980	100.0	100.0	100.0	100.0	100.0	100.0
1990	273.8	252.9	196.9	135.3	234.6	421.9
2000	439.1	247.4	361.6	235.7	415.8	661.8

Data source: Ryoshin Minami and Makino Fumio (2014), p. 439.

industries, and animal husbandry was overlooked. At that time, the rapid population growth put great pressure on food production.

After the reform and opening up, the price index rose relatively evenly, without particularly high or low levels. What is prominent is that the price of industrial oil was relatively low for a long time, indicating that the market competition of such products might be intense or the supply was sufficient and that the price could not be raised. The price of fruit was also relatively low, in contrast to that during the planned economy period, when fruits were luxury goods. Fruits became common products after the reform and opening up. This is partly the result of diversification because some plots of land were suitable for growing fruits. During the planned economy period, such land was used for crop cultivation due to population pressures and the constraints of living standards. On the other hand, the opening up policy facilitated international trade, and the sufficient supply of many varieties of fruits was ensured through imports. For example, the yield of bananas was limited in China due to climatic factors. It was expensive during the planned economy period, and northerners had no access to bananas throughout the year. This situation has changed as a result of imports. Bananas have become commonplace fruit at low prices.

The price of medicinal materials was also relatively low, possibly because of the popularity of Western medicine and the relatively backward traditional Chinese medicine (TCM). Advances in Western medicine are manifested in both treatment effects and price advantages because Western medicines can be easily produced on a large scale while it is relatively difficult for Chinese medicines. Colds can be treated using both Western and TCM methods. If the symptoms are mild, no treatment is required. However, as TCM treatment takes longer and the price is

130 *Processes and characteristics*

not cheaper, Western medicine has the advantage in both respects. Today, people have fast-paced lives, particularly for young people in cities, who make sure that they are in good physical condition every day. Moreover, young people are not as enamored with Chinese medicine as the elderly in rural areas. The prices of aquatic products were slightly higher because of a short supply China. As people's incomes increase, demand for aquatic products is increasing. China's fishery output is insufficient for the need of nearly 1.4 billion people.

Table 8.3 shows the producer price index of industrial and mining products, which can still be observed from the perspective of two periods. It was sometimes high and sometimes low during the planned economy period, but the average value was relatively high, almost the same as the index in 1985. It shows the scarcity of industrial products in this period. Specifically, the prices of timber production, furniture making, ferrous metal mining, tobacco, coal mining, etc. were low, while the prices of machinery, electronic and communication devices, pharmaceuticals, chemical engineering, chemical fibers, nonferrous metal mining, water, electricity and gas supply, etc. were on the high side. The reasons for low prices of the former may be twofold: low cost, such as timber production, coal mining, and furniture manufacturing, and the role of policy, such as tobacco. The reasons for the high prices of the latter are also twofold: one is high production cost, such as pharmaceuticals. China's production technology at that time was backward. The other is limited technical level, which caused a short supply, such as in chemical fibers and machinery sectors.

After the reform and opening up, great changes took place. Price indexes of some products rose fast, while those of other products rose slowly. For example, the price indexes of oil exploration and petroleum processing both exceeded 1,000 in 2000, indicating the importance and scarcity of the oil industry in the reform and opening up period. On the one hand, as China's economy develops, the demand for oil is increasing. On the other hand, the domestic supply of oil is becoming increasingly scarce, and there is more dependence on imports. However, imports are affected by international oil prices, which fluctuate greatly. Except for oil, the increase for industrial and mineral products was not large, and it even declined for individual products. For example, electronic and communication equipment were scarce during the planned economy period. After the reform and opening up, great progress was made in terms of these products, which were typical products with fast technological progress, high efficiency, and great cost reduction.

We then examine the overall changes in agricultural as well as industrial and mining products. Figure 8.1 shows the long-term changes in both. It shows two tendencies. First, the price level during the planned economy period was very stable as a whole. Both agricultural and industrial and mining products showed a trend of horizontal or slight increase, especially for agricultural products. Key changes have occurred after the reform and opening up. There has been rapid price rises, with basically the same upward trend. Second, during the planned economy period, the price index of agricultural products was substantially lower than that of industrial and mining products, indicating a certain level of the scissors movement of prices between industrial and agricultural products. After reform and opening up, this

Table 8.3 Producer price index of industrial and mining products (1985 = 100)

Year	Average	Coal mining	Oil exploitation	Ferrous metal mining	Nonferrous metal mining	Timber production	Food manufacture	Tobacco	Textiles
1952	95.4	40.9	60.5	27.0	100.0	19.2	77.2	37.8	84.5
1960	111.7	53.0	108.9	35.3	86.2	17.6	85.6	51.6	81.4
1970	93.8	63.0	91.5	38.9	91.8	32.4	87.1	62.3	82.0
1980	93.7	80.4	92.5	67.5	97.5	49.0	92.0	63.6	89.9
1990	159.0	121.9	144.9	135.1	229.7	211.0	146.7	113.6	175.5
2000	303.1	323.0	1,185.8	275.3	335.5	358.2	281.5	177.5	283.6

Year	Furniture making	Papermaking	Water, electricity, and gas supply	Oil processing	Chemical engineering	Pharmaceuticals	Chemical fibers	Machinery	Electronic and communications equipment
1952	33.8	64.3	93.8	71.9	171.0	780.1	93.1	260.1	375.3
1960	36.4	68.7	105.0	94.3	133.0	336.7	81.0	181.5	306.1
1970	37.6	69.4	94.1	90.0	94.7	127.7	82.8	101.8	229.5
1980	57.4	90.9	92.4	89.1	89.4	111.7	94.6	95.8	111.3
1990	188.0	181.6	125.6	225.8	188.3	166.1	155.0	151.5	107.3
2000	299.4	316.0	461.1	1086.5	308.3	189.1	167.2	236.7	92.7

Data source: Ryoshin Minami and Makino Fumio (2014), pp. 440–442.

Note: There are price indexes for many industries. Only representative ones are selected here.

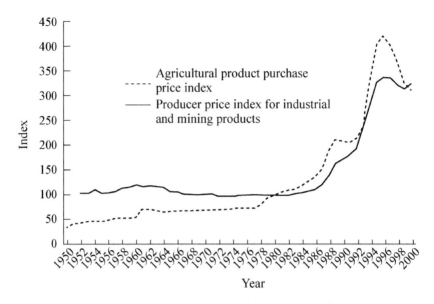

Figure 8.1 Changes in the procurement price index of agricultural products and the producer price index of industrial and mining products (1950–2000)

Data source: Ryoshin Minami and Makino Fumio (2014), pp. 439–440.

situation basically disappeared, and the price index of agricultural products was even slightly higher than that of industrial and mining products, which proved that price changes tended to be more reasonable under market conditions.

Finally, the price changes after the reform and opening up are studied through another form of index. Table 8.4 shows the changes in the main price indexes from 1978 to 2018, including the consumer price index (CPI), the retail price index, the producer price index (PPI), the purchase price index, the price index of fixed asset investment, etc. Due to the different base years for several price indexes, it is not possible to make direct comparison, but they differ little in terms of time, namely in 1978, 1985, and 1990. In general, several price indexes changed within a reasonable range, without too high or too low changes. For example, the CPI rose, especially the urban CPI, which was 100 in 1978 and exceeded 650 in 2018. However, if the increase in residents' income is taken into account, such an increase is acceptable. The latter few price indexes related to production and investment rose slightly, which helped to expand production and investment.

8.3 Standard of living

The people's standard of living after 1949 can still be observed in terms of two periods. Specifically, the standard of living during the planned economy period did not improve much for a host of reasons. First, the population expanded rapidly,

Table 8.4 Changes in various price indexes after the reform and opening up

Year	CPI (1978 = 100) City (1978 = 100)	Rural area (1985 = 100)	Retail price index (1978 = 100)	Producer price index for industrial products (1985 = 100)	Purchase price index for industrial products (1990 = 100)	Price index of fixed asset investment (1990 = 100)
1978	100.0 100.0		100.0			
1985	131.1 134.2	100.0	128.1	100.0		
1990	216.4 222.0	165.1	207.1	159.0	100.0	100.0
2000	434.0 476.6	314.0	354.4	303.1	228.4	198.6
2010	536.1 576.3	403.5	406.3	377.5	347.7	254.6
2018	650.9 702.4	489.0	562.2	389.4	369.8	301.1

Data source: China Statistical Yearbook 2019.

and some of the production achievements were consumed by a bigger population. China's population soared from 550 million in 1950 to 990 million in 1980, an increase of 440 million in 30 years, which is a heavy burden. The population and labor force are productive. However, if the population increases too much, we will see diminishing marginal returns, and productivity will grow more slowly than the population.[2] Second, China's production technology advanced slowly, in stark contrast to rapid population growth. Before 1949, China only had a few mechanized production technologies imported from Western countries, and the level of science and technology as a whole was backward. Despite great progress after 30 years of hard work, it was difficult for China to import advanced technologies from Western developed countries because of the confrontation (cold war) between the two camps in the world. Third, because China adopted a strategy of catching up with the Western countries, the people's living standards were deliberately depressed and more surplus of production was put into the cycle of production. In other words, the standard of living was lowered through policies and institutional arrangements, and investment was made through forced savings. In the long run, this produced good results for China's subsequent development, such as a relatively complete industrial system and a wealth of engineering and technical personnel, but it was a big loss as far as the people's living standards are concerned at that time. This is like the arrangement of consumption and savings by each household today. If you want to spend more, there will be less savings, and vice versa.

Next, the changes in living standards are observed through the per capita income of urban and rural residents as well as the Engel coefficient, as shown in Table 8.5. Despite the incomplete data for the years before 1978, it is possible to gain a general understanding. During the planned economy period, the income of both rural and urban residents did not increase much for a long time. The per capita income of rural residents rose from 73 yuan in 1957 to 133.6 yuan in 1978, an increase of less than two times in more than 20 years. The per capita income of urban residents rose from 235.4 yuan to 343.4 yuan, with a growth rate lower than that of rural

134 *Processes and characteristics*

Table 8.5 Per capita income of urban and rural residents as well as Engel coefficient, Unit: yuan (%)

Year	Per capita disposable income of urban residents (yuan)	Per capita net income of rural residents (yuan)	Engel coefficient of urban residents (%)	Engel coefficient of rural residents (%)
1957	235.4	73.0	58.4	65.8
1964	227.0	107.2	59.2	68.5
1978	343.4	133.6	57.5	67.7
1980	477.6	191.3	56.9	61.8
1990	1,510.2	686.3	54.2	58.8
2000	6,280.0	2,253.4	39.4	49.1
2010	19,109.4	59,19.0	35.7	41.1
2018	39,250.8	14,617.0	33.35	32.71

Data source: *China Statistical Yearbook 2011* for the 1978 to 2010 period and *China Statistical Yearbook 2019* for 2018.

Notes:
(1) The data urban areas in 1957 and 1964 are income available for living expenses, while the data for rural areas in 1964 are actually the data for 1965.
(2) The Engel coefficients for 1957 and 1964 (1965) were calculated on the basis of living expenditures (not shown here).

residents, although the absolute value far exceeded that of rural residents. It shows that the enhancement of people's living standards during the planned economy period was very limited, which verifies our judgment. After the reform and opening up, the per capita income of urban and rural residents rose significantly, increasing from 133.6 yuan in 1978 to 14,617.0 yuan in 2018 for rural residents and from 343.4 yuan to 39,250.8 yuan for urban residents. Although the absolute value of the two is highly different, the increase in the index is close, and the income in rural areas even exceed that in cities. This is an interesting situation: the income gap between rural and urban areas has neither widened nor narrowed during the reform and opening up period, and it is basically synchronized.

In terms of the Engel coefficient, it fell from 58.4 percent in 1957 to 33.35 percent in 2018 for urban residents and fell from 65.8 to 32.71 percent for rural residents. At present, the two are very close, indicating that the economic development after the reform and opening up has improved the lives of residents. Specifically, the Engel coefficient during the planned economy did not decline for a long time. It fell by a negligible proportion from 1957 to 1980 and even increased in the meantime (such as in 1964 and 1965). Even after the reform and opening up, the Engel coefficient did not fall rapidly. In 1990, it was still close to 60 percent for rural areas and more than 50 percent for urban areas. The Engel coefficient did not really decline until after 2000, when it fell below 40 percent for urban areas and below 50 percent for rural areas. At present, the figure for urban areas is close to that of Japan around 1970, and the figure for rural areas is close to that of Japan around 1965.[3]

In addition to the Engel coefficient, other household expenditures can also be observed. Table 8.6 shows the proportion of various cash outlays by urban and rural residents, from which the consumption of various products, including food,

Table 8.6 Proportion of per capita cash outlays of urban and rural residents, Unit: %

Year	Food	Clothing	Housing	Daily necessities and service	Transport and communication	Education, culture and recreation	Medical and healthcare	Others
Urban areas								
1957	58.4	12.0	2.3	7.6	2.4	2.0	1.8	5.4
1964	59.2	11.0	2.6	6.0	1.7	5.8	1.9	6.0
1981	56.7	14.8	1.4	9.6	1.5	8.4	0.6	2.9
1990	54.3	13.4	4.8	8.5	3.2	8.8	2.0	5.2
2000	39.4	10.0	11.3	7.5	8.5	13.4	6.4	3.4
2018	33.4	8.5	9.6	7.6	16.3	14.0	7.5	3.2
Rural areas								
1957	65.8	13.5	2.1	6.9	–	1.7	–	10.0
1965	68.5	10.5	2.8	7.2	–	2.7	–	8.3
1978	67.7	12.7	3.2	6.6	–	2.7	–	7.1
1990	41.6	11.7	21.7	8.2	2.2	8.4	5.1	1.1
2000	36.1	7.4	18.0	5.8	7.2	14.5	6.8	4.1
2018	32.7	6.6	11.0	7.2	17.1	13.2	10.1	2.2

Data source: *China Statistical Yearbook* over the years.

Note: The classification in the 1957–1981 period is different from the current classification. Some of them are recalculated by the author based on the current classification (*China Statistical Yearbook 1984*, p. 464). The numbers are rounded. After 1990, expenditure by residents was cash expenditure.

can be observed. As shown here, the Engel coefficient was lower in rural areas than in cities after 1990, which is unexpected. However, the concept here refers to cash consumption. The consumption situation of rural residents calculated according to this concept is slightly different from what was just described. Except food consumption, the gap between urban and rural areas in terms of clothing consumption is not large, and this figure is relatively low for rural residents after 2000. Housing expenditures accounted for a high proportion after 1990, and this figure was far higher for rural residents than for urban residents, indicating that rural residents spent a large part of their income on housing. Since urban residents began to buy houses and the price was very high after the urban housing reform, why does housing spending account for a small proportion in cash consumption by urban residents? Our understanding is that rural residents build their own houses rather than buying commodity houses. Although the prices of building materials may be lower in rural areas than in cities, house building is still the biggest item of consumption for rural residents whose incomes are far lower than those of urban residents. This can be proved by the comparison of the proportions in 1990 and 2000. Before the housing reform in 1998, the houses of urban residents belonged to the government, and residents spent very little on housing, as manifested by the fact that the proportion of housing expenditure in 2000 was far higher than that in 1990. Although the housing of rural residents is not owned by the government, its proportion has increased since 1990 with the rises in various prices (price reform).

Next is a study of people's dietary structure based on the amount of food purchased by urban and rural residents, as shown in Table 8.7. It is noteworthy that

136 *Processes and characteristics*

Table 8.7 Per capita consumption amount of major food by urban and rural residents, Unit: kg

Year	Grain	Fresh vegetables	Edible vegetable oil	Pork	Beef and mutton	Poultry	Egg	Aquatic products	Sugar	Milk	Fresh melon and fruits	Wine
Towns and cities												
1957	167.2	109.1	4.2	6.7	1.2	1.2	3.3	7.6	1.4	–	–	2.5
1964	155.8	130.3	2.2	8.2	–	0.5	2.0	4.7	1.6	–	–	1.0
1981	145.4	152.3	4.8	16.9	1.7	1.9	5.2	7.3	2.9	–	–	4.4
1990	130.7	138.7	6.4	18.5	3.3	3.4	7.3	7.7	2.1	4.6	41.1	9.3
2000	82.3	114.7	8.2	16.7	3.3	5.4	11.2	9.9	1.7	9.9	57.5	10.0
2018	110.0	99.0	8.9	22.7	4.2	9.8	10.8	14.3	1.3	16.5	56.4	6.9
Rural areas												
1978	248.0	142.0	2.0	5.8	–	0.3	0.8	0.8	0.7	–	–	1.2
1985	257.5	131.1	4.0	10.3	0.7	1.0	2.1	1.6	1.5	–	3.4	4.4
1990	252.1	134.0	5.2	10.5	0.8	1.3	2.4	2.1	1.5	1.1	5.9	6.1
2000	249.5	112.0	7.1	13.4	1.2	2.9	5.0	3.9	1.3	1.1	18.3	7.0
2018	148.5	85.6	9.0	23.0	2.1	8.0	8.4	7.8	1.3	6.9	36.3	10.0

Data source: China Statistical Yearbook over the years.

Note: The figures for beef and mutton are simple means calculated by the author based on the figures for beef and mutton. Wine for 2018 is the figure for 2012.

there is a lack of data for rural areas during the period of the planned economy, and only the situation after 1978 is shown here. First, in terms of grain, the amount of consumption was far higher in rural areas than in cities after 1978, and it even more than doubled in some years. That is to say, the spending on staple food by rural residents is far higher than that of urban residents, indicating that grain accounts for a large proportion in the consumption structure of rural residents. It also shows the great demand for grain in agricultural production and living. Second, the consumption of beef and mutton as well as all commodities on their right except wine is less than in rural areas that in urban areas. The consumption of beef and mutton, poultry, eggs, aquatic products, milk, and fresh melons and fruits is about half of the consumption by urban residents. Third, the absolute number increased for most of the items other than grain in both urban and rural areas, indicating that people's life structure saw diversified changes and that there were more choices and better balance in terms of nutrition.

8.4 Conclusion

This chapter examined China's price issue and the lives of its citizens. After 1949, it is observed in two stages. During the planned economy period, prices rose slightly, and the people's living standards also improved slightly, which reflects the strategy and goals of economic development at that time. Because China's economy was just recovering and a strategy was developed to catch up with the developed countries, it was necessary to pool resources to achieve industrialization. In terms of the lives of its citizens, they had to tighten their belts, and the remaining resources were used to develop industry as much as possible while ensuring subsistence living. Although industry at that time was low-level and extensive in terms of technical level and management from today's standpoint, it could only be so due to the domestic conditions at that time. This had a seriously negative impact on improving the people's living standards.

After the reform and opening up, the state gradually relaxed its control over prices, and it was regulated more through the market rather than planning. Under such circumstances, prices rose rapidly and could really reflect the cost of production and value. Of course, people's salaries and other incomes also increased alongside economic development. Although many people thought that their income increased far more slowly than prices, it is an indisputable fact that the people's living standards improved tremendously as a whole.

Notes

1 There are legions of studies on the scissors movement of prices between agricultural products and industrial products in the planned economy period. Yuan Tangjun (2015) did a good job in organization and analysis.
2 For the population of China, see Guan Quan (2014).
3 See Ryoshin Minami (1981), p. 325.

Part III
Conditions and causes

9 Formation of capital
Savings and investment

9.1 Introduction

There was no concept of capital formation before modern times. Particularly before the First Industrial Revolution, there was no concept of capital equipment and infrastructure, and the vast majority of people lived in rural areas and in a natural economy. The new term "capital formation" emerged as industrialization deepened, factories embraced mechanized production, and transport was developed in modern times. This new term largely represents the level of economic development. The more the capital is formed in a country, the more developed the economy will be, and vice versa.

In modern times, China went through an arduous process in terms of capital formation. Because China suffered domestic strife and foreign aggression before 1949, the country was disintegrated, and the populace had no means to live despite some progress in railways, highways, shipping, and other sectors. This did not befit a country with a population of more than 400 million and a long history. After 1949, infrastructure and production bases were built on a large scale during the planned economy period, laying the foundation for industrialization. However, due to financial and technological limitations, construction was very limited and did not fundamentally change the backward China. After reform and opening up, this situation gradually improved. Especially since the beginning of the 21st century, China's infrastructure development has reached a high level and is not inferior to developed countries in some areas thanks to the rapid improvement in economic power and technological level. For example, China is ahead of other countries in the world in terms of the length of high-speed railways.

In terms of investment enterprises, it can be divided into three categories before 1949: government-run enterprises, foreign-funded enterprises, and private enterprises. The first two were dominant, with a large scale, new technology, and abundant capital. In contrast, private enterprises could only invest in some areas related to people's well-being, such as textiles, matches, brewing, and food processing, and it was difficult to make greater achievements. This monopoly seriously hampered the progress and development of China's economy, and China economically lagged behind other countries as a result.

DOI: 10.4324/9781003410393-12

During the planned economy period after 1949, the government made strenuous efforts to step up investment in order to achieve rapid industrialization and modernization and put forward slogans such as "surpassing Britain and catching up with the United States", "going all out and gong fast", and "making the utmost effort, aiming high, and building socialism with greater, faster, better and more economic results".[1] China introduced 156 major projects from the Soviet Union, engaged in large-scale steel smelting, and mobilized the whole country to learn from Daqing oilfield and Dazhai village, in an attempt to substitute the funds and technology that were scarce at that time through the huge-crowd strategy. China encouraged fertility as it believed that there is strength in numbers. In order to pool superior forces and harness the spirit of collectivism, China vigorously promoted the merger and development of state-run enterprises and collective enterprises and included the whole country in the plan. Gradually, China established an economic structure featuring state-run enterprises, supplemented by collective enterprises, without private businesses or a private sector of the economy. This severely dampened people's initiative and creativity and also reduced investment efficiency. The considerations for investment in this period focused more on political needs than on efficiency. It was largely blind investment without technological innovation, and it was low-level redundant development. Although it spurred economic growth to some extent, it did not improve product quality and the production levels of enterprises, and it focused on quantity instead of quality. The expansion of production and economic growth in this period is usually called "extensive growth".

This situation has changed considerably after the reform and opening up. Original state-owned enterprises and collective enterprises have been restructured, and the vast majority of them have become joint-stock companies. A market economy has been gradually formed. Competition intensifies, resources are effectively allocated, and efficiency has improved. In this case, capital formation not only enhances production capacity but also improves the level of production. In particular, thanks to the introduction of foreign investment, the level of production technology and management has reached a new height, and enterprises have become more internationally competitive. Some new industrial fields, such as new energy, new materials, biopharmaceuticals, electronic instruments, and aerospace, have advanced in leaps and bounds, resulting in more high-quality economic growth. In terms of infrastructure, investment has brought unprecedentedly rapid development in the fields of highways, high-speed railway, airports, ports, urban water, electricity and gas supply, communications, etc. and has greatly built the material foundation for economic development.

9.2 Changes and causes of capital formation

9.2.1 Changes in capital formation

Capital formation in China after 1949 has two characteristics. First, government investment accounts for a large part, particularly during the planned economy period because there was little difference between enterprises and governments at the time.

Even in the early days of reform and opening up, government investment was still highly important because much of infrastructure was state-owned, such as railways, roads, ports, and airports. Second, the proportion of investment has remained high for a long time. The investment rate has been very high, becoming a driver of economic growth. Although many countries and regions (such as Japan and the Four Asian Tigers) also had high investment rates in the early days and middle of economic development,[2] few countries have sustained such a high level of growth as China has. Of course, China has longer rapid economic growth than other countries.

Due to the needs of economic development and national defense after 1949, China stepped up the construction of infrastructure while promoting industrialization. During the First Five-Year Plan period in the early 1950s, the most notable was the 156 major projects introduced from the Soviet Union. The vast majority of these projects were different factories, including automobile factories, tractor factories, rubber factories, steelworks, and power plants. Moreover, there were also some water conservancy projects and other infrastructure, which played an irreplaceable role in the development of China's planned economy. They not only filled a gap in many industries (such as automobiles and aircraft) in China but also boosted the manufacturing capabilities and cultivated a wealth of technical personnel. After a rupture of relations with the Soviet Union, many of China's new enterprises and infrastructure were developed and expanded in imitation of the technology of these projects. In terms of aircraft manufacturing, the earliest was Soviet-aided Shenyang Aircraft Factory (including the engine factory). China built other manufacturing plants in the southwest and northwest regions. The current well known Chengdu Aircraft Industrial Group and Xi'an Aircraft Industry Group are the products of this model. The "three-line construction" that was initiated in the late 1950s was basically conducted through this model. This is the origin of a Chinese characteristic: old enterprises lead new enterprises or provide paired-up support. At that time, a large number of key technical and management personnel moved from the developed regions to the Great Northwest or the Great Southwest for construction, and many people became the key technical personnel there.

Table 9.1 shows the composition of gross domestic product (GDP) calculated according to the expenditure approach from 1952 to 2018. In terms of final consumption expenditure, the proportion of GDP fell from nearly 80 percent in 1952 to 54.31 percent in 2018. The government consumption was relatively stable, and therefore this change was mainly affected by household consumption. Household consumption fell from 65.45 to 39.37 percent, down by about 26 percentage points. This shows that the status of domestic demand in the economic structure gradually declined. The proportion of capital formation (investment rate) rose accordingly, from 22.21 percent in 1952 to 44.85 percent in 2018. Fixed capital formation was dominant in capital formation, while inventories accounted for only a small percentage and declined year by year. In other words, the status of investment in the Chinese economy gradually rose, becoming the pillar of effective demand effect, or the dominant factors in China's economy are consumption and investment rather than imports and exports. The status of consumption is declining while the status of investment is rising, as manifested by the comparison with other countries.

144 Conditions and causes

Table 9.1 Composition of GDP by expenditure approach, Unit: %

Year	Proportion of final consumption expenditure (consumption rate)			Proportion of gross capital formation (investment rate)			Proportion of net exports of goods and services
	Total	Household consumption	Government consumption	Total	Fixed capital formation	Inventory fluctuation	
1952	78.93	65.45	13.48	22.21	11.66	10.55	−1.13
1960	61.85	49.19	12.66	38.14	31.37	6.77	0.02
1970	66.14	54.68	11.46	33.76	24.74	9.02	0.10
1980	65.49	50.75	14.74	35.84	28.80	6.04	−0.32
1990	62.50	48.85	13.65	34.88	24.96	9.92	2.67
2000	63.30	46.44	15.86	35.30	34.28	1.02	2.37
2010	49.08	35.93	13.15	47.24	44.57	2.67	3.67
2018	54.31	39.37	14.94	44.85	43.05	1.68	0.84

Data source: National Bureau of Statistics (1999); China Statistical Yearbook 2019.

9.2.2 Causes of capital formation

The determinants of capital formation are studied next. In other words, by what factors is the size of capital formation?[3] Government investment in capital formation usually relies on noneconomic factors, such as the needs of defense. As the investment behavior in the primary industry is relatively special,[4] the investment function of the secondary industry is primarily studied here. Investment in production equipment can be considered from the perspective of demand and supply, with the demand being more important. It includes sales and its increased share, profits, capital stock, etc. Profits and capital stock are used as variables. Profits are expressed as the return on real capital (r) or the real total profits of industrial enterprises (R). These are expected return indicators, and the increase in these indicators will stimulate entrepreneurs' desire to invest. Furthermore, an increase in the capital stock (K) usually has a negative effect on investment because an increase in K leads to lower demand for production equipment (according to the principle of capital adjustment).

Another determinant of investment lies in the supply side (supply of equipment funds), including the amount of loans, depreciation fees, interest rates, etc. The focus here is on the interest rate. When making investment plans, enterprises consider the real interest rate (i^*), which is obtained after subtracting the rate of price increase $G(P)$ of the industry products from the nominal interest rate i.

$$i^* = i - G(P) \tag{9.1}$$

However, i is often used in practical studies. Two types are used here. We calculated the investment function of the secondary industry for the period from 1982 to 2014, with the results shown in Table 9.2. The data of the previous period are used for explanatory variables.

Table 9.2 Calculation of investment function of the secondary industry

Equation	Variable	Constant	Parameter r_{-1}	R_{-1}	i^*_{-1}	i_{-1}	K_{-1}	R2	D.W
(1)	PCF	−32.470 (−3.58)	0.002 (4.31)	–	0.051 (1.96)	–	4.342 (4.59)	0.79	0.28
(2)	PCF	−17.971 (−5.98)	–	0.877 (20.37)	0.020 (2.35)	–	2.055 (6.08)	0.98	0.55
(3)	PCF	−38.576 (−5.25)	0.001 (2.36)	–	–	−0.446 (−4.54)	5.355 (6.67)	0.86	0.46
(4)	PCF	−14.540 (−3.81)	–	0.934 (12.13)	–	0.013 (0.22)	1.635 (3.36)	0.97	0.67

Sources: China Statistical Yearbook and China Financial Statistical Yearbook over the years.

Notes:
(1) PCF = total fixed assets investment in the secondary industry, K = capital stock of the secondary industry, R = total profits of industrial enterprises, r = real return on capital, i = benchmark interest rate for one-year loans, i* = real interest rate.
(2) PCF, K, r, and R are all prices for 1952; PCF, K, and R are all log values.
(3) Inside the parentheses is the value t.

Although the calculation results are not very satisfactory, it can explain the problem to a certain extent. The return on capital variable is significant and is in line with the theoretical explanation. The total profit indicator is relatively good, which reflects the principle that the higher the profits, the stronger the investment desire. The interest rate variable is not good, and only equation (9.2) (see the next section) is significant and the signs match, showing that the interest rate is not an effective factor for determining Chinese companies' investment, at least not a sensitive factor. The capital stock variable is significant in all four equations, but the signs do not match, possibly because of the fact that China is in a period of capital expansion, and the existing capital stock cannot directly affect investment decisions. However, this statement remains to be further validated.

9.3 The significance of capital formation

Capital formation has effects on economic growth in two areas. First is enhanced potential productivity by the increase in the capital stock, which can be called the production effect. Second is the effective demand effect, which creates effective demand together with consumption and exports, etc. Effective demand, which is gross national expenditure, consists of private consumption expenditure, government consumption expenditure, gross domestic fixed capital formation, inventory investment, and the difference between exports and imports. The rate of economic growth, or the growth rate of real GDP (Y), can be broken down into the following two items:

$$\frac{\Delta Y}{Y} = \frac{CF}{Y} \cdot \frac{\Delta Y}{CF} \qquad (9.2)$$

146 *Conditions and causes*

CF (fixed capital formation) can be roughly seen as the increase (Δ*K*) in the real capital stock. Therefore, the preceding formula can become

$$\frac{\Delta Y}{Y} = \frac{CF}{Y} \cdot \frac{\Delta Y}{\Delta K} \quad (9.3)$$

The first term on the right is the investment rate (α), and the second term is the marginal capital/output ratio (β). Then

$$G(Y) = \alpha \bullet \beta \quad (9.4)$$

In other words, the higher the α is, the higher the *G(Y)*; the higher the β is, the higher the *G(Y)*. However, even if the α is high, *G(Y)* may be low depending on the value of β. The meaning of α is the extent to which current consumption is saved, and savings are made to become capital formation in order to increase future income. Another β indicates the extent to which a certain capital formation can increase income.[5]

Figures 9.1 and 9.2 show these changes in the investment rate and the marginal output/capital ratio, respectively. Except in 1960 or so, the investment rate was

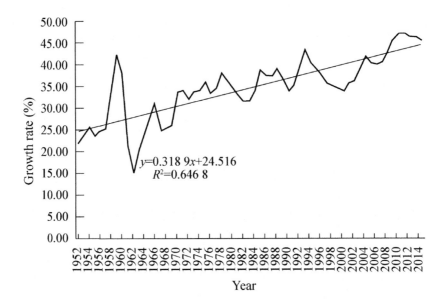

Figure 9.1 Change in investment rate

Data source: *China Statistical Yearbook* over the years.

Note: Investment rate = gross capital formation/GDP calculated according to the expenditure approach × 100.

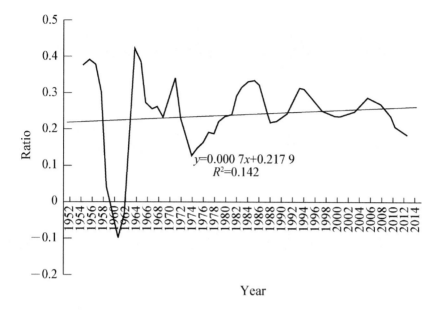

Figure 9.2 Change in marginal output/capital ratio

Data source: *China Statistical Yearbook* over the years.

Note: Marginal output/capital ratio = rate of economic growth/investment rate, which is a 5-year moving average.

almost rising. Although there were fluctuations in the meantime, they were tiny. In summary, the investment rate rose from around 25 to 45 percent, an improvement not achieved by the vast majority of countries. That is to say, China's investment rate exhibits three eye-catching characteristics: the tendency to rise, the level of the investment rate, and small fluctuations, which were small-scale periodic changes. Although this tendency to rise was also observed in the process of Japan's economic development, it is not as high as that in China in both early and late periods.[6]

The marginal output/capital ratio also fluctuated largely from the late 1950s to the mid-1960s, but there were small fluctuations during the reform and opening up period. This can be explained by the fact that the growth rate of output created by investment during the planned economy period was not certain, sometimes high and sometimes low. After the reform and opening up, this relationship was relatively certain. In other words, the growth rate of output created by investment was relatively stable. It can be said that the investment effect during the planned economy period was not certain, while it is easier to evaluate the investment effect in the reform and opening up period.

9.4 Capital accumulation

The productive effects of capital formation are studied here. The fixed capital stock of the previous year plus the fixed capital formation of the current year minus the

148 *Conditions and causes*

capital equipment that has matured is equal to the capital stock of the current year. Capital stock is combined with other factors of production to produce products. Associated with the productive effects of capital accumulation are the capital coefficient (K/Y) and the capital/labor ratio (K/L). The capital coefficient is the reciprocal of capital productivity (Y/K) and is an indicator of the capital productivity, or the capital/output ratio.[7] The smaller this ratio, the higher the production efficiency of capital, and vice versa. The capital coefficients, capital/labor ratios, labor productivity, capital productivity, and labor coefficients of the whole industry from 1953 to 2013 (3-year moving average), three sectors and industry are calculated here (see Table 9.3).

In terms of the industry-wide situation, the capital coefficient has a process of change that rose first and then fell, indicating that the efficiency of capital was low in the planned economy period. In particular, it was at a high level in 1972 and 1982, as well as in 1962 and 1992, reflecting the characteristics of extensive growth at that time. The capital/labor ratio clearly increased, from a very low level to a very high level, despite no significant increase after 1992. This shows that China had labor surplus compared with labor, or at least it did not show a situation of obvious capital advantage. Labor productivity increased markedly. Particularly after the reform and opening up, it rises almost in a straight line, which shows that other factors apart from capital are at play. Capital productivity declined during the planned economy period except in 1953, in contrast to the aforesaid capital coefficient. After the reform and opening up, especially after 2000, there has been an obvious increase. The labor coefficient is the reciprocal of labor productivity. Like the capital coefficient, the larger this number, the lower the production efficiency. In other words, the excessive input of labor reduced productivity. The situation shown here is clear: it was stagnant during the period of the planned economy, without significant increase or significant decline, in contrast to labor productivity. During the period of reform and opening up, the labor coefficient obviously showed a downward trend, and it has fallen to a very low level. This can be said to be an improvement because it at least shows that the increase in production is achieved not by means of the personnel input but by other factors.

The situation of the three industries is examined next. Due to the limited data, the calculation of the three sectors can only start from after 1982 or start from the beginning of the reform and opening up. In terms of the capital coefficient, it generally declined in all three sectors, although not necessarily the case in the meantime. It was the opposite for industry, that is, there was an increase. If the data are correct, it may be due to more capital input and not enough output. On the one hand, the rate of operation might be insufficient due to overcapacity. On the other hand, it is an issue of efficiency. In terms of the capital/labor ratio, it declined in the secondary and tertiary industries, but, of course, it did not always decrease. It began to grow again primarily after 1990 (the secondary industry) and after 2000 (the tertiary industry). It rose for the primary sector and industry, rising prominently and even excessively for industry. If there is no problem of excessive capacity, the increase in capital should lead to an increase in productivity and production efficiency. In terms of labor productivity, it grew fairly well for the primary and tertiary sectors,

Table 9.3 Capital coefficient, capital/labor ratio and labor productivity

Year	Capital coefficient K/Y	Capital/labor ratio K/L (yuan per person)	Labor productivity Y/L (yuan per person)	Capital productivity Y/K	Labor coefficient L/Y (10,000 people per yuan)
All industries					
1953	1.15	417.26	361.95	0.87	27.76
1962	2.51	1,250.66	500.67	0.40	20.08
1972	4.30	2,009.60	467.14	0.23	21.41
1982	3.64	3,516.63	965.79	0.27	10.36
1992	2.67	5,443.36	2,068.15	0.38	4.95
2002	1.04	5,948.51	5,759.30	0.97	1.74
2013	0.40	6,489.83	16,408.02	2.53	0.61
Primary industry					
1982	0.30	137.05	462.45	3.43	21.63
1992	0.13	97.50	760.70	7.98	13.25
2002	0.20	308.90	1,535.14	5.06	6.52
2013	0.11	559.52	4,896.66	8.77	2.05
Secondary industry					
1982	5.13	11,050.48	2,156.14	0.20	4.64
1992	6.50	12,859.12	1,991.90	0.16	5.04
2002	3.14	8,327.30	2,645.48	0.33	3.78
2013	3.34	8,924.69	2,673.69	0.30	3.74
Industry					
1982	0.63	6,067.64	9,718.83	1.63	1.03
1992	3.59	23,766.83	6,562.71	0.29	1.53
2002	7.18	64,356.63	8,974.70	0.14	1.12
2013	21.90	195,702.94	8,909.78	0.05	1.12
Tertiary industry					
1982	7.25	10,048.59	1,390.89	0.14	7.21
1992	7.85	12,865.22	1,635.33	0.13	6.13
2002	6.69	13,995.84	2,089.99	0.15	4.79
2013	3.64	9,454.64	2,596.78	0.27	3.85

Notes:
(1) K = capital stock, Y = real GDP, L = number of employees; K and Y are real values; Y represents the 1952 price before 1978 (inclusive), and the 1978 price after 1979; K represents the 1952 price.
(2) The data on real GDP from the *China Statistical Yearbook*, the data on the number of employees from *China Labor Statistical Yearbook*, the data on capital stock from 1952 to 1994 from Zhang Jun and Zhang Yuan (2003), and the data on the 1995–2014 period are inferred on this basis according to China's total fixed asset investment.
(3) The real industrial GDP refers to the 1990 price; the data on industrial capital stock in the 1981–2002 period are obtained from Lu Baolin (2012), and the data for the 2003–2014 period are inferred based on the data from *China Statistical Yearbook* and are the 1990 price. The data on the number of employed persons in industry from 1981 to 1989 are directly derived from *China Labor Statistical Yearbook*, and the data for the 1990 to 2014 period obtained are based on the number of employees in the secondary industry minus the number of employees in the construction sector. Of this, the number of employees in the construction sector from 1990 to 2002 is directly obtained from *China Statistical Yearbook*, and the data from 2003 to 2014 are calculated based on the data from the *China Statistical Yearbook*.
(4) All are calculated according to the 3-year moving average.

150 *Conditions and causes*

while it was relatively bad for the secondary sector and industry. Since the latter two indicators and the previous ones are mutually reciprocal, no further explanation will be made here.

In summary, China's capital coefficient, capital/labor ratio, and changes in labor productivity are uncertain. The growth of the secondary sector and industry, which should have been better, is not obviously reflected. The capital stock increased a lot while the output did not increase much, showing the problem of inefficiency or the problem of overcapacity. The primary sector, which should not have been so good, showed good results, including both the capital/labor ratio and the labor productivity. Of course, the indicators of the whole industry were also relatively good, showing the characteristics of long-term changes in China's economy.

The long-term changes in the capital coefficient, capital/labor ratio, and labor productivity of each industry are examined here. Figure 9.3 shows the capital coefficient of each sector, from which the following characteristics can be obviously observed. First, the changes in the whole industry are distinct. With 1976 as the dividing line, the capital coefficient rose before 1976 and declined after 1976, with almost no change in the middle. Second, the various industries performed differently. The primary sector was at its lowest level, and the general trend is stability with slight decline or slight fluctuations. If it was drawn separately, it would show a straight decline before 1993, an increase in 2003, and then a decline afterward.

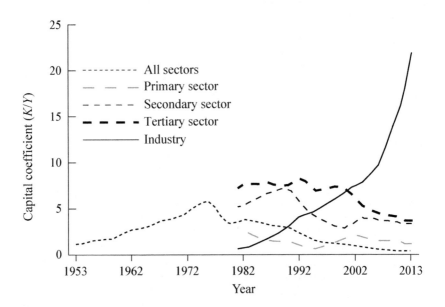

Figure 9.3 Changes in capital coefficients of various industries

Data source: Table 9.3.

Note: The primary industry capital coefficient shown here is the result of multiplying the figures in Table 9.3 by 10.

Some fluctuations occurred in the secondary sector. It rose before 1990, then declined and hit bottom in 2001, then rose again, before falling after 2004. The tertiary sector was largely stable, beginning to decline after 2000. It was a completely different picture for industry, rising all the time, almost in a linear fashion, which is obvious in the figure.

Figure 9.4 shows the change in the capital/labor ratios in various industries. Because the log value is used here, the capital/labor ratio of the whole industry is not obvious. In fact, it rose all the way. In other words, the capital/labor ratio of the whole industry has been increasing or has increased more. However, it stopped increasing around 1994. The primary sector was in a state of horizontal shift before 1992, and there were significant increases afterward. The secondary industry changed in a way wholly different from the primary industry, and it can be said to be full of twists and turns. It rose before 1990, started to decline until 2001, and then rose until 2004. The tertiary sector was even more different, rising before 1993, moving horizontally until 2000, then declining, and moving at a low level after 2011. The changes in industry showed an almost straight climb, which is different from any other industry.

Finally, we take a look at the changes in labor productivity, as shown in Figure 9.5. The curve of industry-wide labor productivity was basically horizontal movement during the planned economy period. For the primary sector, it had a tendency to move horizontally, decline slightly before 1994, and then begin to rise. For the secondary sector, it declined slightly before 1991, then rose afterward, and began

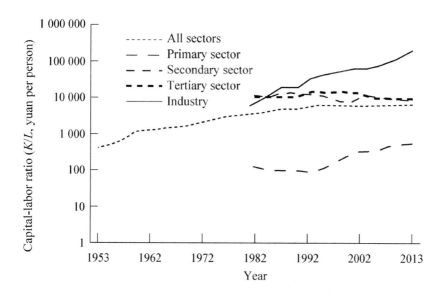

Figure 9.4 Changes in the capital/labor ratio of various industries

Data source: Table 9.3.

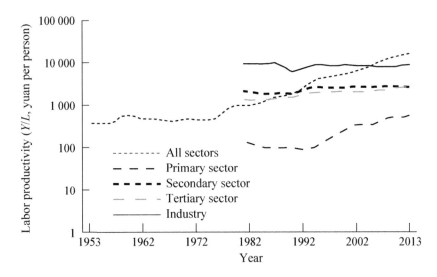

Figure 9.5 Changes in labor productivity of various industries
Data source: Table 9.3.

to move horizontally after 1996. For the tertiary industry, there were basically no great fluctuations. It rose, despite slight fluctuations in the process. For industry, there was a long-term downward trend, with a serious decline in the middle.

9.5 Savings and investment

The funds required for capital formation come from two sources: domestic savings and inflow of capital from abroad (capital inflow − capital outflow). Domestic savings are divided into total savings and household savings. Total savings include household savings, as well as business savings and government savings. Figure 9.6 shows the changes in the gross savings rate, the investment rate, and the household savings rate after 1949. In general, it shows an upward trend, with some fluctuations in the middle. This tendency to rise is what Keynes called normal phenomenon. According to his absolute income hypothesis, the savings rate rises as income per capita increases.[8] This hypothesis fits Japan but not the United States. For other developed countries, it rose for Italy, Denmark, and Canada and also rose slightly for Norway. For the United States, it declined from the end of the 19th century to before World War II. For Britain, it rose somewhat from the mid-19th century to 1900 and then declined until the 1920s. Japanese scholar Ryoshin Minami believes that the savings rate tends to rise in the early days of economic development and then gradually to decline as the economy matures. It can also be considered that the savings rate has a process of inverted U curve change.[9]

Further observations show that total savings and investment rate in China were basically consistent during the planned economy period. In other words, savings

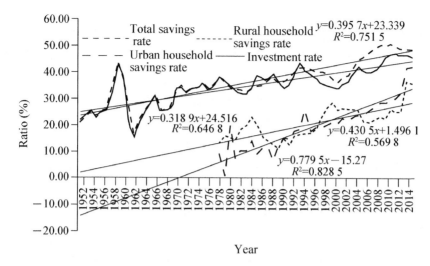

Figure 9.6 Changes in gross savings rate, household savings rate and investment rate
Data source: *China Statistical Yearbook* over the years.

were used for investment, without the need to borrow domestically (actually no such idea at that time) nor to borrow overseas (attract foreign investment). After the reform and opening up, this situation changed. Investment sometimes exceeded savings, and it is necessary to borrow overseas at this time. In most cases, however, the savings rate exceeds the investment rate, and investment needs can be satisfied even without borrowings from abroad. The difference between the two widens as the economy develops and income increases. This tendency can be explained by the growing household savings rate. Savings fluctuate greatly for rural households btu basically increase in a linear fashion for urban households.

The gross savings rate and the household (personal) savings rate are examined above. They generally have a tendency to rise and the savings rate is very high. This shows that the development level of China's economy reaches a stage of high savings rate, which may gradually decline as the economy further develops.[10] The author attempts to calculate the consumption function and the saving function. According to the economic theory on consumption and savings, there are a full variety of hypotheses, the most basic of which are the absolute income hypothesis and the consumption habit hypothesis. The former refers to the extent to which savings will increase as a result of improved living standards. The latter means that consumption habits are generally hard to change and that, even if income increases, consumption does not necessarily increase significantly. How about the consumption habits of the Chinese people? This is related to culture and to economic development and living standards.[11]

The consumption function and savings function for urban and rural households from 1978 to 2014 are calculated here. The basic relationship is as follows: personal savings (PS) = personal disposable income − personal consumption expenditure (PC). The proportion of personal savings to personal disposable income is the personal savings rate (r). The calculation results are shown in Table 9.4. The explained variable personal consumption (PC/N) in equation (1) is explained by per capita income (PY/N) as well as per capita consumption for the previous year. In other words, the explanatory variables are (PY/N) and $(PC/N)_{-1}$. Judging from the results, the effect is obvious for cities and towns, and both variables are significant, indicating that the consumption expenditure of urban residents varies according to the aforesaid variables. However, the effect is not very significant for rural areas, especially for the latter $[(PC/N)_{-1}]$, indicating that farmers' consumption expenditure is not based on previous year's consumption.

Equation (2) is the savings function. The personal savings rate (r) is determined by per capita income (PY/N) and the growth rate of per capita income G(PY/N). The calculation results show that, for both urban and rural areas, the effect of the former (PY/N) is significant, while the latter [G(PY/N)] is not significant, indicating that the income growth rate has little impact on people's savings. It can also be said that China's household savings rate increases mainly based on income. In other words, given sudden or temporary needs, appropriate savings are made even if the income is not necessarily high. To put it another way, this has little to do with future income rises. We call it "absolute demand savings". The expectation of income increase is significantly higher for urban areas than for rural areas, indicating that the rural residents are more inclined to "absolute demand savings", while urban residents more or less expect income increases.

Table 9.4 Calculation of personal consumption function and saving function

Equation	Variable	Constant	Parameter PY/N	$(PC/N)_{-1}$	G (PY/N)	R^2	D.W.
Towns and cities							
(1)	PC/N	81.163 (3.90)	0.318 (4.21)	0.521 (4.67)	–	0.988	1.005
(2)	r	3.992 (2.53)	0.012 (12.19)	–	0.106 (1.13)	0.824	1.806
Rural areas							
(1)	PC/N	25.001 (4.05)	0.758 (5.24)	−0.068 (−0.33)	–	0.990	0.628
(2)	r	14.532 (12.69)	0.020 (8.15)	–	−0.312 (−4.05)	0.730	0.974

Data source: China Statistical Yearbook over the years.

Notes:
(1) Equation (1) is the consumption function, and equation (2) is the savings function.
(2) The unit of PC/N and PY/N is yuan, and the unit of r (personal savings rate) is %; PC/N and PY/N are actual values (1978 prices).
(3) Inside the parentheses is value t.

9.6 Conclusion

The important capital rotation, production equipment, and infrastructure construction issues in economic development were studied in this chapter according to the changes in China's capital formation, savings, and investment after 1949. The following conclusions can be drawn from the summary. First, China's capital formation has a process of increase from low to high. According to international experience, China is still in the middle stage of economic development, which largely depends on investment. There is a lot of room for investment. Railways, highways, aviation, communications, and other infrastructure is not yet developed, and the capital equipment in the industries is not sufficiently advanced and popular. As a result, China still has considerable room and space for investment to drive economic growth, and the rate of investment-driven economic growth is usually high. It can be said that this pattern of economic growth can realize rapid growth, as proved by the experience of Japan and the Four Asian Tigers, as well as China.

Second, the sources of investment are mainly savings. China's savings rate has been trending upward since at least 1949, with no stagnation or decline in sight at present. The reason is that China is still in the middle stage of economic development, the social security system is imperfect, and the personal income is not high. China has not yet reached the stage when economic growth is driven by consumption. Of course, the increase in the savings rate is mainly attributed to the increase in income as a result of economic growth, or it can be said that China is in the middle stage of the inverted U curve savings rate. A high savings rate provides financial support for investment, and this demand can be satisfied even without foreign investment. It is also a financial guarantee that China will see high growth in the years to come.

Third, China's capital formation (investment rate) is higher than in many other countries, while the proportion of consumption is decreasing year by year (although it has just recovered somewhat). This is similar to what Japan experienced. It may be related to the late-mover advantage because capital formation helps spur rapid economic growth and aids the expansion of capital equipment and infrastructure necessary for industrialization. This is favorable to countries that are latecomers and wish to catch up with developed countries rapidly. Consumption is often restricted during this period. After a period of rapid development, an economy will eventually become a consumption-driven economy, but the economic growth will also slow down at this time. China is currently in a period of robust investment-driven economy, and this period may continue for some time because many regions and sectors still lack capital and infrastructure is still weak. However, consumption is rising and has overtaken investment, indicating that China's economy is changing.

Notes

1 The general line of socialism put forward in 1958.
2 The capital formation of Japan in some years after the war is as follows: 29.4 percent in 1970, 27.3 percent in 1980, 29.8 percent in 1990, and 27.9 percent in 1997, see Ryoshin Minami (2002), p. 123.

3 The calculation method refers to the research conducted by Japanese scholar Ryoshin Minami. See Ryoshin Minami (1981).
4 Generally speaking, it is difficult to separate the operation of the primary industry from household life. The investment theory premised on market theory cannot explain the phenomenon of the primary industry. Of course, the rate of returns on capital, a main variable for the industry determining investment, is difficult to calculate.
5 For a discussion and explanation in this regard, see Ryoshin Minami (1981), pp. 142–143.
6 See Ryoshin Minami (2002).
7 This ratio is the most important variable in the Harrod-Domar model on economic growth, see Guan Quan (2014).
8 For various hypotheses on the savings rate, see Guan Quan (2014).
9 Ryoshin Minami (2002), pp. 133–134.
10 Ryoshin Minami studied the situation in Japan, see Ryoshin Minami (2002).
11 Ryoshin Minami argues that the consumption preferences of Japanese people are traditional; that is, there are little changes. In our view, China's savings level may depend more on the extent of economic development and living standards.

10 Human resources
Education and health

10.1 Introduction

China has relatively rich natural resources thanks to its vast territory. However, because China has a large population, and economic development requires a plethora of resources, the resources are not so rich. What about human resources compared to natural resources? We admit that there is strength in numbers, but this is not entirely true because the concept of human resources places a high value on quality rather than quantity. Before 1949, China had a population of more than 500 million,[1] ranking first in the world, but the quality of human resources was not high, and the level of economic development was also very low. Although China also had abundant natural resources at that time, it did nothing to improve the poor and backward China.

For a long time after 1949, China made little of the development of human resources. Instead, China focused more on expanding the population. "There is strength in numbers" is a view that prevailed at that time. It was not until the end of the 1970s that China really realized the problem of overpopulation. Subsequently, China adopted a family planning policy to curb births. However, this does not mean that China attached no importance to the improvement of human resources, only that there was a lack of awareness and capacity. Back in the 1950s, China launched a large-scale anti-illiteracy campaign, laying the foundation for the subsequent universal primary education. Even during the Cultural Revolution period when China's education as a whole was hard hit, China still made great achievements in primary education, particularly in popularizing basic education in rural areas.

The same goes for health, another issue involved in the quality of human resources. As a result of campaigns with Chinese characteristics such as eliminating four pests,[2] eliminating schistosomiasis, and five stresses and four points of beauty,[3] China had greatly raised public awareness of hygiene and health as well as environmental protection. As the economy develops, China has also done a lot to improve the diet structure and has made positive and effective achievements. Thanks to the improved medical services, the life expectancy of the Chinese people has increased significantly, and the level of health has reached a new height.

DOI: 10.4324/9781003410393-13

10.2 Economic development and education

China's education sector underwent an arduous development process after 1949, but it has still made achievements that attract global attention. Two-thirds of the population were previously illiterate, but now the vast majority of people have access to formal education, including many professionals with a high level of educational level and expertise. As a result of the development of education, China has made great strides in human resources. It can be said that China's educational progress has outperformed economic development.

Table 10.1 shows enrollment rate and the proportion of students entering schools of a higher level at all levels of school. The net enrollment ratio of elementary schools rose from 61.7 percent in 1957 to 93.9 percent in 1980. Now, it is close to 100 percent, approaching that in developed countries. That is to say, China's primary education has reached the stage of saturated education. The promotion of elementary school graduates entering high schools (or the enrollment rate of junior high schools) was about 45 percent in the 1950s. It reached 70 to 80 percent from the 1970s to 1990, and increased rapidly after the 1990s. It is now close to that of high-income countries in the world and is consistent with China's GDP per capita. The enrollment rate of high schools was less than 40 percent in the 1950s to 1980s. Although it reached or exceeded 40 percent from 1978 to 1980, it fell back to 31 percent in 1981 and exceeded 40 percent from 1985 to 1986. However, it was still less than 40 percent from 1987 to 1989. It was after the 1990s that it surpassed this threshold. It increased rapidly after 2000 and now reaches about 95 percent. There were no data on the enrollment rate of universities until the 1990s, when the enrollment rate was low. However, thanks to increased university enrollment in 1999, it achieved a quantum leap and is now more than 100 percent, which is higher than

Table 10.1 Proportion of secondary and elementary school graduates entering schools of a higher level as well as enrollment rate of elementary schools, Unit: %

Year	Net enrollment rate of elementary schools	Enrollment rate of junior high schools	Enrollment rate of senior high schools	Enrollment rate of universities
1957	61.7	44.2	39.7	–
1962	56.1	45.3	30.0	–
1970	–	71.2	38.6	–
1980	93.9	75.9	45.9	–
1990	97.8	74.6	40.6	27.3
2000	99.1	94.9	51.1	73.2
2018	100.0	99.1	95.2	101.5

Data source: *China Statistical Yearbook* over the years.

Notes:
(1) Junior high school students entering senior high schools include those entering technical schools.
(2) The proportion of high school students entering universities is the ratio of the number of entrants to regular institutions of higher learning (including the general class of open university) and the number of graduates of regular senior high schools.

that of upper middle-income countries (33 percent in 2010) and even high-income countries (70 percent in 2010).

Table 10.2 shows the number of current students and graduates at all levels of education in China after 1949. Overall, the number of current students and graduates at each level of education has increased significantly, but it should be divided into two stages – the period of planned economy and the period of reform and opening up – because there are obvious differences between the two. In terms of primary education, the numbers of both current students and graduates rose before 1980. It can be said that primary education became popular in China during this period. However, there was a period of relative stability from then until 2000, with few increases or decreases. After 2000, it has basically declined, and this situation is expected to continue, because China has passed the period of popularization of primary education and has reached the period of popularization and development of secondary education. Another factor contributing to the decline in primary education is China's population policy – the family planning policy. China has had family planning policy in place since 1971. Such a policy brought about a change in the age structure of the population: the young population decreases, and the elderly population increases. These demographic changes bring about major changes in China's educational structure: the absolute reduction in the number of elementary school students and the relative decrease in junior high school students. This is a special national condition of China.

Table 10.2 Basic situation of education in China, Unit: 10,000 students

Year	Regular institutions of higher learning	Regular senior high schools	Junior high schools	Secondary vocational education	Primary education
Number of current students (10,000)					
1949	11.7	20.7	83.2	–	2,439.1
1960	96.2	167.5	858.5	230.2	9,379.1
1970	4.8	349.7	2292.2	–	10,528.0
1980	114.4	969.8	4,538.3	45.4	14,627.0
1990	206.3	717.3	3,868.7	295.0	12,241.4
2000	556.1	1,201.3	6,167.6	503.2	13,013.3
2018	2,831.0	2,375.4	4,652.6	1,555.3	10,339.3
Number of graduates (10,000)					
1949	2.1	6.1	21.9	–	64.6
1960	13.6	28.8	142.2	14.9	734.0
1970	10.3	67.6	618.9	–	1,652.5
1980	14.7	616.2	964.8	7.9	2,053.3
1990	61.4	233.0	1,109.1	89.3	1,863.1
2000	95.0	301.5	1,607.1	176.3	2,419.2
2015	753.3	779.2	1,367.8	487.3	1,616.5

Data source: China Statistical Yearbook over the years.

Note: Figures vary somewhat due to changes in the statistical caliber of secondary education.

Unlike primary education, there has been increase in secondary education, both in terms of current students and graduates, despite some fluctuations during this period, particularly for senior high school education. We believe that secondary education holds the key to the country during industrialization and that it should change in sync with economic development. This type of education aims to produce skilled workers and administrative staff suited to industrial production, who are needed in the middle of industrialization. Those who only attended elementary school could not meet the needs, and there was no need for so many graduates of higher education, or there was a lack of scope for their abilities. This is why many countries extend the length of compulsory education from 6 years to 9 years when the economy reaches a certain level. The decline in or slow growth in the number of current students and graduates of secondary education after 1979 is also associated with the aforesaid family planning policy. It does not mean that China's secondary education went wrong and caused a decline.

In terms of higher education, the number of both current students and graduates rose rapidly, except for an absolute decline around 1970. Specifically, higher education went through several dramatic periods. One is the period of rapid development before the Cultural Revolution. Although it did not have a larger scale, and the level of education was not high during this period, it developed relatively fast, similar to that of high school, and exceeded that of elementary schools. During the Cultural Revolution (1966–1976), it was exactly the opposite, with a serious decline and even the closure of schools. Although some schools enrolled students, they were not enrolled through examinations but through the selection of workers, farmers, and soldiers. The criteria for this selection were not academic performance or creativity but political behavior and family background. The quality of students can be imagined accordingly.

After the resumption of the college entrance examinations in 1977, higher education has developed at a fast clip and has produced a wealth of talents, making key contributions to reform and opening up. In 1999, a policy known as increased university enrollment was introduced, and students have been admitted to universities as much as possible within the existing school running capacity. This can promote the development of higher education and has also eased employment pressure. Thereafter, higher education has developed on a large scale. In fact, this campaign is not limited to the existing conditions. In order to increase enrollment, many universities have expanded the scale of school running, and some colleges have been upgraded to universities, which has swelled the number of universities in China. In 2000, there were 1,041 ordinary general institutes of higher education in China, compared to 1,016 in 1985. However, this figure reached 2,663 in 2018. Admittedly, this rapid development has given rise to a host of problems, such as the decline in the quality of faculty and students, a shortage of teaching facilities and dormitories, the huge debt borne by many universities as they built campuses, and the difficulty of employment for university graduates. However, we believe that this has objectively produced a wealth of talents for China's industrialization and economic development, and this must be recognized. In 2000, there were only 950,000 university graduates, but this figure reached 7.533 million in 2018 (more than Hong Kong's population), an increase of nearly seven times in a decade.

We next take a look at the schooling of Chinese people as a result of education. According to the results of the sample survey conducted in 2018, of the 1,064,200 respondents aged above 6 years, 57,500 (5.40 percent) did not receive schooling, 269,000 (25.28 percent) attended elementary schools, 401,900 (37.77 percent) attended junior high schools, 186,800 (17.55 percent) attended senior high schools (including secondary vocational schools), and 149,100 (14.01 percent) attended colleges or those at a higher level. This comparison with the results of the following censuses shows significant educational attainments. According to the fourth population census conducted in 1990, of the total sample of 78.975 million people, 42.0994 million (53.31 percent) attended elementary schools, 26.3144 million (33.32 percent) attended junior high schools, 8.9712 million (11.36 percent) attended senior high schools (including secondary schools), and 1.5899 million (2.02 percent) attended colleges or universities. According to the fifth national census conducted in 2000, of the 1.157 billion people aged above 6 years surveyed, 110 million (9.55 percent) did not receive schooling or had only attended literacy classes, 442 million (38.18 percent) attended elementary schools, 422 million (36.52 percent) attended junior high schools, 138 million (11.96 percent) attended senior high schools (including secondary schools), and 44 million (3.81 percent) attended colleges or universities.

Table 10.3 shows the schooling received by the people according to the censuses since 1949. In terms of the illiteracy rate, the illiteracy rate in China was up to 70 percent before 1949 (1947), but after more than a decade of development, it plunged to 33.58 percent in 1964. However, this is not a tiny proportion, and more than 230 million people were still illiterate.[4] Although the illiteracy rate fell to 22.81 percent in 1982, the number of illiterates did not decrease much due to the

Table 10.3 Length of schooling as shown in previous censuses

Indicators	1964	1982	1990	2000	2010
Colleges and universities	416	615	1,422	3,611	8,930
Senior high schools and technical secondary schools	1,319	6,779	8,039	11,146	14,032
Junior high schools	4,680	17,892	23,344	33,961	38,788
Elementary schools	28,330	35,237	37,057	35,701	26,779
The number of illiterates (10,000)	23,327	22,996	18,003	8,507	5,466
Illiteracy rate (%)	33.58	22.81	15.88	6.72	4.08

Data source: *China Statistical Yearbook* over the years.

Note: The number of people who receive schooling shown in the table is the number of people who receive schooling per 100,000 people.

rapid population growth,[5] and it was still close to 230 million. The illiteracy rate fell to 15.88 percent in 1990, and the number of illiterates fell to 180 million (a total population of 1.14 billion). The two figures fell to 6.72 percent and 85.07 million (a total population of 1.27 billion) in 2000, and to 4.08 percent and 54.66 million (a total population of 1.34 billion) in 2010, respectively.

We then look at the number of people who receive schooling at various levels (number of people per 100,000 people). In terms of elementary schools, there were 28,000 with elementary school education per 100,000 people in 1964, accounting for 28 percent of the 100,000 people. It was roughly about 35 percent from 1982 to 2000. In 2010, it declined significantly, indicating an increase in the number of people who receive education at other levels. This is a kind of progress. In terms of junior high schools, there were only 4,680 people with junior high school education per 100,000 people in 1964, and 17,900 in 1982. This proportion kept rising afterward, reaching 38,800 in 2010, equivalent to 38.8 percent of the total population. It exceeded the peak population of people with elementary school education (1990). It is estimated that this trend will continue. The same goes for senior high schools and technical secondary schools. The number of people who have attended senior high schools or technical secondary schools was just 1,319 per 100,000 people in 1964 but reached 6,779 in 1982 and 14,000 in 2010, equivalent to 14 percent of the total population. If we add up junior and senior high schools (both at the stage of secondary education), it is up to 52 percent, more than half of the population, which is a pivotal achievement because China's stage of development is the period when the demand for secondary education graduates is the highest. as the industrial processing and manufacturing sector is developed and needs a wealth of skilled workers, where are the people who have received a secondary education?

Finally, in terms of people with a college degree or above, the number of people with a college degree or above per 100,000 people was merely 416 in 1964, and only 615 in 1982, indicating not much progress in higher education in these decades. Of course, we must take into account the fact that the total population increased greatly during this period. In 1990, the number of people with a college degree or above more than doubled, reaching 1,422, proving the significance and role of resuming the college entrance examinations, albeit the small progress. This figure more than doubled again in 2000, but it also only accounted for 3.6 percent of the total population. In 2010, it reached 8,930, accounting for 8.9 percent of the total population. Although there is still a huge gap, the absolute number of professionals is considerable, given the total population of China.

Judging from international experience, we have summarized the following regular trends.[6] Figure 10.1 shows the prevalence of primary education, secondary education, and higher education.[7] In the early days of economic development, universal primary education was promoted first, which was easy to achieve due to the simple teaching content, little demand for teaching input, and low requirements for teachers' competence. From the observation of facts, even countries with a very low level of economic development have a high enrollment rate for elementary schools. The countries with the lowest elementary school enrollment rates in 2010 were above 80 percent except for a few countries (45 percent in Eritrea and 60 percent

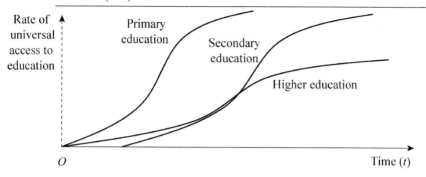

Figure 10.1 Process of universal access to education
Data source: Guan Quan (2014).

in Papua New Guinea). For example, the enrollment rate is 73 percent in Sudan, 87 percent in Yemen, 87 percent in Senegal, 83 percent in Niger, 82 percent in Mali, 89 percent in Jamaica, 83 percent in Gambia, 88 percent in Côte d'Ivoire, 79 percent in Burkina Faso, 87 percent in Albania, and 88 percent in Bosnia and Herzegovina.[8]

The development of secondary education in China was not late, but it developed slowly and it will take a long time to achieve universal access (100 percent). At present, only developed countries have achieved this goal. Even middle- and high-income countries have a completion rate of about 80 percent. Low- and low-middle-income countries are far from meeting this standard. In fact, it is not easy for developed countries to achieve this goal. In 1980, it was only equivalent to that of upper-middle-income countries in 2010. Therefore, it can be inferred that high-income countries and upper-middle-income countries have a 30-year gap in terms of secondary education.

We believe that secondary education is a key step toward achieving modernization because primary education basically teaches general knowledge. In other words, it teaches the most basic knowledge that a modern citizen must master, such as reading, writing, and simple calculations. For secondary education, it is required to master complex knowledge about mathematics, physics, chemistry, biology, history, geography, and foreign languages. This knowledge helps students understand and solve problems. Without the basic knowledge about geometry, trigonometry, and algebra, you cannot operate complex machines (such as numerically controlled machine tools). Without a good knowledge of native language, it is difficult to handle the work as a junior public servant. Without the knowledge of foreign languages, you can't engage in work related to foreign trade and communicate with foreigners, of course.

Higher education is a stage for further studies. Students are required to master the basic knowledge and skills of related specialties, and universities must cultivate senior professionals. Even today's developed countries (high-income

164 *Conditions and causes*

countries) had enrollment rates of only 35 percent for higher education in 1980, which is equivalent to that of upper-middle-income countries in 2010. The two have a 30-year gap in this regard. Whether higher education should or can achieve universal access remains to be seen. At least, no country has achieved this goal. As the times advance, higher education may lead to universal academic qualification, or not exactly professional academic qualification, but may become a stage of learning for cultivation. This is possible. From the perspective of the development trend, undergraduate knowledge is no longer regarded as professional learning, and higher-level research-oriented learning must be pursued at the graduate stage.

10.3 Economic development and health

The life expectancy of the Chinese people has been increasing year by year after 1949. There are incomplete data for the planned economy period, with only scattered statistics for individual regions. In 1950, the life expectancy in Beijing was 53.9 years for males and 50.2 years for females. In 1953, the corresponding figures were 61.2 years for males and 60.5 years for females. In 1957, the average life expectancy for people in one county and 126 townships in 70 cities, 11 provinces, and municipalities was 57.0 years. In 1957, the figure for people in Nanning, Liuzhou, Guilin, and Wuzhou was 64.0 years. In 1964, the figures were 69.3 years for males and 72.3 years for females in Shanghai, and in 1972, the corresponding figures were 71.7 years and 73.8 years, respectively. In 1975, this figure for people in 26 provinces and municipalities was 68.2 years (67.2 years for males and 69.3 years for females). In 1978, the corresponding figure for people in 23 provinces, municipalities, and autonomous regions was 68.2 years (67.0 years for males and 70.0 years for females). In 1980, this figure for people in some of the 25 provinces, municipalities, and autonomous regions was 69.0 years (67.9 years for males and 70.2 years for females). Later, census data were available. The national average life expectancy was 67.77 years (66.28 years for males and 69.27 years for females) in 1982, 68.55 years (66.84 years for males and 70.47 years for females) in 1990, 71.40 years (69.63 years for males and 73.33 years for females) in 2000, and 74.83 years (72.38 years for males and 77.37 years for females) in 2010.[9]

It can be seen that the life expectancy of the Chinese people rose from around 50 years in the early 1950s to nearly 75 years in 2010, an increase of 25 years. Life expectancy in Beijing in 2010 was 80.18 years, about 5 years above the national average. The low figures for the same year was 58.17 years in Tibet, 69.54 years in Yunnan, and 69.96 years in Qinghai. The highest was 80.26 years in Shanghai, slightly higher than that of Beijing. The same situation was available through the 1990 and 2000 censuses. In 1990, the figure was 72.86 years in Beijing and 74.90 years in Shanghai, which was about 5 years higher than the national average. In 2000, the figure was 76.10 years in Beijing and 76.22 years in Shanghai, which was about 5 years higher than the national average.

Table 10.4 shows the names and proportions of the top 10 diseases that cause deaths for urban and rural residents in China in 1990 and 2018. The following two phenomena can be observed: the changes in 1990 and 2018 and the changes

Table 10.4 Diseases as the top 10 causes of death among urban and rural residents in 1990 and 2018

Name of disease	Urban residents Proportion (%)	Ranking	Rural residents Proportion (%)	Ranking
1990				
Malignant tumor	21.88	1	17.47	2
Cerebrovascular disease	20.83	2	16.16	3
Heart diseases	15.81	3	10.82	4
Respiratory diseases	15.76	4	24.82	1
External causes of injury and poisoning	6.91	5	10.65	5
Digestive system diseases	4.02	6	5.01	6
Endocrine, nutritional, and metabolic diseases	1.74	7	1.76 (infectious diseases)	9
Diseases of the genitourinary system	1.58	8	1.48	10
Neonatal disease	1.51	9	2.51	7
Tuberculosis	1.20	10	1.85	8
2018				
Malignant tumor	25.98	1	22.96	3
Heart disease	23.29	2	23.47	1
Cerebrovascular disease	20.51	3	23.19	2
Respiratory disease	10.83	4	11.24	4
External causes of injury and poisoning	5.67	5	7.45	5
Endocrine, nutritional, and metabolic diseases	3.37	6	2.46	6
Diseases of the digestive system	2.31	7	2.11	7
Nervous system disease	1.37	8	1.21	8
Diseases of the genitourinary system	1.09	9	1.08	9
Infectious diseases (including respiratory tuberculosis)	0.95	10	1.05	10

Data source: *China Statistical Yearbook* over the years.

in urban and rural areas. In 1990, the top causes of death among urban residents were very similar to those in developed countries, including malignant tumors, cerebrovascular diseases, and heart disease. The top cause of death in rural areas was respiratory disease, while heart disease ranked fourth. Furthermore, endocrine, nutritional, and metabolic diseases, as well as genitourinary diseases and tuberculosis, were different in urban and rural areas. The rankings and proportions of endocrine, nutritional, and metabolic diseases were higher in cities, while the ranking and proportion of tuberculosis was higher in rural areas. This suggests that tuberculosis still exists in rural areas to some extent but that it was nearly eliminated (though not thoroughly) in cities. By 2018, there was almost no difference between urban and rural areas. The top few causes of deaths are malignant tumors, heart disease, cerebrovascular disease, and respiratory disease. The bottom few are similar, but there are differences in the rankings of several diseases, including

166 *Conditions and causes*

communicable diseases, indicating a gap between rural and urban areas in terms of communicable diseases.

Finally, we take a look at the total spending on health. Table 10.5 shows the situation from 1978 to 2018, including the proportion of government, social, and individual expenditure, as well as the per capita spending and the ratio of total spending to GDP. We first look at the changes in the proportions of various expenditures. The proportion of government spending gradually fell from about one-third to 15.47 percent (2000) and then rebounded, reaching 28.69 percent in 2010 and exceeding 30 percent in 2015 (not shown here) but decreasing slightly in 2018. The proportion of social expenditure had generally been about one-third, with some changes in individual years. It was high (47.41 percent) in 1978, low in 2000 (25.55 percent), and rebounded to more than 43.66 percent in 2018. The proportion of individual cash expenditure showed the opposite tendency to change compared with the proportion of social expenditure, accounting for only 20.43 percent in 1978, reaching 58.98 percent in 2000, and then falling to 28.61 percent in 2018.

In terms of the per capita spending, it showed a rapid rise since 1978, and, of course, rising prices played a part in this. Nevertheless, there is no comparison between the figure in 2018 and that in 1978. An individual's spending on health grows positively as the economy and income grow. Moreover, there is a large gap between rural and urban areas. This gap existed not only in 1978 but also in 2014, only that it gradually narrowed. For example, the per capita spending in urban areas was 4.04 times that of rural areas in 1978 and 2.54 times that of rural areas in 2014. Finally, the total spending on health as a percentage of GDP gradually rose from about 3 to 5.98 percent in 2015. The expenditure on health has indeed increased. This is the result of economic growth and is also a kind of progress, indicating that the fruits of economic growth are shared by citizens.

Table 10.5 Total spending on health

Year	Total spending on health (100 million yuan)	Proportion of government expenditure (%)	Proportion of social expenditure (%)	Proportion of personal cash expenditure (%)	Per capita spending (yuan) Total	Urban areas	Rural areas	Proportion of total spending on health to GDP (%)
1978	110.21	32.16	47.41	20.43	11.45	–	–	3.02
1990	747.39	25.06	39.22	35.73	65.37	158.82	39.31	3.98
2000	4,586.63	15.47	25.55	58.98	361.88	812.95	214.93	4.60
2010	19,980.39	28.69	36.02	35.29	1,490.06	2,315.48	666.30	4.89
2018	59,121.90	27.74	43.66	28.61	4,236.98	3,234.12	1,274.44	6.57

Data source: *China Statistical Yearbook 2019*.

Note: The various expenditure proportions are 100 for the total spending on health. Per capita spending is the 2014 data.

10.4 Conclusion

The following problems can be learned from the preceding simple discussion of human resources in China. First, in terms of education, China has progressed from a very backward state to a level close to that of developed countries, and this is no mean achievement. Education is indispensable for cultivating basic abilities for people in contemporary times. People who do not receive schooling can hardly perform complex work and cannot receive corresponding remuneration. Second, education is irreplaceable for improving the quality of the people as a whole because the educated are more efficient, rational, and tolerant. Therefore, it is more suitable for modern society. The so-called culturally advanced country and society refer to this situation. Third, education can produce high-level personnel who are indispensable in today's highly developed society, such as engineers, analysts, designers, doctors, researchers, and other professionals. These people are engaged in creative work and contribute to social progress.

It should be noted that China has its own characteristics in the education sector and has surpassed the current level of development in some areas. China has higher enrollment rate of higher education than not only upper-middle-income countries but also high-income countries. This phenomenon deserves attention. On the one hand, developed higher education produces a wealth of high-end personnel. On the other hand, it is also easy to cause a waste of talents, or for highly educated people to engage in ordinary work. This is a typical mismatch between investment and return. It is also the improper allocation of human resources. If society does not need so many high-end personnel, there is a surplus of talent supply, and there will also be a lack of middle and low-end labor force.

Another side to human resources is health, which was very poor in China. Before 1949, the Chinese people had a low life expectancy and were severely malnourished, with weak physical strength and energy. As a result of decades of development after 1949, the average life expectancy of the Chinese people today reaches the average level of upper-middle-income countries, and this is consistent with the level of GDP per capita. However, we must be aware that there are still some people living in absolute poverty in China, whose health is bad and needs special attention.

Further, the so-called rich man's diseases are prevalent in China, such as high blood lipids and high blood sugar, which are closely associated with excessive nutritional intake. It indicates the need for a balanced diet as the Chinese people get richer. In particular, the causes of death in rural areas are the same as those for urban residents in developed countries, indicating that as rural areas develop, diseases and causes of death are also "progressing".

Notes

1 493 million in 1930 and 512 million in 1940; Hou Yangfang (2001), p. 443.
2 The "four pests" refer to mosquitoes, flies, rats, and cockroaches.
3 The "five stresses" are stress on decorum, manners, hygiene, discipline, and morals. The "four points of beauty" are beauty of the mind, language, behavior, and the environment.

168 *Conditions and causes*

4 After 1949, the state launched an anti-illiteracy campaign. The number of illiterate people who become literate each year is as follows: 657,000 in 1949, 1,372,000 in 1950, 1,375,000 in 1951, 656,000 in 1952, 2,954,000 in 1953, 2,637,000 in 1954, 3,678,000 in 1955, 7,434,000 in 1956, 7,208,000 in 1957, and 40 million in 1958. See National Bureau of Statistics, ed. (1959), p. 176.
5 By this time China's population reached more than 1 billion, up from 700 million in 1964.
6 Guan Quan (2014) conducted more international comparisons.
7 This is a judgment we made based on the experience of some countries, including Japan and China, but it remains to be confirmed by the experience of other countries.
8 *World Development Indicators 2012*.
9 *China Statistical Yearbook* over the years.

11 Technological advancement
Introduction and innovation

11.1 Introduction

Today, China possesses a vast store of modern scientific and technological knowledge and has the ability to identify the direction and prospects of technological development and to study and develop cutting-edge technologies and innovations in many fields. However, China is not at the forefront of science and technology or R&D for a host of reasons, and there are a multitude of economic, social, political, and cultural obstacles or drawbacks that impede technological progress and innovation. China is still a "semi-industrial and semi-agricultural" country[1] with imbalanced development and has yet to achieve complete industrialization. On the one hand, China has highly developed cities and high-tech industries. On the other hand, China has to improve the living standards of many poor people and ensure the employment of unskilled labor. China must pursue rapid, balanced, and sustainable development and also move with the trend of the world and the times and even stay ahead of others. This is indeed a challenge for China, as well as an opportunity, of course.

China lagged far behind developed countries in terms of science and technology before 1949. As a result, China's economic development lagged, the people's living standards were low, and China was even bulliedl as one of the least developed countries. The famous Needham puzzle was very obvious at the time. Due to a low level of science and technology and a weak economy, China could not show its former glory. After decades of hard work since 1949, China has made sizable progress, ranking among the world's best in terms of ordinary civilian technology and keeping up with developed countries stride for stride in many high-end fields. China's economic development has been largely underpinned by these achievements. Today's achievements would be impossible without the progress and application of science as well as technology. Although China still lags behind the developed countries in some areas, it has the capabilities to catch up.

11.2 Technology introduction

11.2.1 Assistance from the Soviet Union

In the early days of economic development, China lacked the funds to develop modern industry due to a shortage of domestic savings, and it was also difficult to

DOI: 10.4324/9781003410393-14

innovate because of the lack of technological accumulation. In view of these problems, it was often necessary to bring in foreign investment and technology. This chapter mainly focuses on the introduction of technology, while foreign investment will be discussed later in this book. The introduction of technology after 1949 began with the so-called 156 major projects aided by the Soviet Union during the first Five-Year Plan period.[2] These enterprises or factories contributed tremendously to the industrialization and modernization of the People's Republic of China by laying the foundation. Many enterprises later became giants or leaders in their respective fields.

Regarding the Soviet Union aid program, the energy and military sectors occupied a key position, followed by machinery and metallurgical sectors and then the chemical industry. The light industry and pharmaceutical industry accounted for a small proportion. It can be seen that China was primarily short of energy at the time, particularly the coal industry (25) and the power industry (25). The oil industry (2) was not the mainstream at that time. In the metallurgical sector, there were more nonferrous metal sectors (13) than steel sectors (7).[3] Although the steel sector was the basis of industry, the nonferrous metal sector also supported half of the industry. The machinery sector is the core of industrialization, including a variety of machine tools, industrial machinery, and precision instruments. Industrialization would be just empty talk without an advanced machinery sector. The chemical sector is also a key basic industry. Inorganic chemistry (acid, alkali, and salt), petrochemical engineering, material chemical engineering, fertilizers and pesticides, rubber, chemical fibers, coatings, additives, daily-use chemicals, etc. are materials and raw materials indispensable for industrial production. The military industry was particularly important in the context of the international environment at that time.

First, China's military industry was fragile shortly after the founding of the People's Republic of China, which could be felt from wars. Second, in the Cold War period when the world's two major camps were at loggerheads, hostilities might have broken out at any time. Third, as a big country, China had to build armed forces with relatively advanced equipment. China's military sector at that time could hardly support this goal. The 44 military projects are divided into the following fields: 16 for weapons, 12 for aviation, 10 for electronics, 4 for ships, and 2 for aerospace. We can more or less gain a glimpse of China's military industry today from this structure.

Table 11.1 outlines the nonmilitary projects aided by the Soviet Union. From the standpoint of sectors, heavy industries such as coal, nonferrous metals, machinery, chemical engineering, and steel were the core, while there were only a few projects in the light industry and pharmaceutical sectors. It shows that the heavy industry was the focus at the time and that these industries were woefully inadequate in China. In terms of construction time, the vast majority were completed within 10 years, and individual projects were not completed until the late 1960s due to the exit of experts and funds by the Soviet Union.[4] From the perspective of investment funds, the steel sector came first, followed by machinery and electric power. The nonferrous metals and coal sectors also had a considerable proportion. These industries with economies of scale require huge investment. The newly added production capacity is for reference only because this indicator cannot explain the different industries. As it varied greatly from industry to industry, it is difficult to make a direct comparison. Apart from the small number of projects in the pharmaceutical sector and light industry, these had lower production capacity than heavy industry. Another factor not shown here is the siting. Most of the projects were located in the northern and coastal regions, such as Harbin, Qiqihar, Jilin, Changchun, Shenyang, Fushun, Baotou, Xi'an, Luoyang, Taiyuan, Lanzhou, Chengdu, Wuhan, and Zhuzhou. Nearly half (50) of the 106 civilian industries were located in northeast China and 32 in central China. Thirty-five out of the 44 national defense industries were located in the central and western regions and 21 in Sichuan and Shaanxi provinces.[5]

The construction of these projects was accompanied by the transfer of technology, including complete equipment and some devices, as well as the training of technical personnel. According to statistics, the technologies imported from the Soviet Union and Eastern European countries in the 1950s include 420 pieces of complete equipment (including 257 completed) and 152 individual workshops or devices (including 110 completed).[6] Moreover, the Soviet Union furnished a great number of technical data, including factory and product design drawings, process designs, and so on. According to statistics for 1957 alone, there were 3,646 pieces of complete equipment, including manufacturing drawings for 2,207 pieces of machinery and equipment, 751 capital construction designs, and 688 pieces of process descriptions.[7] In addition, the Soviet Union trained thousands of Chinese technical personnel and donated a wealth of science and technology books. More importantly, the introduction of these technologies improved China's technical

Table 11.1 Construction of key projects aided by the Soviet Union

Industry (number of projects)	Construction time	Total investment (10,000 yuan)	Newly added production capacity
Coal (25)	1950–1961	145,804	31.45 million metric tons, 7 million cubic meters
Electricity (25)	1951–1960	224,496	2,986,500 kWh
Oil (2)	1956–1959	36,885	1.7 million metric tons
Nonferrous metals (11)	1952–1962	175,684	467,700 metric tons
Iron and steel (7)	1952–1962	566,344	16.7175 million metric tons
Chemical engineering (7)	1954–1960	108,323	577,400 metric tons
Machinery (24)	1952–1962	283,588	–
Light industry (1)	1953–1957	10,199	50,000 metric tons, 60,000 square meters
Pharmaceuticals (2)	1954–1958	9,542	16,400 metric tons

Data source: Department of Fixed Asset Investment Statistics, National Bureau of Statistics, (1987) pp. 196–205.

Note: The projects also include 44 military projects. As there are no data, these are not shown here. The data on Jiangxi tungsten ore is daily output, totaling 5,026 metric tons per day. Therefore, it is not counted. The units of production capacity of the machinery sector are different, and therefore production capacity is not shown here.

level, and many industrial enterprises were born as a result. In other words, Chinese technicians mastered relevant technologies through study, digestion and imitation and were capable of independently designing and manufacturing many industrial projects. During the First Five-Year Plan period, the machinery sector developed more than 4,000 new products on the basis of imported technology and mapping imitation. Regarding the equipment needed for 156 projects, 52.3 percent were manufactured by Chinese manufacturing plants, and most of the domestically manufactured products and pieces of equipment were made according to Soviet drawings. For example, the Nanjing Automobile Manufacturing Plant imitated the Soviet GAZ 51 2.5-ton truck, and Hongdu Machinery Factory produced the M72 motorcycle produced by the Soviet Union in the early 1950s. Chinese experts also designed and manufactured products based on Soviet technology. In 1957, Harbin Electric Factory designed 10,000-kW hydropower equipment; three major power equipment plants in Shanghai designed 2,500 kW, 6,000 kW, and 12,000 kW steam turbine generator units on the basis of Czechoslovakian drawings; the Dalian Rolling Stock Factory designed 1–5–1 large freight locomotives.[8]

It is also noteworthy that there was the role for Soviet experts because technology transfer requires technical know-how. It would be impossible without professional technicians. Statistics on the number of Soviet experts are unclear. Some studies conducted in the 1960s showed that there were a total of 11,000 experts, while others said that 8,000 Soviet and Eastern European experts came to work in China. The Soviet Union estimated that about 8,500 experts were sent to work in China from 1950 to 1960, and another 1,500 experts worked in the fields of science, education, health, culture, and so on.[9]

11.2.2 Import from Western countries

After 1960, China had no choice but to achieve self-reliance and to establish and work to adjust its foreign policy, and it tried to expand trade with European countries and the United States in an attempt to import advanced technology from these countries. In 1962, China imported the first set of vinylon equipment from Japan. From 1963 to 1966, it signed a contract worth US$280 million with Japan, Britain, France, Italy, the Federal Republic of Germany, and other countries and imported complete equipment and standalone equipment from Eastern European countries for a consideration of US$22 million. Although these facilities were of a small and medium size, they filled a gap. For example, vinylon, synthetic ammonia, polyethylene, fertilizers, oil, and other projects did a lot to ensure that people were warmly clad. Alloy steel smelting, special steel rolling, basic chemical engineering, and so on also played a key role.

According to statistics, China introduced 55 pieces of complete equipment from Western and Eastern European countries (including France, Japan, Switzerland, Italy, the Federal Republic of Germany, the Netherlands, Britain, Sweden, Austria, Poland, Czechoslovakia, and the German Democratic Republic) from 1963 to 1968, covering oil and gas extraction (2), textiles (1), papermaking and paper products (1), printing (1), electricity, gas and water supply (3), petroleum refining (2), chemistry (8), chemical fibers (2), plastic products (1), building materials (2), ferrous metal smelting and processing (9), nonferrous metal smelting and processing (4), machinery (7), transport equipment (1), electronic and communication equipment (9), instruments and measuring instruments (1), and science and technology (1).[10] It is worth mentioning that in terms of industry and profession, it had greater diversity than the 156 projects aided by the Soviet Union, primarily some emerging categories, such as chemical fiber, plastics, electronic and communication equipment, and instrumentation, as well as many traditional industries, such as printing, papermaking, textiles, and building materials.

The introduction of technologies after the 1970s took place mainly as a result of improved relations with major developed Western countries. After 1972, China successively forged or resumed diplomatic relations with major Western countries. As relations improved, China introduced some complete equipment from the Netherlands, France, Japan, and other countries. Petrochemical and chemical fiber enterprises greatly improved China's production capacity and level in these areas. China then launched the reform and opening up a few years afterward. The projects introduced earlier laid the foundation and gained experience for the subsequent introduction of foreign investment and technology.

Table 11.2 shows the overview of 26 and 22 pieces of technologies introduced from Western countries in 1972 and 1978, respectively. The industries include electric power, metallurgy, chemical engineering, light industry, textiles, coal, petroleum, electronics, etc. The chemical sector had the largest number of projects, primarily fertilizers and chemical fibers, as well as other chemical materials. The introduction of these projects well complemented these important industrial sectors, and China improved in terms of both technology and management. In particular, these projects were mostly introduced from developed Western countries, exceeding the level of Soviet-aided projects as a whole. These were basically the most advanced equipment at the time, providing key materials for China's technological progress in these spheres.

Table 11.3 shows the introduction of equipment from 1950 to 1985. The proportion of imported equipment on the left shows the proportion of imported equipment among all equipment. The chemical fiber is the highest, accounting for over 52 percent, indicating that this industry was a completely new industry, based on equipment import. It was followed by plastics as well as electronic and communication equipment sector, which accounted for more than 38 percent and more than 37 percent, respectively. These two industries were emerging industries after World War II, and China had to rely on just imports. Except metallurgy, other industries did not account for more than 20 percent, but most of them were close to 20 percent. Only machinery had a low proportion because this industry involves many categories, and some categories are simple and do not require imports. In terms of the equipment introduced, the most advanced equipment in the 1980s accounted for about one-third on average (with that of the central region as the average). It is worth noting that the proportion of light industry was far higher than that of heavy industry because light industrial equipment was relatively simple and cheap. Some light industries are emerging industries, such as electronics and plastics, and

174 *Conditions and causes*

Table 11.2 Complete projects introduced in 1972 and 1978

Industry (number of projects)	Origin country of imports	Construction time	Total investment (10,000 yuan)	Newly added production capacity
1972 (26 projects)				
Electric power (3)	Italy, Japan, France, Switzerland	1973–1979	141,739	1.69 million kWh
Metallurgy (2)	Japan, the Federal Republic of Germany	1972–1980	276,800	7.08 million metric tons
Chemistry (16)	Japan, the Federal Republic of Germany, the United States, the Netherlands, France	1969–1980	822,675	10.47 million metric tons
Light industry (1)	Italy	1976–1981	26,875	75,000 metric tons
Textile (4)	Japan, the Federal Republic of Germany, France, Italy	1972–1977	731,548	588,000 metric tons, 36,000 kWh
1978 (22 projects)				
Coal (3)	Federal Republic of Germany	1977–1984	81,132	36 million metric tons
Oil (2)	Japan, Britain, the Federal Republic of Germany	1978–	365,309	600,000 metric tons
Metallurgy (3)	Japan, the Federal Republic of Germany, Italy, Finland	1978–1983	1,411,024	19.3 million metric tons
Chemistry (8)	Japan, the Federal Republic of Germany, the Netherlands	1977–1985	380,192	5.625 million metric tons
Light industry (2)	The Federal Republic of Germany and Japan	1980–1985	92,519	80,000 metric tons, 3 million square meters
Textile (3)	The Federal Republic of Germany, Japan, and Britain	1979–1982	346,603	1.253 million metric tons
Electronics (1)	Japan, Switzerland, Italy	1978–1982	71,103	960,000 pieces

Data source: Department of Fixed Asset Investment Statistics, National Bureau of Statistics (1987) pp. 206–211.

Note: The construction time is the earliest commencement time and the latest completion time of each project.

imported technologies accounted for a high proportion. Factory equipment in the 1970s had a slightly higher proportion than that in the 1980s, accounting for 40 percent based on the central region average, which was not bad for 1985. The equipment produced before the 1970s is about one-fourth based on the standard of the central region and was primarily imported during the Soviet aid period.

Table 11.3 Introduction of equipment from 1950 to 1985, Unit: %

Industry	Proportion of imported equipment	Shipped in the 1980s	Shipped in the 1970s	Shipped before the 1970s
Total	18.5	40.4	36.7	22.9
Light industry	19.0	65.6	26.6	7.8
Heavy industry	18.4	32.6	39.8	27.6
Energy	17.7	32.0	38.6	29.4
Metallurgy	25.3	36.2	38.5	25.3
Machinery	14.6	27.4	35.3	37.3
Electronic and communication equipment	37.7	73.0	20.1	6.9
Chemistry	19.6	18.9	66.4	14.7
Chemical fibers	52.2	44.6	50.7	4.7
Plastics	38.2	91.4	6.1	2.5
Textiles	18.2	70.1	21.2	8.7
Eastern region	20.1	47.5	35.1	17.4
Central region	17.2	34.2	40.3	25.5
Western region	16.7	27.5	35.1	37.4

Data source: Office of the State Council Leading Group for Industrial Census, Economic Research Institute of the State Development Planning Commission (1990), p. 124.

After the reform and opening up, China began to implement the strategy of "inviting in and going global". The former means hiring foreign experts and attracting foreign investment, while the latter means sending students and trainees abroad for study. In order to invite foreign experts to China to give lectures or guide work in the early days of reform and opening up, the Chinese government provided preferential treatment, built expert buildings or hotels for long-term rental, and dedicated personnel to serve the experts. China has so far sent millions of students abroad for study, and the number of trainees is innumerable.[11] These students and technicians had acquired advanced know-how in foreign universities or picked up skills at enterprises, having made key contributions to the development of education and enterprises after the reform and opening up. They carry and disseminate knowledge and skills, contribute to China's economic development, and impart knowledge and skills to students and younger workers, so that China's personnel who master modern science and technology as well as knowledge are comprehensively improved.

Figure 11.1 is based on the modified model summarized by Japanese scholars for imported technologies.[12] What mainly sets China and Japan apart is that Japan rarely introduced the most advanced technologies, while making improvements on traditional technologies and directly introducing compromised or intermediate technologies (B_2B_2) were more common practices. In contrast, although China has traditional technologies, the direct introduction of the most advanced or relatively advanced technologies was dominant due to the large gap with foreign countries, and the Japanese approach (form intermediate technologies through the

176 *Conditions and causes*

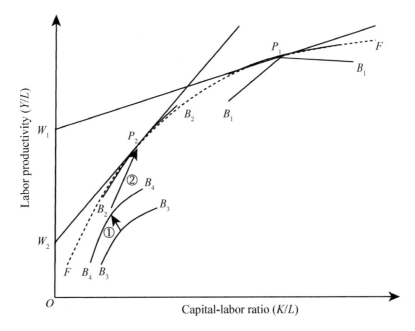

Figure 11.1 Types of technologies imported by China
Note: Improved according to Ryoshin Minami (1981).

modification of imported technologies) was rarely used in China. The figure shows two main differences between China and Japan. First, the gap between the level (distance) of traditional technology (B_3B_3) and the imported technology (B_1B_1) is larger. Second, the gap between technology achieved through improvement and the imported technology is relatively large. In other words, B_4B_4 is not as good as B_2B_2, and what is reflected in the figure is the direction of the arrow (1). That is to say, the gap between traditional technology and modified technology is small, and the gap between the two and the imported technology is relatively large. However, this was mainly the case during the planned economy period. This situation vastly changed after the reform and opening up. As a result of the introduction of foreign investment and the improvement of China's technological level, China moved closer to the situation of Japan, as shown by the movement from B_4B_4 to B_2B_2 [arrow (2) direction] in the figure. Of course, due to the presence of foreign investment and the imported technology, there is still much high-level technology B_1B_1. This diversified pattern with traditional technology as well as advanced technology and compromised technology reflects the current technological system in China.

11.3 Technological innovation

The issue of technological innovation in China's industrial sector should also be discussed based on two periods: the planned economy period and the reform and opening up period. During the planned economy period, China had little dealings with Western developed countries, there was no direct exchange in science and technology fields, and their technology trading market was not open to China. As a result, it was impossible for China to directly acquire state-of-the-art technology from Western developed countries and had to resort to other means. The first way was to obtain these from the Soviet Union and Eastern European countries. These technologies were inferior to those of the Western developed countries but were still better than those of China. The most important technology introduction was 156 major projects. The second way was independent exploration and R&D. By accumulating experience, "learning by doing", and launching the movement-style huge-crowd strategy, China made some achievements, although these were low-level. Despite the fact that the overall technical level was backward, and the system and institutions hampered technological progress during the planned economy period, it was also quite successful though with Chinese characteristics. Mass technological innovation and transformation movements were ongoing. "Levering collective wisdom" and "brainstorming" were popular slogans at that time.

After the reform and opening up, China's technological progress was more attributed to the introduction of technologies from Western developed countries and the realization of technological spillover effects by attracting foreign investment. This effect echoed the domestic market-oriented reforms, creating a symphony for today's technological progress. That is to say, China had the capacity to absorb these advanced technologies. Coupled with the sense of competition and mechanism as a result of marketization, there are sufficient conditions for China's economic and technological progress. From another perspective, many conditions had to be met to create advanced technology, such as technical understanding, manufacturing possibility, and flexible application. Without these capabilities, the technology would be useless. Many developing countries are in this state, but China has long ago addressed this unfavorable situation. China's goal is catching up with the developed countries and competing with then on an equal footing. That is, China must conduct innovation and research and development to lead the world. China has made great strides in this regard.

Table 11.4 shows the situation of patent applications and handling. The total number of patent applications handled from 1990 to 2018 shot up, from more than 40,000 in 1990 to more than 80,000 in 1995, 170,000 in 2000, more than 470,000 in 2005, and 4.323 million in 2018, an increase of more than 100 times in less than three decades. It basically doubled every 5 years, and the number in 2018 increased by 24 times compared with 2000, which indicates accelerating technological progress. The gap between domestic and foreign invention patents in 1990 was tiny, but the number of domestic invention patents in 2018 was already 9 times that of foreign countries.

In terms of domestic inventions, enterprises replaced colleges and universities as well as research institutes as the principal inventors. Back in 1990, scientific research institutes filed far more invention applications than enterprises. That changed by the end of the 1990s and is now totally different. Enterprises have now become the main force in technology R&D and innovation in China. This is a commendable situation because research institutes usually focus on research

178　Conditions and causes

Table 11.4 Number of domestic and foreign patent applications and authorized patents

Index	Number of applications (pieces)				Number of authorized patents (pieces)			
	1990	2000	2010	2018	1990	2000	2010	2018
Total	41,469	170,682	1,222,286	4,323,112	22,588	105,345	814,825	2,447,460
Invention	10,137	51,747	391,177	1,542,002	3,838	12,683	135,110	432,147
Domestic	5,832	25,346	293,066	1,393,815	1,149	6,177	79,767	345,959
Job-related	2,482	12,609	223,754	1,202,100	908	2,824	66,149	322,776
Colleges and universities	509	1942	48,294	226,628	326	652	19,036	74,893
Research institutes	805	2,228	18,254	57,959	331	910	6557	20,508
Enterprises	816	8,316	154,581	896,648	206	1016	40,049	222,287
Government bodies	352	123	2,625	20,865	45	246	507	5,088
Nonjob-related	3,350	12,737	69,312	191,715	241	3,353	13,618	23,183
Foreign	4,305	26,401	98,111	148,187	2,689	6,506	55,343	86,188
Job-related	4,018	25,334	95,517	145,359	2,496	6,222	54,169	85,021
Non-job-related	287	1,067	2,594	2,828	193	284	1,174	1,167

Data source: China Statistical Yearbook over the years.

Note: In addition to invention patents, the total covers utility models and design patents, which are not listed here.

theories and principles, are geared to academic areas, and are therefore not necessarily suitable for the market. Enterprises mainly produce highly applicable products or production equipment and processes, and their innovation achievements are important for boosting corporate competitiveness and spurring economic growth. An interesting fact is that colleges and universities have more achievements than research institutes, indicating that colleges and universities have performed better in the connection between industry and universities, while research institutes are lagging somewhat. Of course, there are far more colleges and universities than research institutes. This situation also basically goes for the granting of invention patents. It is just that license inventions are fewer than the total, accounting for only 17.7 percent of the total in 2018, whereas invention patents accounted for 35.7 percent of the total in terms of the number of applications. This shows either that there are more utility models and design patents in terms of the number of authorized patents or that the examination of invention patents is more stringent.

As just shown, although China has made great achievements in technological innovation, it lags far behind the most developed countries regarding science and technology levels as well as in industrial production capacity. This is primarily manifested in the following respects: First, the foundation of science and technology is relatively backward, and the experimental equipment and scientific research funds are relatively inadequate. Despite considerable improvements in this situation over the years, scientific research and technological R&D require huge investment. Second, the institutions and mechanisms of scientific research are still not competitive and rational. Enterprises have made rapid progress in R&D in recent years, but that progress lags far behind the process of China's economy as a whole. We still need to solve the issues of how to apply the research results of research institutes and universities in the market and how to establish individual invention and social funding systems. Third, the allocation of human resources remains to be addressed. Many highly competent university graduates and graduate students are not willing to engage in scientific research but prefer to work at government bodies and engage in work unrelated to their professions. This is a serious waste of human resources.

11.4 Conclusion

Compared with other countries, there are both similarities and differences in the relationship between China's technological progress and economic development. In terms of similarity, technological progress largely determines the process of economic development, which promotes technological progress. In terms of difference, China's course of development and system are unique. China's economic development and technological progress is a tortuous process. Its unique system has also affected China's technological advance and economic development.

China's technological progress primarily relied on imports from the Soviet Union and Eastern European countries for a long time after 1949. These technologies and equipment laid the groundwork for China's economic recovery and industrialization of heavy industry and also offered a basic guarantee for technological advance after the reform and opening up. In addition to the technological progress caused by the freed productive forces and the introduction of foreign investment, the industrial base and human resources from the planned economy period were also indispensable for China to achieve extraordinarily rapid development after the reform and opening up. This is clear from some comparisons with other developing countries. India and Vietnam also operate open policies and have imported Western technology and attracted foreign investment, but they lag far behind China. One of the main reasons is that the industrial bases of these two countries are weaker. Cambodia, the Philippines, Indonesia, and other countries have also adopted an open policy, but the economy grows slowly due to weaker domestic accumulation (industry and personnel).

Of course, more important is the large-scale introduction of foreign investment and technology after the reform and opening up, which has considerably spurred China's technological advance and economic development. This can be validated by the rapid development of light industry, which was previously ignored, and can also be explained by the emerging industrial sector. Despite the fact that China developed the light textile sector in order to provide the basic necessities for 5 to 1 billion plus people (1949–1980) during the planned economy period, the light textile industry could only provide basic necessities, and there was also no great improvement in quality. After the reform and opening up, the textile industry not only fully meets the needs of the Chinese people but also exports a wealth of products. China even becomes the world's largest producer of a full variety of products, such as textiles and household appliances. Emerging industries thrive.

180 *Conditions and causes*

For example, electronics, communications, aviation, and the universe sectors have achieved a quantum leap and gained a foothold for China in the world. More importantly, in the process of introducing, digesting, and absorbing technology, China has amassed much experience and cultivated a wealth of talented people who can conduct creative work in all fields.

Notes

1 Due to the household registration system, more than half of China's population today is still rural, and China's real urbanization rate is not high.
2 It is usually said that there were 156 major projects, but 150 were actually implemented. See Zhang Baichun et al. (2004) and Dong Zhikai and Wu Jiang (2004).
3 Zhang Baichun et al. (2004), p. 75.
4 Zhang Baichun et al. (2004), pp. 83–87.
5 Zhang Baichun et al. (2004), p. 76.
6 Zhang Baichun et al. (2004), p. 89.
7 Zhang Baichun et al. (2004), p. 91.
8 Zhang Baichun et al. (2004), pp. 93–94.
9 Zhang Baichun et al. (2004), pp. 319–320.
10 Zhang Baichun et al. (2004), pp. 394–400.
11 For the Chinese students sent abroad for further studies, see *China Education Statistical Yearbook*.
12 For the model of technology introduced by Japan, it was first proposed by Akira Ono and later improved by Ryoshin Minami. See Akira Ono (1979), Ono (1986), and Ryoshin Minami (1981).

12 Institution building

Government and market

12.1 Introduction

Like many developing countries, China has also experienced a long-term arduous exploration of institution building, which can be called a process of trial and error. Unlike today's developed countries, China was previously a semicolonial and semifeudal society, indicating that China must start from scratch in every respect. Moreover, the disintegrated state and the deprivation of means of survival in modern China worsened the suffering and hardships of the country.

Some countries that were previously colonies only have the oral language without their own script and now still use English or other strong languages for communication due to the long-term rule of the big powers and colonizers, as well as due to their own history and culture and poor economic development. As a result, these countries and peoples lack self-esteem and self-confidence, so much so that it is difficult to concentrate national spirit and strength to develop the economy and achieve social progress. The institution building of these countries is either fully copied from (and sometimes imposed by) the developed Western countries or has retrograded to the traditional tribal state. For example, the upper classes of some developing countries were fostered by colonial-era suzerains. The upper classes living in a few prosperous cities speak fluent foreign languages, are well educated, and enjoy high positions and large incomes, whereas the vast majority of the populace live in traditional backward rural areas, lack enough food to eat, receive no formal education, have no modern consciousness, and are accustomed to being ruled.[1]

The situation in China is slightly better. First, China has a long history and profound cultural traditions, which cannot be wholly negated by some aggressors, although some of China's traditions are not necessarily suited to modern society. Second, China did not become a colony of the Western powers. Moreover, China learned and integrated the modern (Western) spirit in the long-term struggle. Nevertheless, it must be acknowledged that many negative factors existed in China in modern times. First of all, the long-term feudal society resulted in practices that were contrary to modern ideas, such as resigning oneself to adversity, and there was a lack of the spirit of individuality and independence. Second, some people were at a loss when confronted with the powerful technological and military power

DOI: 10.4324/9781003410393-15

of the Western powers and believed that they could not compete with the West. Two extreme ideas were also held in China at that time for various reasons: self-conceit and an inferiority complex. How come China, a large country with a long history, lagged behind others in modern times? The Chinese people have long been puzzled by this problem. Chinese went to great lengths to seek a path to rapid development and has also put in huge efforts and paid a price.

12.2 Government and markets

12.2.1 General discussion

After 1949, China implemented socialism politically and the planned economy economically, with the salient feature of socialist public ownership of the means of production. In rural areas, the people's commune system was implemented, with the three levels of communes, production brigades, and production teams. The members worked for remuneration, and workpoints were record every day and were settled at the end of the year. The vast majority of the labor in cities worked in governments, public institutions, state-run enterprises, and collective enterprises and received wages. In order to gradually build socialism, a low wage system had been in place for a long time, and benefits other than wages were provided by employers. In brief, guided by the idea of public ownership, individuals basically had no property, except daily articles. Their wage income was only enough for basic living expenses. Rural residents had their own houses and a plot of land for growing crops such as vegetables for their own consumption, but the land could not be traded. In economic terms, this means a lack of property right or the right to dispose of possessions. Farmers had no right to dispose of the land, and urban residents had no right to dispose of housing. Both agricultural products and industrial products were centrally purchased and distributed under the administration of relevant government bodies, and individuals had no right to buy and sell goods. Violation would constitute the crime of speculation and market disturbance, and violators would be sentenced to prison or labor-based reform.[2]

This planned economic system based on public ownership and unclear property rights caused serious inefficiencies and inflexibility. Due to a lack of an incentive mechanism, people thought that good and bad performance was treated equally, and they would engage in slow going. As a result, products were of poor quality, there was no innovation mechanism, and products were not upgraded for a long periods. Externally, as there was no market to allocate resources, goods and services could not realize value on the market, capital and labor as factors of production could not flow smoothly, and land could not be circulated. Because there was no financial institution as the regulator of funds, individuals and enterprises could not take out loans to invest and could only turn to the state for much needed funds. As a result, people became passively reliant on the state, causing a serious obstacle to entrepreneurship and innovation.

In view of this situation, the government put forward the policy of reform and opening up in 1978, which introduced market mechanisms, cancelled public ownership, and allowed people to own and use personal property to invest in order to obtain earnings. The establishment of the securities market, the creation of commercial banks, the dissolution of people's communes, the restructuring of state-owned enterprises and collective enterprises, the formation of the price mechanism, the introduction of foreign investment, the amendment and formulation of laws, etc. are all the achievements of system building. These have greatly promoted economic development and social progress.

Corresponding conditions must be satisfied to ensure the effective operation of the market mechanism. Some conditions involve laws, such as whether privately owned property is lawful, which property can be privately owned, whether the possession has legal effect, and whether property can be transferred (traded) in the market. The market operation also requires people's integrity, which calls for both legal provisions and people's self-consciousness. The law may specify penalties. Breach of contract, frauds, monopoly, rent seeking, etc. must be penalized and perpetrators held accountable. Achieving self-consciousness is more difficult than enacting and observing laws because it requires long-term trial and error and the process of learning the rules of the market. There seems to be no constraints on the market, and you can do what you like. However, it is a bad market if this is the case. A well functioning market should have rules, which must be observed by all. In addition to the rules, people's integrity is also important. China still has a long way to go in terms of both laws and self-consciousness in this regard.

More than 40 years of practice have proved China's reform and opening up policy a success, which should be primarily attributed to the market. In other words, many of the mechanisms under the planned economy that should have been regulated by the market were controlled by the government and planning, but the market role has now been restored. In other words, the government now plays the due roles of managing public resources and formulating policies, as well as monitoring and regulating market mechanisms.

Before China implemented economic restructuring, there had been a strange long-term phenomenon that, if the power was concentrated in the hands of the government or relevant departments, the market mechanism would fail, causing inefficiency. This link of examination and approval has always existed in China, affecting setting up businesses, film and television works, and cadres going abroad. It should be said that examination and approval are necessary in some areas. Some projects that are prone to cause environmental pollution or endanger public safety must go through rigorous approval or review. However, there are also problems of excessive examination and approval and improper examination and approval. "Excessive examination and approval" refers to the situation by which something that can be simply solved involves too complicated procedures and too many departments. "Improper examination and approval" refers to the situation in which some important projects are reviewed by certain government bodies but should have been reviewed by the people's congress.

However, with relaxed regulations and decentralized power, the market indeed will play a role and the efficiency will increase. Nevertheless, it will lead to chaos, such as unauthorized charges, indiscriminate prescriptions, arbitrary fines, and uncontrolled counterfeit and shoddy products. The market originally has the capacity to allocate resources. For example, an increase in pork price means that pork is in short supply, perhaps because pig raisers feel that the price of pork is too low and the price of feed is too high or because there are too many intermediaries. In a sound and perfectly competitive market, there is no monopoly and information asymmetry, or the government does not intervene in price administration. If feed prices are high but normal, it indicates a shortage of feed and a short supply. Unless the price is artificially raised, the relationship between supply and demand can be improved by importing more feed, or pig raisers can increase the price of pork to absorb the rising costs caused by the rising price of raw materials. Pork consumer with limited income can reduce the consumption of pork. Pork can also be imported to increase the supply, thus reducing the price of pork. There is also the possibility that more people join the pig industry because pig raising is profitable, and so on. In brief, the market will react in different ways to make it return to normal levels. However, if there is monopoly or if there are excessive intermediate links, especially in the form of government control, it may disrupt the market. Some people forfeit honor at the sight of money, selling the pork of diseased pigs or making it into meat products. Without strict supervision, public health and safety incidents will occur, upsetting the normal operation of the market as well as harming consumers' trust in the market.

Why did this occur in the early days of economic structural reform? We must start with China's system and habits. First, as a result of the long-term implementation of the planned economy and model, the government and administrators became accustomed to acting as regulators of the market. They believe that all decisions made by the government are correct and should be welcomed by the general public. The more entrenched this idea becomes, the more prone they are to "manage" rather than "decentralize". Second, because China's market economy is not yet perfect and developed, some information is known only to the government but not to the populace, which causes information asymmetry. Third, when the government makes a bad decision or the government believes that it should not be excessively controlled, it will decentralize. In this case, it is prone to cause market chaos because, when the mechanism and principles of the market, as well as the guidelines that should be observed, are not fully known, many people will feel that the market is a place where they can do as they wish. It is rarely realized that the market is a serious environment with high demands. The market, if improperly handled, will not only hurt others but also you.

12.2.2 Interpretation in economic terms

We try to explain in economic terms the transformation of China's economy after 1949. Figure 12.1 shows this transformation, with the horizontal axis representing the production of consumer goods (X) and the vertical axis representing the production of capital goods (Y). China was basically an agrarian country in the early 1950s. It can be considered a country that primarily produced consumer goods, and only a few resources were used to produce capital goods.

Institution building 185

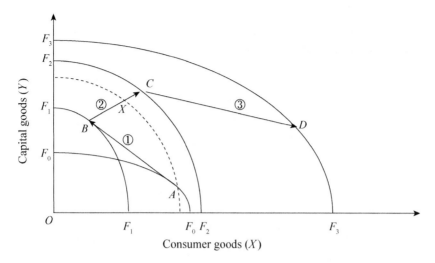

Figure 12.1 Institutional transformation after 1949

After 1952, the socialist transformation of capitalist industry and commerce began. Coupled with the cooperative movement and the people's commune movement in rural areas, China's economy moved toward public ownership within a few years (1953–1957), as shown by the movement of the arrow (1) in the figure. That is to say, it moved from the original point A to point B. It mainly produced consumer goods but now mainly produces capital goods, that is, the shift of the production possibility curve from F_0F_0 to F_1F_1. This transformation is mainly due to two starting points. First, since China embraced socialism, it is theoretically necessary to adopt public ownership, mainly referring to the Soviet system at that time. Second, in order to catch up with the developed capitalist countries as soon as possible, it was necessary to concentrate resources, especially capital goods, such as increasing the output of heavy industry.

This system lasted until around 1978, when the reform and opening up were initiated. Good economic growth was also achieved during this period, manifested as the direction of the arrow (2) in the figure. The production possibility curve expanded from F_1F_1 to F_2F_2, and moved from point B to point C. This expansion followed the original practice with capital goods as the core. After the reform and opening up, China changed the development strategy, focused more on the consumer goods sector, and returned to the original state of resource endowment. Because resources were effectively allocated, economic growth picked up speed. Shown in the figure is a change in the arrow (3), with the production point moving from point C to point D. It is worth noting that because of production inefficiency and unreasonable allocation of resources, the changes in the planned economy period probably did not reach point C but stayed at point X. It is shown as being inside the theoretical production possibility curve F_2F_2, or the part covered by the dotted line.

China's institution building, the relationship between the government and the market, and the fiscal system issues have been examined, leading to the following conclusions. First, China's institution building involves many aspects. Despite great progress, it is still necessary to put in a considerable amount of time and effort. This is primarily related to China's politics, economy, society, and culture and cannot be achieved in a short time. Furthermore, institution building must be carried out simultaneously with economic and social development, and adjustments and revision must be constantly made in this process. Second, the relationship between the government and the market is more complex in China than in other countries. Unlike other developing countries, China experienced a period of planned economy, and Chinese people are unconsciously inclined to rely on the government and are not used to the market, or they do not understand the basic principles of the market. The market is not so simple. It requires people to observe the rules and have integrity and also must be supervised by the government or third parties, especially under the protection of laws. China still has shortcomings in this regard.

12.3 Reform of ownership

12.3.1 From dispersion to concentration

The change in ownership as the main entity of economic activities is discussed here. For China, the core is the issue of state-owned enterprises. The problems of state-owned enterprises are well known in China and one of the key areas of reform. After 1949, China's economic resources were allocated according to planning rather than in a market-oriented manner under the idea of public ownership and the planned economy. During the planned economy period, the allocation of resources had to be thoroughly controlled by the planning authorities, and even the production and sales of a screw had to be arranged by planning departments at all levels. If an enterprise needed 500 metric tons of steel per year, it must apply to the higher-level planning department, which would approve it if it deemed the allocation necessary. According to the approved demand for steel, the planning department issued production commands to the steelworks. If the production capacity of this steelworks was 3,000 metric tons, it also must obtain orders for the remaining 2,500 metric tons of steel from the planning department. The planning department must be clear about which plants needed steel and also know what types and models of steel were needed, such as deformed steel bars, double T-steel, angle steel, and steel plates. Because the quantity and models of steel required by each plant were reported to the planning department, and the planning department also knew which steelworks produced which type of steel, it could arrange the demand and supply of these steel products according to categories. This is a simple circular process of resource allocation under the planned economy.

Under such planning and adjustment mechanism, enterprises could only arrange production according to plans, and this led to a problem: it could not produce too many or too few because excess output could not be absorbed, and inadequate output could not meet demand. Of course, according to the Five-Year Plan set by the government, there must be an increase every year. This must be considered in the production plans of enterprises, such as ordering steelworks to produce an additional 1,000 metric tons of steel next year. In order to produce more, enterprises must install more production equipment. They must apply to the planning department to build a blast furnace and ancillary equipment. They then made investments as arranged by the planning department, and the government paid for it, or the enterprise would use part of its self-retained funds. If all of these plans were realized, there would be economic growth. This form of economic cycle could not involve the private sector because there was no economic benefit. All income was owned by the government, while employees and operators (actually managers) only received wages, with generally higher wages for operators. Private enterprise pursue maximum profits. No private capital would get involved in the absence of profits. Moreover, under the public ownership system at that time, there was no private capital to speak of. Everyone received only wages and remuneration, and there was no private property, not to mention private capital.

After years of enterprise reform, there are not many state-owned enterprises in China, but they are powerful because state-owned enterprises dominant the important sectors of the economy, such as railways, roads, communications, aviation, petroleum, mining, and other sectors. The number of private enterprises is large, but it is not easy for them to become bigger and stronger. On the one hand, it is difficult for them to enter the important sectors in which state-owned enterprises are dominant. On the other hand, they are at a disadvantage in capital, technology, management, and market experience compared with foreign-funded enterprises. Table 12.1 shows the changes in the number of employees in the period of the socialist transformation of capitalist industry and commerce after 1949, including the first Five-Year Plan period. It shows the number of employees, that is, regular employees of enterprises, excluding the rural population and labor force. In this sense, the state sector here had a high proportion from the beginning, rising from 60.7 percent in 1949 to 78.4 percent in 1957. In contrast, the proportion of the private sector fell from 37 percent in 1949 to 11.5 percent in 1955 and further down to

Table 12.1 Number of employees during the period of socialist transformation, Unit: 10,000 people (%)

Year	Total	State-run enterprises	Public–private partnership	Cooperative-run enterprises	Private enterprises
1949	800.4	485.4 (60.7)	10.5 (1.3)	8.8 (1.1)	295.7 (37.0)
1952	1580.4	1,079.7 (68.3)	25.7 (1.6)	107.7 (6.8)	367.3 (23.2)
1955	1907.6	1,440.2 (75.5)	89.9 (4.7)	158.6 (8.3)	218.9 (11.5)
1956	2423.0	1,879.4 (77.6)	352.6 (14.6)	188.2 (7.8)	2.8 (0.1)
1957	2450.6	1,921.9 (78.4)	345.7 (14.1)	180.5 (7.4)	2.5 (0.1)

Data source: Department of Social Statistics, National Bureau of Statistics (1987), p. 83.
Note: The figures in parentheses are proportions, and the total is 100.

188 *Conditions and causes*

0.1 percent in 1956 and 1957. The proportion of the public–private partnership sector, which had been negligible, initially remained at 1.3 percent or so, began to rise since 1954, and soared to 14 percent in 1956. The proportion of cooperative-run enterprises gradually rose from a negligible level to about 7 percent. This situation shows two characteristics. First, the transformation is generally geared to the private sector, with reservations for the public–private partnership and other sectors. Second, the renovation was completed rapidly in 1956 and 1957, despite previous gradual changes.

12.3.2 From concentration to dispersion

Under the planned economy, the vast majority of urban workers, with the exception of the rural labor force, worked either at state-run enterprises or collective enterprises. As we all know, state-run enterprises and collective enterprises operated under the direct intervention of the planning department and had almost no freedom. A worker who began to work in an organization could work until retirement as long as no major problems occurred. Workers had almost no room for mobility. However, this situation changed significantly after the reform and opening up. As shown in Table 12.2, there were previously only state-owned and collective enterprises. Later, organizations with new ownership systems appeared, such as companies limited by shares, private enterprises, self-employed persons, and foreign-funded enterprises. The number of employees of state-owned enterprises plunged from 76.19 percent in 1980 to only 13.22 percent in 2018, and the same figure for collective enterprises also decreased from 23.04 percent in 1980 to 0.80 percent in 2018. In contrast, the number of employees of private enterprises and the self-employed, as well as limited companies, etc. increased significantly, which together have more employees than state-owned and collective enterprises put together.[3]

More notable is the decrease in the proportion of agricultural workers and the increase in the proportion of urban workers. In other words, considerable progress has been made in urbanization. The proportion of urban workers increased from less than 25 to more than 55 percent, and the proportion of rural workers decreased from more than 75 to less than 45 percent. Although it did not change as much as that for the ownership systems of urban enterprises, significant changes actually occurred. Some clarification is needed in this regard. First, in terms of real numbers, the number of urban workers increased more than that of rural workers. The rural population far exceeds that of the urban population, and family planning restrictions were more relaxed in rural areas. The proportion of people born in rural areas should also exceed that in cities. However, the changes in the proportion of employed persons indicates that quite a few people born in rural areas have become urban workers. Second, the above statistics are based on the household registration system, rather than the actual employment. Since the reform and opening up, a wealth of rural surplus laborers has gone to work in nonagricultural sectors in cities every year. If these people are counted, the number of workers in nonagricultural sectors will increase sharply.

Table 12.2 Structure of employees by ownership

Ownership	1980	1990	2000	2010	2018
Real number (10,000 people)					
Total	42,361	64,749	72,085	76,105	77,586
Total for cities	10,525	17,041	23,151	34,687	43,417
State-owned enterprises	8,019	10,346	8,102	6,516	5,740
Collective enterprises	2,425	3,549	1,499	597	347
Limited liability companies	–	–	687	2,613	6,555
Companies limited by shares	–	–	457	1,024	1,875
Private enterprises	–	57	1,268	6,071	13,952
Hong Kong Macao and Taiwan-invested businesses	–	4	310	770	1,153
Foreign investment	–	62	332	1,053	1,212
Self-employed	81	614	2,136	4,467	10,440
Total for rural areas	31,836	47,708	48,934	41,418	34,167
Township and village enterprises	3,000	9,265	12,820	15,893	
Private enterprises	–	113	1139	3347	7424
Self-employed	–	1,491	2,934	2,540	5,597
Proportion (%)					
Total	100.00	100.00	100.00	100.00	100.00
Total for cities	24.85	26.32	32.12	45.58	55.96
State-owned enterprises	76.19	60.72	35.00	18.79	13.22
Collective enterprises	23.04	20.83	6.48	2.01	0.80
Limited liability companies	–	–	2.97	7.54	15.10
Companies limited by shares	–	–	1.98	2.96	4.32
Private enterprises	–	0.34	5.48	17.51	32.13
Hong Kong Macao and Taiwan-invested businesses	–	0.03	1.34	2.22	2.66
Foreign investment	–	0.37	1.44	3.04	2.79
Self-employed	0.77	3.61	9.23	12.88	24.05
Total for rural areas	75.16	73.69	67.89	54.43	44.04
Township and village enterprises	9.43	19.42	26.20	38.38	24.56
Private enterprises	–	0.24	2.33	8.09	21.73
Self-employed	–	3.13	6.00	6.14	16.38

Data source: *China Statistical Yearbook* over the years.

Note: For the figures in the proportion, the urban total and rural total for the total, the figures of state-owned enterprise for the urban total, and rural private enterprises and private businesses for rural total. Regarding the reform of township and village enterprises, no relevant figures have been released since 1912. In addition, stock cooperative enterprises and associated units in cities are not listed, which have 660,000 and 120,000 employees, respectively.

Another noteworthy phenomenon is the increase in the number and proportion of employees of township and village enterprises. The absolute number jumped from 30 million in 1980 to nearly 160 million in 2010, and its proportion in rural workers increased from less than 10 to more than 38 percent. This is important for China, which is a big country with a population of nearly 1.4 billion, and also has hundreds of millions of surplus laborers in rural areas. They must be employed by nonagricultural industries, and go to cities or remain in rural areas. If they remain in rural areas, township and village enterprises will play a decisive role in addressing the issue of labor employment in China as big employers. In fact, more than 280 million migrant workers and their family members face a dilemma. Because of their status, migrant workers, as well as their family members face uncertainty in terms of schooling, healthcare, housing and other social security areas. Medical treatment is more costly in the city than in the rural areas. If a migrant worker gets sick in the city, they hardly afford the high fees. Moreover, many migrant workers leave their children behind in rural areas. Because these children are separated from their parents for a long time, it has a higher negative impact on children's growth, and also increases the living expenses and spiritual burden on migrant workers.

In addition to restrictions imposed by household registration system, migrant workers can oftentimes only engage in simple jobs in construction, catering, security, sanitation, and other sectors due to their limited schooling and experience. Moreover, they have to return to rural areas when they are old or get sick. Although township and village enterprises adopt backward production technology and require a heavy dangerous workload for low wages, they are a key supplementary force for employing rural surplus labor. Even if the household registration system restrictions in large cities are completely lifted, the flow of hundreds of millions of people (labor force and their family members) to cities would be unimaginable. Therefore, more secondary and tertiary industries in small and medium-sized cities are needed to employ rural surplus labor, and township and village enterprises can play a greater role in more areas.

12.4 Conclusion

China's institution building, the relationship between the government and the market, and the problems of fiscal system and state-owned enterprises are examined above. The following conclusions can be drawn: First, China's institution building underwent great changes, with the government holding overall planning power in the early period (planned economy period). Even in the later period (after the reform and opening up), the government also plays a strong role in macroeconomic regulation. However, it cannot be said that the government did not play an active role in the planned economy period. It is precisely because of the strong government force that China did a good job in industrialization. Of course, this does not mean that the government monopoly is good, and that reform is unnecessary.

Second, the relationship between the government and the market is more complex in China than in other countries. Unlike other developing countries, China experienced a period of planned economy, and Chinese people are unconsciously inclined to rely on the government but are not used to the market, or do not understand the basic principles of the market. The market is not so simple. It requires people to observe the rules and have integrity, and also must be supervised by the government or third parties, especially under the protection of laws. China must make further improvement in these areas.

Third, the issue of state-owned enterprises is still sensitive and controversial in China. Although today's state-owned enterprises are no longer what they were, and the number has been slashed through restructuring, they generally exist in the areas are the lifeline of the national economy. Due to the special nature of state-owned enterprises, there are different and even diametrically opposed views on whether to reform or expand state-owned enterprises. The debate is expected to continue for some time to come.

Notes

1 There are many such countries, such as India and the Philippines.
2 Reform through labor is a form of punishment for petty crimes.
3 It should be pointed out that the statistics on the state sector of the economy and the collective economy are somewhat fuzzy. The urban collective economy changed significantly, and it is not strictly defined. Furthermore, there are many government bodies and public institutions as well as related subsidiaries in China, and these are not clearly defined. There is no unified norm in terms of statistics. Besides, many industry institutions become associations, which are neither enterprises nor government bodies but which still wield administrative powers to a certain extent. Some even receive fiscal appropriations.

13 Macro policy
Fiscal and finance issues

13.1 Introduction

The previous chapter examines institution building and mainly discusses the relationship between government and the market. In fact, a key role of the government is to use fiscal policy, which serves the functions of regulating income distribution and the macroeconomy. The former has a longer history than many other economic activities because as long as there is a country, there is a government, and the government needs a fiscal system, including fiscal revenues and spending. Therefore, government funds must be used to regulate income distribution, such as taxing the rich more and the poor less and using the tax collected from the rich to help the poor. The government itself needs money because it needs to employ public servants, make public spending, feed the armed forces, engage in diplomacy, provide education services, keep law and order, and have a certain amount of savings as a precaution. This is similar to a household. A household must have income and also make expenditures, and a portion of the income must be saved.

The latter is mainly the result of Keynesian economics following the Great Depression of 1929. It means that it is necessary for the government to intervene appropriately in economic activities. The means of intervention are primarily fiscal and financial policies. When the economy is good, the government can reduce fiscal expenditures, indicating that the market may be overheated and that investment must be appropriately reduced. When the economic picture is bad, the government can support market activities by spending more, such as building public facilities to promote the production and distribution of various goods and also create jobs. Financial policy has a similar effect. The government can regulate economic activity through the regulatory actions of the central bank. When the economy improves, interest rates can be raised to check corporate loans in order to keep the economy stable. When the economy is bad, the central bank can lower interest rates, thus cutting the cost of corporate loans and stimulating economic activity.

A common feature of the two is the use of funds and currency issues, unlike the activities of the real sector discussed in other chapters, such as agriculture, industry, and services. In terms of the use of funds, the funds belonging to the government are the fiscal responsibility of the government, including revenues and expenditures. Funds that belong to the market operate through financial institutions. There are both state-owned and private financial institutions, which dominate China's state-owned institutions. This strengthens the link with the previous chapter. At the same time, it increases the relevance of fiscal and finance issues in China, which is another common denominator between the two sectors. Of course, the most important common denominator is the macroeconomic control function, which has become the focus of economic policies adopted by various countries, including traditional capitalist countries, after World War II. Such economic policy has far more significance for China than for capitalist countries. Another common denominator is that both have the system and operation. The fiscal system determines the characteristics of fiscal revenue and expenditure and also of operations. The same goes for finance. The financial system determines the characteristics of financial operations and operations.

13.2 Fiscal systems and policies

After 1949, China entered the era of planned economy following several years of economic recovery. The first Five-Year Plan beginning in 1953 marked the official implementation of the planned economy, although it also fell under the planned economy before that. It should be noted that the first Five-Year Plan basically overlapped with the socialist transformation of capitalist industry and commerce. The cooperative campaign was launched in rural areas, progressing the primary communes to the senior communes and to the people's communes. In other words, since the 1950s, China's economy gradually shifted from a decentralized management model to a centralized management model, and this was critical for the establishment and development of the fiscal system. An increasingly centralized economy naturally required more fiscal jurisdiction and influence, which determines that the fiscal issue was far more important than finance during the planned economy period because finance needs the market while the fiscal issue does not necessarily need the market. A centralized fiscal system was implemented throughout the planned economy period, despite a process of power delegation and decentralization in the meantime. This problem of central and local fiscal power has always existed. In a sense, the fiscal problem is largely a problem of central and local governments, although there were also the issues of revenue and expenditure. To increase taxes, the most important is, of course, economic growth. Without rapid economic growth, there will be tax increases to speak of. Assuming that the economy stagnates and fiscal revenues increase, the only way is to raise tax rates under the conditions of no waste. In other words, it is to increase the burden on enterprises and individuals, which is obviously not a good idea. If the burden is too heavy, it will directly affect economic activities, and people will be discouraged from working. The exorbitant taxes and levies during the Republic of China period and the miscellaneous heavy taxes in Chinese history led to social turmoil or even riots or revolutions or there would be at least no stability.

The issue of fiscal decentralization and centralization between the central and local governments is a problem facing many countries. Although the systems and practices vary greatly from country to country, the inconsistency in tax and expenditure between the central and local governments exist in all countries. The same goes for China. It has been a focus in central–local government relations and sometimes has undermined stability. If a region sustains huge fiscal losses, it not only will affect the local economic development but also may spark social problems.

Table 13.1 shows the government's fiscal revenue and expenditure from 1955 to 2018. In terms of the change in the total amount, both income and expenditure have increased by more than 1,000 times in 60 years. Although the figures are based on prices in current years and cannot be directly compared, it still shows that the growth rate is huge. The focus here is the proportions for central and local governments. In terms of revenue, the proportion for the central government rose from more than 20 percent (lower in 1975) to about 50 percent in the early years, except in 1955. In contrast, this proportion fell from more than 70 to about 50 percent for local governments. In terms of expenditure, the proportion for the central government fell from more than 70 to about 15 percent, and the proportion for local governments rose from about 20 to about 85 percent. It is obvious that local governments have an increasing burden but diminishing revenue. There are two possible reasons for this: first, in order to develop the economy, local government invested too much, and revenue fell short of the expenditure. Second, there is a bias in the tax-sharing system between the central and local governments, and it is difficult for local governments to bear normal expenses. In view of this, the central government must transfer funds to local governments through various means. There is also an issue of fairness in the transfer because local development is highly uneven. If it is transferred at equal ratios, it will widen regional disparity. If more is given to backward areas, it will dampen the initiative of the developed areas because the central government's fiscal revenue are collected from local governments. The more developed the regions, the more taxes they pay, and the more they contribute to the central government.

Finally, in terms of the balance of payments, there was deficit finance, or borrowing money, for most of the time, except in the 1970s. In general, this deficit runs mainly relying on the issuance of government bonds or local bonds. As the economy develops, this kind of borrowing has become the norm and is also a common practice in most countries. However, there is a matter of degree here. Many countries have accumulated a huge deficit, which cannot be repaid for a long time. New debts must be obtained to pay off old debts. This will easily cause debt crises. In fact, some countries have already experienced this kind of crisis (such as Greece). China's debt burden is not very heavy thanks to its high economic growth, but it must remain vigilant.

Figure 13.1 shows the proportion of fiscal revenue to GDP and the proportion of tax revenue to fiscal revenue, with the former showing a trend of declining from a high level and then rising again. It is understandable that the proportion of fiscal revenue to GDP is high in the planned economy period because the government at that time played a very great role. It can be said that the government largely played a central role in economic activities. After the reform and opening up, the level of marketization gradually increased, and the role of the government was reduced,

Table 13.1 Government revenues and expenditures, Unit: 100 million yuan (%)

Year	Total revenue (100 million yuan)	Including central Amount (100 million yuan)	Proportion (%)	Including local Amount (100 million yuan)	Proportion (%)	Total expenditure (100 million yuan)	Including central Amount (100 million yuan)	Proportion (%)	Including local Amount (100 million yuan)	Proportion (%)	Balance of payments (100 million yuan)
1955	249.3	193.4	77.6	55.8	22.4	262.7	201.1	76.5	61.7	23.5	−13.5
1960	572.3	142.8	25.0	429.5	75.1	643.7	278.6	43.3	365.1	56.7	−71.4
1970	662.9	183.0	27.6	480.0	72.4	649.4	382.4	58.9	267.0	41.1	13.5
1980	1,159.9	284.5	24.5	875.5	75.5	1,228.8	666.8	54.3	562.0	45.7	−68.9
1990	2,937.1	992.4	33.8	1,944.7	66.2	3,083.6	1004.5	32.6	2,079.1	67.4	−146.5
2000	1,3395.2	6,989.2	52.2	6,406.1	47.8	15,886.5	5,519.9	34.8	1,0366.7	65.3	−2491.3
2010	8,3101.5	42,488.5	51.1	40,613.0	48.9	89,874.2	15,989.7	17.8	7,3884.4	82.2	−6772.7
2018	183,359.3	8,5456.5	46.6	9,7903.4	53.4	220,904.1	32,707.8	14.8	188,196.3	85.2	−37544.8

Data source: China Statistical Yearbook over the years.

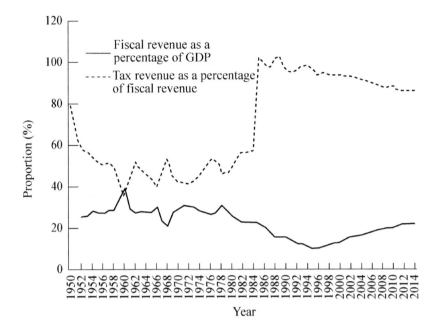

Figure 13.1 Proportion of fiscal revenue to GDP and proportion of tax revenue to fiscal revenue

Data source: *China Statistical Yearbook* over the years.

particularly in the second wave of reforms in the mid-1990s. Later, as the economy further developed, the fiscal revenue continued to increase.

The changes in the latter show the characteristics of the two different periods: the planned economy period and the reform and opening up period. Although the proportion of tax revenue to fiscal revenue in the early period was not low, accounting for about half for a long time, it soared to more than 90 percent and even reached and exceeded 100 percent in some periods in the latter period. This shows that the achievements of China's economic development are enormous. If the economy is bad, tax revenue cannot be collected, or at least there is great difficulty. Of course, this does not exclude the problems of the tax system or an excessively high tax rate. In that case, it would be unsustainable. If the burden on enterprises is too heavy, it will dampen their enthusiasm for production. If the enterprises perform badly, the tax revenue will naturally decrease. The enterprises and the government mutually interact in the tax system. In a sense, it can be said that the amount of tax revenue is determined by the quality of corporate performance. Therefore, it is not advisable to impose heavy taxes because that will significantly suppress the vitality of enterprises.

Figure 13.2 shows the proportions of fiscal revenue by economic types before 1991, which mainly include light industry, heavy industry, commerce, agriculture, transport, and other sectors. It is clear that heavy industry had a large proportion, which exceeded 40 percent since the 1960s, was close to 50 percent for a long time thereafter, and peaked at more than 50 percent, before declining significantly

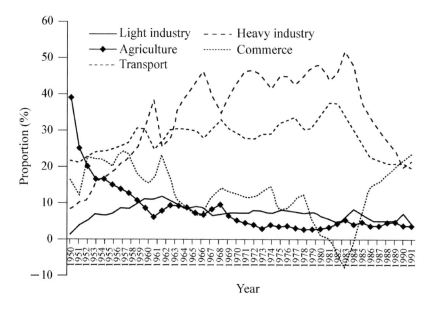

Figure 13.2 Proportion of fiscal revenue by economic types

Data source: Department of Integrated Planning, Ministry of Finance (1992) pp. 34–35.

Note: The construction industry and other two sectors are not shown here. The construction sector was not only small in amount but also contained many negative values.

after the reform and opening up. In general, the high proportion of heavy industry shows that the direction of China's industrialization strategy in the planned economy period was clear. It was not only industrialization but also industrialization of the heavy industry that underpinned China's economic development. The proportion of light industry rose steadily, and it changed in a way highly similar to that of heavy industry, as it also declined significantly after the reform and opening up. Agriculture was the opposite of industry in this regard. The proportion of agriculture was high in the early days but remained at a very low level since the 1970s. In other words, the contribution of agriculture to fiscal revenue was tiny. The proportion of commerce changed widely, declining first and then rising, which was in contrast to that of industry. In the early days when industrial development was at a low level, the income of commerce was high, particularly in the 1950s, and was comparable to that of light industry. It remained at a low level since the 1960s and was even negative in the early 1980s. It then rose significantly afterward, reflecting the vitality of the service sector and market economy.

Table 13.2 shows the sources of the various tax revenues. Tax items changed considerably according to the changing times. What is shown here is incomplete. Some items did not exist in the planned economy period but were important after the reform and opening up, while some items were very important in the planned economy period. For example, before 2000, industrial and commercial taxes accounted for 50

198 Conditions and causes

Table 13.2 Main tax revenue, Unit: 100 million yuan (%)

Year	Total	Industrial and commercial tax	Value added tax	Business tax	Resource tax	Stamp duty	Urban land use tax	Agricultural tax	Customs duties
1950	49.0 (100.0)	26.3 (53.7)						19.1 (39.0)	3.6 (7.3)
1960	203.7 (100.0)	169.6 (83.3)						28.0 (13.8)	6.0 (3.0)
1970	281.2 (100.0)	242.2 (86.1)						32.0 (11.4)	7.0 (2.5)
1980	571.7 (100.0)	510.5 (89.3)						27.7 (4.8)	33.5 (5.9)
1990	2,821.9 (100.0)	1,859.0 (65.9)	661.0 (23.4)					87.9 (3.1)	159.0 (5.6)
2000	1,2581.5 (100.0)	8,885.4 (70.6)	4,553.2 (36.2)	564.0 (20.0)	21.4 (0.8)	10.2 (0.4)	31.7 (1.1)	465.3 (3.7)	750.5 (6.0)
2010	73,210.8 (100.0)		21,093.5 (28.8)	1,868.8 (14.9)	63.6 (0.5)	98.9 (0.8)	64.8 (0.5)		2,027.8 (2.8)
2018	156,402.8 (100.0)		61,530.8 (39.3)	1,1157.9 (15.2)	417.6 (0.6)	1,040.3 (1.4)	1,004.0 (1.4)		2,847.8 (1.8)
					1,629.9 (1.0)	2,199.4 (1.4)	2,387.6 (1.5)		

Year	Corporate income tax	Consumption tax	Personal income tax	City maintenance and construction tax	Vehicle purchase tax	Arable land occupancy tax	Deed tax	Land value added tax	Property tax
1990	731.1 (25.9)			99.6 (3.5)					
2000	999.6 (8.0)	858.3 (6.8)	659.6 (5.3)	352.3 (2.8)	265.8 (2.1)	35.3 (0.3)	131.1 (1.1)	8.4 (0.1)	209.4 (1.7)
2010	12,843.5 (17.6)	6071.5 (8.3)	4,837.3 (6.6)	1736.2 (2.4)	1,792.6 (2.5)	888.6 (1.2)	2,464.9 (3.4)	1,278.3 (1.8)	894.1 (1.2)
2015	35,323.7 (22.6)	10,631.8 (6.8)	13,872.0 (8.9)	4,840.0 (3.1)	3,452.5 (2.2)	1,318.2 (0.8)	5,729.9 (3.7)	5,641.4 (3.6)	2,888.6 (1.9)

Data source: China Statistical Yearbook over the years.

Note: Inside the parentheses are proportions. Due to significant changes in the tax items, what is shown here is incomplete. Before 2000, the "industrial and commercial tax" item included value-added tax, business tax, resource tax, stamp duty, etc., and was the main tax category for many years.

to 90 percent of all tax revenues, while agricultural taxes and tariffs accounted for a small proportion. Agricultural taxes were considerable before the 1970s, began to decline year by year since the 1980s, and finally only accounted for 0.2 percent (in 2005), which confirmed the need to abolish agricultural taxes. Although tariffs fluctuated greatly, it was mostly around 5 percent and never became the main item of taxation.[1] After the reform and opening up, some new categories of taxes have emerged, such as corporate income tax and individual income tax. Corporate income tax is the result of the substitution of tax payment for profit delivery. Profits previously paid by state-run enterprises and collective enterprises to the state become taxes. The proportion of corporate income tax has fallen from nearly 35 percent in the 1980s to about 20 percent now, dropping to a low level in some years (as in 2000).

The personal income tax accounts for 5 to 7 percent. Although the proportion has not changed much, the absolute amount is increasing year by year. This is an important tax category under the market economy, reflecting the achievements of reform and development. However, personal income tax is still a controversial tax category in China because it concerns the income of ordinary people, fairness and justice, as well as income distribution. It has always been a sensitive issue. At present, China collects personal income tax based on conditions, that is, imposing personal income tax on people whose income reaches the lower limit. At present, people with a monthly income of more than 5,000 yuan must pay a personal income tax. The result is twofold. On the one hand, low-income people are exempted from personal income tax, thus increasing their spending power. On the other hand, due to the large number of low-income people in China, many people are not taxpayers of personal income tax.[2] Consumption tax is also a new tax category. As a result of the reform and development, the market has become the center of economic activities, and consumption has also become a key part of daily life. The consumption tax accounts for 5 to 7 percent, primarily reflecting the economic activities in the distribution field, which is a critical part of market economic activities.

Table 13.3 shows the number of fiscal expenditures and respective proportions by functional nature. On the whole, economic development spending has the highest proportion, which is normal. China's socialism and the characteristics of the former planned economy support such fiscal expenditure. Although data for this item are only available for years before 2005, it clearly shows its importance in the planned economy period and its declining status after the reform and opening up, indicating that the market plays a growing role in the economy after the reform and opening up. The proportion of spending on culture, education, science, and health is also large and increases as the economy develops after the reform and opening up. It now accounts for more than 20 percent, compared to 8 to 14 percent in the planned economy period. Defense expenditure accounted for a large proportion in the planned economy period and even accounted for more than 40 percent in the special period (the outbreak of the Korean War in 1950). It gradually declined after the reform and opening up, and in recent years, it has basically remained at 5 to 6 percent. Administrative management costs were not high during the planned economy period, accounting for about 5 percent except in 1950. It gradually increased after the reform and opening up, approaching 20 percent in some years, and it now accounts for almost 10 percent.

Table 13.3 Main items of fiscal expenditure, Unit: 100 million yuan (%)

Year	Total	Economic development	Culture, education, science, health	National defense	Administrative management	Others
1950	68.1 (100.0)	17.4 (25.5)	7.6 (11.1)	28.0 (41.2)	13.1 (19.3)	2.0 (2.9)
1960	643.7 (100.0)	460.7 (71.6)	87.0 (13.5)	58.0 (9.0)	31.4 (4.9)	6.6 (1.0)
1970	649.4 (100.0)	392.6 (60.5)	52.2 (8.1)	145.3 (22.4)	32.0 (4.9)	27.3 (4.2)
1980	1,228.8 (100.0)	715.5 (58.2)	199.0 (16.2)	193.8 (15.8)	75.5 (6.2)	45.0 (3.7)
1990	3,083.6 (100.0)	1,368.0 (44.4)	737.6 (23.9)	290.3 (9.4)	414.6 (13.5)	273.1 (8.9)
2000	15,886.5 (100.0)	5,748.4 (36.2)	4,384.5 (27.6)	1,207.5 (7.6)	2,768.2 (17.4)	1,777.9 (11.2)
2010	89,874.2 (100.0)	—	22,147.1 (24.7)	5,333.4 (5.9)	9,606.4 (10.7)	2,700.4 (3.0)
2018	220,904.1 (100.0)	—	56,119.7 (20.0)	11,280.5 (5.2)	18,961.1 (8.0)	2,312.6 (1.9)

Year	Social security and employment	Urban and rural communities	Agriculture, forestry and water conservancy	Transport	Resources exploration	Environmental protection
2010	9,130.6 (10.2)	5,987.4 (6.7)	8,129.6 (9.1)	5,488.5 (6.1)	3,485.0 (3.9)	2,442.0 (2.7)
2018	2,7012.1 (12.2)	22,124.1 (10.0)	21,085.6 (9.6)	11,282.8 (5.1)	5,076.4 (2.3)	6,297.6 (2.9)

Data source: China Statistical Yearbook over the years.

Note: Inside the parentheses are proportions, and the total is 100. The administrative management in 2010 and 2018 includes "general public service" and "diplomacy". In addition, "public safety" was also included in 2010 and 2018, with spending of 551.770 billion yuan and 1,378.148 billion yuan, respectively, accounting for 6.14 and 6.24 percent of the total, exceeding that of defense expenditure. Expenditure was also high for housing security, reaching 237.688 billion yuan in 2010 and 680.637 billion yuan in 2018.

13.3 Financial systems and markets

13.3.1 Financial system

The period after 1949 is divided into two periods for China's financial system, which has wholly different characteristics and roles. During the planned economy period, the most salient feature was that the People's Bank of China undertook almost all financial business, and the household savings business was managed by the postal system. Due to the needs of economic development and reform after the reform and opening up, China has gradually formed the bank system in which the People's Bank of China is the central bank, and many state-owned and joint-stock commercial banks are the core, as well as a financial market that comprises securities companies, insurance companies, and other financial institutions.

In 1949, China's financial system was divided into three parts: the People's Bank of China, which had been established in the liberated areas; the restructured Bank of China and the Bank of Communications; and the newly established People's Insurance Company of China. A few years later, the People's Bank of China was greatly expanded, and the banks established under the old system were restructured and incorporated into the People's Bank of China. By this time, the biggest threat to the financial sector was hyperinflation. On the one hand, it was caused by the indiscriminate issuance of paper money in the Kuomintang-controlled areas before the founding of the People's Republic of China. On the other hand, the civil war required huge expenditures, and the fiscal deficit of the new regime must be resolved issuing banknotes. A key task was to unify state finances. The government established and improved national finances through the "three balance policy". First is to unify the work on national finances and achieve a balance between state revenue and expenditure. Second is to unify the national work on state-run trade and achieve a balance in the allocation of materials nationwide. Third is to unify the national work on financial affairs and achieve a national balance between cash receipts and payments. Centralized management of foreign exchange was also a key task. Because the Kuomintang government absconded with a wealth of foreign exchange and also because of the blockade imposed by Western countries such as the United States, foreign trade and international cooperation were rare, and foreign exchange funds were scarce. Through foreign currency exchange, the government established designated foreign exchange banks, set a unified renminbi exchange rate, implemented the foreign exchange supply system and the settlement system, and enforced the currency entry and exit management system. Initial progress was made in the establishment of the foreign exchange system through the establishment of new international settlement relations.

The period of the First Five-Year Plan was also the period of time when China progressed from a new democratic economy to a socialist economy and also a period when a highly centralized planned economy was formed. During this period, the state established a centralized planned economy through the socialist transformation of the agriculture, handicraft, and capitalist industry and commerce sectors. Specifically, the following work was done in the financial sector: public–private partnership banks were merged into the People's Bank of China system, the Agricultural Bank of China (1955), and the People's Construction Bank of China (1954) were established, and rural credit cooperatives were developed. During the Great Leap Forward period, a few people advocated the abolition of commodity production and commodity exchange, advocated the abolition of money, and negated the economic leverage role of credit and interest rates. Guided by such thinking, many practices divorced from reality were adopted, causing serious repercussions.

In view of the losses caused by mistakes and errors during the Great Leap Forward period, the state conducted adjustment and rectification after 1961, including freezing the deposits of government bodies and groups, adjusting some financial operations as well as management pattern, and putting forward six-point views on fiscal work and on banking work. The six-point views on banking work include recovering delegated powers, enforcing strict credit management, drawing a boundary between bank credit funds and fiscal funds and banning the use of bank loans as fiscal expenditures, strengthening cash management and enforcing strict settlement discipline, requiring banks at all levels to regularly report to the local government on their work, and strictly managing fiscal affairs while strengthening the work of banks.

The economy and finance recovered somewhat after the rectification, but the Cultural Revolution broke out unexpectedly. The losses caused by this turmoil to China's economy were incalculable. The People's Bank of China merged into the Ministry of Finance to become a department under the Ministry of Finance. Financial work did not get on the right track until after several years of adjustment at the end of the Cultural Revolution. The financial system in the planned economy period can be summarized as financial repression under a high level of centralization and unification. Due to the physical economy implemented under the planned economy, the market mechanism could not be brought into play. The financial system only acted as an auxiliary of fiscal policy, not to mention macroeconomic regulation.[3]

China initiated all-round reforms after 1978. Although the reform was gradually implemented in a way similar to crossing the river by feeling the stones, many reform measures were unprecedented, and it was a difficult and tortuous process. It was no easy job to change from a planned economy that had been implemented for decades to a market economy. The reforms of the 1980s were primarily market-oriented reforms, including the disintegration of rural collective economic organizations, the emergence of the private sector of the economy, the reform of state-owned enterprises, the reform of the price system, and the reform of the fiscal system.

Many reforms were conducted in the financial system. First, the functions of specialized banks and central banks were gradually defined, and specialized banks such as the Agricultural Bank of China, the Bank of China, the China Construction Bank, and the Industrial and Commercial Bank of China were restored or established successively. Joint-stock banks such as the Bank of Communications, China CITIC Bank, China Merchants Bank, Shenzhen Development Bank, Industrial Bank, Guangdong Development Bank, China Everbright Bank, Huaxia Bank, and Shanghai Pudong Development Bank were established. Rural credit cooperatives were also restored. The reform of the financial industry has accelerated since the 1990s. On the one hand, the shareholding system was introduced to state-owned banks, including the introduction of strategic partners and securitization-based listing. On the other hand, the space for the development of joint-stock banks and city commercial banks was expanded. Moreover, the state established policy banks and postal savings banks. Nonbank financial institutions such as insurance companies, securities companies, trust companies, and finance companies of enterprise groups also made great strides. Some problems also occurred during this process, and rectification and improvement were carried out. In particular, there were many problems with trust companies in the early years.

In terms of financial institutions, China has now progressed from the planned economy period when the People's Bank of China was the only bank to a period with diversified banking system in which the People's Bank of China is the central bank, many state-owned banks are the foundation, and joint-stock banks and local banks are the supplements. Several large state-owned banks rank among large enterprises in the world in terms of assets size. The rapid development of joint-stock banks and local banks improves the competition mechanism of the financial market to a certain extent and injects vitality into the financial sector. After more than 20 years of development and reform, the securities system and securities market have developed at a fast clip. China's securities market has become one of the world's important securities markets. The insurance sector has also made great progress after the reform and opening up. In addition to the healthy development of state-owned insurance companies, joint-stock insurance companies and foreign-funded enterprises have also enjoyed opportunities for development.

13.3.2 Financial markets

This section examines incomplete data on the financial sector and discusses long-term changes. Table 13.4 shows the deposits of financial institutions from 1952 to 2010. It can be seen that the amount of deposits in the planned economy period was small, and there is no comparison with the deposits after the reform and opening up. The total deposits were 9.33 billion yuan in 1952 and 193.35 billion yuan in 1980, an increase of 19.7 times, which shows that the amount of deposits also increased significantly in the planned economy period. However, such an increase paled into insignificance when compared to that of the reform and opening up period. The total deposits increased by 370.5 times from 1980 to 2010, although both time periods have a gap of 30 years. There was also a certain degree of inflation in each period, with a far higher inflation in the latter period. Nevertheless, the contrast of this growth rate is clear. We know that in a market economy, economic growth is accompanied by a certain degree of inflation. As long as it is not hyperinflation or as long as inflation is within a healthy range, it even promotes economic growth to some extent.

In fact, deflation is worse than moderate inflation for an economy. Because enterprises believe that the prices of surplus products are lower under deflationary conditions, there is no incentive to step up production, or they will directly reduce output. As a result, the income of enterprises will decrease, the income of

Table 13.4 Deposits of financial institutions, Unit: 100 million yuan

Year	Bank deposits Total	Enterprises	Fiscal	Capital construction	Government bodies and organizations	Savings deposits	Agriculture	Others	Postal savings
1952	93.3	33.0	19.5	4.1	28.1	8.6	–	–	–
1960	502.6	86.0	146.6	29.6	96.3	66.3	77.8	–	–
1970	780.7	226.1	176.8	12.2	141.4	79.5	144.7	9.1	–
1980	1,933.5	563.3	164.5	171.8	229.5	399.5	374.8	30.1	–
1990	14,012.6	4,098.1	380.4	–	614.8	7,119.8	393.1	1,406.4	180.3
2000	123,804.4	44,093.7	3,508.1	–	2,224.3	64,332.4	2,642.9	7,003.0	4,579.2
2010	718,237.9	244,495.6	25,455.0	–	66,175.0	303,302.5	17,244.0	55,101.0	–

Data source: Data for the years before 2000 from Ryoshin Minami and Makino Fumio (2014), pp. 405–406; data for 2010 from *China Statistical Yearbook 2011*.

Note: The "Others" figure for 1970 is the figure for 1971. In 2010, there were no postal savings but "entrusted and trust deposits" (646.5 billion yuan).

employees will be reduced, and enterprises will even lay off employees, resulting in a heightened unemployment rate. Even if there are no layoffs, lower income will cause a decline in purchasing power. This is called a vicious circle of economic depression. Japan has been plagued with deflation since the late 1990s. In view of this, the Abe regime, which came to power in 2012, introduced a slew of policies aimed at achieving inflation of 2 percent, including issuing large amounts of money and lowering the yen exchange rate.

Specifically, the two items that increased the fastest and that accounted for the largest proportion in the total were corporate deposits and personal savings deposits. In terms of the rate of increase, the personal savings deposits increased from 860 million yuan in 1952 to 30,330.25 billion yuan in 2010. Corporate deposits remained basically the same, soaring from 3.30 billion yuan to 24,449.56 billion yuan in 2010. In terms of the role of finance, it was obviously more important in the planned economy period and relatively less important after the reform and opening up, indicating that the market force was growing. The changes in the numbers for government bodies and organizations are basically close to the fiscal situation.

Figure 13.3 shows the money supply, including M2, M1, and M0, which refer to broad money, narrow money, and cash money, respectively. The overall trend of the three was basically consistent, increasing in a linear fashion, but the upward trend is even more prominent after the reform and opening up. Moreover, in the planned economy period, there was basically no difference between broad money and narrow money, which was consistent. After the reform and opening up, the two gradually diverged. One of the key characteristics was that the proportion of deposits as a quasi-money increased year by year. Households

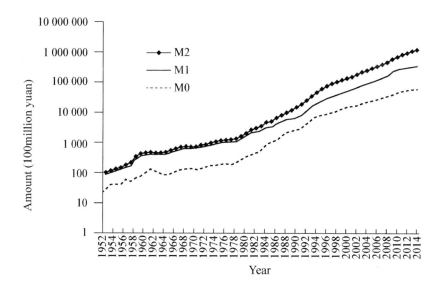

Figure 13.3 Money supply

Data source: *China Statistical Yearbook* over the years.

basically had no deposits during the planned economy period. After the reform and opening up, household deposits rapidly increased as people's incomes rose, leading to the separation of the two. Moreover, the rapid growth of corporate fixed-term deposit also provides the basis for the separation of the two.

13.4 Conclusion

This chapter examined China's fiscal and financial issues, which have both similarities and differences. In terms of difference, fiscal issue consists more of government behavior, while finance belongs to market behavior. In terms of similarity, both are related to capital and currency and do not belong to the physical economy. Moreover, given China's national circumstances, today's finance is closely related to the government in many areas, and the vast majority of banks are state-owned enterprises.

The fiscal system after 1949 was closely related to the country's economic system. Centralized finance operated under the planned economy while decentralized finance operates after the reform and opening up. In the early stage, it was basically arranged according to the five-year plans, including income and expenditure. National finances were inclined to industrial construction while little attention was given to the life of the public in this regard. As a result of fast growth in the latter period, it gradually moved from a biased to a balanced fiscal system. In other words, it shifted from prioritizing a certain industry (such as heavy industry) to taking into account the needs of various industries (including agriculture), thereby effectively supporting economic development.

The same is true of finance. Financial institutions played a supporting role in the controlled procurement and distribution system and almost lost their original functions after 1949 under the planned economy. Not only was there no financial market, but financial outlets were removed as well. People's savings activities were conducted through the postal sector. The People's Bank of China became the sole bank. It nominally shouldered the dual responsibilities as the central bank and a commercial bank but in fact did not undertake business that should be performed by a bank. After the reform and opening up, the banking sector has developed rapidly. In addition to a division of labor between the central bank and commercial banks, a securities market has been built, and insurance business is carried out.

At present, China's fiscal and financial undertakings are developing and improving. Regardless of some problems, fiscal and financial reform as well as development will be greatly promoted as China's economy further develops.

Notes

1 In some developing countries, tariffs are often a key tax category for the day-to-day expenses of governments. Therefore, tariff rates are higher in developing countries than in developed countries. If course, there is also the need to protect local industries.
2 We believe that a key feature of modern society is civil society. Citizens are the masters of society, and the status of citizens as masters is achieved through taxes. If you don't pay taxes, it is difficult to have civic awareness, and you lack responsibility as a citizen.
3 Li Yang (2009), p. 60.

14 International trade

Closed and open

14.1 Introduction

Secluding the country from the outside world is one of the main reasons that China lagged behind the West in modern times because it prevented the Chinese people from keeping abreast of the latest changes in the world. Perhaps it was because we always considered China to be the most powerful, and we were fearless and indifferent to changes in other countries, or perhaps we had not developed the habit of learning about the changes (especially the progress) of others. A country is like a person. For those who are not good at drawing on the merits of others, that means standing still and refusing to make progress, and they will lag behind sooner or later. Judging from human history, it is not that the Chinese people did not understand this rule and principle, or, although they were aware of it, they could not act on it. Empires with a glorious history were eventually defeated by others almost without exception. In a sense, they were defeated by themselves, either because they were not good at learning or because they were overconfident or insatiably avaricious.

China was forcibly invaded by Western powers in modern times and had no choice but to open its doors to the outside world thereafter. This opening up was involuntary and was based on unequal treaties. China benefitted little from this period, and more losses were incurred. China could only export natural resources and local specialties in exchange for industrial products and consumer goods. Trade in resources was clearly predatory. In addition to low prices, China also had no say over prices. China's customs were controlled by foreigners for a long time. Although this structure had a positive effect, such as the introduction of modern management models and standards, it made it easier for foreigners to plunder China's resources.

China could engage in trade independently during the planned economy period after 1949. However, due to the low level of industrialization, coupled with the planned economy and a poor international environment as a result of the Cold War, China suffered setbacks in international trade. In addition to trade, primarily barter trade, with the Soviet Union and Eastern European countries, China also carried out trade with some developing countries. However, due to the limited economic development of these countries (particularly the latter), it was difficult for China

DOI: 10.4324/9781003410393-17

to acquire products from international trade that could boost its industrialization. China made progress in industrialization during this period by relying on self-reliance and Soviet assistance, but the progress was very limited.

After the reform and opening up, China achieved extraordinary development in international trade, which grew faster than the economic aggregate. While bringing great vitality to China's economic development, it has also promoted reform and opening up and has also contributed to the relationship between the two. The policy of reform and opening up cemented China's international economic and trade relations, which in turn promoted reform and opening up. This was proved by China's accession to the World Trade Organization in 2001 and its subsequent development. As a result of China's policy of opening up, great progress was made in international trade and foreign investment, which in turn promoted China to open up wider to the outside world. As a result, China was joined the World Trade Organization. This further accelerated the development of China's international trade and achieved a virtuous circle. China has now become the world's largest trading country and second largest economy.

14.2 Growth in international trade

14.2.1 Changes in trade volume

The economic development strategy was aimed at a domestically oriented economy during the planned economy period after 1949. It was called "independence and self-reliance" at that time. One reason was the blockades and restrictions imposed by foreign countries. Since China is a socialist country, the Western world employed a hostile policy toward China. This situation lasted until after the reform and opening up. China developed in a way beyond people's imagination thereafter.

Table 14.1 shows the import and export trade from 1950 to 2018, which clearly shows the preceding characteristics. The volume of trade did not grow much before 1980, basically remaining at 10 billion yuan (US$3 billion to US$4.5 billion) from 1950 to 1970. In the 1970s, as a result of the establishment of diplomatic relations between China and some Western powers, China's foreign trade made some progress, reaching 57 billion yuan (US$38.1 billion) in 1980. After the 1980s, China formally implemented the policy of reform and opening up, and foreign trade developed by leaps and bounds: trade in 1985 was 3.6 times that of 1980, trade in 1990 was 2.69 times that of 1985, trade in 1995 was 4.23 times that of 1990, trade in 2000 was 1.68 times that of 1995, trade in 2005 was 3 times that of 2000, trade in 2010 was 1.73 times that of 2005, and trade in 2018 was 1.5 times that of 2010. Although these figures are based on prices of the current years, it is still certain that this increase is not only unprecedented for China but also incredible and unimaginable in the world, particularly for a large country. Following the global financial crisis in 2008, China's import and export trade experienced a slowdown in growth due to the decline in demand from other countries.

Table 14.1 Total import and export trade

Year	Renminbi (100 million yuan)				U.S. dollars (US$100 million)			
	Import and export	Export	Import	Difference	Import and export	Export	Import	Difference
1950	41.5	20.2	21.3	−1.1	11.3	5.5	5.8	−0.3
1960	128.4	63.3	65.1	−1.8	38.1	18.6	19.5	−0.9
1970	112.9	56.8	56.1	0.7	45.9	22.6	23.3	−0.7
1980	570.0	271.2	298.8	−27.6	381.4	181.2	200.2	−19.0
1990	5,560.1	2,985.8	2,574.3	410.7	1,154.4	620.9	533.5	87.4
2000	39,273.2	20,634.4	18,638.8	1,996.4	4,742.9	2,492.0	2,250.9	241.1
2010	201,722.1	107,022.8	94,699.3	12,323.5	29,739.9	15,777.5	13,962.4	1,815.1
2018	305,008.1	164,127.8	140,880.3	23,247.5	46,224.2	24,866.8	21,357.3	3,509.5

Data source: China Statistical Yearbook over the years.

From the perspective of trade balance, China's foreign trade was basically in deficit before 1985, but except for a few years (such as 1985, not shown in the table), the amount of deficit was small, and there was basically balance or a surplus in some years. After 1990, there was a surplus and the value is increasing, indicating that China which lacked foreign exchange reserves in the past has now become a large country of foreign exchange reserves and is gradually becoming the top country. Usually developing countries have a trade deficit due to the need to import various machinery and equipment for industrialization and the need to export primary products in exchange for foreign exchange earnings, because the price of primary products is far lower than that of industrial products with high added value. The higher-end the machinery and equipment are, the higher the prices will be. When a country has a large trade surplus (except for oil-exporting countries) and has made some progress in terms of industrialization, it can be said that the country has rapid economic development. To say the least, the country is no longer hampered by insufficient foreign exchange because a lack of foreign exchange is a significant obstacle to the economic development of many countries. Japan and the Asian Tigers, not to mention other developing countries, previously suffered a shortage of foreign exchange. Of course, too much foreign exchange is not necessarily a good thing because it puts pressure on the appreciation of the local currency, and it is prone to causing trade conflicts.

14.2.2 Growth rate of trade

According to these discussions, China's international trade has experienced a process of growing from a low level to a high level since 1949. China was not open enough during the planned economy period. Moreover, few commodities could be exported at the time, and the domestically oriented economy strategy was adopted. Therefore, the trade volume was small, and the growth rate was not high. After the reform and opening up, China has not only gradually expanded trade but has also vigorously introduced foreign investment and developed processing trade through an export-oriented development strategy, providing an important foundation for import and export.

Figure 14.1 shows the growth rates of actual imports and exports after the reform and opening up. The following can be observed. First, the overall growth rate was very high, both for imports and exports, particularly before 2008. Second, the general trend was downward. As China's economy develops, the growth rate of imports and exports is declining. Nevertheless, the growth rate is still high. In recent years, the world economy has experienced a downturn, which also affects China's imports and exports. There is no denying that the growth rate has declined somewhat because the Chinese economy has been in a state of adjustment. Third, the growth of imports is slightly higher than that of exports, even with the exception of 1985, which was a special year. The processing trade is a reason because it requires importing a lot of raw materials and semifinished products.

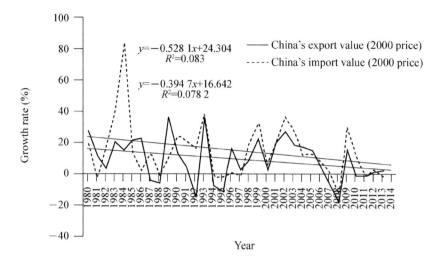

Figure 14.1 Actual import and export growth rate after the reform and opening up

Data source: Data on imports and exports from *China Statistical Yearbook* over the years; the import and export price indices from the United Nations Conference on Trade and Development Statistics.

14.3 Trade dependency

Judging from the history of economic development of various countries, as the economy develops, a country will gradually open up wider to the outside world, including international trade, international investment, and personnel exchanges. A rough measure of a country's economic opening up is the ratio of total volume of import and export trade to GDP. This indicator is called trade dependency. The export dependency (ratio of total exports to GDP) and the import dependency (ratio of total imports to GDP) can also be used.

After studying the laws of trade dependency in developed countries, Kuznets said that there is a negative correlation between trade dependency and the size of a country measured by national income. He also found that in the process of economic development, developed countries experienced a process of increasing and then decreasing trade dependency, except for the United States, Australia, Canada, and other new world countries. Trade dependency in Japan changed in a way similar to that in developed countries in Europe.[1] On this point, Hollis B. Chenery et al. pointed out the same problem through their research on the stages of industrialization in various countries. He believes that trade dependency is low in the initial stage of industrialization because industry is not developed at this time, and the volume of imports and exports is relatively small. In the intermediate stage of industrialization, more imports will lead to an increase in exports because the secondary industry needs more raw materials and equipment, and, as a result, trade dependency will increase. At the advanced stage of industrialization, the proportion of industry declines somewhat, and its trade dependency will also be reduced or remain stable.[2]

In summary, Kuznets raised two questions. One is a static issue, namely the differences between countries in a certain period of time, such as different country size, income difference, and geographical differences. The other is a dynamic issue, the phenomenon of rising first and then falling. We call it Kuznets's "inverted U curve hypothesis" on trade dependency.[3] Regarding this question, many scholars have basically confirmed the existence of this hypothesis based on data from various countries.

What factors influence the degree of trade dependency in various periods or stages? While these factors may be different in various stages, it is necessary to identify the principal factors. Kuznets pointed out two factors: country size and geographical location. Based on the view of Kuznets, the Japanese economist Ryoshin Minami pointed out that even if countries are the same in size, trade dependency is different if productivity or income levels are different. He is of the opinion that, if the productivity is high, there is export competitiveness, and large-scale exports necessarily require the import of a great deal of raw materials. If income levels are high, commodities in more categories are needed, and international trade, especially imports, will be more active. In other words, Ryoshin Minami added a third factor: income level.

Based on Kuznets' research, Ryoshin Minami quantitatively compared Japan's trade dependency with that of other countries. Using population (N, 1,000 persons) to represent the size of the country and GDP per capita (y, U.S. dollars) to represent income levels, he measured the relationship between the trade dependency (δ) of the countries in the world in 1988 and 1999 and the aforesaid two variables. The results show that the smaller the country size (population variable N) or the higher the GDP per capita (income variable y), the higher the level of trade dependency. Ryoshin Minami called these two variables "scale effect" and "income effect", respectively. The theoretical trade dependency (38 percent in 1988 and 52.3 percent in 1999) calculated by substituting Japan's figures into the equation is far greater than the actual values (23 and 19.1 percent, respectively). The world (sample) averages for these two years were 60 and 78.4 percent, respectively. In other words, Japan's trade dependency is far below what should be expected based on its country size and income levels, and even much lower than the world average.[4]

Ryoshin Minami believes that this situation is the result of many conditions. A key reason is that Japan is geographically far from developed countries in Europe and the United States and has no neighboring countries with great productivity and large markets. It can also be said that Japan's low trade dependency is attributed to its economic scale and geographical location. However, he believes that Japan's trade dependency will increase when increased direct investment results in a stagnation (hollowing) of domestic industrial production activities and when the industrialization of neighboring countries leads to the horizontal division of labor.

Based on these discussions, we added the two variables of industrial structure and foreign direct investment (FDI) on the basis of Ryoshin Minami's model. The industrial structure (= the proportion of industrial output to GDP) is used because according to the Petty–Clark theorem and the experience of developed countries, the proportion of a country's industry is expressed as an inverted U curve. In other words, the proportion of industry is very low in the early stage of economic development and high in the middle stage. In the later period, industry is mostly replaced by the service sector. This view is consistent with what Chenery and others claim. Moreover, industrialization will have the effect of correlation among industries. In other words, a great deal of raw materials are needed, and a large product market is also needed. It can be speculated that this situation is closely related to the inverted U curve of trade dependency. The variable foreign direct investment is used because, after World War II, the rise and development of multinational corporations as well as the economic progress of developing countries depended on foreign investment to varying degrees.

Specifically, the explained variable is trade dependency (δ), and explanatory variables are (1) country size, i.e., population (N, 1,000 persons), (2) income level, i.e., GDP per capita (y, U.S. dollars), (3) industrial structure, i.e., proportion of industrial output to GDP (R, %), and (4) the amount of foreign direct investment and as a percentage of GDP (F, million U.S. dollars, %). All variables are converted into logarithmic values to calculate the situation in 2003 and 2013, as shown in Table 14.2.

Judging from the results of regression analysis, the coefficients of each explanatory variable are reasonable, and their significance (value t) is also ideal, indicating that the model performs better after we added two variables. In summary, calculation results better explain that the country size, per capita income, industrial structure, and foreign direct investment all have a significant impact on a country's trade dependency. In other words, a country's trade dependency is largely affected by the aforesaid factors. It is self-evident that trade dependency is also affected by other factors, such as trade policy. We also added tariffs as a trade policy variable to the model, but the calculation results were not ideal. In our view, it is perhaps because the trend of today's international trade policy is toward lower tariffs and replacing them with other nontariff barriers. Nontariff barriers exist in a variety of forms and types, such as allowances, subsidies, technical standards, and environmental standards, and are difficult to quantify. As a result, quantitative analysis was not used.

Table 14.2 Calculation results of the trade dependency function

Year	Definite number	lnN	lny	lnR	lnF	Value F	R^2
2003	3.644 (11.178)	−0.256 (−9.019)	0.134 (4.462)	0.438 (4.711)	0.118 (4.419)	29.899	0.493
2013	4.040 (16.36)	−0.087 (−7.82)	0.034 (1.79)	0.233 (3.30)	0.119 (4.47)	28.180	0.399

Data source: World Development Indicators 2005, 2015.

Notes:
(1) The sample size was 128 in 2003 and 175 in 2013.
(2) Foreign direct investment is the amount in 2003 and the proportion in 2013.
(3) The number in parentheses is the value t.

214 Conditions and causes

Of course, this does not mean that tariffs and other trade-restricting measures and policies have no effect. Theoretically and empirically at least, these should play a great role.

Figure 14.2 shows the change in trade dependency from 1950 to 2014, from which the following characteristics can be observed. It was basically around 10 percent in the planned economy period and lower in some periods. After the reform and opening up, it showed a continuous upward trend. It was about more than 30 percent in the 1990s, rose sharply after China's accession to the WTO in 2001, exceeded 60 percent from 2005 to 2007, and fell below 50 percent after 2009 as a result of the U.S. financial crisis in 2008 and was 41 percent in 2014. Due to the export-oriented development strategy, China is the only large country with the characteristics of a small country. In other words, China is highly trade-dependent in view of China's size. Generally, the trade dependency of major countries is relatively low: 29 percent for the United States, 23 percent for Brazil, and 29 percent for Japan in 2010. However, as globalization has deepened in recent years, various countries have become more interdependent. As a result, this indicator is also rising for large countries that were not previously highly dependent on foreign trade, such as Russia (52 percent) and India (47 percent), compared with only 21 percent

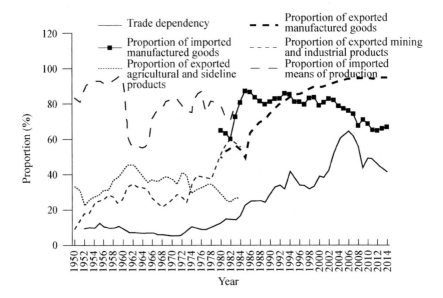

Figure 14.2 Changes in China's trade dependency as well as import and export structure

Data source: *China Statistical Yearbook* over the years.

Note: The industrial and mining products exported from 1950 to 1984 include metal and minerals, machinery and instruments, chemicals, Western medicines, ceramics, and chemical fiber products; exported agricultural and sideline processed products include processed cereal and oil food, textiles, native and livestock products, handicrafts, etc. The classifications of exports in the same period include means of production and means of subsistence.

for the United States, 20 percent for Brazil, and 17 percent for India in 1980.[5] This indicates a trend of growing trade dependency of various countries.

14.4 International trade and industrialization

As industrialization deepens or the economy develops, the structure of international trade will change significantly, usually from mainly exporting primary products to exporting industrial manufactured goods. The import structure is complex – importing primary products as well as industrial manufactured goods. This trend in China can be seen in Figure 14.2. The caliber of statistics before the 1980s is different from that of subsequent years. Two curves are drawn here: the curve representing the proportion of exported industrial and mining products before the 1980s and the curve representing the proportion of exported industrial manufactured goods after the 1980s. The industrial and mining products exported include metal and minerals, and some metal and minerals are primary products. The proportion of industrial and mining products exported should be higher than that of industrial manufactured exports that are commonly used now.

Exports rose from 9.3 percent in 1950 to 34 percent in 1962 and then declined to 21.8 percent in 1968 before rising again. In the early 1980s, it was basically in line with the statistics on manufactured goods. At that time, there was another statistical indicator: the proportion of agricultural and sideline processed products exported. Agricultural and sideline products exported include processed cereal and oil food, textiles, native and livestock products, handicrafts, etc. Textiles and handicrafts should be counted as manufactured goods, and others belong to primary products. It is worth noting that this part of the statistics has two attributes. It changed basically in the same way as industrial and mining exports in the early stage, but it was different afterward – it kept declining without rising. This shows that such products increasingly have the attribute of primary products. China's exports rely more on manufactured goods than primary products. It is noteworthy that mineral fuels, lubricants, and related raw materials as primary products accounted for 23.78 percent of China's exports in 1982, but this figure was 26.1 percent in 1985. Therefore, industrial and mining exports in traditional statistics include many primary products. In the early days, China did not produce so much oil and there were not so much exports, only that data for the early years are not available.

In terms of imports, there is a conceptual issue in the statistics before the 1980s. At the time, imports were only divided into means of production and consumer goods. The means of production can be roughly regarded as manufactured goods, but consumer goods also include such products. Therefore, the figures and proportions of means of production may be underestimated. The proportion of imported means of production fluctuated greatly, rising from 83 percent in 1950 to 95 percent in 1960, suddenly falling to 62 percent in 1961, declining further to around 55 percent, and remaining at a low level until 1965. It began to increase steadily in 1966 and remained at 70 to 80 percent, roughly in line with the statistics after the 1980s. The fluctuations before the 1960s were mainly caused by the relations with the Soviet Union. Since 1959, the import of industrial products from the Soviet

Union and Eastern European countries was badly hurt. From the mid- to late 1960s onward, imports from Western countries gradually increased as a result of the restoration and establishment of diplomatic relations with major Western countries, and therefore this proportion increased.

In terms of exports, the situation after the 1980s is clear. The proportion of manufactured goods exported gradually increased from about 50 percent in 1980 to about 95 percent in 2014. In other words, the proportion of primary products exported fell from about half to about 5 percent in 2014, which was a seismic change in about 40 years. The proportion of 95 percent even exceeds that of almost all industrialized countries. Why did this interesting phenomenon occur? There are two key factors. First, China is in the middle of industrialization. When the share of industrial output is large, there are naturally more exports, which requires competitiveness. China is competitive in this regard. On the one hand, the cost is low. On the other hand, China has certain capability. A second factor is foreign direct investment, indicating that the proportion of processing trade is large. If this part is removed (accounting for about half), the proportion of exports by local enterprises is halved, or about 47 percent, which is more in line with the stage of China's economic development.

The changes in imports differ from those of exports. The proportion of manufactured goods rose from around 65 to 85 percent, then slowly decreased, to about 65 percent in 2014, which was the same as the 1980 levels. That is to say, China's import structure has come full circle after about 40 years of economic development for two reasons. First, in the 1980s, China's technical level was low, and it needed to import a mass of industrial equipment and products. As its capabilities improve, this demand has decreased. Second is still the role of foreign investment. Foreign investment pours into China for the purposes of production and processing, which requires a wealth of raw materials.

Table 14.3 shows the main varieties of imported and exported primary products after the reform and opening up. Food exports increased significantly, and its proportion to total primary products rose from about 33 to about 56 percent, indicating that China's food supply capacity improved greatly. In addition to fully meeting domestic demand, it also increased exports. The absolute value of food imports did not rise much, and its proportion to total imports fell from 42 to less than 11 percent, which also shows China's growing grain and food supply capacity. In terms of nonedible raw materials, the export value increased, but the proportion did not increase or even declined; it basically remained at less than 20 percent. The absolute value of imports increased sharply, but its proportion did not rise, indicating that such products were in short supply, and imports have increased sharply in recent years. Finally, the export value of products such as fossil fuels has increased rapidly since the beginning of the 21st century, but the proportion has declined. The absolute value of imports increased abnormally, from US$200 million to nearly US$200 billion, and its proportion jumped from 3 to 42 percent, indicating that China's demand for imports far exceeds export supply, and this trend is increasing.

Table 14.4 shows the imports and exports of major manufactured goods after the reform and opening up. The volume of chemicals exports increased significantly,

Table 14.3 Import and export structure of primary products after the reform and opening up, Unit: US$100 million (%)

Year	Total	Food	Nonedible raw material	Fossil fuels
Exports				
1980	91.14 (100.00)	29.85 (32.76)	17.11 (18.78)	42.8 (46.96)
1990	158.86 (100.00)	66.09 (29.02)	35.37 (22.27)	52.37 (32.97)
2000	254.60 (100.00)	122.82 (48.24)	44.62 (17.53)	78.55 (30.86)
2010	816.86 (100.00)	411.48 (50.38)	116.03 (14.21)	266.73 (32.66)
2018	1,349.93 (100.00)	654.71 (48.50)	180.21 (13.35)	467.22 (34.61)
Imports				
1980	69.59 (100.00)	29.27 (42.06)	35.54 (51.07)	2.03 (2.92)
1990	98.53 (100.00)	33.35 (33.85)	41.07 (41.69)	12.72 (12.91)
2000	467.39 (100.00)	47.58 (10.18)	200.03 (42.80)	206.37 (44.16)
2010	4,338.50 (100.00)	215.70 (4.98)	2,121.11 (48.89)	1,890.00 (43.57)
2018	7,017.44 (100.00)	648.01 (9.23)	2,721.44 (38.78)	3,493.56 (49.78)

Data source: China Statistical Yearbook over the years.

Note: The real number is outside the parentheses, and the proportion is inside the parentheses. Because the value is small for beverages and tobacco, animal and vegetable oils and waxes, they are not listed here.

but its proportion showed a downward trend. The value of imports increased, but its proportion fell (the proportion of imports was already about double that of exports). The exports of light textiles, rubber, mineral, and metallurgical products share similarities, with a significant increase in value and a sharp decline in proportion. The increase in the volume of imports was not fast, and the proportion decreased greatly. Unlike the aforesaid two types of commodities, the imports and exports of machinery and transport equipment increased significantly, and their proportion also increased, especially for exports. Their imports and exports accounted for half of the manufactured goods, indicating that China's industrialization or economic development in this period is represented by the machinery sector. Why did imports and exports substantially increase simultaneously? The reasons are twofold: One is the progress of China's economy; industrialization requires a great deal of machinery and equipment, which must be imported. Second, the export capacity is greatly enhanced as a result of self-development and the introduction of foreign investment.

Figure 14.3 shows the relationship between the proportion of heavy industry in production and the proportion of heavy industry in trade from 1980 to 2011. Trade includes both exports and imports. Whether it be export or import, their relationship with production is a positive correlation. In other words, as the industrialization of heavy industry deepens, the proportion of heavy industry for exports and imports rises. Further, compared with imports, exports are more closely associated with production (the coefficient of determination is

218 *Conditions and causes*

Table 14.4 Import and export structure of manufactured goods during the reform and opening up period, Unit: US$100 million (%)

Year	Total	Chemicals	Light textiles, rubber, mining, and metallurgical products	Machinery and transport equipment	Miscellaneous
Exports					
1980	90.05 (100.00)	11.20 (12.44)	39.99 (44.41)	8.43 (9.37)	28.36 (31.50)
1990	462.05 (100.00)	37.30 (8.08)	125.76 (27.22)	55.88 (12.10)	126.86 (27.46)
2000	2,237.43 (100.00)	120.98 (5.41)	425.46 (19.02)	826.00 (36.92)	862.78 (38.57)
2010	14,960.69 (100.00)	875.72 (5.86)	2,491.08 (16.65)	7,802.69 (52.16)	3,776.52 (25.25)
2015	23,516.89 (100.00)	1,674.66 (7.12)	4,046.59 (17.21)	12,077.88 (51.36)	5,656.06 (24.05)
Imports					
1980	130.58 (100.00)	29.09 (22.28)	41.54 (31.82)	51.19 (39.21)	5.42 (4.15)
1990	434.92 (100.00)	66.48 (15.29)	89.06 (20.48)	167.45 (38.51)	21.03 (4.84)
2000	1,783.55 (100.00)	302.13 (16.94)	418.07 (23.44)	919.31 (51.55)	127.51 (7.15)
2010	9,623.94 (100.00)	1,497.00 (15.56)	1,312.78 (13.64)	5,494.21 (57.09)	1,135.60 (11.80)
2014	14,339.90 (100.00)	2,236.36 (15.60)	1,513.51 (10.55)	8,396.56 (58.55)	1,437.40 (10.02)

Data source: *China Statistical Yearbook* over the years.

Note: Real number outside the parentheses and proportions inside the parentheses.

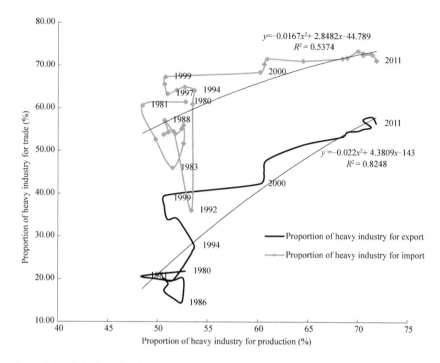

Figure 14.3 Relationship of proportions of heavy industry for production and trade

Data source: *China Statistical Yearbook* and *China Industry Statistical Yearbook* over the years.

Note: The numbers in the figure represent the year.

higher than that of imports). In terms of changes in exports, from 1980 to 1999, it showed a straight climb after stable fluctuations in the early 1980s, exceeding the increase in the proportion of production. It rose from about 20 to about 40 percent. Before 1999, the industrialization of heavy industry for exports rapidly advanced, increasing from 40 to nearly 60 percent. However, industrialization of heavy industry for production also advanced rapidly during this period, increasing from 50 to more than 70 percent.

In terms of imports, its path of change obviously differed from that of exports. Imports exceeded exports from the outset. It fell from 60 percent in 1980 to more than 30 percent in 1992 and then rose rapidly to nearly 70 percent in 1999. This change was similar to that of exports. That is to say, before 1999, the industrialization of heavy industry for exports and imports exceeded that for production. It increased slightly thereafter but basically remained stable. Of course, this is also due to the fact that imports already remained at a high level. In short, compared with exports, imports better mirror the importance of the heavy industry sector, indicating that China needed to import more advanced equipment such as machinery and equipment. The fact that the proportion of exports is lower than that of imports reflects China's gap in industrialization, although it has reached a high level.

14.5 Determinants of international trade

The conduct of international trade is influenced by a slew of factors. In other words, the volume of international trade depends on a number of factors: for example, whether the development strategy adopted is domestically oriented or export-oriented, that is, the degree of openness. Under an export-oriented strategy, the government will implement preferential policies for international trade. Under a domestically oriented strategy, the government will implement a policy of erecting high barriers. Moreover, the prices of imports and exports directly affect the volume of trade. If the price of domestic exports is higher than the price of imports, that is, the terms of trade are improved, the export volume may decrease, but export earnings may rise. Further, an increase in domestic revenue will increase imports in theory because it means an increase in purchasing power. Therefore, it can be used to buy more domestic goods, as well as foreign goods. In terms of exports, an increase in worldwide revenues and in the volume of international trade will boost the volume of exports of various countries. Of course, both exports and imports are restricted by other conditions, such as imports restricted by tariff barriers, and exports restricted by exchange rates.

14.5.1 Terms of trade

The terms of trade are first studied here. Terms of trade is the ratio of the export price index to the import price index. If the export price index increases relative to the import price index, this means an improvement in terms of trade. Otherwise, the terms of trade worsen. An improvement in the terms of trade means that exports are sold at higher prices, that the income will increase in theory, but that the volume of exports may fall due to higher prices. Therefore, it is uncertain whether more revenue can be obtained by improving the terms of trade.

Since the reform and opening up, China's terms of trade have basically declined, from about 1.2 in the early 1980s to 0.8 at present, but it was generally flat – or about 1 – in the 1990s. In other words, after the reform and opening up, China's terms of trade have deteriorated somewhat, but not too much. A modest deterioration in the terms of trade has a role of boosting exports, but if it deteriorates too much, it will reduce incomes. The deteriorating of China's terms of trade is primarily because China's exports are mainly low-end manufactured goods, which have a low added value, and it is difficult to ratchet up export prices. At the same time, imported goods are mainly relatively high-end manufactured goods, which have high added value and can maintain high prices. Although this situation is gradually changing, it will take some time from the standpoint of changes in the terms of trade, and it is difficult to bring about a comprehensive change in the short term.

Figure 14.4 shows two other relative prices: the ratio of China's import price to domestic price and the ratio of China's export price to world export price. The former indicates that imports will increase if import price is cheaper than China's domestic price, and vice versa. It can be seen from the figure that this ratio decreased significantly. In other words, this relative price ratio will boost imports.

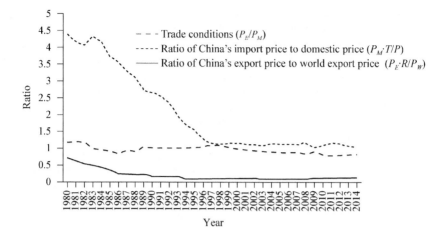

Figure 14.4 Changes in terms of trade, ratio of China's export price to world export price, and ratio of import price to domestic price

Sources: *China Statistical Yearbook 2015*, *China Trade and External Economic Statistical Yearbook 2014*, and the *United Nations Conference on Trade and Development Statistics*.

The latter means that if the price of China's export goods is lower than that of world exports, the volume of China's exports will increase. Otherwise, it will decrease. According to the figure, this ratio also declined, but the decline was larger in the early period (before the mid-1990s) and smaller (or was flat) in the later period (after the mid-1990s). It can be argued that China's exports improved in quality after the mid-1990s, leading to an increase in prices. In this sense, this confirms that the stage of China's industrial development, or, the mid-1990s, was a turning point.

In fact, many countries have a trend of worsening terms of trade in the process of economic development, which occurred in Japan in the first half of the 20th century. It also occurred in other developed countries, such as the United Kingdom from 1800 to 1880 and in Germany from 1870 to 1920. Of course, it remained relatively stable in other countries, such as France and Belgium. It increased in some countries, such as the United States and Sweden.[6] That is to say, various countries have different trends of changes in the terms of trade in the first half of economic development period. It can be considered that the process of economic development may be accompanied by a law in which the terms of trade decline first and then rise.

14.5.2 Calculation of the import and export function

The determinants of import and export are studied next through the calculation of the import and export functions. In general, changes in exports depend on two factors: the income effect and the price effect. The income effect means that an increase in national income of countries around the world will boost the global demand for goods, resulting in an increase in exports to a certain country (China). The indicator of world demand since 1980 is calculated here. Two assumptions are made: the world's total GDP (Y_w) and the world's total trade volume (T_W). The world trade volume index (2000 = 100) rose from 31 in 1980 to 285 in 2014, demonstrating its rate of fast growth. Over the same period, the total world GDP rose from 33 in 1980 to 234 in 2014, which was also an impressive figure. Of course, China's exports increased faster during this period.

The price effect refers to whether the price competitiveness of a country increases compared with other countries, that is, whether its share in the global market has expanded. If the ratio of the domestic export price ($P_E R$) (R = exchange rate of the renminbi to the U.S. dollar) to the world export price (P_W) calculated using the U.S. dollar falls, the domestic export price is lower than the world export price, and exports will increase. In fact, what determines the volume of exports is not the terms of trade just mentioned, but the ratio of domestic export prices to world export prices ($P_E R/P_W$). China's exports as a percentage of world exports rose from 0.9 percent in 1980 to 11.7 percent in 2013. Specifically, this ratio was not high, at only 3.9 percent until around 2000, when it began to rise rapidly.

Changes in exchange rates should also be considered because exchange rates directly affect the prices of imports and exports. The exchange rate of the renminbi has long been controlled, particularly under the planned economy. It has been relatively fixed for a long time even after the reform and opening up, despite some adjustments. From the 1980s onward, the renminbi tended to depreciate substantially against the U.S. dollar, then remained relatively stable until the reform of the exchange rate in 2005, before appreciating significantly afterward. This process shows China's tortuous reform and opening up process and its gradual economic development. China's exchange rate is not entirely regulated by the market, and even today China still operates a managed floating exchange rate, which affects the volume of China's imports and exports to some extent. The depreciation of renminbi in the 1980s promoted an increase in exports because China exports more primary products than manufactured goods at the time. The stability in the 1990s reflects the situation in the adjustment period, when China began to pursue economic internationalization and product competitiveness just emerged. The stable exchange rate actually refers to remaining stable at the low point, which was conducive to exports. After China's accession to the WTO in 2000, the rapid growth of China's economy and its robust export trend have had a great impact on other countries in the world. In the face of great external pressure to appreciate the renminbi, China has made an adjustment after weighing various factors. However, China's economy was already competitive during this period, and the appreciation of the renminbi did not cause a significant decline in exports.

The export function and the import function are calculated according to the income effect and price effect. The export function considers two scenarios: the total world trade as the world demand and the world GDP as the world demand.

The export function (14.1) (with total world trade as the world demand) is

$$\ln E = a + b\ln T_W + c\ln P_E R/P_W + u \tag{14.1}$$

The export function (14.2) (with world GDP as the world demand) is

$$\ln E = a + b\ln Y_W + c\ln P_E R/P_W + u \tag{14.2}$$

where ln is the natural logarithm; E is the actual export value; b is the income elasticity of exports, which is assumed to be positive value, namely how many percentage points E increases when T_W (world trade volume) increases by 1 percent; and how many percentage points E increases when Y_W (real gross world output) increases by 1 percent; c is the price elasticity, which is assumed to be a negative value, indicating the percentage that E increases when $P_E R/P_W$ decreases by 1 percent; u is a disturbance item.

The import function is

$$\ln M = a + b\ln Y + c\ln P_M T/P + u \tag{14.3}$$

where ln is the natural logarithm; M is the actual import value; b is the income elasticity of imports, which is assumed to be a positive value, namely how many percentage points M increases when Y (real domestic GDP) increases by 1 percent; c is price elasticity, which is assumed to be a negative value, indicating the percentage that M increases when $P_M T/P$ decreases by 1 percent; u is a disturbance item.

The calculation results are shown in Table 14.5. Since this period was China's reform and opening up period, the calculation results of the import and export functions are consistent with economic theory. The income effect and the price effect are basically significant and convincing, and the income effect obviously outperforms the price effect. In terms of the export function, there are two functions. In the first function, the total world trade is used as the income variable in the explanatory variables, and this function produced good results. In particular, the income effect is significantly better than the price effect. In other words, the increase in world trade has led to an increase in China's exports. The price effect is also not bad, indicating that the lower the price of China's exports is adjusted by the exchange rate in comparison with the world export price, the more it can promote China's exports. This is consistent with China's reality since the reform and opening up because China's principal exports during this period were inexpensive primary products and primary manufactured products. Of course, the grade of China's exports is also rising, and prices are also rising. It is expected that different effects may emerge in the future. At any rate, the low prices of Chinese goods have promoted China's export growth.

On the second scenario of the export function, the total world trade is replaced with world GDP as a revenue variable and effect variable. It implies that the increase in the economic aggregate of each country will increase the purchasing power and promote export. China, as a large exporter, is no exception. The results of this function are not as good as those of the first. Although the income effect is still good, the price effect is slightly inferior and is not statistically significant enough.

The import function has a result similar to that of the second export function, with a strong income effect and a weak price effect. In fact, China's import prices

224 Conditions and causes

Table 14.5 Calculation of export and import functions

Variable	Intercept	Parameter					R²	D.W.
		lnT_W	lnY_W	lnP_ER/P_W	lnY	lnP_MT/P		
Export function
$lnE(1)$	−3.971	0.849	–	−0.401	–	–	0.9624	0.37
	(−21.07)	(13.51)		(−4.84)				
$lnE(2)$	−5.289	–	1.210	−0.205	–	–	0.9524	0.34
	(−16.62)		(11.73)	(−1.89)				
Import function
lnM	−3.091	–	–	–	1.215	−0.277	0.9749	0.43
	(−4.11)				(12.28)	(−1.56)		

Sources: E, M, R from *China Trade and External Economic Statistical Yearbook 2014*. T_W, P_E, and P_M from United Nations Conference on Trade and Development Statistics; Y_W from the *World Development Indicators 2015*. Y from *China Statistical Yearbook 2015*, T from *China Fiscal Statistical Yearbook 2014*, and P from international financial statistics of the International Monetary Fund; P = GDP reduction index (2000 = 100) calculated according to *China Statistical Yearbook 2015*.

Note: The calculation period is from 1980 to 2014. E = export value, M = import value, Y = China's GDP (the preceding data are all 2000 prices, and the unit is 100 million yuan). T_W = world trade volume index, and T_W, P_ER/P_W, P_M, and P are all 2000 = 100. China's total exports, China's total imports, China's GDP, world trade volume, and world GDP all refer to the 2000 prices; China's export price index, China's import price index, world export price index, and GDP reduction index are 2000 = 100. The tariff rate from 1980 to 1997 is the arithmetic average tax rate and is estimated according to the reform process of China's customs tax system: the average tax rate of 1952 was adopted for 1980 and 1981; the average tax rate of 1982 was adopted for 1982, 1983, and 1984; the average tax rate of 1985 was adopted for 1985, 1986, and 1987; the average tax rate of 1988 was adopted for 1988, 1989, and 1990; and the average tax rate of 1993 was adopted for 1993, 1994, and 1995.

have been declining relative to domestic prices, and the decline is large. Tariffs have also decreased. Theoretically, the price effect should be better.

In brief, these import and export functions basically mirror the determinants of China's imports and exports after the reform and opening up and also prove the principle of market economy to be effective. In terms of exports, the income effect is significant, no matter whether total world trade or world GDP is used as a revenue variable. Although the price effect is not as good as the income effect, it can basically account for the problem. The same goes for the import function. Domestic GDP as a revenue variable performs a key role, and the income effect is significant. Although the price effect is not very significant, it can also explain the problem.

14.6 Conclusion

This chapter discusses China's development strategy and the role of international trade, from which the following lessons can be drawn. First, both economic theory and the practical experience of China's economy testify that a country's economic development is inseparable from the external environment, and self-isolation in any shape or form is detrimental to the local economic development and is also an obstacle to social progress. This is because, although economic and trade relations are, on the surface, trade in goods and services, as well as investment and financial exchanges, these are essentially people-to-people exchanges. People will impart knowledge and technologies as well as experience and lessons learned while engaging in economic and trade exchanges. No one is born wise, and no country can acquire advanced technology and knowledge without interacting with other countries. Complete self-isolation will get you nowhere, as China learned the hard way.

Second, China's opening up is a difficult and tortuous process, and China's economic development was plagued with setbacks. Opening up and international trade can spur economic development, which further promotes international trade. The two complement each other in a virtuous circle. In modern times, China was forced to open up when it lagged behind others. As a result, it had been in a passive situation and mired in a "comparative advantage trap" in international trade.[7] After 1949, the situation changed significantly, and China could conduct international trade independently. However, due to China's limited industrialization shortly after 1949, it could only export primary products and import manufactured goods. In addition, as the Cold War persisted, China could only trade primarily with other socialist countries, and the technology and information obtained from them were limited. After the reform and opening up, China made great strides through gradual development and opening up. After its accession to the WTO in 2001, it has become even more successful, with a quantum leap in both rapid economic growth and comprehensive trade development.

Third, whether international trade can develop well depends on domestic industrialization. If industrialization is successful, international trade can grow smoothly. If domestic industrialization is unsuccessful, or if China can produce only simple industrial products, international trade will be limited to exporting primary products and importing manufactured goods. On the other hand, to bring about domestic industrialization, it also needs good international economic and trade relations to some extent. The two reinforce each other. China has performed excellently in this regard, at least after the reform.

Notes

1 See Kuznets (1989).
2 Chenery and Syrquin (1988).
3 For this statement, see Guan Quan and Kong Jian (2008).
4 Ryoshin Minami (1981, 1992, 2002).
5 *World Development Indicators 2012*.
6 Ryoshin Minami (1981).
7 It refers to the failure to industrialize through long-term production and export of primary products in the international division of labor, leading to economic underdevelopment.

15 Direct investment
"Invite in" and "go global"

15.1 Introduction

As a continuation of the previous chapter, this chapter studies development strategies, or economic development after China opened up. While the preceding chapter deals with international trade, this chapter focuses on international investment, mainly foreign investors investing in China. The reason is crystal clear. In modern times, China had been very backward for a long time and had neither economic strength nor political influence to make outward investment. In the 21st century, China gradually acquired this capacity and soon began to invest abroad, which is called "going global". Although China's current outward investment lags far behind that of developed countries, it is growing rapidly. It is estimated that as China's economy further develops, China's outward investment will gradually shift from the nonmanufacturing to the manufacturing sector, and real multinational operations will be achieved.

The study of foreign investment should also be divided into two stages: the planned economy period and the reform and opening up period. This is particularly important for the discussion on the introduction of foreign investment because the investment environment and conditions are different in the early and later stages. In the early period, China had economic and trade exchanges primarily with other socialist countries, and there were almost no economic and trade exchanges with the developed Western capitalist countries, and therefore there was no possibility of introducing foreign investment from these countries. However, as the international situation and domestic demand changed, China began to import complete equipment from Western countries before the reform and opening up. In the later period, China fully opened up to the outside world. China strives to introduce foreign investment, and foreign investors also hope to take advantage of China's advantages in many areas. China has achieved leapfrog development through the introduction of foreign investment.

15.2 Introduction of foreign investment

After 1949, the introduction of foreign investment began with the 156 major projects aided by the Soviet Union during the first Five-Year Plan period. It should

DOI: 10.4324/9781003410393-18

be emphasized that, although Soviet aid was not necessarily the introduction of foreign investment according to today's standards, it was essentially of this nature. It not only increased China's capital and technology to a certain extent but also offered valuable experience for the subsequent improvement of China's industrial production and technological progress. Even today, the technologies used in some fields in China are from the enterprises introduced at that time.

As China established or resumed diplomatic relations with major Western countries in the 1970s, it opened the way for conducting trade and investment with them. During this period, China introduced a large number of large projects through the state, including chemical engineering, electric power, steel, and other fields. These were mainly introduced from the United States, France, the Netherlands, the Federal Republic of Germany, Italy, Japan, and other countries. These projects featured the production of chemical fertilizers, which laid a key foundation for agricultural production and development, and solved the problem of food shortage for the rapidly expanding population to some extent during this period. Chemical fiber factories produced new chemical fiber clothing, which ensured that some Chinese people were warmly clad. These projects had more advanced technologies than those imported from the Soviet Union. These advanced technologies from Western developed countries played a role in improving China's technological level at the time.

If the introduction of foreign investment in the planned economy period is said to be a special policy to facilitate industrialization, it has become common after the reform and opening up, although this process is as gradual as that of the reform and opening up. Table 15.1 shows the introduction of foreign investment after the reform and opening up. Foreign investment was less than US$2 billion in 1985, exceeded US$37.5 billion in 1995, exceeded US$60 billion in 2005, and exceeded US$126.2 billion in 2015. The number of foreign-funded enterprises increased from less than 5,000 in 1985 to 25,000 in 1990, jumped to 234,000 in 1995, remained at

Table 15.1 Foreign investment and foreign-invested enterprises introduced after the reform and opening up

Year	Investment (US$100 million)	Number of enterprises	Total investment (US$100 million)
1980	–	7	0.05
1985	19.56	4,912	164.12
1990	34.87	25,389	545.74
1995	375.21	233,564	6,390.09
2000	407.15	203,208	8,246.75
2005	603.25	260,000	14,639.93
2010	1,057.35	445,244	27,059.11
2018	1,349.66	593,276	77,738.00

Data source: *China Statistical Yearbook* over the years.

Note: The investment amount is the investment of the current year, and the total investment is the investment made by existing enterprises.

about 250,000 in subsequent years, but increased after 2005 and exceeded 590,000 in 2018, with a total investment in excess of US$7.8 trillion.

Another feature of the introduction of foreign investment is the change in the types of exports, that is, the change in the share of processing trade in all exports. This change was significant since the reform and opening up. It rose from a negligible figure to accounting for about half, as shown in Table 15.2. In 1981, the share of processing trade was tiny in terms of both imports and exports. After China vigorously promoted processing trade in the 1980s, this proportion rose rapidly, rising to 10.1 percent in 1985 to 40.9 percent in 1990. In the 1990s, China continued the reform and opening up and attracted a wealth of foreign investment. The share of processing trade approached 50 percent in 1995 and exceeded 55 percent in 2000. After China's accession to the WTO in 2001, China opened up in more areas, and foreign investment poured into China. This increased processing trade, which accounted for close to 60 percent in some years. However, as a result of the global financial and economic crisis in 2008, this proportion declined somewhat. In 2010, exports fell below 50 percent and imports fell below 30 percent. In 2015, exports declined to 35.1 percent, and imports remained only at 26.6 percent.

Next, we observe the proportion of the import and export value of foreign-invested enterprises to the total import and export value as well as the proportion of the industrial output value of foreign-invested enterprises to the national industrial output value, as shown in Figure 15.1. It can be seen that both proportions first rose and then fell, but not significantly. In terms of imports and exports, these were insignificant in the early 1980s and increased all along the way and peaked during the economic crisis in 2008, before declining. It peaked at 60 percent, and now remains at about 50 percent, which reflects the characteristics of China's processing trade mode after the reform and opening up. In addition, there were slightly more imports than exports, especially before 2008, and then there was a reversal. It can be said that imports come more as a result of the need for foreign-funded enterprises to import parts and raw materials.

Table 15.2 Changes in China's trade mode, Unit: %

Types	1981	1985	1990	1995	2000	2005	2010	2015
General trade								
Exports	94.5	86.8	57.1	48.0	42.2	41.4	45.7	53.4
Imports	92.5	88.2	49.1	32.9	44.5	42.4	55.1	54.9
Processing trade								
Exports	5.1	12.1	40.9	49.6	55.2	54.7	46.9	35.1
Imports	6.8	10.1	35.2	44.2	41.1	41.5	29.9	26.6
Other trade								
Exports	0.4	1.1	1.9	2.5	2.6	4.0	7.4	11.5
Imports	0.7	1.7	17.6	23.0	14.4	16.1	15.0	18.5

Data source: *China Trade and External Economic Statistical Yearbook* over the years.

Note: The total is 100, which is not shown here.

Direct investment 229

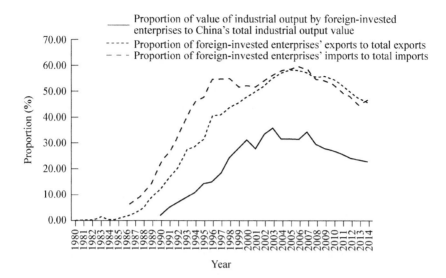

Figure 15.1 Proportion of imports and exports of foreign-invested enterprises to total imports and exports as well as the proportion of industrial output value of foreign-invested enterprises to the total industrial output value

Sources: *China Statistical Yearbook* and *China Industry Economy Statistical Yearbook* over the years.

We then examine the second proportion – the proportion of industrial output value. Although its proportion was not as high as that of imports and exports, it rose all the way and then slightly declined. It peaked at 35 percent and is now about 23 percent. It remained high in the period from 2000 to 2008, which shows the golden period of economic development after China's accession to the WTO. Judging from the preceding proportions, the importance and contribution of foreign investment to China's economic development are significant.

Next, we observe the proportion of foreign direct investment to domestic fixed asset investment and capital formation, as shown in Figure 15.2. Although the two proportions are slightly different, they show a trend of first rising and then falling. It was 2 to 4 percent in the early and late periods, peaking at 14 percent. It was the highest in the 1990s and low in the 1980s and after 2000. This is because China had just initiated reform and opening up in the 1980s, and few foreign investors entered China. As China further opened up after 1993, foreign investors began to enter China on a large scale. Because China had a low level of industrialization at the time, the proportion of foreign investment was high. After 2000, although foreign investment increased in China, the proportion of foreign investment was not so high because China has made key progress in industrial development.

As mentioned, China introduced foreign investment on a large scale after the reform and opening up. As China opens up wider and the economy gallops forward, especially after China's accession to the WTO, foreign investment has also

230 Conditions and causes

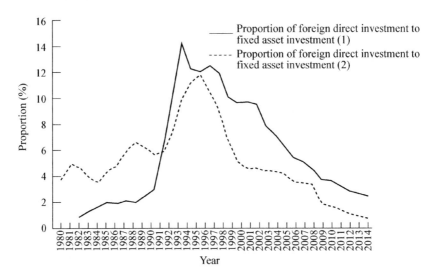

Figure 15.2 Proportion of foreign direct investment to fixed asset investment (capital formation)

Data source: *China Statistical Yearbook* over the years.

Note: (1) is the proportion of foreign investment to capital formation, and (2) is the proportion of foreign investment to fixed asset investment (foreign investment/total of state budgetary funds, domestic loans, self-financing, and other funds).

gradually increased. There is comprehensive foreign investment in terms of both regions and sectors, although there is a great bias in distribution.

Table 15.3 shows the distribution of industries for FDI enterprises in China from 2000 to 2018. The manufacturing sector has kept an overwhelming advantage for a long time, accounting for about half – sometimes even more – of total investment. This shows that foreign investment is attracted to China for its manufacturing and processing capacity and the vast market. It also includes the purpose of exports, as well as the cost and quality factors of China's labor. It is followed by the real estate industry, which is also a key industry in the Chinese economy. Especially after the housing reform in 1998, China's real estate sector showed an unprecedented momentum of development, and foreign investors would certainly not miss this opportunity. Other sectors that account for a large proportion include electricity, gas, and water supply, leasing and business services, scientific research, technical services, and geological exploration, transport, warehousing, and postal services. These sectors have their respective advantages. The electricity, gas, and water supply sector is a typical infrastructure sector that requires huge capital and offers good returns. Leasing and business services are emerging sectors in recent years. As urbanization deepens and the real estate sector emerges, this sector has also developed apace, becoming a key service sector. Scientific research and technical services are obviously a more forward-looking and promising sector, and foreign investors are primarily involved in research and development as well as

Table 15.3 Distribution of industries for foreign direct investment enterprises, Unit: US$100 million (%)

Industry	2000 Real number	2000 Pro-portion	2005 Real number	2005 Pro-portion	2010 Real number	2010 Pro-portion	2018 Real number	2018 Pro-portion
Total	8,246.75	100.00	14,639.93	100.00	2,7059	100.00	7,7738	100.00
Agriculture, forestry, animal husbandry, and fishery	92.15	1.12	234.63	1.61	325	1.21	9,549	12.28
Mining	27.70	0.34	63.86	0.44	151	0.56	221	0.28
Manufacturing	4,536.32	55.01	8,955.06	61.17	1,4306	52.87	23084	29.69
Electricity, gas, water supply	491.05	5.96	759.54	5.19	1,396	5.16	2,792	3.59
Construction	221.31	2.69	287.86	1.97	644	2.38	1,308	1.68
	332.05	4.03	459.11	3.14	907	3.36	2,061	2.65
			297.86	2.04	1,063	3.93	2,570	3.31
	252.83	3.07	285.07	1.95	1,032	3.82	4,879	6.28
Transport, warehousing, postal services			275.73	1.89	372	1.38	569	0.73
	19.99	0.25	46.77	0.32	437	1.62	4,023	5.18
Information transfer, computer services, software	1,512.47	18.34	1,851.67	12.65	3,570	13.20	8,556	11.01
			247.28	1.69	1,367	5.06	1,0119	13.02
	26.73	0.33	256.95	1.76	914	3.38	5,924	7.62
Wholesale and retail	41.81	0.51	99.83	0.69	170	0.63	590	0.76
Accommodation and catering	554.00	6.72	97.10	0.67	93	0.35	380	0.49
			6.98	0.05	9	0.04	83	0.22
Finance	24.38	0.30	20.01	0.14	25	0.10	258	0.33
Real estate	14.95	0.19	150.58	1.03	142	0.53	531	0.68
Leasing and business services	99.01	1.20	250.80	1.72	134	0.50	60	0.08
Scientific research, technical services, geological exploration								
Water conservancy, environment, public facilities management								
Resident services and other services								
Education								
Health, social security, social welfare								
Culture, sports, entertainment								
Other								

Data source: China Statistical Yearbook over the years.

Note: Some classifications in 2000 are different from those in subsequent years and are not shown here. For example, education is included in culture and sports; for another example, resident services belonged to the social service sector in 2000.

technical consulting sector, which is developing at a fast clip. Transport, warehousing, and postal services also belong to the infrastructure sector, which requires a lot of funds. Warehousing is an emerging sector in China. As the distribution industry develops rapidly, this sector has become one of the new areas of growth.

15.3 Calculation of the foreign investment demand function

Given the fact that China introduced foreign investment after the reform and opening up, the foreign investment demand function is calculated here, in the hope of explaining the influencing factors of foreign investment through quantitative relationship. Specifically, the explained variable is the amount of FDI actually utilized (F, US$ 100 million); explanatory variables are divided into income effect and price effect. The income effect includes (1) gross domestic product (Y, 100 million yuan) indicating market size, and (2) economic growth rate (GY, %) indicating potential (future) market size. The price effect uses labor costs, that is, (3) the average wage of employees of urban employers (W, yuan). Moreover, the dummy variable D is used to measure the impact of policy changes on FDI inflows. The numeral 1 represents the year in which national policies influence FDI, and 0 represents other situations. In 1992, Deng Xiaoping comprehensively expounded his ideas on the relationship between opening up to the use of foreign capital and socialism in his remarks on the tour of the South. The 14th National Congress of the Communist Party of China, held in the same year, set the reform goal of establishing a socialist market economy. These policies accelerated China's introduction of foreign investment. The number of foreign investment projects and contract amount approved by China in 1992 alone exceeded the sum for the previous 12 years. Besides, China officially became a member of the WTO on December 11, 2001. After China's accession to the WTO, market access restrictions on foreign investors (except for specific industries) and non-national treatment were reduced. These policies created good conditions for China to introduce FDI. China's FDI ranked top in the world in 2002. Accordingly, the value after 1992 (including 1992) is set to 1, and the value for previous years is 0. The function of FDI is as follows:

$$\ln F_t = a + b\ln Y_{t-1} + cGY_{t-1} + d\ln W_{t-1} + eD + u \qquad (15.1)$$

All variables except the economic growth rate are converted into log values for calculation. It is generally believed that the FDI of the current year depends on the market size, economic growth, and labor cost of the host country in the previous year. Therefore, all explanatory variables were regressed with one lag period. The situation from 1980 to 2014 is calculated here, with the calculation results shown in Table 15.4.

Judging from the calculation results, the foreign investment demand function is good and effective as a whole and is illustrative. First of all, the significance (value t) of the economic aggregate is very high, indicating that the economic aggregate has a great impact on FDI. The bigger the Chinese economy, the more attractive it is to FDI. Second, the economic growth rate is significant, and the symbols are also

Table 15.4 Calculation results of the foreign investment demand function

Variable	Definite number	Parameter				R^2
		lnY_{t-1}	GY_{t-1}	lnW_{t-1}	D	
lnF_t	−7.963 (4.23)	1.138 (−8.01)	0.054 (10.74)	−0.00003 (3.44)	0.901 (−4.53)	0.9846

Data source: China Statistical Yearbook 2015.

Note: The number in parentheses is the value t.

consistent, indicating that China's rapidly growing economy is attractive to FDI. Foreign investment will be based on the prospects of China's economic growth. Third, the calculation results of the labor cost variable are also significant, and the symbols are also in line with the (negative) logical relationship. In other words, the rise in labor costs in China has a negative impact on FDI. Finally, the symbols and significance of dummy variables are valid, indicating that different levels of reform and opening up before and after 1992 directly affect the trend of FDI.

15.4 Attempts at outbound investment

We also need to discuss China's outbound investment in recent years. As China's economy rapidly develops and China opens up wider to the outside world, China is not limited to exporting light textile products and introducing foreign investment or to being the world's largest country in terms of international trade volume and surplus. China has embarked on a new journey. China begins to invest in other countries, as developed countries do. In other words, China has gradually changed from a big country that attracts foreign investment to a big country that makes outbound investment. This is of decisive significance, marking a shift from borrowing money from others and learning technology to lending money and transferring technology to others.

China put forward a strategy of "going global" shortly after joining the WTO. As China's international trade rapidly increases and foreign investors enter China on a large scale, China's strength has greatly improved, and some Chinese industries and enterprises are willing and able to go global. Of course, China's labor costs are rising, and there is a need to find more suitable investment destinations. This generally takes two forms: One is the investment for resource development, mainly by large state-owned enterprises. The other is outward FDI, which is mainly undertaken by private small and medium-sized enterprises.

Statistics on China's outward FDI first appeared on *China Statistical Yearbook 2005*, which shows data for 2003 and 2004, with US$2.855 billion and US$5.498 billion, respectively. By the end of 2004, the net direct investment was US$44.777 billion. Leasing and business services had the largest share in the net amount, reaching US$ 16.446 billion, or 36.73 percent of the total. Ranking second is wholesale and retail trade, which reached US$7.843 billion, accounting for 17.52 percent. The mining sector ranked third, with an investment of US$5.951 billion, accounting for

13.29 percent. Ranking fourth is transport, warehousing, and postal services sector, with US$4.581 billion, accounting for 10.23 percent. Ranking fifth is the manufacturing sector, with US$4.538 billion, accounting for 10.14 percent. Ranking sixth is information transfer, computer services, and software sector, with US$1.192 billion, accounting for 2.67 percent. Ranking seventh is resident services, repairs, and other services sector, with US$1.093 billion, accounting for 2.44 percent. Ranking eighth is the water conservancy, environment, public facilities management sector, with US$911 million, accounting for 2.04 percent. Ranking ninth is agriculture, forestry, animal husbandry, and fishery sector, with US$834 million, accounting for 1.87 percent. Ranking tenth is the construction industry, with US$818 million, accounting for 1.83 percent. In terms of the proportion of industries, the manufacturing sector accounts for only 10 percent, the mining sector 13 percent, and the rest are all service sectors, indicating that China's outbound investment was dominated by the service sector at this point in time.

Table 15.5 shows the distribution of industries for China's outward direct investment in 2005, 2010, and 2018. Due to limited space, the table shows only the proportions of a few industries with large investment. In terms of amount and proportion, the largest investment was made in the leasing and business services sectors, accounting for about 30 percent or even more than 40 percent. It was followed by wholesale and retail trade, mining, and finance sectors. The wholesale and retail trade as well as financial sectors belong to the service sector. If leasing and business services are added, China's outbound investment is dominated by the service sector. The mining sector belongs to the development of resources. China must import resources because of the rapidly growing economy. Given limited domestic resources, developing resources overseas becomes inevitable. It is followed by the manufacturing industry. Unexpectedly, the proportion of this important industry declined, indicating that China's manufacturing sector is not strong enough to go global, and it needs to be transformed and upgraded.

As Table 15.5 shows, the investment in 2018 was US$143.037 billion. The net investment value by the end of 2018 was US$1,982.266 billion, which is obviously far more than that 10 years ago. Based on net worth, in 2018, the leasing and business services sector had the highest amount, with US$50.778 billion, accounting for 35.50 percent of the total. Ranking second is the financial sector, with US$21.717 billion, accounting for 15.18 percent. Ranking third is the manufacturing industry, with US$19.18 billion, accounting for 13.36 percent. Ranking fourth is wholesale and retail trade, with US$12.238 billion, accounting for 8.56 percent. As these figures show, although the manufacturing sector had a share of more than 13 percent, it still fell below that in 2005. It can be seen that China's current outbound investment is still mainly in the service sector. This is the case for the amount of investment in the current year and the net investment by the end of the current year. This is clear when compared to foreign investment in China. In 2018, foreign investment in China totaled US$134.966 billion. In terms of industry, the manufacturing sector ranked first, with US$41.174 billion, accounting for 30.51 percent of all investment. The real estate sector ranked second, with US$22.467 billion, accounting for 16.65 percent. The leasing and business services sector ranked third, with

Table 15.5 Distribution of industries for China's outward direct investment, Unit: US$ million (%)

Industry	2005	Net investment value by the end of 2005	2010	Net investment value by the end of 2010	2018	Net investment value by the end of 2018
Total	12,261.27	57,205.62	68,811.31	317,210.59	143,037.31	1,982,265.85
Agriculture, forestry, animal husbandry, and fishery	105.36	511.62	533.98	2,612.08	2,562.58	18,773.18
Mining	1675.22 (13.67)	8,651.61 (15.13)	5,714.86 (8.31)	44,660.64 (14.08)	4,627.94 (3.24)	173,480.81 (8.75)
Manufacturing	2,280.40 (18.60)	5,770.28 (10.09)	4,664.17 (6.78)	17,801.66 (5.62)	19,107.68 (13.36)	182,305.88 (9.20)
Electricity, gas, water supply	7.66	287.31	1,006.43	3,410.68	4,702.46	33,694.71
Construction	81.86	1,203.99	1,628.26	6,173.28	3,618.48	41,632.29
Wholesale and retail	2,260.12 (18.44)	11,417.91 (19.96)	6,728.78 (9.78)	42,006.45 (13.25)	12,237.91 (8.56)	232,692.68 (11.74)
Transport, warehousing, postal services	576.79 (4.70)	7,082.97 (12.38)	5,655.45 (8.22)	23,187.80 (7.31)	5,160.57 (3.61)	66,500.33 (3.35)
Accommodation and catering	7.58	46.40	218.20	449.86	1,353.96	4,404.34
Information transmission, computer services, software	14.79 (0.12)	1,323.50 (2.31)	506.12 (0.74)	8,406.24 (2.65)	5,631.87 (3.94)	193,574.56 (9.77)
Financial industry	–	–	8,627.39 (12.54)	55,253.21 (17.42)	21,717.20 (15.18)	217,895.44 (10.99)
Real estate	115.63	1,495.20	1,613.08	7,266.42	3,066.00	57,340.96
Leasing and business services	4,941.59 (39.49)	16,553.60 (28.94)	30,280.70 (44.01)	97,246.05 (30.66)	50,778.13 (35.50)	675,464.58 (34.08)

(*Continued*)

Direct investment 235

Table 15.5 (Continued)

Industry	2005	Net investment value by the end of 2005	2010	Net investment value by the end of 2010	2018	Net investment value by the end of 2018
Scientific research, technical services, geological exploration	129.42	604.31	1,018.86	3,967.12	3,801.99	44,245.64
Water conservancy, environment, public facilities management	0.13	910.02	71.98	1,133.43	178.63	3,131.08
Resident services, repairs, and other services	62.79	1,323.38	321.05	3,229.74	2,228.22	1,6715.29
Education	–	–	2.00	23.94	573.02	4,761.11
Health, social security, social welfare	–	0.11	33.52	36.16	524.80	2,996.97
Culture, sports, entertainment	0.12	5.38	186.48	345.83	1,165.86	12,655.99
Public administration and social organizations	1.73	18.03				

Data source: *China Statistical Yearbook* over the years.

Note: The numbers in parentheses are the proportions. Only industries with large proportions are shown here.

US$18.875 billion, accounting for 13.98 percent. The information transmission and software services sector ranked fourth, with US$11.661 billion, accounting for 8.64 percent. The wholesale and retail trade sector ranked fifth, with US$9.767 billion, accounting for 7.24 percent. The financial sector ranked sixth, with US$8.704 billion, accounting for 6.45 percent.[1] In this sense, China is not a really big country in terms of outbound investment, although China's outbound investment has exceeded foreign investment in China. Judging from the experience of developed countries, only a country with the capacity to invest abroad in the manufacturing sector can be called a real power in terms of outbound investment. China still has a long way to go in this regard.

15.5 Conclusion

This chapter examines the introduction of foreign investment and outbound investment. After 1949, China experienced two periods. In the planned economy period, China had almost no normal external relations due to domestic and foreign situations at that time, not to mention the introduction of foreign investment. Of course, China had imported a lot of technology and equipment and even the construction of the whole factory from the Soviet Union, which laid the foundation for China's industrialization to some extent.

After the reform and opening up, China's economy has rapidly developed largely as a result of opening up and the introduction of foreign investment. China is the world's most attractive country for foreign investment, and enterprises from more than 100 countries and regions have invested in China. While promoting China's economic development, it brings handsome benefits to these countries and regions. However, as we introduce foreign investment, we must be aware that, although foreign investment has played a role in the development of China's economy, overreliance on foreign investment will lead to contraction. This issue must be taken seriously. That is to say, more foreign investment is not necessarily better. Excessive competition in China should be avoided. Moderate competition is good, and, more importantly, the competition should be horizontal rather than vertical.

Finally, we examined China's "going global" situation in recent years. Since the early 21st century, China has gradually acquired the capacity to invest abroad. Through preliminary investigation, we see that China's going global is mostly for the service sector and resource development, but it is difficult for China to invest in the manufacturing sector. This issue deserves great attention.

Note

1 *China Statistical Yearbook 2019.*

Part IV
Summary and outlook

16 China's experience and prospects

16.1 Introduction

After 70 years of development, China now has a high level of economic development, although China still lags far behind the world's most developed countries. It is still worth summarizing experience[1] because three-fifths of the countries in the world have not yet developed, and a considerable number of them need to industrialize. Moreover, the experience of developed countries is outdated in some areas, and the development conditions of countries are also different. China is not only an emerging country but also a big country. A big country has both pros and cons. It is a miracle that a populous country like China has achieved such successful development. India, a populous country like China, obviously lags behind China economically and has not yet become a middle-income country, and its industry is not strong enough. It is difficult for it to summarize the development experience. China's development experience is both general and special. In terms of generality, the late-mover advantage hypothesis applies to some European countries and is often used metaphorically to describe the success of Japan and the Asian Tigers. The economic development of these countries and regions depended on the use of foreign investment and the introduction of foreign technology to a certain extent. They successfully achieved industrialization by digesting, absorbing, and improving foreign technologies. China also realized rapid economic development through the introduction of foreign investment and technology after the reform and opening up. In terms of the special nature, the relationships between the government and the market and between the government and enterprises have obvious Chinese characteristics, such as local governments promoting economic growth. Furthermore, it is rare for a big country to adopt an export-oriented development strategy. Generally, large countries tend to adopt a domestically oriented development strategy, while small countries are likely to adopt an export-oriented one. China's success as a big country in implementing an export-oriented development strategy is a valuable case that merits special mention. Moreover, a big country has a potential economies of scale effect. If the corresponding conditions are met, such as industrial base and human resources, the role of a huge market will be brought into play. If an export-oriented development strategy is also adopted, the country can become a key player in the international market. This is also a key reason that China becomes

DOI: 10.4324/9781003410393-20

the workshop of the world. The following is the discussion around these issues. It is hoped that China's experience in industrial development and even economic development can be summarized.

This final chapter sums up China's development experience, although China's economy has problems in many areas, and reform is needed to achieve further development. However, it is a miracle that a populous country can achieve such a high level of development, and therefore it deserves careful summary. This experience helps us to gain an insight into the laws of China's economic development and is also of reference value for other countries.

16.2 China's experience in economic development

16.2.1 Development model combining government and the market

As we know, China's economic development has always been dominated by the government in both the planned economy period and the reform and opening up period, only that it is only a matter of extent. Needless to say, during the planned economy period, the government played a role throughout, enterprises only worked for the government, factory directors had to obey the plans and arrangements made by the planning departments, and there was neither market nor decision-making power. A serious problem with the planned economy was the lack of market mechanisms. Enterprises lacked the motivation and capacity to do what they wanted to do. Planning departments developed economic plans according to rigid concepts, and enterprises were prone to slow going due to the lack of initiative. This resulted in insufficient supply. Some people call the economy in the planned economy period the "shortage economy".[2]

After the reform and opening up, the role of market forces comes into play. Enterprises can invest and produce (serve) according to their capabilities and market expectations, and the price signal of the market also comes into play, which is conducive to the effective allocation of resources and improved efficiency. Of course, the Chinese government intervenes appropriately in the market. The main means include supporting the lifeline of the national economy through state-owned enterprises, supporting the development of certain industries through industrial policies, participating in enterprise operations through government funds, and conducting macroeconomic regulation through financial and fiscal policies. In view of these, it can be considered that China is a "semimarket country" in which the market plays a role in some areas but is restricted in others. The areas in which the market role is restricted are generally key sectors related to the national economy and people's well-being, such as telecommunications, railways, aviation, shipping, military, oil, and finance. This practice aids economic stability but also leads to inflexibility and dependence on the government. Although state-owned enterprises have been greatly downsized, they still dominate important sectors. This limits the overall development and progress of China's economy. Because state-owned enterprises usually lack the initiative for operations, they passively work for the government in many cases. Due to the visible influence of the government, it is difficult to bring into play the due role of enterprises, particularly the entrepreneurial spirit. On the other hand, because the government restricts the participation of private enterprises in some areas, the development of private enterprises in China is restricted. Private enterprises can only conduct activities in areas related to people's daily lives and find it difficult to operate in key industrial sectors. As a result, China's private enterprises are rarely seen in some key arenas of increasingly fierce international competition. Enterprises that have developed in some fields also go it alone, without being able to create a huge industrial chain and industrial network. We rarely see state-owned enterprises in the cutting-edge fields of science and technology, while private enterprises find it difficult to become bigger and stronger in these fields due to a lack of funds, technology, and policy support because the positioning of private enterprises has been vague in China. However, such relationships between the government and the market and between the government and enterprises in China are objectively in line with China's reality and therefore have produced unexpected results. Although the government and state-owned enterprises occupy a favorable position and greater resources, the market is unlimited, and private enterprises can become successful in those sectors that are associated with the people's well-being. This can also be seen as a model of division of labor and cooperation. It is a matter of extent. If the government interferes in the market excessively, the market will react and cause the failure of the government. Therefore, the government will correct the mistakes and deregulate appropriately. China's economy has developed rapidly in this process of trial and error as well as error correction. It is also a model of development. Of course, this approach has many drawbacks, which will be exposed as the economy further develops. If connection is not made, the economy will run into trouble, and the government will make improvements. However, this model of error making and error correction has costs. It is expected that this model can become more efficient.

16.2.2 Outward-looking development strategy and economies of scale effect of a big country

As a big country, China should have adopted a domestically oriented development strategy, but it adopted an export-oriented development strategy after the reform and opening up. This helps China develop the world's resources and markets, promoting China's rapid development, especially making China the world's largest trading country and manufacturing powerhouse. According to the general law, a big country usually tends to use domestic resources because this benefits domestic employment and resource development. During the planned economy period, China adopted a domestically oriented development strategy and advocated self-reliance. One reason is the severance of ties with Western countries as a result of the Cold War between the East and the West. Another reason is that it has abundant resources. Admittedly, China is rich in resources. Were it not for a large population, China would have no shortage of resources, but China is a country with insufficient resources because of the large population. This is different from big countries in a general sense. Several of the world's countries with a vast territory have a relatively small population, including Russia, Canada, the United States, Brazil, and Australia. Only India is similar to China, with a large population density.

After the reform and opening up, China learned the lessons from the planned economy period and adopted a new development strategy. Drawing on the experience of the Asian Tigers, China began to implement an export-oriented strategy and to use external resources as much as possible. China attracted foreign investment and earned foreign exchange through processing exports and then imported equipment and technology for its own development. This has injected development vitality into the southeast coastal areas. Through overseas Chinese capital and later foreign investment, southeast coastal areas used the cheap labor to form huge processing trade areas. These areas not only earned foreign exchange but also led to labor mobility as well as the formation and development of industrial zones.

The export-oriented development strategy of the Asian Tigers is characterized by being small and flexible. They leverage the world's resources and markets to provide abundant opportunities for their own development. China, in contrast, is a huge market in its own right. However, its abundant resources and vast territory are not comparable to the world market and resources, which can be verified by comparison with the United States, Canada, Australia, and Russia. The United States, Canada, and Australia are highly open countries, where there is no artificial restriction on the utilization of external resources. However, these countries have a small population relative to their territorial areas and are rich in resources, and therefore they are not highly dependent on trade. Canada and Australia have small populations and rich resources. Russia has a vast territory and a relatively small population, and its manufacturing sector is unevenly developed. According to the characteristics of the aforesaid countries, it can be said that China is the only big country that adopts the strategy generally adopted by a small country. It is precisely because of this that China has become what it is today. If China still adopted the domestically oriented strategy as it did in the planned economy period, it would not have such a high level of development.[3]

It is important that China is a big country in terms of both territorial area and population. Only two countries in the world have this population size, the other being India. However, India's territorial area is only one-third of China's territorial area. The significance of emphasizing a populous country is that once a populous country develops, it may become the manufacturing center of the world. China has gradually become such a center since the 1990s. Despite the fact that being such a world processing factory does not mean being powerful and advanced, the economies of scale is unrivaled. As a result of China's export-oriented development strategy after the reform and opening up, export processing zones have been established in coastal areas, and a huge production and processing capacity has been developed. Together with the productive capacity of the inland areas, China has a huge economy of scale. This can be manifested in two areas: the domestic market and the international market.

Previously, the domestic market was only potential. As the hinterland also achieves rapid economic development, various enterprises have also emerged in the hinterland, as evidenced by the widespread township and village enterprises throughout the country. In addition to township and village enterprises, other types of enterprises, particularly private enterprises, have mushroomed, which lays the foundation for the development of the domestic market. As people's income levels rise, the level of domestic consumption is rising. Therefore, the effect of domestic production and sales has been expanded, which provides "logistical support" for China to become the world's processing factory.

The international market is enormous and is largely in a state of perfect competition. Therefore, the participation of small countries in the international market is inconspicuous because they are a bit player in the world market, such as the Asian Tigers. China is a different case. Once China has the capacity to produce a certain product, it is possible to become a huge producer. Although it is not fully sure that China has a kind of monopoly power in the international market, there is no denying that China is the world's top country in terms of the production of many industrial products. For example, China's textile exports, such as clothing to the United States, account for about 80 percent of the U.S. imports, while Vietnam, which ranks second, accounts for only about 5 percent. China may not have a monopoly over textiles due to the characteristics of some commodities and other market factors, but its market share abundantly illustrates its influence. This is not to say that China has the power to monopolize the market but only that China has this capacity to provide commodities to the world. In this sense, China brings into play its comparative advantages due to the division of labor and also has the effect of economies of scale. This is a phenomenon deserving attention and study.

16.2.3 Late-mover advantage and social capacity

With regard to how a backward country can catch up with developed countries, there is a famous "late-mover advantage" hypothesis put forward by the American economic historian Gerschenkron in 1962. Through his research on several European countries that were relatively backward in modern times, such as Italy and Russia, he concluded that backward countries can catch up by introducing technologies from developed countries rather than by starting from scratch. Thereafter, many scholars have interpreted this hypothesis in various ways. The Japanese scholar Ryoshin Minami confirmed Gerschenkron's hypothesis – the more backward the country, the higher the economic growth rate – by comparing the development rate of Japan in about 100 years after the late 19th century with that of the world's major developed countries.

No matter whether the calculations begin in 1949 or 1978, China was one of the most backward countries in the world at the time. China's GDP per capita was less than US$50 in 1949 and US$155 in 1978, both of which values were among the lowest in the world rankings. The proportion of the rural labor force was high (91.52 percent in 1949 and 76.13 percent in 1978), and the urbanization rate was very low (10.64 percent in 1949 and 17.92 percent in 1978).[4] However, the economic growth was relatively high after 1949 and even reached 5 to 6 percent in the planned economy period. After the reform and opening up, the growth rate was up to 9 percent or so. No other country has achieved such a high growth in the past

70 years. As a result, China has evolved from a poor and backward country into an upper-middle-income country with GDP per capita of nearly US$10,000. It can be said that China is one of the typical countries that proves the late-mover advantage hypothesis, especially as a populous country.

As Ryoshin Minami pointed out, the late-mover advantage is not manifested in all developing countries because it requires many conditions. "Social capability" is one of the key factors. Kuznets pointed out one reason – namely, social capability – for Japan's economic development and the absorption of advanced Western technology.[5] However, Kuznets did not explain what exactly social capability meant. Later, Kazushi Okawa and H. Rosovsky explained and argued that improved social capability played a key role in introducing technology and enhancing technological progress, thereby promoting economic growth.[6] On this basis, Ryoshin Minami listed four categories by way of explanation. First, human resources, including entrepreneurs and excellent labor, particularly technicians. Second, the ability to collect information on foreign science and technology as well as industrial development. Japan's comprehensive commercial companies play an important role in this regard. Third, the construction of infrastructure, which has promoted the formation and development of the national market. Fourth, promising government. In particular, the industrial revitalization policies implemented by the government in the Meiji period provided a guarantee for industrialization. The provision of compulsory education and higher education has cultivated a wealth of high-quality personnel. He also stressed that social capability is not static but improves as industrialization deepens.[7]

Except for the second item that Ryoshin Minami described, which is currently uncertain, China has the other three capabilities. In terms of human resources, Chinese entrepreneurs have made outstanding contributions to economic development and industrialization, which is evident to all, after the reform and opening up. Chinese people are business-savvy, studious, able, efficient, and hard-working. Given a good environment, many people with entrepreneurial spirit will devote themselves to economic activities. There is no shortage of outstanding ordinary workers in China. There is a wealth of highly skilled workers in the industrial sector as a result of training during the planned economy period. There is also no shortage of technical personnel. Many engineers and technicians had been trained in various ways during the planned economy period. China's higher learning institutions and secondary vocational schools are relatively developed, providing a guarantee for the cultivation of technical personnel. Infrastructure was built on a large scale even in the planned economy period. After the reform and opening up, China has built highways, as well as aviation and shipping infrastructure at a fast clip. Railway speed increased several times in the 1990s. The electrical multiple units (EMUs) and high-speed railways have been built since the early 21st century, becoming a new ambassador of China. The fourth is the promising government.[8] It means that the government can mobilize all forces in society to make tireless efforts to promote economic development. China's government has this willingness and capacity. This was absolutely the case during the planned economy period. After the reform and opening up, the government has also spared no effort to promote economic development. Of course, it is not that the more government intervention there is, the better. Oftentimes, excessive government intervention may cause market distortion and failure. It is a fact that the Chinese government's excessive intervention in the economy is often criticized. Therefore, government intervention should be limited to a certain scope. For example, the government should not be directly involved in economic activities, and state-owned enterprises should exit from more industries so that private enterprises can operate in their place.

In addition to what Ryoshin Minami said, several areas are worth discussing. First is whether there is a traditional business culture. China has a time-honored business culture. Although businesspeople do not have a high social status and doing business is not considered a noble profession in traditional society, Chinese businesspeople have emerged one after another, and a developed commodity economy has been formed. Well-known merchant groups, such as Shanxi merchants, Anhui merchants, Fujian merchants, and Zhejiang merchants, have previously emerged in China. After modern times, overseas Chinese can be seen all over the world. They are known for being hard-working, capable, and efficient. In contrast, some countries lack this business culture and business-savvy merchants. As a result, it is difficult for them to engage in business operations in the industrial era. The fact that overseas Chinese in many Southeast Asian countries can dominate the lifeline of the local economy is attributed to China's business culture, while foreign locals lack this ability.

Second is whether there is a traditional market. China is steeped in history. Because of the long-standing farming culture, trade in agricultural products is highly developed, with agricultural products trading markets all over the country. Through such markets, farmers and craftsmen exchange agricultural products, handicraft products and, more importantly, information. As a result of this exchange, people get better acquainted, enhance understanding, and keep abreast of the latest news. This seemingly inconspicuous market broadens people's horizons. Although this exists in most countries, the nature and size of the market are different because of the different national conditions and styles.

Third, the fact that China lagged far behind the developed countries in terms of economic development and industrialization in modern times does not mean that no progress was made. With the rise of the Self-Strengthening Movement and the establishment of a large number of small and medium-sized private enterprises during the Republic of China period, modern industries centered on cities emerged throughout the country, laying the groundwork for formal industrialization after 1949. After 1949, the government-led industrialization movement kicked off. Impressive results were achieved, although China adopted the planned economy, the development strategy was domestically oriented, and the strategy of prioritizing heavy industry and neglecting light industry was implemented in defiance of the general practice. After about 30 years of development, a complete industrial system has basically been put in place, which could produce the vast majority of industrial products. A wealth of engineers and technicians, as well as skilled workers with certain knowledge and experience has been cultivated. This foundation of industrialization facilitated the introduction and digestion of advanced foreign technologies after the reform and opening up, laying the foundation for China to become the world's processing factory.

16.3 Extension of China's development experience

These are several cases of China's experience in economic development. In this section, the general laws affecting economic development are studied in conjunction with China's experience, in the hope of providing reference value for other countries. Based on earlier studies by others and the author's understanding, a relationship chart was produced for the economic development of later developing countries, especially industrial development. Figure 16.1 shows the influence of various factors on economic development. In other words, the role of these factors is required for industrial development. This concerns two players: the market and the government, or the mutual influence and role of the market and the government. They contain six factors, with certain correlation for some factors.

We first examine the market factor. The first is the development level of the market, that is, whether there is a national market. Some countries have tribes and are self-sufficient, without a unified national market (as in some African countries), which works against economic development, especially industrial development. Industrial development requires clusters, or urbanization. It also requires a wealth of labor forces, which are transferred from rural areas. Without a unified national market, each tribe lives in a narrow space and is influenced by an independent religion and culture. It is difficult for them to leave tribes and become citizens and industrial workers. Second, the absence of a unified market means an underdeveloped business culture. A key role of business culture is to pass on information. Merchants carry goods from one place to another, so that people can consume products not available locally. They also transmit cultures and messages, allowing people to broaden their horizons. Moreover, as businesspeople are savvy, well informed, shrewd, and well travelled, and are interested in new things, they can

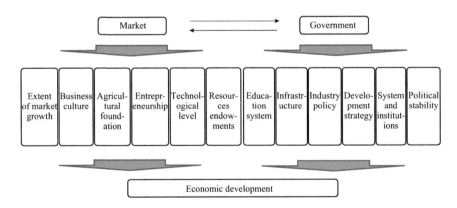

Figure 16.1 Factors influencing economic development

easily become a key force in promoting industrialization. Furthermore, merchants are usually richer than ordinary farmers and urban residents. In the early days of industrialization, many merchants invest in industry, either independently or in cooperation with others. Of course, business culture alone is not enough. Agricultural foundation is also needed. The level of agricultural development largely holds the key to successful industrialization in the early stage because agriculture contributes to industrialization in many areas. For example, the surplus agricultural funds are used for industrial construction; surplus labor from agriculture is transferred to industry; foreign exchange earnings from agricultural exports are used to buy industrial equipment; agriculture provides food for industrial workers and urban dwellers; and agriculture provides industry with raw materials and markets as industrial products.[9] As some countries (such as Africa) are not agriculturally developed enough and remain at a state of primitive tribes, it is difficult for them to achieve industrialization. It is universally recognized that entrepreneurs play a central role in industrialization and economic development and are the most important factor. According to J. A. Schumpeter, entrepreneurs, unlike ordinary business operators, are a group of innovative people. Innovation refers to "creative disruption", which means smashing the old framework and introducing new technologies. Ordinary operators only pursue maximum profits, and this is not enough to promote economic development.[10] Of course, the development of industry requires technical reserves and related knowledge. There is generally no developed technology in the early days, most of which are traditional technologies, notably handicrafts. Industrialization requires the introduction of modern industry, namely mechanized production. It usually starts with light industry (like food and textiles) and gradually extends to heavy industry (such as metallurgy, chemical engineering, and machinery). This must be grounded in a country's resource endowment. The technology adopted and industries developed are different due to the varying national conditions of countries. Some countries are sparsely populated but have a vast territory, while some are small in size but large in population. Other countries are landlocked and find it difficult to engage in international trade. Some countries are woefully short of resources to develop their own industries and must rely on international trade.

In terms of these market factors, China outperforms other developing countries. First of all, China has a long-standing farming culture and commercial civilization. Even in a traditional society which has no modern means of transport, the markets in rural areas are highly developed, not to mention the role of merchant culture. Famous merchant groups have emerged throughout China, who have travelled to all corners of the country and have greatly promoted the formation of a unified national market and the transmission of information. These merchant groups have travelled extensively, and some have even participated in international trade. China is a major agricultural country with an agricultural civilization that has lasted thousands of years. Farmers were the main group before industrialization, and agricultural production technologies are well developed. Some areas become lands of agriculture and fishery with abundant resources. Entrepreneurship came into play during the Republic of China period. Many small and medium-sized enterprises were established throughout the country, particularly in coastal areas. They achieved great success in silk reeling, textile, papermaking, matches, flour, machinery, chemical engineering, and other sectors, and the first group of entrepreneurs emerged, making a key contribution to the formation and development of industry in the Republic of China period.[11] The market was abolished under the planned economy after 1949, and entrepreneurs disappeared. This disrupted the continuation of entrepreneurship. After the reform and opening up, entrepreneurs emerged again and rose rapidly. They now become a key force to promote China's economic growth. In terms of the level of technology, modern industrial technologies were introduced at the end of the 19th century, but mainly the military industry and a small proportion of heavy industries. During the Republic of China period, light industry technologies were introduced to China. Chinese people gradually mastered many of these technologies. Following the Japanese occupation of northeast China, many enterprises were established, mainly in heavy industry, which made important contributions to industrial development after the founding of the People's Republic of China. The 156 major projects aided by the Soviet Union in the 1950s also laid the foundation for industrial development during the planned economy period, particularly the development of heavy industries and military sector. The "three-line construction" in the 1960s reinforced the foundation of heavy industries and the military sector. These industrial bases provided technical support for absorbing imported technologies and developing emerging industries after the reform and opening up. In terms of natural resource endowments, China is a large and resource-rich country. However, due to the rapid population growth and industrialization after 1949, China suffered a shortage of resources. In terms of production factors, during the planned economy period, China, a populous country, was mainly an agricultural country, with a low level of industrialization and inadequate industrial labor, which made it difficult to achieve rapid industrialization. Funds were scarce, and technology was backward at this time. Progress was made in some areas, but it mainly took place in heavy industry. Heavy industry was not an industry that developed in accordance with market principles but was developed as a result of development strategies.

The market cannot completely determine economic development. In many cases, government assistance or promotion was needed. The market foundation is weak in most countries, which lack a unified market, business culture, and entrepreneurship, not to mention technology. Most of today's developed countries are European countries, and the residents of North America and Australia are mostly descendants of Europeans. Europe possesses the aforesaid market characteristics, such as business culture, entrepreneurship, and technology. Japan, the first developed country in East Asia, also meets these conditions compared with other backward regions and countries. Nevertheless, the role of government in Japan's economic development is also clear.[12] In other words, the vast majority of countries in the world lack the conditions to rely solely on market forces to achieve economic development. In many cases, government involvement is required and sometimes dominant, as evidenced by the Asian Tigers and China. Of course, the role of the government has been contentious. What the government should do and should not do can only be determined in light of national conditions.

Next, we examine the role of the government. First of all, the government needs to put in place a modern education system to cultivate personnel needed for economic development, whether it be primary education or higher education. As the economy develops, the private sector will also evolve to contribute to education. Second is the construction of infrastructure, including roads, railways, aviation, electric power, communications, as well as providing running water and gas in cities. These sectors are usually natural monopolies that require abundant capital. Private capital is powerless in this regard. Moreover, private capital pursues private interests and cannot guarantee services of a public nature. Of course, with the development of the economy and social progress, these areas may also become part of the private sector. There is a better environment at the legal level and supervision level by this time, and the private sector may perform better. Third is industrial policy, which is controversial, particularly in China. In fact, industrial policies are also implemented in developed countries, but not of on the scale and with the influence they have in China. The United States also protects those vulnerable industries and enterprises and subsidize farmers. Japan is the birthplace of industrial policy. To catch up with European and American countries after World War II, Japan implemented many industrial policies, including foreign exchange control, support for certain industries, and the combination of industry, officials, and universities. In China, which is a socialist country, the government controlled the lifeline of the economy in addition to industrial policy in the planned economy period. After the reform and opening up, the Chinese government gradually delegated some powers to the market, such as price setting. The number of state-owned enterprises was slashed, and almost all collective enterprises have become private enterprises. Nevertheless, the willingness and capacity of the Chinese government to engage in economic activities remain unchanged. It not only participates in but often dominates economic activities in various forms, including preserving state-owned enterprises in key sectors. Industrial policy is also a key means. This arouses great controversy, with some saying that industrial policy distorts market prices and leads to unfair competition. Others argue that industrial policy is necessary for catching up with developed countries because it is impossible to rely on market forces alone in the face of powerful opponents. In addition to industrial policy, the government does the more important job of formulating development strategies. Compared with industrial policy, the development strategy is more important and has a greater effect. There are usually two types of development strategies: domestically oriented and outward-looking. The former strategy makes use of existing domestic resources, while the latter focuses on the use of external resources. The two have their respective advantages, focus, and effect, and various countries formulate appropriate or inappropriate strategies in light of national conditions and the nature of the government. For example, small countries are often suited to outward-looking development strategies because they lack the basic resources that support economic development, such as natural resources and land. Large countries have a considerable quantity of resources (such as natural resources and labor force) and are inclined to domestically oriented development strategies. However, even large countries (such as China and India), should adopt an outward-looking strategy because the large population increases resource pressures. Of course, what kind of development strategy to adopt at what stage of development is worthy of study. According to the experience of the Asian Tigers and China, they were not open from the outset. Instead, they adopted a protectionist policy, set high tariffs, and supported the development of infant industries. When some industries become competitive, the country begins to open up. In this way, it will not be monopolized by high-level technology and markets from developed countries. China adopted an inward-looking development strategy during the planned economy period, which laid the industrial foundation to some extent. Although there was a process of a painful adaptation after the reform and opening up, and some enterprises and industries took a hard hit, it still has grown up.

System and institutions can also be important, which is a complicated issue. Here, it mainly refers to government-led or market-led. In other words, it is to what extent and how the government should play a role. Because China has experienced both the planned economy period and the reform and opening up period, and the economy has obviously performed better after the reform and opening up, it is unnecessary to discuss which is better. It is important to understand why a certain system is better. The economy performs better after the reform and opening up for a number of reasons. First, the market mechanism has been put in place through reform. Resources can be effectively allocated, and people have the initiative for work. Second, China integrates itself into the international market through opening up and uses its comparative advantage to engage in trade, while introducing foreign investment and technology. Moreover, the Chinese people are diligent and intelligent, and China already had a good industrial base. The issues of how the government should play a role, how to position itself, and what economic activities it should participate in deserve serious study. It depends on the national conditions and stage of development of each country. Generally speaking, the government should be responsible for redistribution, maintaining public order and the public sector, overseeing the market conduct according to laws and regulations, and appropriately regulating the economic cycle through macroeconomic policies, while other activities should be left to the market and entrepreneurs.

Finally, we talk about political stability, which is a very important issue, but it is difficult to give a clear explanation. To develop the economy, a country must first have political stability. A chaotic political situation, a coup d'état, or the scramble for political power is obviously detrimental to economic development. After 1949, China also went through an unstable period such as the Cultural Revolution, which played havoc with economic activities and led to social chaos. After the reform and opening up, China has stability and has boldly carried out reforms, and foreign investors enter China without fear. Many countries that gained independence after World War II did not have the political stability that China enjoys because of head-on clashes or armed battles among different political forces or even direct coups. It is also noteworthy that the goal of governments or political parties in some developing countries is not to develop economies and enhance their people's living standards but to keep their own rule. This easily breeds corruption and social injustice. Economic benefits are mostly shared among a few rulers, and ordinary people lack the ability to oppose or resist them. They have no choice but to resign themselves to the situation, flee the country, or participate in the rebel forces, as is the case in some African countries. China has done a good job in this regard. Corruption was almost nonexistent in the planned economy period. Although rampant corruption occurred after the reform and opening up, it was put right in a timely manner. In addition, we give our views on the political systems of developing countries that do not adopt Western-style democracy, and many governments of developing countries do not adopt Western-style democracy. Instead, only one party or a few leaders have the final say. This system is often referred to as "authoritarianism". In our view, if the goal of the government or ruling party is to develop the economy and bring benefits to the people, it can be called an authoritarian government. If it is to simply maintain rule, suppress the opposition, and indulge in corruption, it is an authoritarian regime or an authoritarian system.

The relationship between the market and the government, as well as the factors related to both, have been studied. In fact, there are other factors. For example, the population issue is not discussed here. Moderate population growth is one of the necessary conditions for economic growth and development. Because it belongs neither to the market nor to the government, it is not shown in the chart. According to economic theory and population theory, as well as the experience of various countries in development, population growth should be neither too slow nor too fast. Too slow a population growth cannot meet the demand for labor in industrial and urban development. Too fast a population growth will easily cause negative effects, such as high unemployment, which will impose a burden on society and the government. During the planned economy period, China experienced excessive population growth. Cognizant of this problem, the government adopted a family planning policy in a timely manner to keep the population growth rate at a low level. Although this policy has negative effects in many areas, it is generally more positive than negative in terms of economic growth. Compared with China, many developing countries that gained independence after World War II experienced rapid population growth known as "population explosion", but few countries adopted a family planning policy and went on to achieve rapid economic growth. India adopted the family planning policy, but to little avail. India will have a bigger population than that of China, and this is undoubtedly a negative factor for India's economic growth.

There are social, cultural, geographical, and other factors, such as religion and values, whether it is collectivism or individualism and whether it is a landlocked country or a maritime state. However, these factors cannot be changed in a short time and can only be discussed as a social foundation. Some factors indeed impede the process of economic development. For example, too strict religious beliefs are detrimental to economic development, and the geographical environment of tropical countries is also detrimental to industrialization.[13]

16.4 Conclusion

From the perspective of long-term development, this chapter gives a detailed summary and evaluation of China's economic development over approximately 70 years since 1949, including experiences and lessons learned, as well as achievements and problems. Our goals are to sum up experience, build on achievements, learn lessons, and have a forward-looking vision. The 70-year-plus development course since 1949 is an arduous and challenging process, but there are also hope and impressive achievements. We still lag behind Japan and South Korea, which are also East Asian countries, and we must keep working. However, we have achieved a roaring success and have become the world's processing factory, and no other country can replace China in the short term. This is unmatched by India, which has national conditions similar to those of China. Nevertheless, we must be aware of our own problems and shortcomings and realize that many countries have also achieved what we have accomplished. We have done right in many areas, but that doesn't mean smooth sailing in the future. We hope that China will achieve the goal of becoming a moderately developed country by the middle of this century, but it is uncertain because we face domestic problems and international interference, which must be resolved one by one. Domestic problems include institutional limitations, low quality of population, insufficient labor supply, lack of innovation capacity, and lack of high-level technology. International interference includes restrictions and suppression imposed by Western countries, exclusive groups organized by certain countries, challenges from emerging powers, and uncertainty in international relations. Challenges include the recent trade war waged by the United States, Japan replacing the United States to establish the Comprehensive and Progressive Agreement for Trans-Pacific Partnership (CPTPP), a new trade agreement reached by Japan and the United States, a new free trade agreement reached by Japan and the European Union, the redefined North American Free Trade Agreement (NAFTA), and the rapidly developing Vietnam and India. In short, a period of 70 years is a turning point. Even as we look back at the past, we must also be forward-looking. Past achievements do not represent the future. There was no smooth sailing in the past, and the lessons learned are worth summarizing. The development experience of other countries also deserves our learning. We must free our minds and move forward boldly. The future is bright, but the road ahead has twists and turns.

Notes

1 For achievements and issues in China's industrial development, see Guan Quan (2019a).
2 For the views of the Hungarian economist Kornai, see Kornai (1986).
3 For issues related to trade dependency, see Guan Quan (2005), Guan Quan and Kong Jian (2008).
4 *China Statistical Yearbook 1984*.
5 Kuznets (1968).
6 Ōkawa Kazushi and Rosovsky (1973).
7 Ryoshin Minami (1981), pp. 122–123.
8 See Lin Yifu (2014).

9 For the role of agriculture in the early days of industrialization, see Guan Quan (2014, 2018a).
10 For Schumpeter's innovations, see Schumpeter (1990); it was partially supplemented by Guan Quan (2014, 2018a).
11 For the development of China's industry and entrepreneurship during the Republic of China period, see Guan Quan (2018a).
12 For the development of the Japanese economy, see Ryoshin Minami (1981).
13 For information in this regard, see Guan Quan (2014, 2018a).

References

Literature of the Chinese edition

Cai Fang. *Demystifying the Economic Growth in Transition China*. Beijing: China Social Sciences Press, 2012.

Cai Fang and Wan Guanghua. *Income Disparity and Poverty in Transition China*. Beijing: Social Sciences Academic Press, 2006.

Dong Zhikai and Wu Jiang. *The Cornerstone of Industry in the People's Republic of China: Study of 156 Projects*. Guangzhou: Guangdong Economy Publishing House, 2004.

Du Runsheng, editor-in-chief. *Agricultural Cooperative System in Contemporary China* (Parts 1 and 2). Beijing: Contemporary China Publishing House, 2002.

Gan Li, et al. *China Household Finance Survey*. Chengdu: Southwestern University of Finance and Economics Press, 2012.

Guan Quan. "Crossing the Lewis Turning Point: The Japanese Experience and Its Inspiration". In *Nankai Japan Studies*, edited by Mang Jingshi. Beijing: World Affairs Press, 2010.

Guan Quan. *Development Economics: China's Economic Development*. Beijing: Tsinghua University Press, 2014.

Guan Quan. "See 'Child Power' for Economic Development from the Perspective of 'Universal Two-Child Policy'". *PKU Business Review*, Vol. 138, 2016.

Guan Quan. *Development Economics*. Beijing: China Renmin University Press, 2018a.

Guan Quan. *Industrial Development in Modern China: Comparison with Japan*. Beijing: China Renmin University Press, 2018b.

Guan Quan. "The Role and Significance of Rural Industrial Development in China". *The 8th International Symposium on the History of Indigenous Knowledge*. Kyushu University, Japan, November 2018c.

Guan Quan. "70-year Industrial Development in China". *Economic Theory and Business Management*, Vol. 9, 2019a.

Guan Quan. *China's Economic Development: A Century History*. Beijing: China Renmin University Press, 2019b.

Guan Quan and Kong Jian. "A study on trade dependency". *Open Economic Review*, Vol. 1, 2008.

Hou Yangfang. *History of China's Population: Volume 6*. Shanghai: Fudan University Press, 2001.

Kim Changnam. "Structural changes and Turning Points in the Korean Labor Market". In *A Turning Point in China's Economy*, edited by Ryoshin Minami, Makino Fumio, and Hao Renping. Beijing: Social Sciences Academic Press, 2014.

Li Shi, Luo Chuliang, et al. *An Empirical Analysis of Income Gap in China*. Beijing: Social Sciences Academic Press, 2014.

Li Shi, Sato Hiroshi, Terry Sicular, et al. *Analysis of the Change in Income Gap in China: Research on Income Distribution in China IV*. Beijing: People's Publishing House, 2013.

Li Wei. *Agricultural Surplus and Industrialized Capital Accumulation*. Kunming: Yunnan People's Publishing House, 1993.

Li Yang. *Finance Over 60 Years in the People's Republic of China*. Beijing: China Financial and Economic Publishing House, 2009.

Lin Yifu. *System, Technology and Agricultural Development in China*. Shanghai: Shanghai Sanlian Bookstore, Shanghai People's Publishing House, 1992.

Lin Yifu. *New Structural Economics*. Beijing: Peking University Press, 2014.

Liu Foding, Wang Yuru, and Yu Jianwei. *The Economic Development of Modern China*. Jinan: Shandong People's Publishing House, 1997.

Liu Foding (Ed.). *Modern Economic History of China*. Beijing: Higher Education Press, 1999.

Lu Baolin. "Estimation of China's Industrial Capital Stock: 1981–2009". *Journal of Zhengzhou University of Light Industry (Social Science)*, Vol. 5, 2012.

Song Xiaowu, Wang Tianfu, Li Shi, and Wang Feng. *China Faces Inequality: Studies in Income Distribution*. Beijing: Social Sciences Academic Press, 2013.

Xu Dixin and Wu Chengming. *History of the Capitalist Development in China: Volume 2*. Beijing: People's Publishing House, 1990.

Xu Dixin and Wu Chengming. *History of the Capitalist Development in China: Volume 3*. Beijing: People's Publishing House, 1993.

Yang Zihui. *Study on Demographic Data of China*. Beijing: Reform Press, 1996.

Yao Shuben. *Overview of the Development of Employee Wages in 35 Years*. Beijing: Labor and Personnel Publishing House, 1986.

Yuan Tangjun. "Poverty among Chinese Farmers: What the Government Should Do". In *Unfinished Reform of China's Economy*, edited by Zhang Jun. Beijing: Dongfang Publishing House, 2015.

Zhang Baichun, Yao Fang, Zhang Jiuchun, and Jiang Long. *The Transfer of Soviet Technology to China: 1949–1966*. Jinan: Shandong Education Press, 2004.

Zhang Dongsheng. *Annual Report on China Household Income Distribution: 2010*. Beijing: Economic Science Press, 2010.

Zhang Jun. *China's Industrial Reform and Economic Growth: Issues and Explanations*. Shanghai: Shanghai Sanlian Bookstore, Shanghai People's Publishing House, 2003.

Zhang Jun and Zhang Yuan. "Re-estimation of China's Capital Stock K". *Economic Research Journal*, Vol. 7, 2003.

Zhou Yunbo and Qin Yan. *Empirical Analysis of Gap in China Household Income Distribution*. Tianjin: Nankai University Press, 2008.

Translated literature

[[U.S.] Chenery Hollis and Moises Syrquin. *Patterns of Development: 1950–1970*. Translated by Li Xinhua, et al. Beijing: Economic Science Press, 1988.

[France] Delaunay Jean-Claude and Jean Gadrey. *Services in Economic Thought: Three Centuries of Debate*. Translated by Jiang Xiaojuan. Shanghai: Shanghai People's Publishing House, 2011.

[Sweden] Jansson Jan Owen. *The Economics of Services*. Translated by Shi Xiancheng. Beijing: China Renmin University Press, 2013.
[Hungary] Kornai János. *Economics of Shortage*. Beijing: Economic Science Press, 1986.
[U.S.] Kuznets Simon. *Modern Economic Growth*. Translated by Dai Rui and Yi Cheng. Beijing: Beijing University of Economics Press, 1989.
[U.S.] Kuznets Simon. *Economic Growth of Nations: Total Output and Production Structure*. Translated by Chang Xun, et al. Beijing: The Commercial Press, 1999.
[U.S.] Lewis (W.A.). *Development Plan*. Beijing: Beijing University of Economics Press, 1989.
[Britain] Maddison Angus. *Development Centre Studies Chinese Economic Performance in the Long Run, 960–2030 AD* (2nd edition). Translated by Wu Xiaoying, et al. Shanghai: Shanghai People's Publishing House, 2008.
[Japan] Minami Ryoshin. *Turning Point in Economic Development: The Japanese Experience*. Translated by Guan Quan. Beijing: Social Sciences Academic Press, 2008.
[Japan] Minami Ryoshin, Makino Fumio, and Luo Huanzhen. *Education and Economic Development in China*. Translated by Guan Quan. Beijing: Social Sciences Academic Press, 2012.
[Japan] Minami Ryoshin and Ma Xinxin. "Changes in China's Labor Market and the Lewis Turning Point". In *The Turning Point of China's Economy: Comparison with East Asia*, edited by Ryoshin Minami, Makino Fumio and Hao Renping. Translated by Jingwenxuejian. Beijing: Social Sciences Academic Press, 2014.
[U.S.] Rawski Thomas G. *Economic Growth in Prewar China*. Translated by Tang Qiaotian, et al. Hangzhou: Zhejiang University Press, 2009.
[U.S.] Rostow W. W. *The Economics of Take-Off into Sustained Growth*. Translated by He Liping, et al. Chengdu: Sichuan People's Publishing House, 1988.
[U.S.] Rostow W. W. *Stages of Economic Growth: A Non-Communist Manifesto*. Translated by Guo Xibao and Wang Songmao. Beijing: China Social Sciences Press, 2001.
[U.S.] Schumpeter Joseph. *The Theory of Economic Development*. Beijing: The Commercial Press, 1990.

English literature

Bai Moo-Ki. "The Turning Point the Korean Economy". *Developing Economies, Institute of Developing Economies*, Vol. 20, No. 2, 1982.
Baumol W. "Macroeconomics of Unbalanced Growth: The Anatomy of an Urban Crisis". *American Economic Review*, Vol. 57, pp. 415–425, June 1967.
Fei John C. H. and Gustav Ranis. *Development of the Labor Surplus Economy: Theory and Policy*. Homewood: Richard D. Irwin, 1964.
Gerschenkron A. *Economic Backwardness in Historical Perspective: A Book of Essays*. Cambridge, MA: Harvard University Press, Belknap Press, 1962.
Kuznets S. "Notes on Japan's Economic Growth". In *Economic Growth: The Japanese Experience since the Meiji Era*, edited by L. Klein and K. Ohkawa. Homewood: Richard D. Irwin, 1968.
Lewis W. Arthulr. *The Theory of Economic Growth*. Homewood, IL: Irwin, 1955.
Lewis W. Arthulr. "Economic Development with Unlimited Supplies of Labour". In *The Economics of Underdevelopment*, edited by A. N. Agarwala and S. P. Singh. London: Oxford University Press, 1958a.

Lewis W. Arthulr. "Unlimited Labour: Further Notes". *Manchester School of Economic and Social Studies*, Vol. 26, No. 1, January 1958b.

Minami R. *The Turning Point in Economic Development: Japan's Experience*. Tokyo: Kinokuniya, 1973.

Ono Akira. "Technical Progress in Industry in Prewar Japan – The Types of Borrowed Technology". *Hitotsubashi Journal of Economics*, Vol. 27 No. 1, 1986.

Todaro Michael P. "A Model of Labor Migration and Urban Unemployment in LDCs". *American Economic Review*, Vol. 59, pp. 138–148, 1969.

Japanese literature

Ara K. *Economic Growth Theory*. Tokyo: Iwanami Shoten, 1969.

Hayami Y. *Development Economics*. Tokyo: Sobunsha, 1995.

Guan Quan. "Industrial Production in Manchukuo: Estimates from the 'Factories Statistical Tables'". *Journal of Tokyo Keizai University: Economics*, 2005.

Minami R. *The Turning Point of the Japanese Economy*. Tokyo: Sobunsya, 1970.

Minami R. *Economic Development of Japan* (1st edition). Tokyo: Toyo Keizai Inc, 1981.

Minami R. *Economic Development of Japan* (2nd edition). Tokyo: Toyo Keizai Inc, 1992.

Minami R. *Economic Development of Japan* (3rd edition). Tokyo: Toyo Keizai Inc, 2002.

Minami R. and F. Makino. *Asian Historical Statistics: China*. Tokyo: Toyo Keizai Inc, 2014.

Nakagane K. *Studies on the Chinese Economy: Political Economics of the Relation between Agriculture and Industry*. Tokyo: University of Tokyo Press, 1992.

Okawa K. and H. Rosovsky. *Japanese Economic Growth: Trend Acceleration in the Twentieth*. Tokyo: TOYO KEIZAI INC, 1973.

Ono A., S. Fujino, and A. Ono. "Advances in Silk Manufacturing Technology and Improvements in Labor Productivity". In *The Textile Industry (Long-term Economic Statistics – Estimation and Analysis)* (volume 11). Essay. Tokyo: Toyo Keizai Inc, 1979.

Ryoshin M. and M. Fumino. *Economic Development in China*. Tokyo: Nippon Hyouron Sha, 2012.

Yanotsuneta-Kinenkai, ed. *100 Years of Japan in Figures: A Databook for Understanding the 20th Century* (Nihon kokusei zue, Long-term Statistical Edition) (4th edition). Tokyo: Kokuseisha, 2000.

Yutaka K. *The Era of High Speed Growth*. Tokyo: Nippon Hyouron Sha, 1981.

Referred statistics

Chinese Academy of Social Sciences, Central Archives. *Selected Economic Archives of the People's Republic of China from 1952 to 1957: Industry*. Beijing: China Wuzhi Press, 1998.

Department of Comprehensive National Economy Statistics of the National Bureau of Statistics. *Compilation of Statistical Data of the People's Republic of China Over 50 Years*. Beijing: China Statistics Press, 1999.

Department of Comprehensive Planning, Ministry of Finance. *China Finance Statistics: 1950–1991*. Beijing: Science Press, 1992.

Department of Fixed Asset Investment Statistics, National Bureau of Statistics. *Statistics on China's Fixed Asset Investment: 1950–1985*. Beijing: China Statistics Press, 1987.

Department of National Economic Accounting, National Bureau of Statistics. *Data of Gross Domestic Product of China: 1952–1995*. Dalian: Dongbei University of Finance and Economics Press, 1997.

Department of Population Statistics, National Bureau of Statistics, Third Bureau of the Ministry of Public Security. *Compilation of Demographic Data of the People's Republic of China 1949–1985*. Beijing: China Financial and Economic Press, 1988.

Department of Social Statistics, National Bureau of Statistics. *Chinese Social Statistics*. Beijing: China Statistics Press, 1987.

Department of Trade and Material Statistics, National Bureau of Statistics. *China Commercial Foreign Trade Statistics: 1952–1988*. Beijing: China Statistics Press, 1990.

Maddison Angus. *The World Economy: Historical Statistics*. Translated by Wu Xiaoying, et al. Beijing: Peking University Press, 2009.

Ministry of Agriculture of the People's Republic of China. *Statistics on Agriculture in the People's Republic of China over 60 Years*. Beijing: China Agriculture Press, 2009.

National Bureau of Statistics. *The Great Decade: Statistics on the Achievements of Economic and Cultural Development in the People's Republic of China*. Beijing: People's Publishing House, 1959.

Index

Note: Page numbers in *italic* indicate a figure and page numbers in **bold** indicate a table on the corresponding page.

accumulation of capital 147–152, **149**, *150–152*
age structure 89–91, **89**
agriculture 27–28, 47–48; development in 28–37, **29**, *31*, **33**, **35**; institutional changes 37–43, **37**, **40–42**; role and significance of rural industry 43–47, *47*
analysis: household registration system and family planning policy 102–105, *103–104*; rate of economic growth 9–19, **10**, **12**, **14**, *16*, **17**, **19**
assistance from Soviet Union 169–172, **171**

calculation of the import and export function 221–224
capital, accumulation of 147–152, **149**, *150–152*; *see also* formation of capital
causes of capital formation 144–145, **145**
change in agriculture 27–28, 47–48; development 28–37, **29**, *31*, **33**, **35**; institutional changes 37–43, **37**, **40–42**; role and significance of rural industry 43–47, *47*
changes: capital formation 142–143; industrial structure 19–22, **20–21**, 60–62, *60*; institutional (agriculture) 37–43, **37**, **40–42**; institutional (industry) 62–68, **63–64**, **66**, *67–68*; institutional (service sector) 79–82, **80–82**; structural (service sector) 76–79, **77–79**; trade volume 208–210; *see also* change in agriculture; demographic changes; price changes
citizens' lives 126–127, 136–137; changes in prices 127–132, **128–129**, **131**, *132*; standard of living 132–136, **133–136**
collectivization 39–43, **40–42**
concentration 186–190

demographic changes 85–86, 95–96; age structure 89–91, **89**; demographic transition 88–89, *88*; labor supply 92–95, *93*, **94**; population increase 87–88, **87**, 91–92
dependency, trade 211–215, **213**, *214*
determinants of international trade 220–224, *221*, **224**
development *see* development in agriculture; development in service industry; development strategy; economic development; industrial development
development in agriculture 28–37, **29**, *31*, **33**, **35**
development in service industry 71–72, 83–84; growth in the service sector 72–76, *72*, **73**, **75**; institutional changes 79–82, **80–82**; structural changes 76–79, **77–79**
development strategy 243–245
direct investment: attempts at outbound investment 233–237, **235–236**; calculation of the foreign investment demand function 232–233, **233**; introduction of

Index

foreign investment 226–232, **227–228**, *229–230*, **231**
dispersion 186–190
distribution *see* income distribution

economic analysis: household registration system and family planning policy 102–105, *103–104*
economic development 3–4, 22–23; analysis of the rate of economic growth 9–19, **10**, **12**, **14**, *16*, **17**, **19**; changes in industrial structure 19–22, **20–21**; economic take-off 4–9, **5**; and education 158–164, **158–159**, **161**, *163*; experience in 242–253, *248*; and health 164–166, **165–166**
economic growth, analysis of the rate of 9–19, **10**, **12**, **14**, *16*, **17**, **19**
economic take-off 4–9, **5**
economies of scale 243–245
education 157, 167; and economic development 158–164, **158–159**, **161**, *163*
experience 241–248, 254; extension of 248–253, *248*
export: calculation of the import and export function 221–224

family planning policy: economic analysis 102–105, *103–104*
finance issues 192–193, 201–206, **204**, *205*
fiscal issues 192–200, **195**, *196–197*, **198**, **200**
foreign investment 226–232, **227–228**, *229–230*, **231**; calculation of the foreign investment demand function 232–233, **233**
formation of capital 141–142, 155; capital accumulation 147–152, **149**, *150–152*; causes of 144–145, **145**; changes in 142–143; savings and investment 152–154, *153*, **154**; significance of 145–147, *146–147*

GDP 9–13
GDP per capita 9–13
"go global" 233–234
government 181–186, *185*, 190–191; development model combining market and 242–243; reform of ownership 186–190, **187**, **189**
growth, economic 9–19, **10**, **12**, **14**, *16*, **17**, **19**

growth in agriculture: output and input 30–36, *31*, **33**, **35**
growth in industry 51–55, *52*, **54–55**
growth in international trade 208–211, **209**, *211*
growth in service sector 72–76, *72*, **73**, **75**
growth rates: agriculture 36–37; economic 9–19, **10**, **12**, **14**, *16*, **17**, **19**; industry 53–55; trade 210

health 157, 167; and economic growth 164–166, **165–166**
household registration system: economic analysis 102–105, *103–104*
human resources 157, 167; education 158–164, **158–159**, **161**, *163*; health 164–166, **165–166**

import: calculation of the import and export function 221–224; from Western countries 172–176, **174–175**, *176*
income distribution 110–121, **114–115**, *116–117*, **118**, *119–121*, 123–124
individual operations: agriculture 39–43, **40–42**
industrial development 50–51, 68–69; growth of industry 51–55, *52*, **54–55**; institutional changes 62–68, **63–64**, **66**, *67–68*; shifts in the model of growth 55–60, *57–59*; structural changes 60–62, *60*
industrialization 215–219, **217–218**, *219*
industrial structure, changes in 19–22, **20–21**
industry, growth of 51–55, *52*, **54–55**; *see also* rural industry; service industry
innovation 176–180, **178**
input: agriculture 30–36, *31*, **33**, **35**
institutional changes: agriculture 37–43, **37**, **40–42**; industry 62–68, **63–64**, **66**, *67–68*; service sector 79–82, **80–82**
institution building 181–182, 190–191; government and markets 182–186, *185*; reform of ownership 186–190, **187**, **189**
international trade 207–208, 224–225; dependency 211–215, **213**, *214*; determinants 220–224, *221*, **224**; growth in 208–210, **209**; and industrialization 215–219, **217–218**, *219*
investment 152–154, *153*, **154**; *see also* direct investment

labor migration 100–102
labor mobility 97–98, 107–108; household registration system and family planning policy 102–105, *103–104*; Lewis turning point 105–107; and urbanization 98–102, *99*
labor supply 92–95, *93*, **94**
late-mover advantage 245–248
Lewis turning point 105–107

macro policy 192–193; financial systems and markets 201–206, **204**, *205*; fiscal systems and policies 193–200, **195**, *196–197*, **198**, **200**
market/markets 181–186, *185*, 190–191; development model combining government and 242–243; financial 203–206; reform of ownership 186–190, **187**, **189**
migration, labor 100–102
mobility *see* labor mobility
model of development: combining government and market 242–243
model of growth: shift in 55–60, *57–59*
modern economic growth 4–6, **5**; *see also* economic growth

opening up 207–208, 224–225; determinants of international trade 220–224, *221*, **224**; growth in international trade 208–210, **209**; and industrialization 215–219, **217–218**, *219*; trade dependency 211–215, **213**, *214*
outbound investment 233–237, **235–236**
output: agriculture 30–36, *31*, **33**, **35**; industry 51–53; service sector 72–74
outward-looking development strategy 243–245
ownership, reform of 186–190, **187**, **189**

policy: family planning 102–105, *103–104*; fiscal 193–200, **195**, *196–197*, **198**, **200**; population 91–92; *see also* macro policy
population increase 87–88, **87**
population policy 91–92
poverty issues 110–111, 121–124, **122–123**
price changes 127–132, **128–129**, **131**, *132*

rate: agriculture growth 36–37; economic growth 9–19, **10**, **12**, **14**, *16*, **17**, **19**; industry growth 53–55; service sector growth 74–76; trade growth 210
reform, ownership 186–190, **187**, **189**
rural industry 43–47, *47*

savings 152–154, *153*, **154**
service industry 71–72, 83–84; growth in the service sector 72–76, *72*, **73**, **75**; institutional changes 79–82, **80–82**; structural changes 76–79, **77–79**
significance of capital formation 145–147, *146–147*
significance of service industry 71–72, 83–84; growth in the service sector 72–76, *72*, **73**, **75**; institutional changes 79–82, **80–82**; structural changes 76–79, **77–79**
social capacity 245–248
Soviet Union 169–172, **171**
standard of living 132–136, **133–136**
status of agriculture 28–30
strategy *see* development strategy
structural changes: industry 60–62, *60*; service sector 76–79, **77–79**
supply, labor *see* labor supply

technological advancement 179–180; technology innovation 176–179, **178**; technology introduction 169–176, **171**, **174–175**, *176*
terms of trade 220–221
trade: changes in trade volume 208–210; dependency 211–215, **213**, *214*; growth rate of 210; *see also* international trade

upgrading 50–51, 68–69; growth of industry 51–55, *52*, **54–55**; institutional changes 62–68, **63–64**, **66**, *67–68*; shifts in the model of growth 55–60, *57–59*; structural changes 60–62, *60*
urbanization 97–102, *99*, 107–108

views on China 7–9

Western countries: import from 172–176, **174–175**, *176*

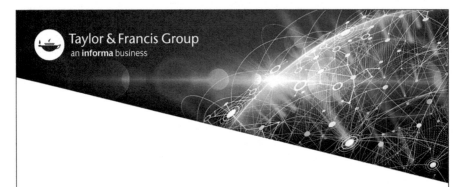